Lecture Notes in Computer Science 2571

Edited by G. Goos, J. Hartmanis, and J. van Leeuwen

Springer
Berlin
Heidelberg
New York
Barcelona
Hong Kong
London
Milan
Paris
Tokyo

Sajal K. Das
Swapan Bhattacharya (Eds.)

Distributed Computing

Mobile and Wireless Computing

4th International Workshop, IWDC 2002
Calcutta, India, December 28-31, 2002
Proceedings

 Springer

Series Editors

Gerhard Goos, Karlsruhe University, Germany
Juris Hartmanis, Cornell University, NY, USA
Jan van Leeuwen, Utrecht University, The Netherlands

Volume Editors

Sajal K. Das
University of Texas at Arlington
Center for Research in Wireless Mobility and Networking (CReWMaN)
Department of Computer Science and Engineering
P.O. Box 19015, Arlington, TX 76019-0015, USA
E-mail: das@cse.uta.edu

Swapan Bhattacharya
Jadavpur University
Department of Computer Science and Engineering
Calcutta 700 032
E-mail: bswapan2000@yahoo.co.in

Cataloging-in-Publication Data applied for

A catalog record for this book is available from the Library of Congress.

Bibliographic information published by Die Deutsche Bibliothek
Die Deutsche Bibliothek lists this publication in the Deutsche Nationalbibliografie;
detailed bibliographic data is available in the Internet at <http://dnb.ddb.de>.

CR Subject Classification (1998): C.2, D.1.3, D.2.12, D.4

ISSN 0302-9743
ISBN 3-540-00355-X Springer-Verlag Berlin Heidelberg New York

Springer-Verlag Berlin Heidelberg New York
a member of BertelsmannSpringer Science+Business Media GmbH

http://www.springer.de

© Springer-Verlag Berlin Heidelberg 2002
Printed in Germany

Typesetting: Camera-ready by author, data conversion by PTP Berlin, Stefan Sossna e. K.
Printed on acid-free paper   SPIN: 10872271   06/3142   5 4 3 2 1 0

General Chairs' Message

Welcome to the proceedings of IWDC 2002. This workshop provides a relatively new forum for researchers in distributed computing to exchange their ideas, and contribute to the advancement of the state-of-the-art. With guidance from the advisory committee members, we kept the vision and the focus of the workshop relevant and practical. The magic combination of ubiquitous computing, nanotechnology, and wireless computing has opened up a brave new world of applications, which has a profound influence on the way we live and do our business. This year's topics emphasize traditional as well as the emerging areas in distributed computing, with special emphasis on wireless and mobile computing. This year's workshop was made possible by the dedication and the hard work of many people. The program chairs Sajal Das and Swapan Bhattacharya deserve special credit for having the workshop proceedings published by Springer-Verlag. This is a major milestone that adds to the visibility of the workshop, and highlights the exclusiveness that it deserves. We are grateful for the leadership of the organizing committee chair by Asok K. Bhattacharya in coordinating the local arrangements. We also counted on the skills of the finance chair Jaya Sil in handling registration matters and conference expenses. Finally, it is a pleasure to acknowledge the support of the industry chairs Subhasis Mitra and Diptendu Dutta in building the much needed bridges with the real world that harvests the fruits of our research. When the dust settles down, the quality of a workshop is determined by the quality of the papers, tutorials, talks, and the interaction among the participants. Sajal Das deserves special thanks for his help with publicity, and for his efforts in contacting the keynote speakers. The program chairs put together a solid program. Finally, we thank all the authors who submitted papers – without them there would be no workshop.

November 2002

Subhansu Bandyopadhyay
Pradip K. Das
Sunil R. Das
Sukumar Ghosh

Program Chairs' Message

Welcome to the proceedings of IWDC 2002, the *4th International Workshop on Distributed Computing* which was held on December 29–31, 2002, in Kolkata (formerly Calcutta), also called the City of Joy. Kolkata, once the capital of India, is a culturally vibrant city with over 300 years of rich history.

With the help of an international Program Committee, we were glad to present an excellent technical program containing high-quality research on various aspects of distributed computing, mobile computing systems, and wireless and optical networks. This year experienced the highest number of submissions ever in response to the general call for papers and solicitations from well-known researchers around the world. Each submitted paper was reviewed by at least two program committee members and one or two external referees. Only about 35% of the regular papers were accepted for presentation. You would agree with us that the quality of the proceedings speaks for itself. Due to the single-track nature of the workshop, we could not accommodate many excellent papers.

The technical program was divided into nine sessions spanning three full days. In addition, the program included three keynote addresses by internationally known experts in the field. We would like to thank Prof. Imrich Chlamtac (University of Texas at Dallas), Prof. Narsingh Deo (University of Central Florida, Orlando), and Prof. Satish Tripathi (University of California at Riverside) for kindly agreeing to deliver keynote talks. The second day (December 30) of the workshop was designated as the *Mobile Computing Madness Day*. Two pre-workshop tutorials on exciting topics were also planned.

Many people contributed toward the tremendous success of IWDC 2002. Our heartfelt thanks go to the members of the Program Committee and external referees who worked very hard to get the reviews on time. We would like to thank the General Chairs for their confidence in us. We gratefully acknowledge the hard work of the team in Kolkata: N. Chaki, S. Neogy, S. Choudhury, S. Setua, J. Sil, A. Chakraborty, S. Das, and B. Saha. Special thanks are also due to Nabendu Chaki (Calcutta Univ.) for his dedication and timely responses, and to Wook Choi (Univ. of Texas at Arlington) for the needed help with the final manuscripts. We are grateful to Springer-Verlag for its cooperation in publishing the proceedings in such a short time. We also acknowledge the moral support of IEEE Computer Society (Kolkata Chapter), IEEE India Council, Calcutta University, Jadavpur University, and the Center for Research in Wireless Mobility and Networking (CReWMaN) at the University of Texas at Arlington.

Last, but not least, thanks to all the authors and attendees for making this workshop a grand success. We sincerely hope that the three-day program of IWDC 2002 fostered the exchange of new ideas and provided an opportunity for lively discussions/collaborations among the participants.

November 2002   Sajal K. Das
                                                          Swapan Bhattacharya

Organization

Advisory Committee

General Chair: S. Bandyopadhyay, Univ. of Calcutta, India
P.K. Das, Jadavpur Univ., India
S.R. Das, Univ. of Ottawa, Canada
S. Ghosh, Univ. of Iowa, USA

Other Advisors: A.K. Banerjee, Vice Chancellor, Univ. of Calcutta, India
A.N. Bose, Vice Chancellor, Jadavpur Univ., India
D.K. Bose, Vice Chancellor, Tripura Univ., India
T. Mukherjee, Pro-Vice Chancellor, Univ. of Calcutta, India
A. Thakur, Pro-Vice Chancellor, Jadavpur Univ, India

Program Committee

Program Chair: S.K. Das, Univ. of Texas at Arlington, USA
S. Bhattacharya, Jadavpur Univ., India

Convenor: N. Chaki, Univ. of Calcutta, India
S. Neogy, Jadavpur Univ., India

D. Agrawal, Univ. of Cincinnati, USA
S. Agarwal, Usha Martin Telekom Limited, India
M. Agustin, Univ. of New Mexico, USA
A. Bagchi, Univ. of Texas at Dallas, USA
P. Banerjee, Northwestern Univ., USA
V. Berzins, Naval Postgraduate School, Monterey, USA
B. Bhattacharya, Indian Statistical Inst., India
R. Biswas, NASA Ames Research Center, USA
M. Broy, Technical Univ. of Munich, Germany
B. Bryant, Univ. of Alabama at Birmingham, USA
J. Cao, Hong Kong Polytechnic Univ., Hong Kong
N. Chatterjee, Jadavpur Univ. India
S. Chattopadhyay, Jadavpur Univ., India
D. Das, Jadavpur Univ., India
N. Das, Indian Statistical Inst., India
S. Das, State Univ. of New York, Stony Brook, USA
R. Dasgupta, Technical Teachers Training Inst., Kolkata, India
A. Datta, Univ. of Nevada at Las Vegas, USA

N. Deo, Univ. of Central Florida, USA
Z.F. Ghassemlooy, Sheffield Hallam Univ., UK
J. Ghosh, Univ. of Texas at Austin, USA
R. Guha, Univ. of Central Florida, USA
P. Gupta, IIT, Kanpur, India
O. Ibarra, Univ. of California at Santa Barbara, USA
A.K. Mondal, Jadavpur Univ., India
Luqi , Naval Postgraduate School, Monterey, USA
C. Majumder, Jadavpur Univ., Kolkata, India
S. Majumder, Carleton Univ., Canada
S. Majumder, Colombo Staff College, Manila, Philippines
C. Pinotti, Univ. of Trento, Italy
V. Prasanna, Univ. of Southern California, USA
S.K. Rath, Regional Engineering College, Rourkela, India
D. Saha, Indian Inst. of Management, Calcutta, India
S. Sahani, Univ. of Florida, USA
A. Sen, Indian Inst. of Management, Calcutta, India
I. Sengupta, Indian Inst. of Technology, Kharagpur, India
D. Sinha, Univ. of Calcutta, India
B. Sinharoy, IBM Watson Research Center, USA
T. Srikantham, Nanyang Technological Univ., Singapore
S. Tripathi, Univ. of California at Riverside, USA
Y. Zhang, Univ. of Tsukuba, Japan

Organizing Committee

Chair: A.K. Bhattacharya, Univ. of Calcutta, India

Convenor: B. Saha, Univ. of Calcutta, India
                    S. Setua, Univ. of Calcutta, India

Finance Committee

Chair: J. Sil, Univ. of Calcutta, India

Convenor: S. Choudhury, Univ. of Calcutta, India
Industry Chair: S. Mitra, Compaq India, India
                    D. Dutta, Aunwesha Knowledge Technologies, India

List of Referees

A. Agarwal, Univ. of Windsor, Canada
M. Auguston, New Mexico State Univ., USA
S. Bandyopadhyay, Indian Inst. of Management, Calcutta, India
S. Bandyopadhyay, Univ. of Windsor, Canada
S. Banerjee, Jadavpur Univ., Kolkata, India
A. Basu, Indian Inst. of Technology, Kharagpur, India
K. Basu, Univ. of Texas at Arlington, USA
S. Bhattacharya, Indian Inst. of Management, Calcutta, India
B.B. Bhattacherya, Indian Statistical Inst., Kolkata, India
M. Broy, Technical Univ. of Munich, Germany
B. Bryant, Univ. of Alabama at Birmingham, USA
U. Chakravarty, Univ. of Missouri, St. Louis, USA
S. Chattopadhyay, Jadavpur Univ., Kolkata, India
D. Das, Jadavpur Univ., Kolkata, India
N. Das, Indian Statistical Inst., Kolkata, India
P. Kumar Das, Jadavpur Univ., Kolkata, India
S.R. Das., Univ. of Ottawa, Canada
A. Dutta, Univ. of Calcutta, Kolkata, India
H. Evans, Univ. of Glasgow, UK
Z.F. Ghassemlooy, Sheffield Hallam Univ., UK
S. Ghose, Jadavpur Univ., Kolkata, India
J. Ghosh, Univ. of Texas at Austin, USA
S. Ghosh, Univ. of Iowa, USA
P. Gupta, Indian Inst. of Technology, Kanpur, India
J.M. Jaam, Univ. of Qatar, Qatar
C. Majumder, Jadavpur Univ., India
A. Mohanty, Indian Inst. of Management, Calcutta, India
A.K. Mondal, Jadavpur Univ., Kolkata, India
A. Mukherjee, Univ. of Central Florida, USA
A. Pal, Indian Inst. of Technology, Kharagpur, India
C.M. Pinotti, Univ. of Trento, Italy
S. Prakash, Indian Inst. of Technology, Madras, India
D. Saha, Indian Inst. of Management, Calcutta, India
A. Sen, Indian Inst. of Management, Calcutta, India
A. Shende, Roanoke College, VA, USA
B.P. Sinha, Indian Statistical Inst., Kolkata, India
S. Thambipillai, Nanyang Technological Univ., Singapore
S. Surkoley, Indian Statistical Inst., Kolkata, India

Table of Contents

Keynote Talk III

Session III: Wireless Networks

Session IV: Mobile Ad Hoc Networks

Session V: Wireless Mobile Systems

Session VI: VLSI and Parallel Systems

Session VII: Optical Networks

Session VIII: Distributed Systems

Session IX: Student Papers

Bandwidth Management in Community Networks

Imrich Chlamtac and Ashwin Gumaste

Center for Advance Telecommunications Systems and Services
The University of Texas at Dallas, TX 75083, USA
chlamtac@utdallas.edu

Abstract. The downturn in the economy and related telecom activities has led to the accelerated development of a new concept of Community (owned) Networks. A Community network represents a unique business model whose returns encompass social, economic as well as technology issues of a community. The new concept also provides a platform for multiple vendors to sell products and services, to reach out a larger customer base at a lower cost structure, and new opportunities to providers to work in tandem directly with customers/communities. For OPEX and CAPEX considerations and for better services, in community networks the issue of bandwidth management that supports provisioning in real time on a per demand real-time basis, is a critical issue for the future success of such networks. We address the various issues that need to be considered in designing a unified management scheme in these networks, accompanied by a detailed discussion of the concepts and challenges related community networks.

1 Introduction

Recently, several cities and towns in USA and Europe have started to experiment with Fiber-to-the-home (FTTH), Fiber-to-the-curb (FTTC) and Wi-Fi deployments, organized around an optical backbone, to build their own networks supporting high-speed Internet access and new services to their businesses and homes with the goal of improving quality of life, creating more jobs and bringing new businesses into the city. There are many business and technology issues that need to be resolved before the undertaking of building a community network can be started. Financing a fiber-optic network in the corporate sector carries significant risks, as evidenced by the recent demise of Global Crossing, and its inability to become profitable after spending 15 billon dollars in its five years of operation. Communities, municipalities or local governments, are therefore venturing into the endeavor of building a community owned metro optical networks based on a different business model. Their solution targets a significantly reduced effort, focusing on investment in infrastructure only, combined with the outsourcing of management and active network deployment, and the premise of a much longer term for return on investment traded for longer term socio-economic benefits to their community. Improving the quality of life, growing local business, improving education and citizen health care, increasing security and numerous other facets of regional daily and economic life yield a slower and lower rate of financial return, but are justified by being accompanied by significant non-tangible as well as long term tangible benefits is the communities game. To build a community network with fiber at its core, that enables new services, the optimization

S.K. Das and S. Bhattacharya (Eds.): IWDC 2002, LNCS 2571, pp. 1–11, 2002.
© Springer-Verlag Berlin Heidelberg 2002

of the metro core's network bandwidth management is a key component to success. A more than incremental change is needed to demonstrate the benefits of truly high bandwidth optical network to the curb or home. In other words not only high bandwidth, but bandwidth on demand is needed for home, for enterprise customers and communications service providers to make the community network attractive. In the optical segment of the network, on-demand bandwidth can be obtained by real time provisioning of wavelength and sub-wavelength, enabling high speed real time services to be effectively offered throughout the community. However, an optical metropolitan area network is often characterized by a diverse operational environment, consisting of various topologies and vendors that current optical bandwidth management systems fail to optimize. Traditional service provisioning, or circuit switching, systems offer limited choices and rates, and are very slow. Even today, customers can wait days to obtain a new high speed optical connection. To create a competitive environment in which providers can offer the community real time, on demand provisioning, along with the more traditional value-added services of network and protocol conversion, exchange services, including peering, aggregation, and protocol conversion, including SONET, ATM, IP, or Ethernet, traffic engineering and aggregation, bandwidth management, network security, (Service Level Agreements) SLAs and private network connections with diverse network carriers, the emerging community providers are in acute need of new and better bandwidth provisioning solutions. Currently, the metro core relies on provisioning in which circuits are allocated, service-level agreements (SLAs) managed, and compliance enforced, all via a central point. While the centralized operation yields a simplified management environment, it is generally agreed that a metro optical network today cannot provide true optical connectivity, high efficiency, low delays and low data loss, real time settlement for bandwidth trading, or bandwidth on demand, or real-time provisioning and pricing using extant centralized bandwidth management solutions. Under current economic conditions, better utilization of current bandwidth in terms of lower capital expenditures and operating cost expenditures, as well as improved bandwidth granularity are essential for viable communication solutions. It is necessary, therefore, to develop solutions with added bandwidth management intelligence needed to provide a new bandwidth management platform that can support the emerging broadband applications while delivering the necessary bandwidth efficiency. Under such conditions the need for advanced services at customer premises can justify the deployment of community optical networks that bring new telecommunication products, improve the quality of life and open new markets that can lay the basis for accelerated regional development through advanced telecommunications environments.

2 Community Networks

A network infrastructure built by a representative authority for the deployment of broadband based services represents a generic community network. A community network is a classic example of a centralized investment by the Government / Municipality for the betterment of the general e-lifestyle of the population. The community network becomes a platform for multiple service oriented vendors to offer a plethora of services to engage enterprise and residential users on a voluminous basis. Community networks are being developed with past optical experience in mind.

The recent downturn in the economy has led to a severe situation for telecommunication companies and in particular optical networking vendors due to various reasons. This period of instability, referred to as "the photonic winter", has caused tremendous turmoil in the telecommunications industry leading to doubts regarding the business aspects of broadband communications per se. The business model, of carriers taking on huge capital investments and creating abundant network infrastructure did not achieve the primary target of a fast ROI. The failure of this business model was partially due to a lack in foresight as well as the costing structure of the network infrastructure, and an incorrect assessment in the projected demands and revenue models of the carriers. A additional problem faced by carriers was the inability to provide the multitude of services, many requiring efficient on-demand real time basis bandwidth provisioning. The inability to support this type of bandwidth management stemmed from a number of reasons, but primarily from the vast number of technologies that interacted with each other in a generic long haul network. The above factors cumulatively wrecked the all optical vision for global optical networking.

Over the same period metropolitan area networking has seen some successes. Newer optical technologies such as WDM and optical cross-connects etc. were successfully applied in the metropolitan area and hence seemed to be a better investing ground for good returns. Firstly, the fiber represented a medium to carry significantly large amounts of data. This was seen as a paradigm shift from conventional network mediums such as copper and wireless. Secondly, the envisaged huge available bandwidth was seen as a safe revenue multiplier. Thirdly, by keeping data in the optical domain, the network infrastructure was expected to be greatly simplified. Optical switching of bit streams was much easier and lower cost than in electronic domain. This led to projecting lower capital expenditure and lower operating expenditure. By keeping data in the optical domain, network planning, and deployment became simpler as well as more cost effective. These projections led the telecommunications industry to believe that optical technologies were mature enough to cause a revolution. These projections were however quite overoptimistic too. Data streams were indeed easier to be switched in the optical domain; however the switching was purely between ports for end-to-end optical paths or lightpaths. Technological limitations prevented the deployment of packet switching in the optical domain. A trade-off between conventional lightpath switching and packet switching – the recently emerged paradigm on optical burst switching – was still a technology on paper. There is no architecture that could support such highly flexible schemes as expected from burst switching. Grooming traffic from multiple bit-streams onto a homogenous high capacity bit-pipe or lightpath was not possible in the optical domain. Getting the desired granularity at an incumbent optical node meant time division de-multiplexing of the lightpath and segregating to create multiple slower rate streams. This could only be done in the electronic domain. Often creating issues like synchronization etc to facilitate TDM and lead to a surge in the cost of provisioning such multiple bitrate pipes. These technological barriers demonstrated that no simple technology solution will provide bandwidth at high granularity on demand, similar to electronic switching in the near future. On the other hand, purely electronic networking at high data rates do not provide a cost effective solution, hence a mix of the two under a proper management suite offers the only cost-effective solution today. In the community network area, specifically, the metro core needs to be augmented by a last mile solution, often built around a wireless network. The resulting integration of multiple technologies to suite the end-user requirement is highly challenging. Wireless networks built on top of the optical backbone primarily for voice and secondarily for data need to be provisioned keeping in mind the intricacies of both optical as well as wireless technologies, and the discrepancy in the speeds of optical and wireless transmission. Keep in mind, the entire wireless spectrum is a few Gigahertz while a single strand of optical fiber can cover more and yet have reuse.

The emerging community network models, draw on this experience when building a new type of modular, centralized telecommunication distribution framework. *The community network model, in short, is a hierarchical implementation by a central authority to facilitate exchange of information between resident and business users, and create a uniform platform for service providers to invest in the most appropriate manner for optimized services that would be offered.*

The three factors which most critically dictate the success or failure of an infrastructure of a project are invariably the social, economic and technological implications involved. While balancing the effects of each of these factors a central authority (government / municipality / corporation) has to decide on the best technique to build a network infrastructure. The built network infrastructure called Community network is further intended to create a level playing field for carriers and other Telcos to provision their services in the best possible cost structure for the ultimate benefit of the community.

The Community network by technology classification is a metropolitan area network on account of its proximity to the metro area and its multi-service capability. By provisioning multiple classes of service through a multi-vendor open system, a community network is intended to derive the best possible results in terms of economic, technological and social implications, the justification for its deployment, as discussed next.

2.1 Social and Technical Implications

A Community network acts as a single unifying strata to reach a large population in the least expensive as well as most efficient manner. The community network showcases, by definition, an open system architecture for business and residential customers and provides for various access services. To develop a broad segmented network infrastructure to reach a broad population profile, having a varied requirement, can be facilitated by only a governing authority like Municipality etc which has the necessary and sufficient resources (both financial and otherwise). The central authority which commits to such an exercise benefits from the multiple service advantages stemming from Community Network deployment. Purely from a business case perspective the central authority creates an optical backbone for further leasing/renting of network resources to various specialized providers. Though slow to begin with, the return on investment in a community network for both the leaser (central authority) as well as the lessee (the service provider) is expected on account of the broad structure of the network deployment strategy (discussed in technology section) as well as the multi-service platform. The community network business model, also takes into account the fact that multiple service classes can exist to serve the various economic strata's of society to alleviate network bandwidth requirements from a long term perspective. The community network can then be understood as a unified framework for carriers to provision their individual services and offer these services to specialized customers as well as consumers, consolidating the market share of the carriers, and assuring fixed minimum revenue to the providers. The business model, also drives a need for carrier investment only at places where such investment is absolutely necessary thus saving overall CAPEX. From a management perspective, the community network represents a unified management scheme with multiple technologies and services on the same high bandwidth backbone. The services and technologies on the optical backbone can be managed from a wavelength or wave-service perspective leading to resilient, scalable and efficient networks with low operational costs (OPEX).

The single homogenous backbone in a geographic community created by a central authority represents a wide panorama of technologies coalesced into the backbone to exude user confident services. From a community network perspective the network backbone is an optical network, spread geographically across the community with various points of presence (POP) to interact with users. The current level of technology for optical networks, places this class of optical networks in the third generation optical networks.

From a historical perspective, the first generations of optical networks were legacy SONET networks, with tributary and distribution feeder lines. These were predominantly catered for voice traffic, and represented a synchronous TDM hierarchy. With the advent of data communication and primarily the Internet, voice services were outnumbered by data services, and pure SONET networks were an inefficient (cost as well as technological) for this kind of information transport. A multi-services platform paved the evolution of the second generation optical networks, which were now based on multi-channel WDM systems. The benefit in efficiency of packetizing voice and data and maintaining a packet oriented network created data networking on WDM a strong contender for second generation optical networks. The packetized form of transport as well as the bursty profile of Internet (IP) traffic created a unique requirement for Quality of Service (QoS) for transport of information. QoS was now, more than ever before considered a strong pre-requisite for good service guarantee in packet based communication modes. ATM and much later MPLS served as two generic protocols to insure QoS to the traffic flows. These types of QoS protocols over optical backbone, through Gigabit Ethernet or Packet over SONET, were still part of the second generation of optical networks. The third generation of optical networks is currently being consolidated as an amalgamation of new and old technologies to offer a class of services that are well defined. The data transmission oriented third generation of optical networks promotes a number of new technologies such as Gigabit and 10 Gigabit Ethernet, POS, MPLS and RPR to create efficient transport over an intelligent optical layer. Despite these advances, traffic grooming and high speed packet switching are still technologies in their infancy.

Intelligent Optical Layer: As opposed to past manifestations of optical networks, whereby stagnated optical boxes had the primary function of data transport and providing elementary resiliency, the optical layer today serves as an intelligent means for transport of service oriented data. WDM networking has now matured enough to provide smart features for seamless integration of the higher layer services on the WDM physical layer. Among them, high density, high speed optical cross connect architecture, highly granular optical multiplexing technology, and a smart provisioning layer are the key for the popularization of WDM networking. Among the biggest challenge in the third generation of optical networks is the ability to manage the vast number of different services according to network classification and user requirement. From an implementation perspective-metropolitan area optical networks are the closest classification to community networks. Metro networks represent a class of networks which have multi-service platforms and have a sizable amount of inter-network as well as intra-network traffic. Metro-networks also have multiple providers sharing the backbone through wavelengths and wave services creating a niche market for themselves. From a commercial perspective metro networks represent a single high growth area. Despite the recently witnessed downturn in the optical segment, metro networks still continue to experience steady growth, on account of their strong impact on user's needs.

2.2 Economic Implications

A community network represents a single broad based infrastructure and level playing field for multiple vendors to provide service to consumers. As opposed to a typical application specific network, a community network has both consumers and customers as end-users and both service providers and application specific providers as the vendors. Moreover it is built and managed by a central authority, which has the authority to regulate the billing and costing structure of the network commodity-bandwidth. The community business model is a slow return model, with emphasis on surety of returns rather than a quick return high-risk model. From the perspective of returns, it has to be noted that in present economic climate only a central authority like the Government or a local administration can take part in such an exercise on account of the very high investment initially needed in the network. The returns though slow are expected to be guaranteed in this environment, as bandwidth is now a secondary commodity with applications being the primary requirement. To draw an analogy we consider the following: The network infrastructure can be envisioned as the 'roads' in a remote area of a city suburb. Upon completion of this basic transport infrastructure, a section of the population would move to this part of the city on account of the ease of access (analogous to good bandwidth availability). The inhabitants can move only when there are houses and residential buildings on the periphery of the roads (access points). The access point creates revenue- realtors sell property, flats, furniture (application services). As traffic increases, and vehicles, pedestrians use the roads they pay tax to the government.

Business is conducted through this network of roads (analogous to a Community network), and the Government benefits through indirect taxation also. Over a period of time the government is able to recover the entire investment through direct (to inhabitants and business owners) as well as indirect taxes. Moreover by creating this infrastructure a level playing field is formed for different business entities to sell their specialized services. The average lifestyle of the inhabitants is also bettered through such an exercise, showcasing the importance of building an infrastructure by a central authority. If a private entity were to build a township, the amount of resources it would need would be tremendous. Moreover due to fear of competition and lack of trust, not many other companies would be willing to join such a private venture (analogous to service provider monopoly in the US). In such a case a model built by the central authority opens up the entire market to competition. The same principle can be applied to community networks also. Community networks from an economic perspective therefore showcase a single efficient model for revenue generation and creation of a BoD network for the end user.

3 Management in Community Networks

The third generation of optical networks has found new application in community networks. One of the key issues in creating community networks and ensuring their overall success is the management of such networks. From management perspective, community networks, pose a multi-faceted problem. Amongst the many issues that direct special attention are: multi-service platforms, issues in multi-vendor (interoperability), and data and voice bundling. Though far from complete, this list represents the key management bottleneck for provisioning services on a real time basis in community networks.

The primary issue in managing a Community network is the wide distribution of technologies on the same network backbone. Data and voice, packetized and TDM technologies, coalesced on the same platform, create several challenges for management and provisioning. From a management perspective, it is desirable to provide efficient service as well as create a resilient network. While from a provisioning perspective, it is desirable to make available third generation network features like bandwidth on demand (BoD), multi-service platform, and scalability. The wide range of network protocols that serve as transport mechanisms create difficulties in provisioning such type of networks. Packet and TDM protocols when multiplexed together on separate wavelengths are quite easy to provision and manage, but issues arise when there is interconnection of multiple technologies in an end-to-end scenario. The problem escalates when there is some additional QoS requirement for the end-to-end traffic flow. The right amount of grooming and the adequate QoS guarantees accorded are two critical issues in provisioning such services. An end-to-end user lightpath may pass through several nodes some oblivious of the data that flows through while, some resorting to O-E-O conversion and creating protocol variations. These interconnecting nodes have the unique responsibility of ensuring seamless delivery of the data and creating a unique framework to facilitate good QoS based communication.

Another issue in management is the equipment/element management system (EMS). Due to the slowdown in the economy and the absolute resolve by network planners to utilize every available piece of network equipment for deployment, a typical metro optical network may have multi-generation network equipment. On average a metro network may consist of equipment from at least two of the three known generations of optical networking. Managing such networks can become extremely difficult, as each generation creates its own functionality and hence promotes an entirely different set of network parameters. Hence such networks must be based on industry standards. For most known protocols standardization is a key to their global acceptance. In other words, as long as network equipments are within the conformity of a standard the possibility of good inter-networking and hence provisioning is high. Despite adherence to standardization process, networks today may still not be manageable due to protocol non-conformity or overhead wastage. For example the overhead wastages in ATM and SONET are different creating a mismatch for transport of data first over ATM and then over SONET. On the other hand by employing a statistical TDM scheme like Gigabit Ethernet or 10 Gigabit Ethernet, the bandwidth utilization issue gets partially solved.

The multi-layered approach to internetworking by itself creates a serious management problem. To provision services on an end-to-end basis, the network has to be so managed that the selected services through multiple technologies can be optimized to yield the best results. This can be done using a generalized framework for management at the optical layer. When IP routing was transformed into high speed Gigabit capable routers, there was a need to have a smart provisioning scheme for the router ports, to map ingress and egress ports in an efficient way. This scheme termed MPLS, or multi-protocol label switching, is a method to create forward equivalence classes (FEC) for different traffic schemes and switching packets (provision) in routers by purely looking at layer 2 scheme rather than decoding the entire layer 3 header. This results in shorter routing cycles, as well as accorded good QoS when desired. This scheme, when extended to a larger spectra from just switching to the optical layer as well as the multiple technologies is now being standardized as GMPLS or Generalized Multi-protocol Label Switching. GMPLS stands for a generalized framework

Historically optical network management itself has evolved in synchronous and asynchronous methods: TDM and LAN technologies. The TDM technology management, i.e. management of SONET networks was done by TL-1 commands. On account of the difficulty in deploying TL-1 commands universally, TL-1 was replaced with a more prolific method-CMIP or common management information protocol. CMIP is a machine to machine language, intended to be vendor neutral. CMIP has been popular in SONET networks, but it did not spread beyond SONET technologies. For packet based technologies like routing, switching etc. SNMP became the accepted standard. With the integration of packet and TDM technologies, there also emerged a need to integrate the management schemes of the two. In principle CMIP and SNMP were incompatible. CMIP uses a connection oriented model of operation, while SNMP by virtue of being packet mode, is connectionless. Moreover CMIP executes management strategies and actions through a handshake protocol, thus creating a chronological hierarchy for execution. On the other hand in SNMP, being entirely connectionless, there is no need for a hierarchy to establish communication between clients and servers. With the need for maximum utilization of the network, and the wide spread of data traffic through the Internet, the integration of the two technologies became necessary. SONET networks originally designed to carry voice circuits now were transformed for packet based communication to maximize their bandwidth utilization. Likewise, established packet networks could carry packet based voice (VoIP etc.) and hence avoid the need for expensive additional deployment of SONET gear. This created an additional bandwidth management problem. Another fundamental difference between packet and TDM networks is that of availability and reliability. TDM networks like SONET are very reliable. They have excellent resiliency. By having carrier class reliability (50 ms restoration etc) SONET networks are good for voice communication. Packet based networks, in contrast operate on the principle of availability (best effort) Resiliency in packet based networks is not fully automated as in TDM networks. The times required for locating and correcting failures may vary. Such networks hence may not ideally be suited for voice traffic. To ensure voice communication in packet networks, it is then important to have QoS of the packet streams. Newer technologies like differentiated services (DiffServ) and integrated services (IntServ). Provisioning such packet based network with the hierarchy of the protocols is a management challenge.

The evolutionary model in networks today clearly emphasizes a scheme which begins and ends with Ethernet like technologies at the ingress and egress of a network periphery. SONET networking may now only exist in the core of such networks creating all optical pipes on WDM channels. The end-to-end flow in a network needs to be provisioned across these multiple segments of Ethernet, SONET and back on Ethernet through a WDM compatible core. Another issue here is that of routing and wavelength assignment in the WDM core. Having a fixed number of wavelengths can be a bottleneck. More so if we consider the limitations in tunable laser technology and the bottleneck of finding the right transponder cards to provision wavelengths on demand. Opto-electronic conversion based transponder cards are typically not bit rate independent thus creating a management optimization problem for traffic grooming. All this means the necessity to increase the equipment stock at network elements.

4   The Mobility Management Issue

In a community network, wireless happens to be an important revenue generating segment. The wireless network runs on the optical backbone for transport. Many of the wireless services are voice based. This creates an intricate end-to-end model. The wireless traffic has to be sent seamlessly across the optical backbone. The management strategies in the optical backbone have to be now extended to incorporate this extra delay-sensitive wireless traffic. Wireless traffic by itself may be geographically very diverse and provisioning in the backbone might have to be done at very fast speeds. The constant changes in wireless traffic create management problems for the entire network. On average wireless circuits for voice etc. do not have a long duration. Access points for wireless are generally quite well defined, however the traffic variation is unclear. Allotting bandwidth to such access points on a real-time basis is a challenge. Wireless data networks based on principles such as the 802.11b standards need a separate provisioning procedure. Moreover as pointed out earlier, there is a serious bandwidth mismatch between the optical layer and the wireless technologies. Scheduling and routing wireless traffic through interconnects of these two layers is a bandwidth management issue.

Since most of the wireless traffic is mobile oriented, the requirement for bandwidth at access points keep changing drastically. In such a case, optimizing the network for bandwidth is not always possible. A vision of an ultra-broad GMPLS layer, can be viewed, as the best possible alternative to provide management of such unified networks. Assigning bandwidth on a real-time basis to end-to-end traffic flows, spread across geographically as well as protocol varied networks is a classic problem. Optimizing such networks for real-time bandwidth means creating a management platform which has good interaction with the various technologies as well as the protocols involved. Each network may have a management system well tailored to meets its specification, while still able to interact with other networks. This type of micro and macro level management creates an appropriate platform for optimization of the entire network as well as the sub-networks in the access and the core. The management plane must be aware of the various resources the network to create the optimal virtual connection topology for facilitating good end-to-end communication.

Once the management plane constructs the virtual topology, it has then to provision traffic paths.

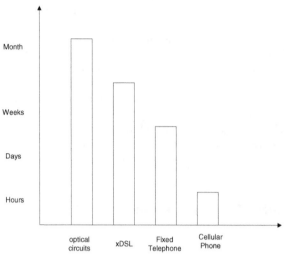

Fig. 1. Provisioning times for services today Ref: "The need for flexible Bandwidth in the Internet Backbone" by Peter Sevcik and Rebecca Wetzel, May 2001 IEEE Network.

5   Potential of Effective Bandwidth Management

The automated scheme of managing networks by discovering the resources, creating a connection topology and then managing or provisioning traffic can yield significant benefits in community networks. This scheme results in significant advantages amongst which are: the subscriber is billed most appropriately only for the specific services that are used. In contrast, earlier schemes created billing anomalies due to multiple management planes and no unification. Secondly, the provisioning time required for networks with a non-unified management schemes can be very high. As can be seen from Fig. 1, the provisioning time decreases with efficient management schemes. A unified management scheme also allows carriers to better utilize the network infrastructure. The management plane has full knowledge of the network infrastructure and can efficiently utilize each network resource to create the best connection topology. This can result in a significant cost saving. In [3] we see a mean 30 % cost saving in optical equipment for provisioning lightpaths by having a unified control algorithm for routing and wavelength assignment in an interconnected ring network. A unified management strategy also avoids duplication of network resources this eliminating undue redundancy. Redundant inventory creates undue surges in capital expenditure. This can be avoided by having a unified management strategy. Another effect of an efficient unified management scheme is the facilitation of growth of the network. A strong management scheme, allows for modular and incremental growth. A unified scheme also fine tunes the network, to best place network resources to create homogeneity of resource utilization throughout the network.

A good management scheme should provide a resilient network with low protection times. The management scheme should be able to provision the network in the least required time, under different loads (variations). Despite a diverse range of protocols the management plane has to interact efficiently with each protocol. Apart from the economic objectives of saving costs and optimizing network resources, the management scheme has to minimize the blocking probability of connection oriented services. The call admission probability has to be maximized to ensure maximum traffic in the network.

Despite an efficient management scheme, dynamic network provisioning may be suboptimal, if the network was initially not well planned. Although outside the scope of this overview article, network planning and capacity planning serve as a necessary framework for network optimization.

Signaling is yet another important aspect of a good management scheme. While reserving bandwidth, efficient and bipolar signaling creates fast provisioning of the resources. Efficient signaling helps secure bandwidth on demand and is a key tool for a good management policy.

6 Conclusion

We have presented an overview of bandwidth management in Community Networks. The importance of community networks is in creating an efficient business model, which further can be best optimized by a good management scheme. The design of a unified management scheme is complicated by the diverse range of protocols and technologies that interact in producing the network hierarchy. A good management scheme results in cost savings for capital as well as operational expenditure. We summarized the needs and properties of a good management scheme necessary for operating a community network with low opex and capex and providing a suitable platform for fast provisioning of community networks.

References

1. Chlamtac, A. Ganz and, G. Karmi, "Purely Optical Networks for Terabit Communication," IEEE INFOCOM, 1989.
2. G. Xiao, J. Jue and I. Chlamtac, "Lightpath Establishment in WDM Metropolitan Area Networks", SPIE/Kluwer Optical Networks Magazine, special issue on Metropolitan Area Networks, 2003.
3. A. Gumaste et. al. 'BITCA: Bifurcated Interconnection of Traffic and Channel Assignment,' Proc of OFC 2002 Anahiem CA
4. http://www.cnuce.pi.cnr.it/Networking2002/conference/chlamytac.pdf Talk by I. Chlamtac, Networking 2002 Pisa, Italy

A Generalised Cost-Aware Caching Scheme for Caching Continuous Media Objects in Best-Effort Network Environments

W.H.O. Lau[1], M. Kumar[2], and S. Venkatesh[1]

[1] Department of Computer Science, Curtin University of Technology, GPO Box U 1987,
Perth 6845, Western Australia
{lauhow, svetha}@cs.curtin.edu.au
[2] Department of Computer Science and Engineering, University of Texas at Arlington,
Box 19015, Arlington TX 76120, Texas, USA
kumar@cse.uta.edu

Abstract. In this paper, we investigate the potential of caching to improve QoS in the context of continuous media applications over wired best-effort networks. We propose the use of a flexible caching scheme, called GD-Multi in caching continuous media (CM) objects. An important novel feature of our scheme is the provision of user or system administrator inputs in determining the cost function. Based on the proposed flexible cost function, Multi, an improvised Greedy Dual (GD) replacement algorithm called GD-multi (GDM) has been developed for layered multi-resolution multimedia streams. The proposed Multi function takes receiver feedback into account. We investigate the influence of parameters such as loss rate, jitter, delay and area in determining a proxy's cache contents so as to enhance QoS perceived by clients. Simulation studies show improvement in QoS perceived at the clients in accordance to supplied optimisation metrics. From an implementation perspective, signalling requirements for carrying QoS feedback are minimal and fully compatible with existing RTSP-based Internet applications.

1 Introduction

The growing use of on-demand *continuous media* (CM) in the Internet has created much interest in designing solutions to scale and enhance the Internet's infrastructure to accommodate CM flows. As outlined by Aras *et al.* [1], the performance requirements of real-time communications include low jitter, low latency, adaptability to dynamically changing network and traffic conditions, good performance for large networks and large numbers of connections and low processing overhead per packet within the network at the end systems, which are difficult to achieve in best-effort networks. Currently, the solutions available to enhance CM delivery include end-to-end congestion control techniques, Quality-of-Service (QoS) provisioning architectures, multicasting, error correction mechanisms, traffic engineering and network proxies. However, such schemes only work well if the level of congestion is low.

A promising technique in alleviating serious congestion problems is the use of network proxies. Specifically, this paper focuses on proxy caching of CM objects in various network environments. The motivation of this paper is due to the following

S.K. Das and S. Bhattacharya (Eds.): IWDC 2002, LNCS 2571, pp. 12–23, 2002.

facts. In recent years, proxy caching has been employed effectively to enhance web services on the Internet. To date, no technology for enhancing on-demand client-server applications (e.g. web) has equivalently matched up to proxy caching in terms of reducing server workload, reducing bandwidth consumption and improving perceived QoS at the clients. Like the web, proxy caching, an incrementally deployable technology, will have great impact in improving on-demand CM applications. Specifically, this paper focuses on developing a suitable caching scheme for CM objects.

Cost-based caching policies [2, 3] represent the state-of–the-art in caching algorithms. Unfortunately, the nature of cost-based schemes, such as the *Bolot/Hoschka* scheme [4], is that they force caches to become application specific, which is fundamentally too restrictive for CM caching. Using generic cost-based schemes such as SLRU [5] and GD [6] does not circumvent the problem, as such schemes are incapable of managing objects with different optimisation parameters within the same cache. To overcome this limitation, it is necessary to deploy separate caches for every application they wish to support caching on, thus creating additional management problems particularly in provisioning storage resources for each cache. In addition, having separate caches is not feasible in resource constrained environments, such as ad-hoc networks.

2   Greedy Dual-Multi

In this section, we discuss the details of the GDM caching scheme. GDM essentially comprises of the GD [6] cache replacement algorithm and a multiple metric cost function called *Multi*. The GD algorithm was devised to deal with systems that exhibit heterogenous transfer costs. Details explaining the GD algorithm can be found in several publications [2, 6, 7]. GD in essence allows a bias to be applied to each object in its cache so as to give higher priority to objects that incur higher retrieval costs. In this section, we discuss a generalisation of GD, which allows multiple cost factors/metrics to be considered. The two key points to note are: i) Many factors such as packet loss, delay, jitter and area [7] affect the quality of a CM stream, and ii) The degree of influence due to each factor largely depends on the nature of each CM session.

In essence, the caching scheme should offer sufficient flexibility for specific cost factors and weights for each cost factor to be stated by users of the cache. For example, a user in a typical CM session could state that loss rate and delay are cost factors that the cache should consider with delay being the more important of the two factors.

Fig. 1 is a conceptual depiction of our proposed idea. We propose that the session feedback mechanism be implemented within the RTSP signalling protocol. We propose the addition of a *Session-Feedback* header to carry out feedback. This information can be conveyed through piggybacking TEARDOWN messages which are issued at the end of sessions. According to the RTSP specification [8], unsupported headers should be ignored by the recipient. Thus, the inclusion of the *Session-Feedback* header does not break existing RTSP implementations. Proxy

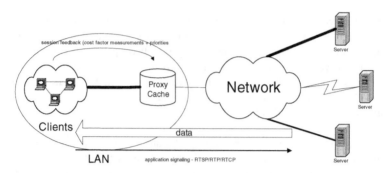

Fig. 1. Proxy cache feedback mechanism

caches that do not support the *Session-Feedback* header, simply ignore it. In addition, the additional header does not include any additional states to RTSP. Thus, the implementation requirements to include the header are straightforward. In addition, signalling overhead for carrying feedback is extremely lightweight.

The GD algorithm alone does not have the capability to consider multiple cost factors. Thus, we propose the *Multi* algorithm, (see Fig. 2) which allows a feedback mechanism to input two tuples into GDM:

i.   A tuple *M*, which is a set of pre-normalised measurements, such as loss rate and jitter. These measurements are derived from sample traces gathered at the client.

ii.   A tuple *W*, where each element w_i in *W* is a weight corresponding to element m_i in *M*. Each weight w_i is an indicator of m_i's relative importance to the other elements in *M*.

Using the above-mentioned inputs, *Multi* employs a two phase approach to computing $R(p)$ in GD. The first phase involves a statistical normalisation process, which normalises the value of each cost factor considered, and the second combines these normalised values through a weighting process. The purpose of the normalisation process is to provide normalised measurements across the types of cost factors being considered, since cost factors can have different distribution characteristics between themselves. The purpose of the weighting process is to allow the user to specify bias amongst several cost factors that a user wishes the caching scheme to consider.

- **Normalisation Phase** – Due to the online nature of caching, *multi* requires a computationally and spatially efficient procedure to normalise its inputs. In addition, the normalisation procedure should converge as quickly as possible. We have developed a normalisation procedure called *RANGE*, which attempts to normalise cost factors in accordance to their corresponding distribution range. The RANGE normalisation procedure is as follows:

$$1. \quad n_i = \begin{cases} m_i / t_i & : \text{ if } \quad m_i / t_i \leq 1 \\ 1 & : \text{ if } \quad m_i / t_i > 1 \end{cases}$$

$$2. \quad \text{if } (m_i / t_i > 1)$$
$$t_i = m_{ii}$$

(1)

where m_i refers to a pre-normalised measurement from set *M*, t_i refers to the right tail-end of measurement m_i's corresponding distribution and n_i refers to the normalised result. If m_i is higher than t_i, RANGE updates t_i with the current m_i value.

- **Weighting Phase** – The normalised values are combined to form a single measure of utility by using a weighted function. As an example, we will discuss the case when GDM considers loss, delay and jitter. Let n_l, n_d, n_j, and n_a represent the normalised values for loss, delay and jitter and area respectively, and w_l, w_d, w_j and w_a represent corresponding weights. $R(p)$ is derived as follows:

$$R(p) = (n_l w_l) + (n_d w_d) + (n_j w_j) + (n_a w_a)$$ (2)

where $w_l + w_d + w_j + w_a = 1$.

The revised GD caching algorithm with the RANGE normalisation scheme called GDM is shown in Fig. 2.

---

1. $L = 0$
2. If p is already cached
3. $H(p) = R(p)$
4. If p is not cached
5.   While there is not enough space
6.   Evict q from X where $q = \min H(x)$ and $x \ni X$
7. $\forall\ a \ni X, H(a) = H(a) - H(q)$
8. $R(p) = 0$
9.

$$\forall m_i \ni M$$

$$N_i = \begin{cases} m_i / t_i & : \text{if} \quad m_i / t_i \le 1 \\ 1 & : \text{if} \quad m_i / t_i > 1 \end{cases}$$

$$\text{if } (m_i / t_i > 1)$$

$$t_i = m_{ii}$$

$$R(p) = R(p) + w_i n_i$$

$\}$ Multi

10. $H(p) = R(p)$
11. Insert p into cache

where
   i. $R(p)$ denotes the retrieval cost for object p,
   ii. $H(p)$ denotes the worthiness of object p relative to other objects in GD's cache
   iii. M denotes the tuple of cost factor measurements at the client where m_i refers to an element in M,
   iv. W denotes the tuple of cost factor weights specified by the client, where each element w_i in W, corresponds to the weighting of measurement m_i,
   v. t_i denotes the threshold for cost factor i,
   vi. n_i denotes the normalised value for measurement m_i.

Fig. 2. Greedy Dual-multi

3   Evaluation of Greedy Dual-Multi

In the context of this paper, we propose three single metric GD-based schemes- *GD-lossrate*, *GD-delay* and *GD-bitrate*. Using these schemes, comparisons are made against the proposed multi-based schemes, *GDM-lossrate, GDM-delay, GDM-*

lossrate-single and *GDM-delay-single* which takes into account a combination of loss rate, delay, jitter and area cost factors. Three special cases of single metric GDM schemes have also been evaluated against the above-mentioned schemes- *GDM-lossrate-single, GDM-delay-single* and *GDM-bitrate-single*. It is important to note that the simulation outcomes of the single metric GD schemes serve as the outcomes for the single metric GDM schemes if the distribution-range of the cost factors are known.

We use simulation-based studies to investigate the performance of GDM. We have extended the *NS* network simulation package to simulate Internet-based CM scenarios, which is described comprehensively in [7]. To evaluate the effects of cost-aware caching, we compare the results in the various proposed GD and GDM schemes (GD-lossrate, GD-delay, GD-bitrate, GDM-lossrate, GDM-lossrate-single, GDM-bitrate-single, GDM-delay and GDM-delay-single) against LRU, which is the most commonly used caching algorithm today. We used loss rate, delay, jitter and area [7] as cost metrics in the GDM simulations. We evaluated the characteristics of GDM by comparing GD-lossrate and GD-delay against 4 GDM cases with biased cost functions- GDM-lossrate, GDM-lossrate-single, GDM-delay and GDM-delay-single. This is achieved by adjusting the weights of our cost function to the 'preferred' metric. The link attributes in all scenarios are depicted in Fig. 3.

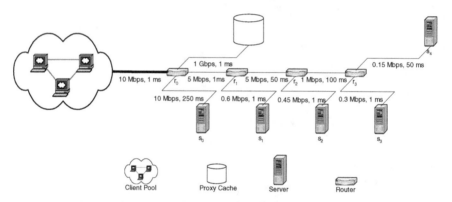

Fig. 3. Simulation topology and link parameters

The number of clients varies between 10 and 50. We assume that all streams are smoothed, thus exhibiting CBR-like inter-departure rates. The simulated time for all cases is 24 hours. The number of layers in each stream is uniformly distributed between 1 and 12. Frame sizes are uniformly distributed between 100 and 1500 bytes. Object distribution is uniformly distributed amongst the 5 servers. Resource popularity is modelled using the Zipf distribution with parameter $z = 1$. Resource size is modelled using the lognormal distribution with input parameters $\mu = 16.6$ bits and $\sigma = 0.5$ bits. Inter-session time for each client is modelled using exponential distributions with $\lambda = 10$ seconds. Session duration is modelled using a shifted exponential distribution (30 seconds added to the result) with $\lambda = 165$ seconds. GDM based schemes require a few extra parameters. Weight values for the GDM schemes are shown in Table 1.

Table 1. Weights for various GDM schemes

Scheme	Lossrate	Delay	Jitter	Area
GDM-lossrate	0.7	0.1	0.1	0.1
GDM-lossrate-single	1.0	0	0	0
GDM-delay	0.1	0.7	0.1	0.1
GDM-delay-single	0	1.0	0	0

4 Simulation Results

We focused our analysis on two main areas. Firstly, we examined the proportion of hits per server based on the various schemes. The purpose is to observe how the cost functions affect hit ratio and how they in turn affect QoS at the clients in the latter part of the analysis. We used the network topology and link characteristics described in Fig. 3 in all scenarios. Each simulation run consists of 4500–22000 sessions depending on the number of clients.

4.1 Proxy Trace Results

The first set of experiments compares the GD-based schemes against their single metric GDM counterparts, namely GD-lossrate, GD-delay, GDM-lossrate-single and GDM-delay-single. The hit ratio profile for GD-lossrate and GD-delay are depicted in Fig. 4a and Fig. 5a respectively. Likewise, we collected results for the single metric GDM based schemes; GDM-lossrate-single and GDM-delay-single (see Fig. 4b and Fig. 5b).

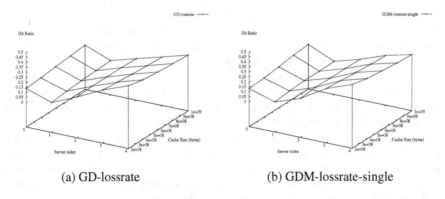

(a) GD-lossrate   (b) GDM-lossrate-single

Fig. 4. Hit ratio

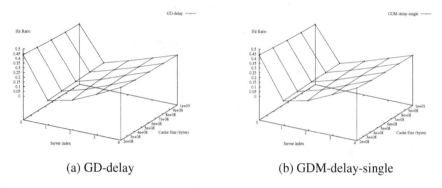

(a) GD-delay   (b) GDM-delay-single

Fig. 5. Hit ratio

The hit ratio profiles depicting GD-lossrate and GD-delay in Fig. 4a and Fig. 5a respectively indicate that GD managed to optimise its cache in accordance to each cost factor. We see very similar results with the single metric GDM counterparts, GDM-lossrate-single and GDM-delay-single (see Fig. 4b and Fig. 5b). Both GD and GDM schemes managed to rank the importance of each server correctly. For the loss rate based schemes, we see increasing hit-proportion with increasing server IDs. Fig. 4 and Fig. 5 also depict the effect of hit ratio with respect to cache size. In these plots, as cache size increases, hit ratio across the servers converges to a more uniform-like distribution, since bigger cache sizes allow GD to accommodate more objects that are of lesser value, thus inducing uniform-like hit ratio characteristics.

The plots for the multiple metric versions of GDM, GDM-lossrate and GDM-delay are shown in Fig. 6a and Fig. 6b respectively. In comparison to their single metric GDM equivalents, there are some subtle differences due to the weighting of other cost factors. The differences are depicted in Fig. 7. The z-axis in Fig. 7a shows the difference in hit ratio between the corresponding schemes depicted in Fig. 4b and Fig. 6a. Similarly the z-axis in Fig. 7b shows the difference between the z-axes of Fig. 5b and Fig. 6b. For instance, due to the additional delay bias, we can see that GDM-lossrate (see Fig. 7a) is caching approximately 6% more objects in server 0 as compared to GDM-lossrate-single. Similarly, due to the loss rate factor considered, we can see GDM-delay (see Fig. 7b) caching approximately 7% less objects in server 0 compared to GDM-delay-single (see Fig. 5b). Based on the above-mentioned observations, we can see *multi*'s weighting function working as intended. By altering the weights of a particular parameter based on the type of scheme (e.g. the delay parameter in GDM-delay), GDM is able to improve performance.

Through examining hit ratio characteristics, we have seen that the proposed schemes are able to appropriately cache objects according to the given optimisation criteria. However, it is still not clear from the above observations that a cost aware caching scheme improves overall QoS. Due to GD's biased behaviour, there is a potential problem of the GD based schemes serving less hits compared to LRU, which in turn induces lower QoS. This rest of the investigation in this paper is focused on whether the proposed schemes improve overall QoS.

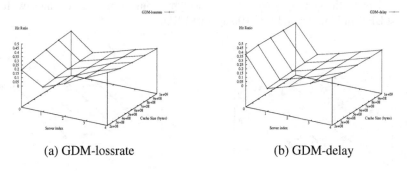

(a) GDM-lossrate   (b) GDM-delay

Fig. 6. Hit ratio

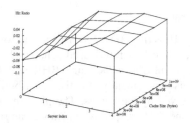
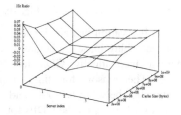

(a) Difference: Hit ratio(GDM-lossrate-single) – Hit ratio(GDM-lossrate)

(b) Difference: Hit ratio(GDM-delay-single) – Hit ratio(GDM-delay)

Fig. 7. Hit ratio differences

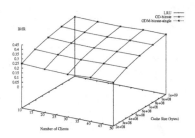
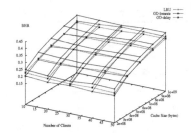

Fig. 8. BHR comparisons between LRU, GD-bitrate and GD-bitrate-single schemes

Fig. 9. BHR comparisons between LRU, GD-lossrate and GD-delay

We investigate GDM's byte-hit-ratio (BHR) performance [3, 9], which is a common benchmark for evaluating caching schemes. The plots in Fig. 8 indicate that for unbiased cost factors, GD and GDM perform similarly to LRU. However, the schemes with biased cost factors (see Fig. 10) tended to have lower BHR than LRU.

Fig. 9 depicts this observation more clearly by comparing the schemes with the highest BHR in Fig. 10a and Fig. 10b against LRU.

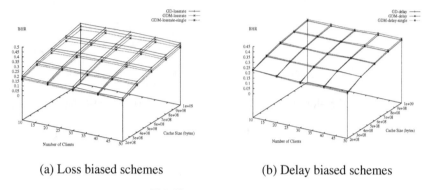

(a) Loss biased schemes   (b) Delay biased schemes

Fig. 10. BHR comparisons

Another observation that can be noted from Fig. 10 is that BHR performance between the various delay biased schemes is marginal, while loss rate biased schemes have higher variance. Ideally, GDM-lossrate-single should have the same BHR as GD-lossrate. The reason for this discrepancy is due mainly to the distribution characteristics between loss rate and delay observed by the clients. The plots in Fig. 11a and Fig. 11b depict the CDFs for loss rate and delay respectively. As we can see, the loss rate distribution is more positively skewed compared to the delay distribution, which in turn causes RANGE to converge slower. We have seen that GDM can potentially induce lesser BHR due to its biased nature. The next section involves verifying if GDM can outperform LRU despite having lower BHR.

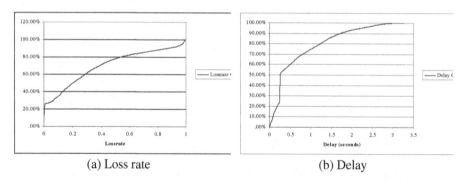

(a) Loss rate   (b) Delay

Fig. 11. QoS observations at the clients

4.2   Quality of Service Measurements at Clients

To determine spatial QoS characteristics, we investigate the loss rate measurements recorded at the clients. The plots depicting mean loss rate measurements (see Fig. 12

and Fig. 13), clearly reflect the measured hit profile of their corresponding schemes. More importantly, despite LRU exhibiting highest BHR and loss rate-biased schemes exhibiting lowest BHR, all loss rate-biased schemes outperform LRU. This indicates that BHR is not a strong indicator of caching performance when QoS factors have to be considered. Predictably, GD-lossrate had the lowest loss rates, due to aggressive caching of objects from server 4 (see Fig. 4a) and higher BHR compared to the other loss rate-biased schemes. GD-losssrate-single does not perform on par with GD-lossrate.

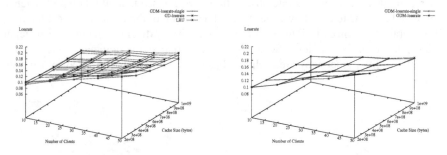

Fig. 12. Mean loss rate comparisons with schemes considering single cost factors   **Fig. 13.** Mean loss rate comparisons

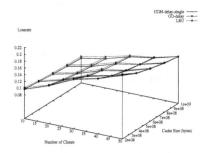

Fig. 14. Mean loss rate comparisons between single metric delay-biased schemes

The reason is due to the highly skewed loss rate distribution (see Fig. 11) which caused RANGE to take longer periods to converge. Due to the slow convergence, there was little difference between GDM-lossrate-single and GDM-lossrate (see Fig. 13). Even when compared to delay-biased schemes (Fig. 14), LRU still exhibited the worst loss rate. The reason is due to LRU caching more objects between server IDs 1-3 and compared to the other schemes. Since the loss rate observations (see Fig. 11a) indicate that a large portion of sessions involved low losses, there was little difference between various schemes in general. It is clear from the above-mentioned plots and the hit-profiles discussed in the previous section that GDM outperforms LRU.

To determine the temporal QoS aspects of the various schemes, we investigate delay and jitter observed at the clients. Delay was measured by recording the time taken for data packets to travel between source and receivers. The plots depicting mean and standard deviation delay observations are shown in Fig. 15 and Fig. 16. As we can see from Fig. 15a, unlike the disparity between GDM-lossrate-single GD-lossrate, GDM-delay-single performs on-par with GD-delay. This is due to the lower skew of the delay distribution compared to loss rate (see Fig. 11). Again, LRU performs worst despite its high BHR. The plot in Fig. 16 depicts the differences between the GDM-delay-single and GDM-delay schemes. The key point to note in this plot in comparison to the hit profiles of GDM-delay-single and GDM-delay (see Fig. 5) is that by altering the weights supplied to GDM, we are able to achieve the desired QoS characteristics. Like the loss rate observations, we can see that all GD-based schemes compared to LRU tend to lower the standard deviation of their dominant cost factor.

In general, differences in jitter (see Fig. 17) are insignificant as there is insufficient jitter induced in the topology. Schemes with loss rate as the dominant factor tend to exhibit less jitter since they are caching objects predominantly further away from the proxy.

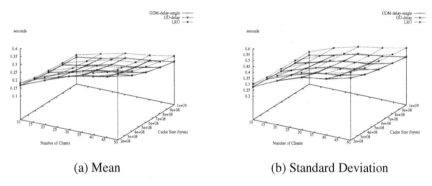

(a) Mean   (b) Standard Deviation

Fig. 15. Delay comparisons between single metric delay-biased schemes

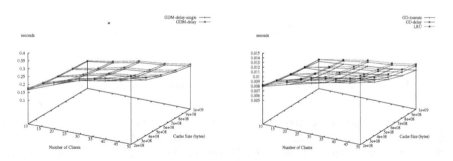

Fig. 16. Mean delay comparisons between   **Fig. 17.** Mean jitter comparisons
GDM-delay and GDM-delay-single

To summarise, this section, we note following two key points:

i.   The outcomes of the dominant factor x (i.e. loss rate, delay), of all GDM based schemes is upper bounded by GD-x. We restate that the GDM-x-single schemes would perform on par with GD-x if the t_i values are known.

ii.   The payoff for managing objects in a cache according to their dominant factors results in lower QoS than the other factors. One such example is the difference in loss rate and delay measurements between GD-lossrate and GD-delay. However, since a combination of factors can affect the quality of CM applications, GDM is a more suitable caching scheme compared to other single metric schemes.

5   Conclusion

In this paper, we have shown the benefits of using QoS feedback from clients to tailor a cache's decisions on caching. Specifically, we have generalised GD by extending it with a fast converging multi-metric and accurate cost function, *multi*. We stress the point that network caches should provide greater flexibility, allowing users the option of influencing the cache's eviction policy. The huge advantage that we see in a receiver driven approach to caching is that it allows the cache to individually prioritise each cached object according to the optimisation metrics supplied by the user. By that, we mean users decide on the metric set they find that affects their applications most. This approach is most suitable for the heterogeneous nature of Internet applications, since GDM does not make any hard assumptions on users' needs. In addition, the implementation requirements for the session feedback mechanism are fully compatible with existing RTSP-based Internet applications.

References

1.   Aras, C.M., Kurose, J.F., Reeves, D.S., Schulzrinne, H.: Real-Time Communication in Packet-Switched Networks. Proceedings of the IEEE, **82**:1 (1994) 122–139
2.   Cao, P., Irani, S.: Cost-aware WWW Proxy Caching Algorithms. in USENIX Symposium on Internet Technology and Systems. (1997) 193–206
3.   Wang, J.: A Survey of Web Caching Schemes for the Internet. ACM SIGCOMM Computer Communication Review, **29**:5 (1999) 36–46
4.   Bolot, J.C., Hoschka, P.: Performance Engineering of the World Wide Web: Application to Dimensioning and Cache Design. Computer Networks and ISDN Systems, **28** (1996) 1397–1405
5.   Aggarwal, C., Wolf, J.L., Yu, P.S.: Caching on the World Wide Web. IEEE Transactions on Knowledge and Data Engineering, **11**:1 (1999) 94–107
6.   Young, N.E.: The K-Server Dual and Loose Competitiveness for Paging. Algorithmica, **11**:6 (1994) 525–541
7.   Lau, W.H.O., Kumar, M., Venkatesh, S.: A Flexible Receiver-Driven Cache Replacement Scheme for Continuous Media Objects in Best-Effort Networks. in IEEE Hawaii International Conference on System Sciences. (2001)
8.   Schulzrinne, H., Rao, A., Lanphier, R.: Request For Comments 2326: Real Time Streaming Protocol (RTSP), Internet Engineering Task Force. (1998)
9.   Krishnamurthy, B., Rexford, J.: Web Protocols and Practice: HTTP 1.1, Networking Protocols and Traffic Measurement. (2001) Addison Wesley.

Improving Web Access Efficiency Using P2P Proxies

Ratan K. Guha[1] and James Z. Wang[2]

[1]SEECS- Computer Science, University of Central Florida
Orlando, FL 32816, USA, 407-823-2956, guha@cs.ucf.edu
[2]Department of Computer Science
Clemson University, Clemson, SC 29634, USA
864-656-7678, jzwang@cs.clemson.edu

Abstract. Recent studies have shown that caching data at the proxy server can improve the user response time for web document retrieval. However, a single cache proxy has a limited cache space, thus the amount of data that can be cached is limited. In this paper, we organize the distributed proxy servers into a group of peer-to-peer cache proxies. By exploiting the aggregate cache space and computing power, we can reduce the average user response time and improve our quality of services. Unlike some previous works that achieve the similar results by replacing the single proxy server with a cluster of servers, we simply link the existing distributed proxy servers using a set of rules for connection, data cache and data routing to build a self-organized scalable distributed P2P proxy caching system. Our simulation has proven the feasibility and effectiveness of our cache system. In addition, our P2P proxy cache system is configured using individual based model and is easy to implement in a large scale distributed environment.

1 Introduction

Although the Internet backbone capacity increases as 60% per year, the demand for bandwidth is likely to outstrip supply for foreseeable future as more and more people blend the WWW into their daily life. The WWW contains a wide range of information, such as news, education, sports, entertainment, shopping. Due to the bandwidth limitation, the performance of Web surfing is suffering from network congestion and server overloading. Especially when some special event happens, the web servers who have the related information always experience unordinary number of HTTP requests on those information. Recent studies have shown that caching popular objects at locations close to the clients is an effective solution to improve Web performance. Caching can reduce both network traffic and document access latency. By caching replies to HTTP requests and using the cached replies whenever possible, client-side Web caches reduce the network traffic between clients and Web servers, reduce the load on the Web servers and reduce the average user-perceived latency of document retrieval. Because HTTP was designed to be stateless for servers, client-driven caching has been easier to deploy than server-driven replication.

S.K. Das and S. Bhattacharya (Eds.): IWDC 2002, LNCS 2571, pp. 24–34, 2002.
© Springer-Verlag Berlin Heidelberg 2002

Caching can be implemented at various points on the network. Since early 90's, a special type of HTTP servers called "proxy" has been used to allow users hiding behind a firewall to access the internet [1]. Although using caching proxy server can reduce both network traffic and document access latency, researchers have found that a single proxy cache can be a bottleneck due to its bandwidth and storage limitations. As the number of clients increases, the proxy server tends to overloaded and hence causes a lot of cache missing. In a heterogeneous bandwidth environment, a single naive proxy cache system might actually degrade the Web performance and introduce instability to the network. [2] To solve the problem, organizations normally use many servers to serve as the cooperative proxies.

There are many different cache architectures proposed in cooperative web caching. Hierarchical Web caching cooperation was first introduced in the Harvest project [3]. The Harvest cache system organizes caches in a hierarchy and uses a cache resolution protocol called Internet Cache Protocol (ICP) [4] to search the cached document. Adaptive Web Caching [5] extends the Harvest cache hierarchy by grouping the cache servers into a tight mesh of overlapping multicast groups. There are many problems associated with the hierarchical cache systems [6,7]. To setup a hierarchy, cache servers often need to be placed at the key access points in the network. It requires some manual configuration or significant coordination among the participating servers. In addition, higher levels of the hierarchy sometimes become the bottlenecks. To solve the problems, some distributed caching systems have been proposed. In distributed web caching systems [7,8,9,10,11,12,13,14,15], all cache proxies are viewed as the same level within the caching system. Several approaches have been proposed to design cooperative caches in a distributed environment. Internal Cache Protocol (ICP) [4] supports discovering and retrieving documents from sibling caches as well as parent caches despite its hierarchical origin. Adaptive Web Caching (AWC), an extension of Harvest cache hierarchy, is a cluster based distributed cooperative caching architecture. AWC relies on multicasting to discover and retrieve the cached documents. Similar to the idea of AWC, LSAM [8] is also a multicast based distributed web cache architecture providing automated multicast push of web pages to self configuring interest groups. Cache Array Routing Protocol (CARP) [9] divides the URL-space among an array of loosely coupled caches and lets each store only the documents whose URLs are hashed into it. Provey and Harrison proposed a hierarchical metadata-hierarchy [10], in which directory servers are used to replace the upper level caches in hierarchical cache structure, to efficiently distribute the location hints about the cached documents in proxies. Push Caching [7] proposed a similar distributed internet cache using a scalable hierarchy of location hints combined with caching of these hints near clients. CRISP [11] cache adopts a centralized global mapping directory for caches. Cachemesh [12] builds a routing table for clients to forward the Web requests to the designated server who was selected to cache documents for a certain number of web sites. Proxy sharing [13] tries to make multiple servers cooperate in such a way that a client can randomly pick a proxy server as the master server and the master server will multicast the requests to the other cooperative caches if it can not satisfy the client's request. Summary Cache [14] and Cache Digest [15] keep local directories to locate cached documents in the other caches. The cooperative servers exchange summary or digests of the documents in their caches.

In hierarchical caching architectures, not only organizing and maintaining a cache hierarchy require a significant amount of administrative coordination between the institutions, but also increasing levels of hierarchy tend to create bottleneck at higher levels. In distributed caching architectures, most schemes focus on maximizing the global cache hit ratio by implementing sophisticated directory look up or search schemes. But increasing global hit ratio does not always imply reduction of request latencies in distributed environment. In those caching schemes, not all cache hits are good for user request latencies [16]. Those protocols also create hot spots when some web servers become very hot sometimes. To solve the hot spot problem, Karger et al proposed a consistent hashing technique to construct per-server distribution trees to balance the work load among the proxy servers [17]. However implementing consistent hashing and random tree requires a lot of changes of current internet infrastructure [18]. Some problems associated with distributed caching schemes that use multicast or directory servers to locate the documents include high connection times, higher bandwidth usages and administrative issues [6]. On the other hand, because most those schemes concentrate on reduce the miss rates, load balance among the proxy servers are not thoroughly discussed. In reality, balancing the workloads is very important in quality and fairness of services. Load balancing are not only affected by the user request patterns, but also by the characteristics of the servers, such as storage capacity and network bandwidth of the cooperative servers [19].

The essential features for an ideal proxy cache system include minimized access latencies, robustness, transparency, scalability, efficiency, flexibility, stability, load balancing, and simplicity. It is important to design and implement a Web caching scheme to satisfy all those properties. However, scalability and simplicity are the biggest problems in the current Web cache schemes as discussed earlier. To solve the aforementioned problems, we propose a novel caching scheme using P2P concept. In this proxy caching system, the cooperation between proxy servers is handled naturally by simulating an ecological system. The load balance is achieved by data caching and data replication based on an economical model. The design of this Web cache system is unique that it satisfies reasonably well all desirable properties mentioned above. The rest of the paper is organized as follows. In section 2, we discuss the fundamental of the proposed proxy caching system and explain the design details. In section 3, we design a simulation model to examine our observations and to check the feasibility of the caching system. The simulation results are presented in section 4. Finally we have our conclusion and future study in section 5.

2   Cache Ecology – A Novel Proxy Caching Scheme

A distributed proxy cache system consists of many proxy servers inter-connected through network. Each server or a cluster of servers normally serve a group of clients within an institution. Figure 1a typical distributed proxy caching system on the internet.

Proxy servers serve the requests from their clients as well as the requests from the peer servers. On the other hand, they download the requested documents either from

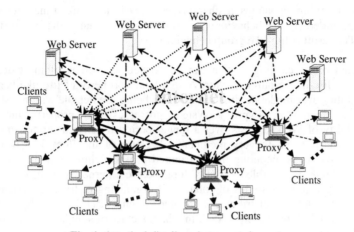

Fig. 1. A typical distributed proxy cache system.

the web servers or from its neighbor proxies to minimize the latencies for their clients. There are many factors contributing to the complexity of implementing a large scale distributed proxy caching system. Institutions have their own business agenda and economic policies hence the common interests of all institutions are different. Thus the available caching resources, such as storage capacity and network bandwidth, vary dramatically in different proxy servers. Hence, the routing of requests and caching data in a distributed proxy system, as shown in Figure 1 are complicated and the complexity of management grow exponentially with the growth of the network. Further more, using complex caching scheme adds more complexity to the system and in turn hinders the scalability of the system.

2.1 An Individual-Based Design Model

In real world, there are two proven mechanisms that can successfully manage a massive cooperative system. One is the economic system in which millions of clothes can be distributed among the same magnitude number of people without the centralized control. The distribution of clothes follows a simple supply and demand model. The other is the ecological system where within a specific environment natural selection creates cumulative advantages for evolving entities. For many years, people have enjoyed the beauty of bird flocks and fish schools in natural world. Researchers have tried to find a simple model to simulate the nature flock in computer animation until the paper "boids"[1] published at SIGRAPH in 1987 [20]. Since then the boids model has become an oft-cited example of principles of Artificial Life. Flocking is a particularly evocative example of emergence: where complex global behavior can arise from the interaction of simple local rules. In the boids model, interaction between simple behaviors of individuals produce complex yet organized group behavior. The component behaviors are inherently nonlinear, so mixing them gives

---

[1] http://www.red3d.com/cwr/boids/index.html

the emergent group dynamics a chaotic aspect. At the same time, the negative feedback provided by the behavioral controllers tends to keep the group dynamics ordered. The result is life-like group behavior.

A distributed proxy caching system can be viewed as a flock of individual cache nodes having life-like group behavior. A significant property of life-like behavior is unpredictability over moderate time scales while being predictable within a short time span. Data caching in a proxy system possesses this property due to the unpredictability of Web requests over a longer period time. In a shorter time frame, the Web requests seem to very predictable because of the flock like behavior of human interests. Thus modeling the distributed proxy caching system using similar approach as boids is feasible. Actually long before Internet flourished, flocks and schools were given as examples of robust self-organizing distributed systems in the literature of parallel and distributed computer systems [21]. The boids model is an example of an individual-based model[2], in which a class of simulation used to capture the global behavior of a large number of interacting autonomous agents. Individual-based models are also used in biology, ecology, economics and other fields of study. In this paper, we use individual-based model to design a self-configured, self-organized proxy ecology in which individual cache nodes exchange data and information using some simple rules. The aggregate effect of caching actions by individual cache nodes automatically distributes the data to nearest clients and also automatically balances the workload.

2.2 Self-Configuration of Proxy Network

Self-configured network architecture is the most important part of our proxy cache system. When a proxy server decides to join the proxy network, it broadcasts a request-for-join message to the existing cache nodes; the existing cache nodes reply the request-for-join message with the characteristics of their own. Those characteristics include storage capacity, network bandwidth, the number of linked neighbors or the IP addresses of the neighbors who link to the exiting node. Then the requester decides which existing nodes it wants to link to. Many factors determine the number of links that the requester can establish. Besides its own storage capacity, network bandwidth and user tolerance to response latencies, the characteristics of the exiting nodes, such as distances to the requester, storage capacities, network bandwidths and average number of links per nodes, all contribute to the final decision. After the decision is made, the new added node informs the other nodes who it wants to link with to update their neighbor database. It also builds a neighbor table for later lookup. An entry in the neighbor table includes an ID which is normally an integer and the IP address to the neighbor. If the IP addresses of the neighbor nodes for all the existing nodes have been sent to the requester, the requester can actually build a proxy graph and store it for later reference. If a proxy graph is required to store in every proxy servers, the newly added node has to send the IP addresses of its neighbors to all the other nodes in the system so that the other nodes can update the proxy graph on their sites. Because our individual based model does not require the individual proxy aware of all the nodes other than its neighbors, storing the proxy graph is only an

---

[2] http://www.red3d.com/cwr/ibm.html

enhancement option. However, with the proxy graph stored locally, we can improve the performance in searching the cached documents. Once the links have been virtually established, the new added node is restricted to only exchange information and data with its neighbors. This constraint guarantees the simplicity of the management on each individual cache nodes. Figure 3 demonstrates a proxy graph with 7 nodes.

2.3 Data caching and data flow

In our proxy cache system, the cached data may be transmitted to current node from its neighbors instead of directly from the original Web server. To cope with the new data type, we extend the traditional cache line to include data ID, Metadata and state bytes. An ID of the cache line can be the URL of the cached document. Metadata should include some simple descriptions of the document. State bytes contain information for cache coherency control as well as some other statistical data, such as number of replicas of the document in the proxy system known to this node, shortest distance to a replica. Figure 2 depicts a Web cache line in our proxy cache system.

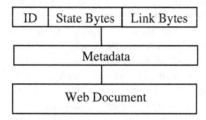

Fig. 2. A web cache line.

The cached document might be replicated from other nodes in the proxy caching system or from links of other nodes that had previously accessed this document. Additional fields are needed in cache line to provide the link information. A distance-to-replica field must pair with the links to tell the distance from this node to the nearest replica along the link.

The heart of our proxy cache system is to link the data across the proxies by flowing metadata or data among the neighbors. We explain the rules for each individual proxy node to handle the data caching and data flow instead of the algorithm. We generate a flock effect as seen in boids model by controlling the caching and flow of data on demand as in an economic system. Figure 3 shows how cached documents flow among the proxies in a 7-node proxy graph.

Assume document *a, b* and *c* are originally cached in nodes 3, 7 and 2 respectively. When client at proxy node 1 requests for document a, node 1 does not have the document cached in its site; it asks its neighbors for a cached copy. In turn, the neighbors ask their neighbors and finally find document *a* in node 3. Node 3 sends document *a* to node 2. Node 2 then sends the data to node 1 where the request was originated. Most importantly those proxy nodes could replicate the document for

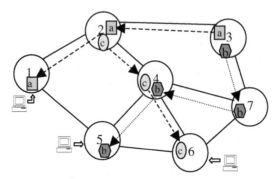

Fig. 3. Data flow among the proxies

serving later requests along the way that data routed through. Actually those nodes that sit on the path between the query originator and data source do not need to cache the Web document if it is not necessary by its own local policy. However it needs to cache the ID, state bytes, links and metadata. By caching the information, the later requests for the same Web document from its neighbors or itself can be quickly routed to the cached replicas. The number of replicas passes along the nodes and increases when a node on the path replicates the document. When a proxy decides to replicate the document, it updates the shortest distance to a replica in state bytes and sends a message to its neighbors for them to update their state bytes and link bytes accordingly. Then the neighbors notify their neighbors if their shortest distances to a replica are modified. All updates on one node are based on the information passed in by its neighbors and the information stored locally. Similarly when client at proxy node 5 request for document *b*, document b is passed to and possibly replicated along path 3-7-4-5. When client at node 6 requests document c, it is replicated and linked on path 2-4-6. The accumulative result of the data caching and data flow distributes the data to where they are mostly demanded and hence reduces the user response latencies.

2.4 Searching the Cached Replicas

With the cache strategy described in the previous subsection, when a new request for a document comes in to certain proxy, the proxy node first checks if the document is cached in its site or if the link information is cached in its site. If the document is already cached, the request from the client is satisfied. If the proxy node contains only the link information, the proxy sends a request to its neighbor that the link points to. The nodes linked by cached link information relay the request to eventually reach the node that has a cached replica. The cached replica is then transmitted to the requesting node along the path that the request was replayed. However, if the proxy node contains neither the requested document nor the link information, then this proxy node has to issue a query to its neighbors. The query message includes the ID of the requested document, a timestamp, maximum waiting time. The timestamp tells the time when the query was issued. The maximum waiting time indicates how long the requester will wait for response. The proxy node who initiated the query waits for the query results until the waiting time expire. If a node receives a query that passed the maximum waiting time, it discards the query message. Once a node finds a cached document or link information matching the ID given in query message, it sends a response to its neighbor where the query message comes from. The neighbors then route the response all the way back to the query originator. A response must include a field to indicate the distance to the cached replica. This field is updated along the way that the response propagates back to the requester. For instance, assume a client at node 7 request for document c, a query is sent to its neighbors, including nodes 3, 4, and 6. Some time later, node 7 gets responses back from nodes 3, 4, and 6. Node 7 then decides the route to obtain the document based on the distance information provided in all responses. If a node, after it issues a query to its neighbors, does not get responses within the maximum waiting time, the node will contact the original Web server for the document.

3 Simulation Model

There are many metrics that need to be studied to evaluate a proxy cache system. Those metrics include hit ratio, average user response time, load balance, management complexity, etc. In this paper, we focus on study the feasibility of our proxy ecology scheme. Without loss of generality, we configure a proxy system based on some simple assumptions. Then we examine the hit ratios and user response times on this simplified simulation model. First we assume there are 64 proxy servers existing in the network. The distribution of those 64 servers is so uniform that we can automatically configure them into a mesh-like proxy graph so that all proxy servers have 4 neighbors each, excepting that those servers on the edge and the corner have 3 and 2 neighbors each respectively. We further assume all the servers are identical in computation power, storage capacity and network bandwidth. The distances between the neighbors are all equal.

We assume the users have equal probability issuing Web requests at any proxy servers. We also assume all Web documents have equal size. The response time for a Web document is the time when first part of the document arrives at client's workstation. We compare the user response times using our proxy cache system with that using a single proxy server. First we assume the distance from a client to its proxy server is 100ms. If the requested document is cached in the proxy server, the user response time is 200ms ignoring the other overheads. We assume the distance between the neighbor proxies is 200ms, which is double the distance from client to its proxy server. So if a requested document is found in a neighbor node, the user response time is 600ms. We also assume there are 10,000 distinct web documents on the web servers. The average distance from the clients to the web servers is 1500ms. Thus the user response time for a cache miss is 3000ms ignoring all other overheads. We further assume each proxy can cache 1% of total web documents. Based on our observation [19] and some other studies [22], web requests follow a Zipf-like distribution. The access frequency for each Web document i is determined as follows:

$$f_i = \frac{1}{i^z \cdot \sum_{j=1}^{m} 1/j^z},$$

where m is the number of Web documents in the system, and $0 \leq z \leq 1$ is the zipf-factor [19]. We assume $z = 0.7$ in our simulation. We use the aforementioned parameters as our default simulation parameters unless explicitly specified otherwise. In this simulation, each node performs as a proxy server. When the proxy server receives a request from its client, it sends the document to the client if the document is cached in the proxy. Otherwise, it routes request to the Web server as well as to its neighbor proxies. The first response from either the original web server or from the neighbor nodes will be used. Because user response time is the most important metric for customer service from proxy server's point of view, simultaneously sending requests to its neighbors and to the original web server yields better response times. We use a simple LRU algorithm as our cache replacement algorithm in simulation.

4 Simulation Results

We study the system performance on various cache rates. Our simulator simulates the 64 proxy nodes in either individual mode or cooperative mode. We collect the results of our simulations running in those two modes. As most of the Web cache system, we use hit ratio and average response time as system performance metrics. We issue 200,000 web requests to the cooperative proxy cache simulator. We start to collect statistic data after the first 50,000 web requests have been processed to avoid the inaccurate results due to the startup of the simulation. We observe the user response times and cache hit ratios at all nodes. The simulation results are presented in Figure 4 and Figure 5.

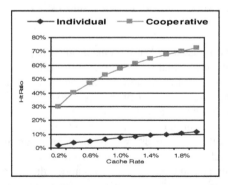
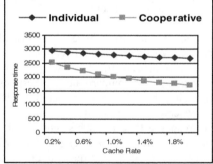

Fig. 4. Hit ratios under various cache rates.   **Fig. 5.** Response times in various cache rates.

As expected, increasing the cache rate increases the cache hit ratios and in turn improves the system average response time for requests. This is true in both individual proxy cache system and cooperative proxy cache system. As shown in Figure 4, Our P2P cooperative proxy system increases cache hit ratios tremendously over the individual proxy cache. In our simulation, the average hit ratio for individual proxies is only 7%. On the other hand, the P2P cooperative cache system yields 57% hit ratio. In terms of user response times, Figure 5 shows our P2P cooperative cache system outperforms individual proxy cache by large margin. For instance, when each individual proxy caches only 1% of the total web documents, the average response time for individual proxy is 38% more than that for our cooperative proxy cache system.

5 Conclusion

In this paper, we proposed a novel P2P cooperative proxy system using an individual based model. Each proxy node needs only to communicate with its neighbors. The accumulative results of the individual actions by all proxy nodes automatically distribute the data close to the clients. The system can be self-configured into a proxy graph using simple rules. Based on the demand, data cache and data movement in our proxy cache system create an ecological proxy system. This unique system design simplifies the management of a large-scale cooperative proxy cache system. Our simulation results indicate the effectiveness and feasibility of our cache system.

Acknowledgment. This work has been partially supported by ARO under grant DAAD19-01-1-0502. The views and conclusions herein are those of the authors and do not represent the official policies of the funding agency or the University of Central Florida, or Clemson University.

References

[1]   A. Luotonen and K. Altis, World Wide Web proxies, Computer Networks and ISDN systems, First International Conference on WWW, 27(2):147–154, April 1994.
[2]   A. Feldmann, R. Caceres, F. Douglis, G. Glass and M. Rabinovich, Performance of Web Proxy Caching in Heterogeneous Bandwidth Environments, Proceedings of InfoCom (1), pages 107–116, 1999.
[3]   A. Chankhunthod, P. B. Danzig, C. Neerdaels, M. F. Schwartz, and K. J. Worrel, A Hierarchical Internet object cache, proceedings of USENIX Annual Technical Conference, pp. 153–164, San Diego, CA, January, 1996.
[4]   Duane Wessels, K Claffy, ICP and the Squid Web Cache, IEEE Journal on Selected Areas in Communication, 16(3):345–357, 1998.
[5]   Scott Michel, et al., Adaptive Web Caching: Towards a New Caching Architecture, the 3rd International WWW Caching Workshop, Manchester, England, June 1998.
[6]   P. Rodriguez, C. Spanner and E. W. Biersack, Web Caching Architecture: Hierarchical and Distributed Caching, the 4th International WWW Caching Workshop, San Diego, CA, March 1998.
[7]   R. Tewari, M. Dahlin, H. Vin and J. Kay, Beyond Hierarchies: Design Consideration for Distributed Caching on the Internet, Technical Report: TR98-04, Department of Computer Science, University of Texas at Austin, February 1998.
[8]   Joe Touch, The LSAM Proxy Cache – a Multicast Distributed Virtual Cache, the 3rd International WWW Caching Workshop, Manchester, England, June 1998.

[9]   V. Valloppillil and K. W. Ross, Cache array routing protocol v1.0, Internet Draft, <draft-vinod-carp-v1-03.txt>, February 1998.

[10]   D. Dovey and J. Harrison, A Distributed Internet Cache. In 20th Australian Computer Science Conference, February 1997.

[11]   S. Gadde, M. Rabinovich and J. Chase, Reduce, Reuse, Recycle: A Approach to Building Large Internet Caches, in Workshop on Hot Topics in Operating Systems, pp. 93–98, May 1997.

[12]   Zheng Wang, Cachemesh: A Distributed Cache System for World Wide Web, the 2rd NLANT Web Caching Workshop, June 1997.

[13]   R. Malpani, J. Lorch and David Berger, Making World Wide Web Caching Servers Cooperate, the Fouth International World Wide Web Conference, Boston, MS, December 1995.

[14]   L. Fan, P. Cao, J. Almeida and A. Broder, Summary Cache: A Scalable Wide-Area Web Cache Sharing Protocol, IEEE/ACM Transactions on Networking, 8(3):281–293, 2000.

[15]   Alex Rousskov and Duane Wessels, Cache Digests, Computer Networks and ISDN Systems, 30(22-23):2155–2168, June 1998.

[16]   M. Rabinovich, J. Chase and S. Gadde, Not All Hits Are Created Equal: Cooperative Proxy Cache Over a Wide-Area Network, Computer Networks and ISDN Systems, 30(22-23):2253–2259, November 1998.

[17]   David Karger et al., Consistent hashing and random trees: Distributed cachine protocols for relieving hot spots on the World Wide Web. In Proceedings of the Twenty-Ninth Annual ACM Symposium on Theory of Computing, pages 654–663 , 1997

[18]   David Karger et al., Web Caching with Consistent Hashing, the 8th international WWW conference, Toronto, Canada, May 11–14, 1999.

[19]   James Z. Wang and Ratan K. Guha, Data Allocation Algorithms for Distributed Video Servers. In Proceedings of ACM Multimedia, pages 456–459, Marina del Rey, California, November 2000.

[20]   Craig W. Reynolds, Flocks, Herds, and Schools: A Distributed Behavioral Model, in Computer Graphics, 21(4) (SIGGRAPH '87 Conference Proceedings) pages 25–34, 1987.

[21]   L. Kleinrock, Distributed System, invited paper for ACM/IEEE-CS Joint Special Issue: Communications of the ACM, Vol. 28, No. 11, pp. 1200–1213, November 1985.

[22]L. Breslau, P. Cao, L. Fan, G. Phillips and S. Shenker, Web Caching and Zipf-like Distributions: Evidence and Implications, in proceedings of IEEE INFOCOM'99, pp. 126-134, March 1999.

Web Recency Maintenance Protocol

K. Satya Sai Prakash and S.V. Raghavan

Dept. of Computer Science and Engineering
Indian Institute of Technology Madras, India.
ssai@acm.org, svr@cs.iitm.ernet.in

Abstract. In this paper, we propose a new protocol namely Web Recency Maintenance Protocol (WRMP) that employs "push" mechanism to maintain the currency of the World Wide Web (WWW) at Search Engine (SE) site. As of this writing SEs are adopting "pull" technology, by employing search bots to collect the data from WWW. Pull technology can no longer cater to the growing user base and the information explosion on the web. In view of the gigantic structure and dynamic nature of the WWW, it is impractical to maintain the currency using this technology. This practical limitation makes SEs yield stale results. WRMP ensures the real time update by initiating an update agent as and when the server is modified or updated. The availability of high processing speed enables the SE to maintain the currency of the whole WWW in real time. This protocol cuts down the unwarranted roaming of the search bots and takes the real purpose of the web server establishment i.e. reach the public over Internet as the motivating factor. This protocol gives an additional advantage to the SE by enabling it to prioritize the Web sites based on the change frequency. We have given a formal specification for the protocol and an M/M/1 model based analysis.

1 Introduction

WWW is a constantly changing entity with doubling period less than 24 months [3]. Web is a huge repository of information. SE is one of the most sought after tools to search the information on the WWW. SE has three key functional phases namely, *Web Data Acquisition (WDA), Web Data Indexing (WDI)* and *Web Data Rendering (WDR)*. In WDA phase, SE employs pull technology by sending Search bots to spider the web. In WDI phase the collected data is indexed using a customized page-indexing algorithm. Usually the algorithm is a variant of Vector based indexing. Vector contains keyword frequency, keyword occurrence position (like title, heading, sub-section etc.), proximity parameter in case of 'multi word' keyword and the link popularity (e.g. Google). After indexing, URLs are sorted based on the page rank. In WDR phase, SE accepts the keyword from the user and retrieves the closely matched documents and renders it to the user.

In user's point of view SE need to fulfill two important specifications.

Recency: "It is the policy of the SE to render the most recent web document". Any document d_i rendered by SE with timestamp t_i should have the same timestamp at the original web site

S.K. Das and S. Bhattacharya (Eds.): IWDC 2002, LNCS 2571, pp. 35–44, 2002.

Relevancy: "It is the policy of the SE to render precise document the user is looking for". Any document d_i rendered for the input keyword(s) must be exact match to the user expectation.

Recency and *Relevancy* are the two sustaining core features of any SE. An *ideal* and *successful* SE must render absolutely recent and relevant information.

(α, β) – Currency metric was proposed in [3]. It gives a probabilistic metric for the Recency and carries out an analytical analysis to get an estimate of the bandwidth requirement to maintain the β currency with a probability α. To give away the most current information, Stock Quote Servers, News Servers are deploying the push technology. It is clear from above that the Recency is a primary factor for SE and to maintain the Recency it is essential to employ the push mechanism. The best form of ensuring such norms is in the form of a *protocol*. Protocol ensures a formal and clear specification of the tasks and requirements. It enables the transactions to flow smoothly and regulates the communication process between the server and the clients. Hence as the Recency requirements become stringent, it calls for a new protocol and WRMP is aiming to fulfill the criterion for real-time web updates.

In this paper we have given the formal description of the protocol and highlighted the need for such a protocol. We also show that this protocol has number of advantages like, a) Elimination of the staleness in SE hits, b) Reduction of spider activity, c) Focused crawling, d) Efficient utilization of the computing and communication resources. This protocol can be incorporated in Stock Quote Servers and News Servers.

The limitation of this work is implementation of the protocol in real Internet scenario. We are hopeful that the contributions in the paper are valuable and motivate the Web server and SE developers to adapt to this protocol.

The rest of the paper is organized as follows. In Section 2, we survey the related work. Section 3, gives a formal specification and description of the proposed WRM Protocol. We gave an M/M/1 based model for WRMP and illustrated with a numerical example in Section 4. Finally in Section 5, we discuss the results and the future work.

2 Related Work

WWW is a highly dynamic and unstructured entity. Yet it is modeled as Web and lot of characterization [1] and various studies have been carried out. [10] gives an analytical substantiation of Internet topology using power-laws. A formal definition for freshness of a web page, freshness metric and a page refresh strategy are discussed in [2]. In [9] we find a comprehensive survey of the existing SE and web growth. It also talks about the crawlers and the indexing capacities of some popular SEs and [11] gives the approximate size of the WWW as about 2 billion pages and also provides with various statistics such as indexing of web by some popular search SEs, rating of SEs etc. The bandwidth requirement for the WWW assuming that there are 1 billion pages and each page is of 12k size (approximately) to be indexed everyday is about 1Gbps [5]. To handle such an explosive growth and to maintain the Recency [5] proposes a meta-computer based technique. Authors in [6] indicated that the inability to index the whole web by any single SE is causing the inconsistency in the result set and also staleness. A holistic view of SE anatomy is discussed in [12] and a SE technology over view in [17]. Crawling speed is improving and literature reports that the fastest crawler can index about 10 million pages a day. But this cannot ensure the absolute Recency because the lower bound on the web change is about 12%, which amounts to indexing about 240 million pages a day. Initially maintenance of the freshness of SE with the help of Web servers is proposed in [16]. It was studied just as an algorithm but our proposal is more generic and substantial in the sense that it will be an integral part of the Web servers and SEs. [4][7][14] give an insight into protocol proposal, specification, description, testing, implementation and conformance. [15] in accordance with [3] highlights the dynamic nature of web, especially with reference to the page modifications and creations. [15] also makes a reference to the "push" based technology, which is a major influencing factor in our work. Traditional study of maintaining the Recency of the web is by optimizing the number of search bots and an elegant study is made in [13].

All this related work has motivated us to characterize the core features of SE. In this paper we have proposed the protocol that will ensure the Recency of the web data and in our future work we focus on the relevancy of the web data. We have chosen to incorporate this feature at protocol level to make it long lasting, simple to incorporate and manage and can be used by all the application servers, which give primary importance to the currency of the data.

3 Web Recency Maintenance Protocol (WRMP)

WRMP is an application layer protocol designed to maintain the Recency of the WWW at SE site. This section gives a formal specification and description of the protocol.

3.1 Overview of WRMP

In Client – Server architecture, there are three possible ways of event notifications namely

- Instantaneous Notification: Client instantaneously notifies the server and the server immediately updates the events. This mechanism is realized by *interrupt* mechanism.
- Periodic Notification: Server periodically checks for the notifications and updates the events, if any. This is termed as *polling* technique.
- On Request: On client's request, server updates the event.

Present SEs are employing the *periodic* updating policy with some customization. In this proposal we advocate the usefulness and feasibility of the *instantaneous* notification technique. In this protocol, what we call as URL_Update can be the total modified/created page as the available technology barriers are eliminated.

Client – Server Notification Mechanisms:

Table 1. Listing of notification mechanism properties

Type/Properties	No. of Requests	Change Frequency	Periodicity
On Demand	Yes	No	No
Periodic	No	Yes	Yes
Instantaneous	No	Yes	No

No. of Clients to SE (Web Servers): n, No. of Requests: m, Change Frequency: c
Periodicity: p, Data Transfer Time: t, Time Period: T
Total Time for the Mechanism: T_{demand}, $T_{periodic}$, $T_{instantaneous}$
$T_{demand} = 2*(m/T)*n*t$ (100% Recent)
$T_{periodic} = 2*(p/T)*n*t$ (P% Recent, where P = p/c)
$T_{instantaneous} = (c/T)*n*t$ (100% Recent)
Since m >> c, $T_{instantaneous}$ << T_{demand} also since m >> p, $T_{periodic}$ << T_{demand}
Hence T_{demand} is discarded.
To maintain the cent percent Recency in the case of Periodic Updates, p = c, which in turn clearly makes $T_{instantaneous}$ << $T_{periodic}$.
Thus the superiority of the Instantaneous Update technique is established.
<u>Algorithm to find the periodicity:</u>

Upper bound on periodicity $(k) = T/n*t$
 Let the time stamp be denoted by τ
 for i = 1 to k
       for j = 1 to n
             find τ_{ij}
 for each j, compare τ_is (i.e i = 1, while (i < k) {if diff(τ_i, τ_{i+1}) d_j++; i++;}) Where d_j is the difference count at j^{th} server.
 m = d_j;
 if m < k
   Periodicity is m
 else
   Periodicity is k (upper bound)

In this protocol WRMP server resides in the SE server and the WRMP client resides in the Web server.

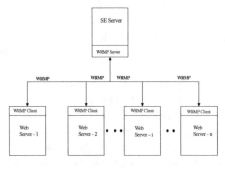

WRMP: Web Recency Management Protocol

Web Server Functionality (Protocol Client):

- Invoke *Information Agent (IA)* whenever there is a creation or modification of web page
- Update IA with the URL Tag, Timestamp and key words.

Search Server Functionality (Protocol Server):

- Read the IA update
- Update the time-stamp
- Read the content description
- Get the change frequency of the URL
- Rank the URL
- Invoke the Download Agent

3.2 Specifications for WRMP

We give Finite State Machine (FSM) based protocol specification for WRMP. Initial handshake for connection establishment, connection closing and abort procedures are in accordance with the other application layer protocols. Hence no explicit mention is made in this paper.

WRMP Server States:

- Idle: Starting state in which the server waits for the client update.
- Receive_Update: Upon receiving the client update, Server gets into this state. In this state it reads the packet header to check for the correctness. On success, it moves to next state (Process_Update) or *On_Error* it goes to Reject_Update state.
- Process_Update: Parses the update packet and checks the correctness and validity of the update. Upon which it either moves to next state (Update_DB) or *On_Error* goes to Reject_Update state. It may invoke the *spam* guard functions incase of spurious updates in terms of content or frequency.
- Update_DB: In this state, server opens a connection with the database and updates the obtained information. Incase of any error, throws an appropriate error flag and moves to Idle state or Receive_Update state to process the next update request (if any)
- Reject_Update: This state looks for pending requests in the queue and on finding them it moves to Receive_Update state otherwise settles in Idle state.

WRMP Server Functions:

- Read_Header (): A function to read the Update packet sent by the information agent from the client. If the header is not conforming to the protocol, an error flag is raised by this function.
- Parse_Packet (): This function parses the Update packet and looks for the protocol conforming URL, Timestamp and Description fields. Incase of incompatibility raises the appropriate error flag.
- Write_DB (): An important function that opens the connection with the local Database and writes the updated information.

Special Functions:

- Spam_Guard(): This special function is invoked if the SE is flooded with spam packets (both in terms of spurious frequency and/or keywords).
- Block_Sender(): This function is invoked as a remedy for spamming.

WRMP Client States:

- Idle: Start state in which the client is waiting for the OS to raise an Update interrupt.
- Prepare_Update: In this state the client prepares the Update packet in the prescribed format.
- Dispatch_Update: Sends the prepared Update packet with the help of the *information agent.*

WRMP Client Functions:

- Create_Update (): This is the function that enables the client (web server) to fill the packet with the correct information.
- Send_Update (): Enables the client to send the Update packet to the server.

The FSM for WRMP is as follows:

WRMP Server:

The FSM for WRMP Server is a quintuple $<I, O, S, \delta, \lambda>$, where
$I = O = \{I_1, I_2, I_3, I_4, I_5, I_6, I_7\}$, $S = \{S_1, S_2, S_3, S_4, S_5\}$, $\delta = I \times S \rightarrow S$ and
$\lambda = I \times S \rightarrow O$. Further,
I_1 = On_Receive_Interrupt, I_2 = On_Receive_Update, I_3 = On_Process_Update,
I_4 = On_Update_DB, I_5 = On_Reject_Update, I_6 = On_Error_Update,
I_7 = On_Completion_Update. And S_1 = Idle, S_2 = Receive_Update,
S_3 = Process_Update, S_4 = Update_DB, S_5 = Reject_Update

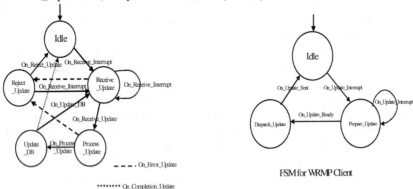

FSM for WRMP Server

FSM for WRMP Client

State Transition Tables for WRMP Server and Client:

Inputs States	I_1	I_2	I_3	I_4	I_5	I_6	I_7
S_1	S_2	-	-	-	-	-	-
S_2	S_2	S_3	-	-	-	S_5	-
S_3	-	-	S_4	-	-	S_5	-
S_4	-	-	-	S_2	-	-	S_1
S_5	S_2	-	-	-	S_1	-	-

Inputs States	I_1	I_2	I_3
S_1	S_2	-	-
S_2	S_2	S_3	-
S_3	S_1	-	S_1

Problems related to the Database update are not highlighted in this protocol. Server takes the necessary measures for successful writing of the data to the database.

WRMP Client:

The FSM for WRMP Client is a quintuple $<I, O, S, \delta, \lambda>$, where
$I = O = \{I_1, I_2, I_3\}$
$S = \{S_1, S_2, S_3\}$
$\delta = I \times S \rightarrow S$ and
$\lambda = I \times S \rightarrow O$
Further, I_1 = On_Update_Interrupt, I_2 = On_Update_Ready, I_3 = On_Update_Sent
And S_1 = Idle, S_2 = Prepare_Update, S_3 = Dispatch_Update

WRMP Errors
WRMP101 – Invalid Update Packet
WRMP201 – Invalid URL
WRMP202 – Invalid Timestamp
WRMP203 – Invalid Data
WRMP301 – Blocked URL for Keyword Spam
WRMP302 – Blocked URL for Repeated Update
WRMP401 – Error Opening Database
WRMP402 – Error Reading/Writing Database
Description of WRMP
WRMP Update packet has the following format: <URL, Timestamp, *>
To be more specific, including the packet header, the complete format is given below.

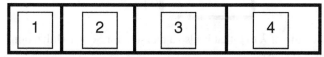

1 – WRMP Header: Contains the protocol header to distinguish from other application layer packets
2 – URL: Contains the complete URL string that is modified or created.
3 – Timestamp: This field takes the time stamp in a prescribed format.
[mm/dd/yyyy-hh/MM/ss-GMT(24 hours clock)]
4 – Description (Keywords, Abstract, Meta Tags): A brief description about the *url* that may contain the keywords, meta tags etc.

3.3 WRMP Implementation

A working model for the WRM Protocol is developed using JDK 1.3.1 and Oracle 8i WRMP Client sends the URL updates in the above given format and the WRMP Server accepts after validation and writes to the Recency_Database.
The Database schema used to store the URL update is as follows:
Database Name: Recency_Database
[*URL_ID, URL_STRING, TIMESTAMP, DESCRIPTION, UPDATE_FREQUENCY*]
With this protocol in order, the SE invokes an up-to-date module while throwing the result set to the user for the given keyword (s). As the result set is being rendered the corresponding URL freshness is checked with the Recency_Database and incase it is found to be stale, no cached data is given. Instead user is either directed to the site or the site is indexed on the fly. More stress and light is thrown in this aspect in our future work that concentrates on *Relevancy* aspect of the SE.

4 Model & Analysis

This section gives a basic m/m/1 based queuing model at SE server to process the arrived *information agent* updates. A simple numerical illustration is given in the analysis sub section to substantiate the power of the protocol.

The WWW content creation and the modification is an independent activity. Creation/Modification of one web site has no bearing or influence on the other web sites. Hence the update arrivals from various Web servers to the SE site are Poisson with arrival rate λ. Let the service rate of the SE server be μ. As long as $\lambda < \mu$ the system is under control.

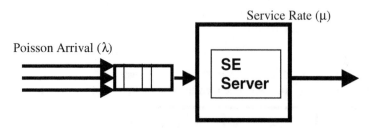

Traffic Intensity (ρ) is the ratio of λ to μ that is also a measure for Server Utilization.

Mean number of requests = $\rho/(1-\rho)$

Average response time = $(1/\mu)/(1-\rho)$

Mean number of requests waiting to be processed: $\rho^2/1-\rho$.

In the present web scenario, the volume of the server-initiated updates is much less than the available bandwidth and processor speed. We are not dwelling into the SE architecture because indexing and rendering are not the primary issues in this paper. We will report the performance analysis of SE and web server ranking, based on the *change frequency* in our future work.

Illustration:

Today in the computing industry Giga hertz processors and Megabits bandwidth are available. To illustrate the efficiency of WRMP, consider a typical scenario.

Let the percentage change of the web be 25%. That amounts to 500 million pages a day are subjected to change.

Let the available bandwidth be 1Mbps and the processor speed is one Giga hertz.

Assuming that each *information agent* request is about 50 bytes and the processing time is about 500 clocks, the system can process about 2 million URL updates per second.

But with the 25% change of the web, the server needs to process about 5000 URL updates per second that comes to .25% utilization of the actual capacity. This highlights the fact that the protocol overhead is insignificant with the available computation power.

5   Results & Future Work

This section describes results obtained in this work, the limitations of the protocol acceptance and the future scope of the work. The plots given in the results section are for visualization of the numeric values available today.

5.1 Results

WRMP neatly fit into the M/M/1 model. Hence numerical study on Web change, processor speed and bandwidth requirements have shown that the available computing and communication infrastructure is sufficient for the real-time maintenance of the Web Recency.

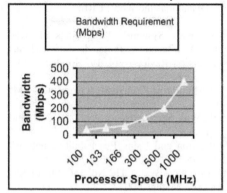
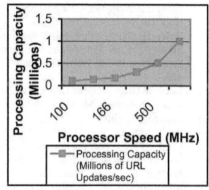

Fig. 1. Speed versus Bandwidth requirement   **Fig. 2.** Processor Speed versus Capacity

Even if the whole web changes every day and sends the updates, it requires only 23.2 kbps bandwidth on a 1GHz processor. On the average a lookup program to process an incoming *URL Update* contains about 250 instructions. Hence it needs about 1000 clock cycles. Each *URL Update* is about 50 bytes. In this scenario for various processor speeds an estimate of the number of *URL Updates* that can be processed is given in figure 1. Balance between computing and communication resources is essential to achieve the optimal throughput. As the processor speed increases we find that the capacity to process the number of updates increases and so is the bandwidth requirement.

5.2 Limitations

The client specification of the protocol needs to be incorporated in the Web server and the server specification of the protocol in SE server.

5.3 Future Directions

Since there are quite a few popular SEs, the protocol needs to be extended for a Multicast environment. As the SE site has more Web servers dedicated for WWW data acquisition, it can be modeled as *M/M/n* and study the performance improvement. Based on the update frequency, SE server can schedule the resources to index the site and develop a ranking system.

References

[1]   Andrie Broder et.al, "Graph Structure in the Web", URL:
      www9.org/w9cdrom/160/160.html
[2]   Aravind Arasu et.al, "Searching the Web", ACM Transactions on Internet Technology,
      Vol. 1, No. 1, August 2001, pp: 2–43
[3]   Brian E Brewington, GeorgeCybenko, "How Dynamic is the Web", URL:
      www9.org/w9cdrom/264/264.html
[4]   Colin H. West, "Protocol Validation in Complex Systems", Proceedings of ACM
      SIGCOMM' 89 Symposium: Communications Architecture & Protocols, Austin, Texas,
      September, 19-20, 1989. Computer Communication Review, Vol. 19, No. 4, pp: 303–
      312.
[5]   Jacob W Green, "Hyper Dog: Up to date Web Monitoring through Meta Computers", MS
      Report, Baltimore, Maryland, October 2000.
[6]   Lawrence S, Giles C. L, "Searching the World Wide Web", Science, Vol. 280, No. 5360,
      April 1998, pp: 98–100 URL: www.sciencemag.org
[7]   Lin F., Chu P and Liu M., "Protocol Verification and Using Reachability Analysis",
      Proceedings of ACM SIGCOMM'87 pp: 126–135.
[8]   W. May, G. Lausen, "Information Extraction from the Web", TR. No. 136, Institute for
      Informatics, Albert-Ludwigs University, Germany, March 2000
[9]   Mei Kobayashi, Koichi Takeda, "Information Retrieval on the Web", ACM Computing
      surveys, Vol. 32, Issue 2, June 2000, pp: 144–173
[10] Michalis Faloutsas et al, "On Power-Law Relationships of the Internet Topology",
      Proceedings of ACM SIGCOMM, Cambridge, USA, August 1999, pp: 251–262
[11] URL: www.searchenginewatch.com
[12] Sergy Brin, Lawrence Page, "The Anatomy of Large Scale Hyper textual Web Search
      Engine", URL: www7.scu.edu.au/programme/fullpapers/1921/com1921.htm
[13] J Talim et al, "Controlling the Robots of Web Search Engines", Proceedings of ACM
      SIGMETRICS 2001, pp: 236–244.
[14] K. Tarnay, "Protocol Specification and Testing", Plenum Press, ISBN: 0-306-43574-8
[15] Venkat N Padmanabhan, Lili Qiu, "The Content Access Dynamics of a Busy Web Site:
      Findings and Implications", Proceedings of ACM SIGCOMM 2000, pp: 111–123
[16] Vijay Gupta, Ray Campbell, "Internet Search Engine Freshness by Web Server Help",
      TR –UIUCDCS–R–2000–2153, Digital Computer Library.
[17] Wen-Chen Hu, Yining Chen, "An Overview of World Wide Web Search Technologies",
      In the proceedings of 5th World Multi Conference on Systems, Cybernetics, Informatics,
      SCI2001, Orlando, Florida, 22-25 July 2001.

Tools and Techniques for Measuring and Improving Grid Performance

Rupak Biswas[1], Michael Frumkin[1], Warren Smith[2], and
Rob Van der Wijngaart[2]

[1] NAS Division, NASA Ames Research Center, Moffett Field, CA 94035
[2] Computer Sciences Corp., NASA Ames Research Center, Moffett Field, CA 94035

Abstract. To better utilize its vast collection of heterogeneous resources
that are geographically distributed across the United States, NASA is
constructing a computational grid called the Information Power Grid
(IPG). This paper describes various tools and techniques that we are
developing to measure and improve the performance of a broad class
of NASA applications when run on the IPG. In particular, we are investigating the areas of grid benchmarking, grid monitoring, user-level
application scheduling, and decentralized system-level scheduling.

1 Introduction

NASA has a vast collection of unique and powerful resources such as wind tun-
nels, flight simulators, massive data storage systems, and state-of-the-art su-
percomputers located at centers around the United States and connected by
high-performance networks. To better utilize these heterogeneous distributed
resources singly and in groups, NASA is constructing the Information Power
Grid (IPG) (www.ipg.nasa.gov). It is one of several instances of computational
grids [4] intended to provide ubiquitous and uniform access, through a convenient interface, to a wide range of resources, many of which are specialized and
cannot be replicated at all user sites. The overall goal is to create a scalable,
adaptive, robust, and transparent environment that unifies multiple physically
separated resources into a single virtual entity. As part of the IPG project, we
are investigating techniques and developing tools to measure and improve the
performance of a broad class of applications when run on such distributed grids.

One question often asked is what types of applications can run well on grids
and, in particular, how well do they run on a specific grid? We are developing
the NAS Grid Benchmarks (NGB), a suite of representative distributed tasks,
to answer this question. Details of NGB are given in Section 2. Another important issue is to determine how well a grid is performing. To address this, we are
building a software framework called CODE for observing the performance of
resources (computers, storage systems, networks), services (databases, file transfers), and applications (convergence rate, time per iteration) in computational
grids. CODE is described in Section 3.

In addition to measuring grid performance, we are attempting to improve
it by devising better techniques for scheduling applications to resources. These

S.K. Das and S. Bhattacharya (Eds.): IWDC 2002, LNCS 2571, pp. 45–54, 2002.

scheduling strategies are based on predictions of application resource usage. Using these predictions, we are developing algorithms for user-level grid scheduling where the primary goal is to minimize application turnaround time (see Section 4). However, while reducing turnaround time is the aim of individual users, organizations operating grids typically want to maximize throughput. We are addressing this problem by developing decentralized system-level scheduling algorithms that balance the load across multi-resource (e.g., CPU, memory, and I/O) computer systems with the ultimate goal of minimizing the time required to completely process all the submitted jobs (see Section 5).

2   Grid Benchmarking

Apart from transparent access to remote resources, the most important property of a computational grid, from a user perspective, is how quickly a certain job or collection of jobs can be finished. A number of tools have been available for a long time that help rate the qualities of computing resources, such as processor speed, memory bandwidth, disk I/O bandwidth, and point-to-point communication bandwidth and latency. However, the performance of an application code is typically a nonlinear function of system characteristics, which is why user-level benchmarks such as the NAS Parallel Benchmarks (NPB) [3], despite their inadequacies, have gained popularity among application engineers. Applications that can benefit most from execution on computational grids are often complex, which makes the task of predicting their turnaround time more difficult, even when all system characteristics are available.

Thus, we have developed a set of prototypical grid applications, based on NPB, called the NAS Grid Benchmarks (NGB) [6]. These applications have been released as a set of paper-and-pencil benchmarks [13], to be implemented by groups developing grid middleware, computer vendors, as well as organizations operating grids. Their significance is that they specify standard tasks to be executed, allowing comparisons between different grids or different resource pools within a single grid. We briefly describe the benchmarks here, and provide a rationale for their design, scaleup properties, and verification.

2.1   NGB Design

Applications that are naturally suited for execution on computational grids fall broadly into two categories. The first is large collections of independent (non-communicating) processes that would overwhelm a single computing resource. An example is parameter studies, in which many instances of the same process or group of processes with slightly different input data are run independently. The second is collections of communicating processes with different processing characteristics. An example of this much broader category is a numerical computation producing sizable raw data sets, followed by a postprocessing step filtering the data, and a visualization step. These two examples are captured in two of the four NGB, namely Embarrassingly Distributed (ED) and Visualization Pipe

Visualization Pipe (VP)

Embarrassingly Distributed (ED)

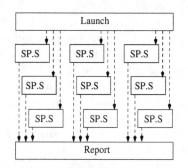

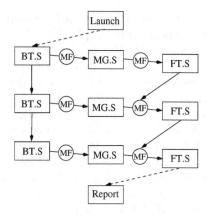

Fig. 1. Data flow graph of parameter study, sample size (class S).

Fig. 2. Data flow graph of visualization pipeline, sample size (class S).

(VP). The remaining two NGB, Helical Chain (HC) and Mixed Bag (MB) [6], are also examples of collections of communicating processes.

Each NGB is defined by means of a Data Flow Graph (DFG), whose nodes consist of computations, and whose arcs indicate communication and control. The DFGs representing ED and VP are shown in Figures 1 and 2. Dashed arrows signify control flow only, while solid arrows signify both data and control flow. The nodes "Report" and "Launch" signify start and wrap-up (including verification) of the benchmarks, respectively. Other graph nodes shown in rectangular boxes indicate benchmark tasks derived from NPB. SP and BT are kernels of Computational Fluid Dynamics (CFD) codes that represent regular scientific computations. MG, which contains a multigrid solver that includes data smoothing, represents post-processing. Finally, FT, which contains a Fast Fourier Transform (FFT) component, symbolizes visualization.

Changes made to NPB to accommodate NGB are kept to a minimum. For ED, the only change is the variation of a constant used to initialize a flow field in SP, thus producing a parameter study. VP features communications between BT, MG, and FT nodes (solid arrows). Each modified NPB outputs its entire solution array, which is used for initialization by its successor node(s) in the DFG. Some data transformations need to be performed to accomplish this. BT produces a field of vectors with five components per mesh point, whereas MG operates on a scalar field. Hence, a reduction operation is required; we choose the local speed of sound as the scalar computed from BT's five-vector. FT, in turn, operates on a complex field. MG's real scalar output field constitutes the real part of the FT input field. The complex part is a spatially filtered copy of the real part. In addition to different data formats, BT, MG, and FT also use different size meshes. We use trilinear interpolation, indicated by the nodes in round boxes labeled "MF" in Figure 2, to adjust to different mesh sizes. When multiple inputs are used for a single graph node, we take their arithmetic average.

2.2   NGB Problem Sizes

Like NPB, NGB features different problem sizes—called classes—to accommodate grids of various capabilities. The classes, ranked in ascending order of data
set sizes, are S, W, A, B, C, and D. An NGB problem of class X uses NPB
of class X as well, as indicated by the suffix "S" in Figures 1 and 2. The NPB
classes, except W and D [12], were determined in a fairly ad hoc manner, and we
will not try to retrofit them with a justification. For determining NGB problem
sizes, we use the following rationale. Let a critical path in an NGB DFG be
determined by the summed total amounts of arithmetic work along a directed
path from Launch to Report (i.e. ignoring concurrency within DFG nodes), save
pipeline startup experienced by, for example, VP, and save interpolation work.
We now postulate that an NGB should not have more work along a critical path
than any unmodified NPB of the corresponding class used in the construction
of the NGB DFG. That means that if full inter-node concurrency is exploited,
an NGB will take no more time than a corresponding NPB of the same class.
This requirement is met by determining the number of DFG NPB nodes along
a critical path, its *length*, and dividing the number of iterations or time steps
within each original NPB by that length. For VP.S, the length is three.

2.3   Verification, Usage, and Availability

A benchmark specification should always contain a verification test to assure that
all required tasks were executed correctly. This places some unusual restrictions
on NGB, most notably that there should be a directed path from any node in
the DFG to the Report node where verification takes place. The arcs between
FT nodes in VP (via MF) are an artifact of this requirement.

In addition to system performance, stability, and variability, NGB can be
used to gauge scheduling efficiency (including gang scheduling, advanced reservation, and load balancing), middleware expressivity, queueing policies, etc. While
early grids will probably show large variability in turnaround times due to interference, it is expected that this will be reduced significantly as they mature, and
as tools like NGB allow users to do quantitative regression tests. NGB reference
implementations in Fortran and Java can be obtained from the NAS software
repository at www.nas.nasa.gov/Software under the name GridNPB3.0.

3   Grid Monitoring

As organizations begin to deploy large computational grids, it has become apparent that systems for observation and control of the resources, services, and
applications that make up such grids are needed. Administrators must observe resources and services to verify that they are operating correctly and must control
them to ensure that their operation meets the needs of users. Users are interested
not only in the overall performance of their applications but also in the proper
operation of resources and services to be able to choose the most appropriate

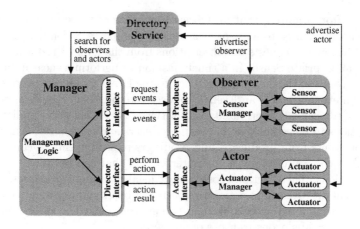

Fig. 3. Architecture of the CODE framework.

ones for their purposes. In this section, we first describe our software framework for distributed monitoring and management that addresses these requirements. It is called CODE (Control and Observation in Distributed Environments) [9]. We then briefly discuss how CODE can be used in a variety of ways.

3.1 CODE Framework

CODE is a framework because it contains the core code necessary for performing monitoring and management. Users only need to add components to CODE and commence execution. For example, if a user wants to create a host monitor, she would create components to monitor processes, files, network communications, etc. The user would then add these components to the framework and instruct it to begin monitoring the host. This same process is used for adding components to perform management actions. In fact, a typical process will be easier because CODE provides a set of commonly used components for observing certain properties and performing relevant actions, and all a user will have to do is select the specific components to use. The CODE architecture is shown in Figure 3. The logical components are Observers that perform and report observations, Actors that perform actions, Managers that receive observations, make decisions, and request actions, and a Directory Service for locating Observers and Actors.

An Observer is a process on a computer system that provides information that can be obtained from the system it is executing on. This could be about the system itself, services or applications running on the system, or even information that is not directly related but is accessible from the system. An Observer provides information in the form of events. An event has a type and contains data in the form of (name, value) pairs. An Observer allows a Manager to query for an event or subscribe to a set of events. A subscription is useful, for example, if a user wants to be periodically notified of the load on a system or whenever some fault condition occurs. Access to events is controlled based on user identity and user location on both a per-observer and a per-event type basis.

Notice from Figure 3 that an Observer consists of three main components. First, Sensors are used to sense or measure some property. Second, a Sensor Manager receives event requests or subscriptions from the Event Producer Interface, uses the appropriate Sensor in a timely fashion to perform a measurement, and sends the result of the measurement back to the Event Producer Interface in the form of an event. Finally, an Event Producer Interface provides an interface for Observers to access a distributed event service. This event service allows event subscriptions to be established between producers and consumers, consumers to query for events from producers, and producers to send events to consumers.

An Actor is a process on a computer system that can be asked to perform specific actions. These actions could affect local or remote resources, services, and applications. Access to actions is controlled based on user identity and user location on both a per-actor and a per-action type basis. The three components of an Actor are analogous to those of an Observer.

A Manager is a process that asks Observers for information, reasons upon that information, and then asks Actors to take appropriate actions. A Manager also consists of three main components. Management Logic receives events from the Event Consumer Interface, reasons upon this information to determine if any actions need to be taken, and then takes the necessary actions using the Director Interface. The Event Consumer Interface is used to request and then receive events from Observers. The Director Interface is used to instruct Actors to perform certain actions and to receive the results of those actions.

The final component of CODE is a Directory Service that stores the locations of all Observers and Actors, describes the types of observations and actions they provide, and allows Managers to search for the necessary Observers and Actors.

3.2   CODE Applications

We are using the CODE framework in several different ways. First, we have developed a prototype Grid Management System [10] to assist with the administrative monitoring and management of a Globus-based [5] grid such as the IPG. This system monitors the resources and services that make up a grid, detects a variety of problems, and supports limited management functions such as stopping/starting daemons and adding/deleting grid user ID to Unix user ID mappings. Second, CODE is being used by grid services to notify clients of events such as when an application begins to execute or completes execution.

There are several other areas where we may use the CODE framework in the future. For example, it could be used as a base information gathering system for a grid information service. Or, CODE could be embedded within applications so as to dynamically monitor or steer them. An application might generate events showing its progress or to report any error conditions that occur.

4   User-Level Scheduling

Grid computing software toolkits, such as Globus [5], provide mechanisms for executing applications on remote computer systems by submitting applications to the schedulers on the remote computers. An active area of research is how to schedule applications across many computer systems with local schedulers so as to minimize the individual application turnaround times. In this section, we describe our approach to this problem using a technique called resource brokering.

We define a resource broker to be a service that can intelligently select where to execute an application when there are many possible target computer systems to choose from. The broker does not have control over these computers and must use local schedulers to execute the application. It therefore selects a computer system based on user requirements and desires. For example, a user may only have executables of an application for certain operating systems, may need a minimum amount of memory or CPUs, or may wish to minimize the cost of executing the application. Typically though, a user's ultimate goal is to obtain the results of the application as soon as possible; so a broker that minimizes turnaround time given user constraints is most desirable.

The two most important factors that determine application turnaround time are the time spent waiting in the scheduler queue and the actual execution time. The resource broker must have a good estimate of these two times in order to select an appropriate computer system on which to execute the application. We are thus developing novel techniques for predicting application run times on space-shared parallel computers, as well as for predicting queue wait times before the applications are given access to the requested resources.

4.1 Application Execution Time Prediction

We predict the execution time of applications using instance-based learning techniques [2] where a database of experiences, called an experience base, is maintained and used to make predictions. Each experience consists of input and output features. Input features describe the conditions under which an experience was observed while the output features describe what happened under those conditions. When a prediction is to be performed, a query point consisting of input features is presented to the experience base. The entries in the experience base are then examined to determine their relevance to the query by computing the "distance" between an experience and the query. Among many possible distance functions [14], we use the Heterogeneous Euclidean Overlap Metric. We also include feature weights that allow the feature space to be stretched, thus giving less or more importance to different features.

Estimates for the output features of the query point are calculated using a distance weighted average of the output features of the experiences. This allows experiences that are more relevant to the query to have a larger contribution. We have chosen a simple Gaussian function as our weighting kernel. We have also inserted a kernel weight that stretches or compresses the kernel function so that greater or fewer experiences are used to form an estimate.

We also specify the maximum size of the experience base and the number of nearest neighbors when making an estimate. Specifying the latter quantity reduces the estimation time but may negatively impact its fidelity. In order to determine the best values for these parameters, we use a search based on genetic

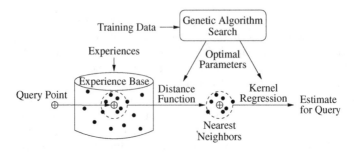

Fig. 4. Instance-based learning technique.

algorithms [7] to try different values and attempt to minimize the prediction error for training workloads. A schematic of the entire process is shown in Figure 4.

In our approach, each scheduled job can be an experience or a query. When a job finishes executing, it is inserted as an experience into the experience base. The experience consists of input features such as the name of the user, the application that was executed, the number of CPUs requested, etc. The execution time of the job is the only output feature. When a user wants a prediction for how long a job will execute, the job is posed as a query with the relevant input features. An estimate for the execution time output feature of the query is then provided.

Results indicate that our execution time predictions are significantly more accurate than user estimates and more accurate than other prediction techniques. For workloads recorded from SGI Origin systems at NASA Ames, the mean error of our execution time predictions is between 36 and 39 percent of the mean run time while the error of the user estimates is between 87 and 149 percent.

4.2   Queue Wait Time Prediction

To predict when applications submitted to scheduling systems will begin executing, we use a relatively simple strategy: We perform a simulation of the scheduling algorithm which results in estimated start times for each of the applications waiting in the queue. This simulation is performed using predicted run times of the applications because the actual run times are not known.

Preliminary experiments show that our start time predictions are much more accurate when our run time predictions are used instead of user estimates of run time. For example, the average error is 95 percent of the mean wait time when using our execution time predictions as opposed to 222 percent when user estimates are used. We expect to improve our start time predictions by tuning the run time prediction techniques for the estimates requested by the start time predictor. Further details of our prediction methods are available in [11].

5   System-Level Scheduling

Almost all system-level scheduling techniques suffer from significant deficiencies when extended to a grid environment: some use a centralized approach that renders the algorithm unscalable, while others assume the overhead involved in searching for appropriate resources to be negligible. Furthermore, classical scheduling algorithms do not consider a grid node to be multi-resource rich and merely work towards maximizing the utilization of one of the resources. We are therefore developing a new decentralized and scalable scheduling algorithm [1,8] for general heterogeneous computational grids that addresses these drawbacks.

Two important aspects of any grid scheduler are its transfer and location policies. The transfer policy decides if there is a need to initiate job migration, and is typically threshold based. Using workload information, it determines when a node becomes eligible to act as a sender or a receiver. Our algorithm is sender initiated and completely dynamic. The location policy selects a partner node for a job transfer transaction to improve overall system performance. The overhead involved in capturing the status of potential partner nodes before making a scheduling decision can be a major issue negating the advantages of job migration. Our algorithm therefore overlaps the time spent looking for appropriate nodes with the actual execution of the ready jobs.

We assume that an Internal Queue (IQ) and an External Queue (EQ) exist in each node of the computational grid. IQ consists of the ready jobs which would be executed by this particular node only; they cannot be migrated. Instead, EQ contains jobs that have been initially submitted to this node, but are yet to be mapped and scheduled for execution. We also assume that each node knows the communication overhead to all of its neighbors. Finally, we postulate that each job has specific requirements for each of the N resources available at a node.

Whenever a job is submitted to a node P_i, the node decides whether the job should be migrated. If so, a request is recursively sent to all adjacent nodes that can respond before IQ is depleted. This strategy overlaps the task of looking for receiver nodes with actual processing, thus hiding the overhead. The transfer policy uses a simple triggering heuristic: greater the load at a node, the less inclined would it be to accept future loads. A node P_j, having received a request for the status of its resources, responds to P_i along the route the request came. Since more than one job may have to be scheduled and multiple nodes may satisfy the requirements, our algorithm first schedules jobs that have the fewest choices. The process continues until all jobs have been scheduled (moved to IQ) or until no more can be mapped because of the lack of resources.

We have conducted extensive simulations for 100 nodes to evaluate the performance of our algorithm and help substantiate the approach. A single performance metric called normalized throughput (η) was used. Basically, η measures the effectiveness of our strategy and is computed as

$$\eta = \frac{T_{\text{single}} - T_{\text{ouralg}}}{T_{\text{single}} - T_{\text{ideal}}}$$

where T_{single} is the time required to completely process all the jobs on a single node; T_{ideal} is T_{single} divided by the total number of nodes; and T_{ouralg} is the time needed by our algorithm. Clearly, $\eta = 1$ in the ideal case. Heterogeneity in resource capabilities and communication cost was maintained while repeating the set of experiments for 1-, 2-, and 3-resource nodes (and jobs). The metric η was 0.79 for 3-resource nodes and as high as 0.85 for 1-resource nodes. These performance levels are very encouraging and could be attained only by overlapping some of the scheduling overhead with the actual execution of the jobs.

6   Summary

In this paper, we gave an overview of the various tools and techniques that we are developing to measure and improve the performance of a wide spectrum of NASA applications when run on computational grids. NASA's instantiation of a computational grid is called the Information Power Grid (IPG) that links its vast collection of heterogeneous resources geographically distributed across the United States. As part of this project, we are investigating the specific areas of grid benchmarking, grid monitoring, user-level application scheduling, and decentralized system-level scheduling.

References

1. Arora, M., Das, S.K., Biswas, R.: A De-centralized Scheduling and Load Balancing Algorithm for Heterogeneous Grid Environments. Proc. Workshop on Scheduling and Resource Management for Cluster Computing (2002) 499–505
2. Atkeson, C.G., Moore, A.W., Schaal, S.: Locally Weighted Learning. Artificial Intelligence Review **11** (1997) 11–73
3. Bailey, D.H., Barton, J.T., Lasinski, T.A., Simon, H.D. (Eds.): The NAS Parallel Benchmarks. NASA Ames Research Center TR RNR-91-002 (1991)
4. Foster, I., Kesselman, C. (Eds.): The Grid: Blueprint for a New Computing Infrastructure. Morgan Kauffmann (1999)
5. Foster, I., Kesselman, C.: Globus: A Metacomputing Infrastructure Toolkit. International Journal of Supercomputing Applications **11** (1997) 115–128
6. Frumkin, M., Van der Wijngaart, R.F.: NAS Grid Benchmarks: A Tool for Grid Space Exploration. Cluster Computing **5** (2002) 247–256
7. Goldberg, D.E.: Genetic Algorithms in Search, Optimization, and Machine Learning. Addison-Wesley (1989)
8. Leinberger, W., Karypis, G., Kumar, V., Biswas, R.: Load Balancing Across Near-Homogeneous Multi-Resource Servers. Proc. 9th Heterogeneous Computing Workshop (2000) 60–71
9. Smith, W.: A Framework for Control and Observation in Distributed Environments. NASA Ames Research Center TR NAS-01-006 (2001)
10. Smith, W.: A System for Monitoring and Management of Computational Grids. Proc. 31st International Conference on Parallel Processing (2002) 55–62
11. Smith, W., Wong, P.: Resource Selection Using Execution and Queue Wait Time Predictions. NASA Ames Research Center TR NAS-02-003 (2002)
12. Van der Wijngaart, R.F.: NAS Parallel Benchmarks Version 2.4. NASA Ames Research Center TR NAS-02-007 (2002)
13. Van der Wijngaart, R.F., Frumkin, M.: NAS Grid Benchmarks Version 1.0. NASA Ames Research Center TR NAS-02-005 (2002)
14. Wilson, D.R., Martinez, T.R.: Improved Heterogeneous Distance Functions. Journal of Artificial Intelligence Research **6** (1997) 1–34

Coarse-Grained Parallelization of Distance-Bound Smoothing for the Molecular Conformation Problem

Narsingh Deo and Paulius Micikevicius

School of Electrical Engineering and Computer Science,
University of Central Florida, Orlando, FL 32816-2362
{deo, pmicikev}@cs.ucf.edu

Abstract. Determining the three-dimensional structure of proteins is crucial to efficient drug design and understanding biological processes. One successful method for computing the molecule's shape relies on the inter-atomic distance bounds provided by the Nucleo-Magnetic Resonance (NMR) spectroscopy. The accuracy of computed structures as well as the time required to obtain them are greatly improved if the gaps between the upper and lower distance-bounds are reduced. These gaps are reduced most effectively by applying the tetrangle inequality, derived from the Cayley-Menger determinant, to all atom-quadruples. However, tetrangle-inequality bound-smoothing is an extremely computation intensive task, requiring $O(n^4)$ time for an n-atom molecule. To reduce the computation time, we propose a novel coarse-grained parallel algorithm intended for a Beowulf-type cluster of PCs. The algorithm employs $p \ n/6$ processors and requires $O(n^4/p)$ time and $O(p^2)$ communications. The number of communications is at least an order of magnitude lower than in the earlier parallelizations. Our implementation utilized the processors with at least 59% efficiency (including the communication overhead) – an impressive figure for a non-embarrassingly parallel problem on a cluster of workstations.

1 Introduction

Determining a macromolecule's shape is important in drug design as well as in understanding biological processes [1]. However, determining the structure remains one of the grand challenge problems in computational biology [24]. Experimental methods, such as X-ray crystallography and Nucleo-Magnetic Resonance (NMR) spectroscopy, account for the majority of protein structures known today [4]. We present a coarse-grained parallel algorithm for tightening inter-atomic distance-bounds – a critical step in structure computation from NMR data. The algorithm is intended for a Beowulf-type cluster of PCs. For an n-atom molecule it requires $O(n^4/p)$ time and $O(p^2)$ communication steps with $p \leq n/6$ processors. Parallelization of the tetrangle inequality bound-smoothing is a challenging problem since atom-quadruples sharing more than one atom cannot be processed concurrently [19]. Previous parallelizations [19,20,22] either do not scale beyond a few processors or require shared-memory architecture, making them unsuitable for distributed systems.

S.K. Das and S. Bhattacharya (Eds.): IWDC 2002, LNCS 2571, pp. 55–66, 2002.
© Springer-Verlag Berlin Heidelberg 2002

1.1 Distance-Bound Smoothing

For an n-atom molecule bounds for a small fraction of all $\binom{n}{2}$ inter-atomic distances are provided by NMR spectroscopy. A number of heuristics have been employed to solve the molecular conformation problem utilizing NMR data [2, 7,16,8,15]. For example, in [12] the structure of the 109-atom polypeptide was computed from the bounds on just 23 (out of the total of 5886) distances. The accuracy of computed structure as well as the time required to obtain it are greatly improved if the gaps between the upper and lower distance-bounds are reduced.

An n-atom molecule is modeled with K_n, a complete graph on n nodes, where nodes represent atoms. Each edge (i, j) is assigned two labels u_{ij} and l_{ij} – the upper and lower bounds, respectively, on the distance between the ith and j^{th} atoms.

The triangle inequality can be applied to all atom-triples to tighten the distance-bounds. Likewise, the tetrangle inequality, derived from the Cayley-Menger determinant [5,18], can be applied to quadruples of atoms to further reduce the gaps. Given four points a, b, c, d, the Cayley-Menger [5,9] determinant is denoted by $CM(d_{ab}, d_{ac}, d_{ad}, d_{bc}, d_{bd}, d_{cd})$, where d_{ij} is the distance between points i and j.

$$CM(d_{ab}, d_{ac}, d_{ad}, d_{bc}, d_{bd}, d_{cd}) = \begin{vmatrix} 0 & 1 & 1 & 1 & 1 \\ 1 & 0 & d_{ab}^2 & d_{ac}^2 & d_{ad}^2 \\ 1 & d_{ba}^2 & 0 & d_{bc}^2 & d_{bd}^2 \\ 1 & d_{ca}^2 & d_{cb}^2 & 0 & d_{cd}^2 \\ 1 & d_{da}^2 & d_{db}^2 & d_{dc}^2 & 0 \end{vmatrix}.$$

The tetrangle inequality $CM(d_{ab}, d_{ac}, d_{ad}, d_{bc}, d_{bd}, d_{cd}) \geq 0$ is both a necessary and sufficient condition for these six non-negative real numbers to be pair-wise distances of four points in Euclidean three-dimensional space [5]. If d_{cd} is being tightened, expanding the Cayley-Menger determinant results in 32 inequalities for u_{cd} and 32 for l_{cd}. Havel and Easthope [12] determined that only 7 of the 64 inequalities are non-redundant if the bounds already satisfy the triangle inequality. It has been shown that the tetrangle-inequality bound-smoothing results in substantially tighter bounds than the triangle inequality [9,12,17], therefore resulting into more accurate three-dimensional structures.

2 Previous Parallel Algorithms

Tetrangle-inequality bound-smoothing is an extremely computation intensive task, requiring $O(n^4)$ time for an n-atom molecule. Even for a relatively small 2000-atom molecule it requires over 45 days of continuous computation on a single 2GHz IA-32 processor. Computation time can be reduced through parallelization, however, no two quadruples sharing an edge can be processed concurrently [20,23]. Thus, the number of processors employed cannot exceed the maximum number of edge-disjoint quadruples, $D(n, 4, 2)$.   Brouwer [6] established that $D(n, 4, 2) = \left\lfloor \dfrac{n}{4} \left\lfloor \dfrac{n-1}{3} \right\rfloor \right\rfloor + \varepsilon$,

where $\varepsilon < 4$.

A parallel master-slave approach was proposed by Rajan, Deo, and Kumar [23]. The master processor distributes a set of edge-disjoint quadruples among the processors, which apply the tetrangle inequality and return the improved distance-bounds. The process is repeated until all quadruples are considered. Only $O(1)$ speedup is possible with this approach since the master-processor must generate and send all the quadruples.

Rajan and Deo [20,22,23] also proposed an alternative parallelization, intended for a shared memory architecture. The method iteratively constructs difference sets with up to n edge-disjoint quadruples, which are then used to generate packings containing at most n K_4's. A single pass through all quadruples requires $O(n^3(n + p \log p)/p)$ computation time with $p \leq n$ processors. The efficiency is $O(1)$ if $O(n/\log n)$ processors are utilized. Since the algorithm is not cost-optimal, the efficiency decreases as the number of processors is reduced. On a distributed architecture the algorithm would require $O(n^3(n + p \log p)/p)$ communication steps, each an all-to-all broadcast, making it unsuitable for a Beowulf-type cluster of PCs.

3 Proposed Algorithm

The proposed algorithm is intended for the Beowulf-type cluster of PCs [3,25] which imposes high communication overhead and provides no centralized control. It is assumed that p, the number of processors, is significantly smaller than n.

A copy of the distance matrix is stored on each processing node. Processors update their local distance matrix by applying the tetrangle inequality. A communication step, during which each processing node sends its updated distance-bounds to every other node, follows each computation step. The nodes of K_n are partitioned into s subsets $S_0, S_1, \ldots, S_{s-1}$. It is assumed that $s \mid n$ and that $S_i = \{i(n/s), \ldots, (i + 1)(n/s) - 1\}$. Due to partitioning, node-quadruples can be classified into five types:

Type A: quadruples $\{a, b, c, d\}$, where all four nodes belong to the same subset: $a, b,$ $c, d \in S_i$, for $0 \leq i < s$. Given s subsets there are $s \dbinom{n/s}{4}$ Type A quadruples.

Type B: quadruples $\{a, b, c, d\}$, such that three nodes belong to one subset and the fourth node belongs to another one: $a, b, c \in S_i$ and $d \in S_j$, where $i \neq j$. Given s subsets there are $n(s-1)\dbinom{n/s}{3}$ Type B quadruples.

Type C: quadruples $\{a, b, c, d\}$ containing pairs of nodes from two different subsets: $a, b \in S_i$ and $c, d \in S_j$, where $i \neq j$. Given s subsets there are $\dbinom{s}{2}\dbinom{n/s}{2}^2$ Type C quadruples.

Type D: quadruples $\{a, b, c, d\}$, where the nodes belong to three different subsets: a,
$b \in S_i$, $c \in S_j$, and $d \in S_k$, where $i \neq j \neq k$. Given s subsets there are
$$s\binom{s-1}{2}\binom{n/s}{2}\left(\frac{n}{s}\right)^2 \text{ Type D quadruples.}$$
Type E: quadruples $\{a, b, c, d\}$, such that the nodes belong to four different subsets.
Given s subsets there are $\binom{s}{4}\left(\frac{n}{s}\right)^4$ Type E quadruples.

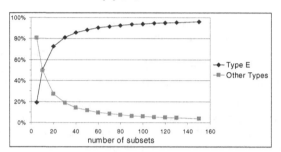

Fig. 1. Percentage of quadruples that are Type E

The percentage of Type E quadruples increases with the number of subsets, reaching 100% when $s = n$. This trend is shown in Figure 1 for $s \leq 150$ as $n \rightarrow \infty$. The following sections describe parallel algorithms for each type of quadruples. See [10] for the proofs of correctness and detailed complexity analysis.

3.1 Bound-Tightening with Type A Quadruples

All nodes in a Type A quadruple belong to the same subset. Thus, given s subsets there are $s\binom{n/s}{4}$ Type A quadruples. The algorithm employs up to s processors but is included only for completeness sake as Type A, C and D quadruples are processed by the same function in the implementation.

   1.   **for all** P_i, where $0 \leq i < p$, **do in parallel**
   2.   **for** each subset S_j, where $i(s/p) \leq j < (i+1)(s/p)$, **do**
   3.   tighten Type A quadruples given subset S_j
   4.   **communicate**

Fig. 2. Algorithm for generating Type A quadruples

Complexity. The algorithm requires $O(n^4/(s^3p))$ computation time. The speedup is p and efficiency is 100% if $p \mid s$. A single all-to-all-broadcast communication step is required after tightening Type A quadruples.

3.2 Bound-Tightening with Type B Quadruples

Three nodes in a Type B quadruple belong to subset S_j, the fourth node to S_k, where $j \neq k$. Given s subsets there are $n(s-1)\binom{n/s}{3}$ Type B quadruples. The proposed algorithm utilizes $p \leq (s-1)$ processors, where $(2p) \mid (s-1)$.

The algorithm executes in two stages. In the first stage quadruples are generated (and tightened) by iteratively combining each node-triple from subset S_j with every node from subsets S_{j+1}, S_{j+2}, ..., S_{s-1}. Thus, no quadruple contains a node-triple from subset S_{s-1}. Similarly, in the second stage quadruples are generated by combining every node-triple from subset S_j with the nodes from subsets S_1, S_2, ..., S_{j-1}.

In both stages the $(s-1)$ subsets used to generate node-triples are distributed evenly among the processors, which then independently tighten Type B quadruples. Note that during the first stage node-triples from subset S_j are combined with nodes from $(s-j)$ subsets. Thus, naïve subset-distribution where the first s/p subsets are assigned to processor P_0, the following s/p subsets are assigned to P_1, etc., causes processor P_{i+1} to idle while P_i finishes processing. The workload can be perfectly balanced if $(s-1) \equiv 0 \pmod{2p}$: in the first stage processor P_i is "assigned" subsets S_j, where $i\dfrac{s-1}{2p} \leq j < (i+1)\dfrac{s-1}{2p}$ and $(2p-i-1)\dfrac{s-1}{2p} \leq j < (2p-i)\dfrac{s-1}{2p}$, which means that if a processor is assigned subset S_j then it is also assigned subset S_{j-k-2}. For example, if $s = 13$ and $p = 3$, then P_1 generates node-triples from subsets S_2, S_3 and S_8, S_9. Such subset distribution ensures that every processor tightens exactly $\dfrac{n(s-1)}{2p}\binom{n/s}{3}$ quadruples. Similarly, in the second stage processor P_i is assigned subsets S_j, where $i\dfrac{s-1}{2p} < j \leq (i+1)\dfrac{s-1}{2p}$ and $(2p-i-1)\dfrac{s-1}{2p} < j \leq (2p-i)\dfrac{s-1}{2p}$.

1. **for all** P_i, where $0 \leq i < p$, **do in parallel**

2.   **for each** subset S_j, $i\dfrac{s-1}{2p} \leq j < (i+1)\dfrac{s-1}{2p}$ and

         $(2p-i-1)\dfrac{s-1}{2p} \leq j < (2p-i)\dfrac{s-1}{2p}$, **do**

3.   **for each** S_k, where $k > j$, **do**

4.   TightenB(S_j, S_k)

5. **communicate**

Fig. 3. Algorithm for the first stage of tightening with Type B quadruples

Only the first stage of the algorithm is described in Figure 3 since the second stage is identical except for the bounds of the loops on lines 2 and 3. The pseudo-code specification calls function *TightenB(S_j, S_k)*, which generates and tightens all Type B quadruples by combining each node-triple from subset S_j with every node in S_k. The loop on line 2 iterates through each subset S_j assigned to the processor, while the loop on line 3 iterates through every subset S_k where $k > j$. Thus, only Type B quadruples are tightened on line 4.

Complexity. When $2p \mid (s - 1)$ the algorithm requires $\dfrac{n(s-1)}{p}\dbinom{n/s}{3}$ or $O\left(\dfrac{n^4}{s^2 p}\right)$ time to process all Type B quadruples and each processor tightens the same number of quadruples. The algorithm requires two communication steps, one after each stage.

3.3 Bound-Tightening with Type C Quadruples

Two nodes in a Type C quadruple belong to subset S_i, the other two to S_j, where $i \neq j$. Given s subsets there are $\dbinom{s}{2}\dbinom{n/s}{2}^2$ Type C quadruples. The proposed algorithm employs up to $(s - 1)/2$ processors, where $(2p) \mid (s - 1)$.

For simplicity of presentation we assume that $p = (s - 1)/2$. The proposed algorithm can be modified for any p, where $p \mid (s - 1)$, without increasing the number of communications [10]. The algorithm executes in $(2p + 1)$ iterations and is based on the near-one-factorization of K_{2p+1}, where vertices represent subsets. A near-one-factorization of K_{2p+1} partitions the edges into near-one-factors – edge sets such that $2p$ vertices have degree 1 and one vertex is isolated [27]. During each iteration a processor is assigned a different subset-pair: in j^{th} iteration processor P_i calls the function TightenC to tighten Type C quads given the $(i + j)^{\text{th}}$ and $(2p - i - 1 + j)^{\text{th}}$ subsets, where addition is carried out modulo $(2p + 1)$. This corresponds to $(2p + 1)$ near-one-factors of a near one-factorization of K_{2p+1}.

1.   **for each** processor P_i, where $0 \leq i < p$, **do in parallel**
2.   **for** $j \leftarrow 0$ **to** $2p$ **do**
3.   TightenC($S_{(i+j)\bmod(2p+1)}$, $S_{(2p-i-1+j)\bmod(2p+1)}$)
4.   **communicate**

Fig. 4. Parallel algorithm for tightening Type C quadruples

The **for** loop on lines 2 through 4 iterates through the $(2p + 1)$ near-one-factors of K_{2p+1} (each corresponding to p disjoint pairs of subsets), ensuring that each pair of subsets is used as a parameter to function TightenC exactly once.

Complexity. The loop on lines 2 through 4 has $(2p + 1)$ iterations, each tightening $\dbinom{n/s}{2}^2$ quadruples. Thus, the algorithm in Figure 4 requires $O\left(\dfrac{n^4 p}{s^4}\right)$ computation time. The algorithm requires $(2p + 1)$ communication steps, one after each iteration.

3.4 Bound-Tightening with Type D Quadruples

A Type D quadruple contains nodes from three different subsets. Given s subsets there are $s\binom{s-1}{2}\binom{n/s}{2}\left(\frac{n}{s}\right)^2$ Type D quadruples. The algorithm employs up to $p = (s - 1)/2$ processors, where $(2p) \mid (s - 1)$.

For simplicity we assume that $p = (s - 1)/2$. Similarly to the algorithm for tightening Type C quadruples the algorithm is based on the near-one-factorization of K_{2p+1} and executes in $(2p + 1)$ iterations, each corresponding to a near-one-factor of K_{2p+1}. Every processor is assigned an "edge" of the current near-one-factor: processors assigned disjoint pairs of subsets. During the jth iteration processor P_i is assigned the $(i + j)^{th}$ and $(2p - i + j - 1)^{th}$ subsets (arithmetic is carried out modulo $(2p + 1)$).

	$k = 1$	$k = 2$	$k = 3$	$k = 4$
P_0	S_1, S_4	S_2, S_3	S_6	$\emptyset$
P_1	S_2, S_3	S_6	$\emptyset$	S_0, S_5
P_2	S_6	$\emptyset$	S_0, S_5	S_1, S_4

Fig. 5. Near-one-factor of K_7 and assignment of remote subsets

For example, consider the case where $p = 3$ and there are 7 subsets. The first near-one-factor of K_7 is shown in Figure 5. In the first iteration of the algorithm processor P_0 is assigned subsets S_0 and S_5, processor P_1 is assigned S_1 and S_4, processor P_2 is assigned S_2 and S_3. The processors consider subsets assigned to remote processors in $(p + 1) = 4$ steps as shown in Figure 5 (symbol $\emptyset$ indicates the idle step). During each step a processor calls TightenD function with the assigned subsets as the first two arguments, and each of the remote subsets it is currently considering as the third argument. Thus, any two processors' arguments share at most one subset.

```
1.  for all P_i, where 0 ≤ i < p, do in parallel
4.      for j ← 0 to 2p do
6.          for k ← 1 to (p + 1)  do
7.              rp ← (i + k) mod (p + 2)
8.              if rp = p then
9.                  TighenD(S_{(i+j) mod (2p + 1)}, S_{(2p-i-1+j) mod (2p + 1)}, S_{(2p+j) mod (2p + 1)})
10.             else if rp < p then
11.                 TightenD(S_{(i+j) mod (2p + 1)}, S_{(2p-i-1+j) mod (2p + 1)}, S_{(rp+j) mod (2p + 1)})
12.                 TightenD(S_{(i+j) mod (2p + 1)}, S_{(2p-i-1+j) mod (2p + 1)}, S_{(2p-rp-1+j) mod (2p + 1)})
13.             communicate
```

Fig. 6. Parallel algorithm for tightening Type D quadruples

The variable rp denotes the processor whose clusters P_i is considering in the current step. The loop on line 4 iterates through the $(2p + 1)$ near-one-factors. The loop on line 6 iterates through subsets assigned to the remaining processors (lines 11 and

12) and the subset not assigned to any processor in the current iteration (line 5). In order to avoid edge-conflicts a processor idles when $rp = (p + 1)$.

Complexity. The statements on lines 7 through 12 are executed $(p + 1)(2p + 1)$ times, each time processing up to $2\left(\dfrac{n}{s}\right)^2\left(\dfrac{n/s}{2}\right)$ quadruples. Thus, the algorithm requires $O\left(\dfrac{n^4 p^2}{s^4}\right)$ computation time. A total of $(p + 1)(2p + 1)$ communication steps are required. Even though the algorithm was described for $p = (s - 1)/2$, it can be modified for any p, where $(2p) \mid (s - 1)$, without increasing the number of communications [10].

3.5 Bound-Tightening with Type E Quadruples

Each node in a Type E quadruple belongs to a different subset. There are $\left(\dfrac{s}{4}\right)\left(\dfrac{n}{s}\right)^4$ Type E quadruples. The algorithm utilizes up to $p = (s - 1)/6$ processors, where $(3p) \mid (s - 1)$.

Given four distinct subsets, a total of $\left(\dfrac{n}{s}\right)^4$ Type E node-quadruples are easily constructed. If any two processors concurrently generate node-quadruples from *subset-quadruples* that share at most one subset, then any two node-quadruples, generated by different processors, are edge-disjoint. Thus, in the remainder of the section we consider the problem of assigning subset-quadruples to processors.

A processor *extends* three given subsets S_a, S_b, S_c (without loss of generality let $a < b < c$) by iteratively considering every subset S_d, where $c < d < s$, and generating all Type E node-quadruples from the four subsets S_a, S_b, S_c, S_d. Thus, a total of $(s - c - 1)$ subset-quadruples are processed.

1. **for all** P_i, $0 \leq i < p$, **do in parallel**
2.   **for each of** $(3p - 1)(3p - 2)/2$ one-factors **do**
3.   let (a, b, c) be the hyperedge assigned to processor P_i, where $a < b < c$
4.   **for** $d \leftarrow (c + 1)$ **to** $(s - 1)$ **do**
5.   tighten Type E quadruples given subsets S_a, S_b, S_c, S_d
6.   **communicate**

Fig. 7. Parallel algorithm for tightening Type E quadruples

Assuming that $p = (s - 1)/3$, all Type E node quadruples are generated by the algorithm in Figure 7. The algorithm utilizes one-factorization of the complete 3-uniform hypergraph on $3p$ vertices [11]. One-factorization of a complete 3-uniform hypergraph on $3p$ vertices is a partition of all $\left(\dfrac{3p}{3}\right)$ hyperedges into disjoint *one-factors* (hyperedge-sets such that each vertex is incident to exactly one hyperedge). Thus, in our case, there are $(3p - 1)(3p - 2)/2$ one-factors, each containing p subset-triples.

Note that subset-triples are generated only from the first $(s - 1)$ subsets (hence $s = 3p + 1$) so that at least one subset always remains for *extension*.

The **for** loop on line 2 iterates through all one-factors, thus, every hyperedge (in this case a triple of the first $(s - 1)$ subsets) is assigned to some processor. Every processor extends the assigned subset-triple on lines 4 and 5.

Complexity. There are $\binom{3p-1}{2}$ iterations of the loop on line 2. Since in a single iteration any processor considers a maximum of $s - 3$ subset-quadruples, each resulting in $(n/s)^4$ node-quadruples, the algorithm in Figure 7 requires $O(n^4 p^2 / s^3)$ computation time. A total of $\binom{3p-1}{2}$ communication steps (all-to-all broadcasts) are required, one after processing each one-factor. While the preceding description assumes that $p = (s - 1)/3$, the algorithm can be modified for any p, where $(3p) \mid (s - 1)$, without increasing the number of communications.

3.6 Overall Complexity and Comparison with Previous Parallelizations

In practice, the algorithms for tightening Type A, C, and D quadruples are combined to reduce the number of inter-processor communications [10]. The algorithms for tightening Type C and D quadruples are inherently similar since they are both based on near-one-factorization of K_{2p+1}. Type A quadruples are tightened by the processor P_0 when it would otherwise be idling.

The algorithms for tightening Type B and A-C-D quadruples require that $2p \mid (s - 1)$, while the algorithm for Type E quadruples requires $3p \mid (s - 1)$. We chose $s = 6p + 1$, the lowest s-value that satisfies both divisibility conditions. Consequently, combined algorithms require $O(n^4/p)$ computation time and

$$2 + (p+1)(2p+1) + \binom{3p-1}{2}$$ or $O(p^2)$ communication steps. At most $p = (n - 1)/6$

processors can be utilized. When $p = (s - 1)/6$ the worst case efficiency approaches 45.8% from above as n increases. The best case efficiency approaches 92% from above. Refer to [10] for derivations.

The algorithm proposed by Rajan *et al.* [19] utilizes up to n processors and requires $(n^3(n + p \log p)/p)$ computation and communication steps. During a computation step every processor tightens a single quadruple and each communication is an all-to-all broadcast (if implemented on cluster architecture). Note that reducing the number of processors increases the required number of communications. In contrast, our proposed algorithm requires $O(p^2)$ communications. For example, when $O(1)$ and $O(n)$ processors are employed, the algorithm due to Rajan requires $O(n^4)$ and $O(n^3 \log n)$ communications, respectively. In comparison, the proposed algorithm requires $O(1)$ and $O(n^2)$ communications for $O(1)$ and $O(n)$ processors, respectively. Therefore, the proposed algorithm requires at least an order of magnitude fewer communications than any previous parallelization and is more suitable for the cluster architecture.

4 Experimental Results

The proposed algorithms were implemented on the SCEROLA cluster at University of Central Florida. Each processing node contains a 900MHz AMD Athlon processor, 256MB RAM, and runs Red Hat Linux operating system. The nodes are interconnected via switched Fast Ethernet network. Algorithm implementation was tested with $p = 3, 7, 9, 15$, and 21 processors.

Given p processors, the nodes are partitioned into $s = (6p + 1)$ subsets, dummy nodes are used for padding if necessary. Only the updated distance bounds are transmitted to reduce the required network bandwidth. Each processor maintains a list of updated distances, as well as an array to indexe the list. Thus, checking whether a given distance has been updated requires $O(1)$ time and there is no need to scan the entire distance matrix for updated bounds before each communication.

The algorithms were implemented using MPI message passing interface [25]. Experiments were conducted with NMR distance-bounds for two molecules: Phage 434 CRO Protein (PDB code: 1zug, restraints involve 370 atoms), Ribonuclease A (PDB code: 2aas, restraints involve 635 atoms), both obtained from the Protein Data Bank [4]. Execution times for each experiment were averaged over several runs. Wall-clock time was used to compute the speedup and efficiency of implementation (*i.e.* overhead due to parallelization and communication is included).

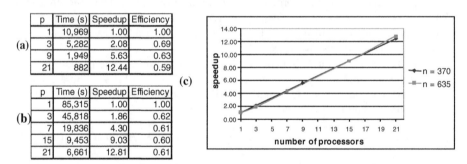

(a)

p	Time (s)	Speedup	Efficiency
1	10,969	1.00	1.00
3	5,282	2.08	0.69
9	1,949	5.63	0.63
21	882	12.44	0.59

(b)

p	Time (s)	Speedup	Efficiency
1	85,315	1.00	1.00
3	45,818	1.86	0.62
7	19,836	4.30	0.61
15	9,453	9.03	0.60
21	6,661	12.81	0.61

(c)

Fig. 8. Timing results: (a) $n = 370$, (b) $n = 635$, (c) speedup

Empirical timing results for the Phage 434 CRO protein are shown in Figure 8a. The wall-clock time is given in seconds. Timing results for the Ribonuclease A appear in Figure 8b. Speedups for both experiments are compared in Figure 8c. In both experiments the observed efficiency is well above the theoretical lower bound of 42%. The decrease in efficiency as the number of processors is increased is due to several factors. While the algorithms for tightening Types A, B, C, and D are nearly 100% efficient, the fraction of all quadruples that belong to these types decreases rapidly with increasing number of processors (see Figure 4). Both the lower and upper bounds on the efficiency for tightening Type E quadruples approach their respective limits of 42% and 92% from above.

5 Conclusions

We proposed a parallel algorithm for tightening the inter-atomic distance-bounds for the molecular conformation. The coarse-grained algorithm is suited for a cluster of PCs, whereas the previous parallelizations were designed for tightly-coupled parallel computers and required exchange of updated bounds after processing every quadruple of atoms. We have minimized the number of inter-processor communications in order to reduce the parallelization overhead. Empirical tests of the implementation with up to 21 processors exhibited efficiency of at least 59%, an impressive result for a non-embarrassingly-parallel problem on a cluster of PCs.

References

1. C. B. Anfinsen. Principles that govern the protein folding chains. *Science*, vol. 181, pp. 233–230, 1973.
2. A. Aszödi, M. J. Gradwell, W. R. Taylor. Global fold determination from a small number of distance restraints. *Journal of Molecular Biology*, vol. 251, pp. 308–326, 1995.
3. D. J. Becker, T. Sterling, D. Savarese, E. Dorband, U. A. Ranawake , C. V. Packer. BEOWULF: A parallel workstation for scientific computation. *Proceedings of the 1995 International Conference on Parallel Processing (ICPP)*, pp. 11–14, 1995.
4. H. M. Berman, J. Westbrook, Z. Feng, G. Gilliland, T. N. Bhat, H. Weissig, I. In. Shindyalov, P. E. Bourne. The Protein Data Bank, *Nucleic Acids Research*, vol. 28, pp. 235–242, 2000.
5. L. M. Blumenthal. *Theory and Applications of Distance Geometry*. Chelsea Publishing Company, Bronx, New York, 1970.
6. A. E. Brouwer. Optimal packings of K_4's into a K_n. *Journal of Combinatorial Theory*, vol. 26, pp. 278–297, 1979.
7. F. E. Cohen, I. D. Kuntz. Tertiary structure prediction. In G. D. Fasman, editor, *Prediction of Protein Structure and the Principles of Protein Conformation*, pp. 647–705, Plenum Press, New York, 1989.
8. G. M. Crippen. A novel approach to the calculation of conformation: Distance geometry. *Journal of Computational Physiology*, vol. 24, pp. 96–107, 1977.
9. G. M. Crippen, T. F. Havel. *Distance Geometry and Molecular Conformation*. Research Studies Press Ltd., Taunton, Somerset, England, 1988.
10. N. Deo, P. Micikevicius. Coarse-grained parallelization of distance-bound smoothing. Computer Science Technical Report CS-TR-02-06, University of Central Florida, 2002.
11. N. Deo, P. Micikevicius. On cyclic one-factorization of complete 3-uniform hypergraphs. *Congressus Numerantium*, to appear, 2003.
12. P. L. Easthope and T. F. Havel. Computational experience with an algorithm for tetrangle-inequality bound-smoothing. *Bulletin of Mathematical Biology*, vol. 51, pp. 173–194, 1989.
13. P. Güntert. Structure calculation of biological macromolecules from NMR data. *Quarterly reviews of biophysics*, vol. 31, pp. 145–237, 1998.
14. T. F. Havel. The sampling properties of some distance geometry algorithms applied to unconstrained polypeptide chains: a study of 1830 independently computed conformations. *Biopolymers*, vol. 29, pp. 1565–1585, 1990.
15. T. F. Havel. An evaluation of computational strategies for use in the determination of protein structure from distance constraints obtained by nuclear magnetic resonance. *Prog. Biophys. Mol. Biol.*, vol. 56, pp. 43–78, 1991.

16. B. A. Hendrickson. The molecule problem: Exploiting structure in global optimizations. *SIAM Journal on Optimization*, vol. 5, pp. 835–857, 1995.
17. N. Kumar, N. Deo, R. Addanki. Empirical study of a tetrangle-inequality bound-smoothing algorithm. *Congressus Numerantium*, vol. 117, pp. 15–31, 1996.
18. K. Menger. New foundation of Euclidean geometry. *Amer. J. Math.*, vol. 53, pp. 721–45, 1931.
19. P. Micikevicius. *Parallel Graph Algorithms for Molecular Conformation and Tree Codes*. Ph.D. thesis, University of Central Florida, Orlando, Florida, 2002.
20. K. Rajan. *Parallel Algorithms for the Molecular Conformation Problem*. Ph.D. thesis, University of Central Florida, Orlando, Florida, 1999.
21. K. Rajan, N. Deo. A parallel algorithm for bound-smoothing. *Proceedings of the 13ᵗʰ International Parallel Processing Symposium*, April 12–16, San Juan, Puerto Rico, 1999, pp. 645–652.
22. K. Rajan, N. Deo. Computational experience with a parallel algorithm for tetrangle inequality bound smoothing. *Bulletin of Mathematical Biology*, vol. 61(5), pp. 987–1008, 1999.
23. K. Rajan, N. Deo, N. Kumar. Generating disjoint t-$(v, k, 1)$ packings in parallel. *Congressus Numerantium*, vol. 131, pp. 5–18, 1998.
24. D. K. Searls. Grand challenges in computational biology. In *Computational Models in Molecular Biology*, S. L. Salzberg, D. K. Searls, S. Kasif, editors. Elsevier, 1998.
25. M. Snir, S. Otto, S. Huss-Lederman, D. Walker, J. Dongarra. *MPI: The Complete Reference*. MIT Press, Cambridge, Massachusetts, 1996.
26. T. Sterling, D. Savarese. A coming of age for Beowulf-class computing. *Lecture Notes in Computer Science*, vol. 1685, pp. 78–88, 1999.
27. W. D. Wallis. *Combinatorial Designs*. Marcel Dekker, Inc., New York, 1998.

Concurrent Reading and Writing with Mobile Agents

Sukumar Ghosh* and Alina Bejan

University of Iowa, Iowa City IA 52242, USA
{ghosh,abejan}@cs.uiowa.edu

Abstract. This paper presents a method using which a set of reading and writing agents concurrently read and update the global state of the network. In addition to the consistency of the snapshot and the reset states, our protocol preserves the atomicity of the reads and writes, despite the fact these operations are non-blocking. Potential applications include the design of multi-agent protocols for self-stabilization, self-healing and adaptation.

1 Introduction

Observing the computation of an asynchronous distributed system from within the system is a difficult task, though often needed in distributed computations. An example of such an observation is the task of obtaining an instantaneous picture of the global state of a distributed system from partial observations of the local states of processes over a period of time, as the system continues to run an application. Turning off the application program during the measurement will trivialize the problem, and is often unacceptable. If we intuitively define a configuration to be a set of the states of the individual processes and the channels of the network, then an arbitrarily taken snapshot does not provide valuable, or even correct information about the configuration. Algorithms for taking *correct* or *consistent* snapshots are discussed in [2] and [3].

While snapshots can be viewed as *reading* the state of a distributed system, *distributed reset* can be compared with *writing* the state of a distributed system, and is useful when the system undergoes a transient failure, including that of coordination loss among processes. One way out would be to use a self-stabilizing system in which the recovery from transient failures is guaranteed by design. However, in absence of a built-in guarantee, snapshot and global reset are the only mechanisms for recovery from failures. Despite network latencies, we intend to make the snapshot and reset operations *look like* instantaneous operations. The non-trivial nature of the reset operations well as an algorithm for implementing distributed reset are described in [4].

---

* This research was supported in part by the National Science Foundation under grant CCR-9901391.

S.K. Das and S. Bhattacharya (Eds.): IWDC 2002, LNCS 2571, pp. 67–77, 2002.

Our goal is to study the problems of reading and writing the global state of a distributed system using the *agent model* proposed in [5]. An agent is a *program*, that can migrate from one node to another, read the local states of processes or update them as and when necessary, and can take autonomous routing decisions. The agent model supports a framework that separates the execution of the application from the supervisory functions of the systems. Processes running the application may not even be aware of the agents visiting them, whereas the activities of fault detection and correction are delegated to the agents. This has the potential to make the solutions simpler and scalable. A formal model appears [1].

We assume that the reading and writing operations on the global states of a distributed system are carried out by *reading agents* and *writing agents* respectively. We furthermore propose to study how reading and writing operations can be performed when multiple agents are active in the network at the same time. The network reduces to a *concurrent object* that can be accessed by the *read* and the *write* operations. There are numerous possible applications. Multiple reading agents may work simultaneously to speed up data retrieval, multiple reading and writing agents may work together to expedite fault recovery. In parallel programming languages like *Linda* [11], processes communicate with one another via a tuple space. On a network of processes, the tuple space will consist of a part of the network state that will be read or written in overlapped time by two or more agents. In the area of electronic commerce, multi-agent protocols are rapidly growing.

The classical approach to implementing concurrent objects consists of the use of *critical sections* and a mechanism to *mutual exclusion*. This approach involves waiting, since at most one process is allowed in the critical section at any time. A side-effect is deadlock – if one process is stuck in the critical section, then it indefinitely blocks all processes waiting to enter the critical section. For asynchronous, fault-tolerant distributed systems, it is much more desirable to design a *non-blocking* or *wait-free* [7] solution, where each access by an agent is completed in a finite number of steps, regardless of the execution speeds of other agents or processes. In this paper, we explore *non-blocking* solutions to the problem of concurrent reading and writing, using the agent model. The basic correctness condition relevant to our solutions is that even though the operations of reading and writing by two different agents may overlap, the results of the reading must insure as if the operations are atomic, and consistent with what was written by the writing agent(s). Readers might note that similar algorithms have already been proposed for shared registers by Lamport [8].

The paper is organized in five sections. Section 2 introduces the model of computation. Section 3 gives an overview of the individual protocols for the single-reader and the single-writer cases. The concurrent reading and writing protocol is described in Section 4. Finally, Section 5 contains some concluding remarks.

2   The Model of Computation

2.1   Introductory Concepts

We represent a distributed system by a *connected undirected graph* $G = (V, E)$, where $V = \{V_0, V_1, \ldots, V_{n-1}\}$ is the set of nodes representing processes, and $E = \{E_0, E_1, \ldots, E_{m-1}\}$ is the set of edges representing channels for interprocess communication. Processes are asynchronous, and do not have access to a common global clock. Interprocess communication uses message passing. The channels are fifo and half-duplex: at any time a channel can be used for communication along one direction only.

The program for each process consists of a set of rules. Each rule is a guarded action of the form $g \to A$, where g is a boolean function of the state of that process and those of its neighbors received via messages, and A is an action that is executed when g is true. An action by a process involves several steps, these include: receiving a message, updating its own state, and sending a message. The execution of each rule is atomic, and it defines a step of the computation. When more than one rule is applicable, any one of them can be chosen for execution. The scheduler is unfair. A *computation* is a sequence of atomic steps. It can be finite or infinite.

Definition 1. *A global state S of the system G is a tuple $(s(0), s(1), \ldots, s(n))$, where $s(i)$ is the state of process i, together with the states of all channels incident on it.*

From [2], a consistent snapshot only approximates a global view, that corresponds to a global state that is reachable from the initial state of the system through a valid computation. In the presence of network latencies, a consistent snapshot can be constructed from the local snapshots recorded at different moments, such that no two recording events are causally related.

Definition 2. *A consistent global snapshot of a network includes a set of local snapshots of all the processes, such that there is no causal order between the recordings of the local snapshots of any two processes i and j $(i \neq j)$.*

While a snapshot reads the global state of a system, a *reset* operation restores the global state to a known configuration. Like a snapshot state, a reset state is only approximate in presence of network latencies. The following definition from [4] captures the notion of a consistent reset:

Definition 3. *Let a reset operation try to update the global state of a distributed system to W. Then the reset will be called consistent, if the system is reset either to W, or to any global state that is reachable from W through a valid computation.*

A crucial aspect here is the state of the computation when the reset is in progress. A consistent reset operation prohibits all messages that propagate between nodes that have been reset and nodes that have not been reset - such messages are rejected by the receiver. Consequently, there is no causal order between the resetting events of the local states of two different processes i and j $(i \neq j)$.

2.2   The Agent Model

We propose to investigate a system in which processes run the application program, but all supervisory activities like the reading or resetting of the global state for the sake of fault recovery, synchronization, or any other objectives are delegated to mobile agents. We define a mobile agent (or simply an agent) as follows:

Definition 4. *An agent is a program that can migrate from one node to another, execute a piece of code at these nodes, and take autonomous routing decisions.*

An agent is a mobile supervisor that patrols the network infinitely often. We will represent an agent by a tuple consisting of the following five components: (1) the *id*, (2) the agent program P, (3) the briefcase B containing the agent variables, (4) the previous node PRE visited by the agent, and (5) the next node $NEXT$ to be visited by the agent.

Each agent has a designated *home* which is one of the processes in the network. The home generates the agent, initializes the briefcase variables prior to the next traversal, and sends it out to one of its neighbors. Therefore, for every protocol, there is an agent computation, which is the program P executed by the agent while visiting a node. P has a set of guarded actions: a *guard* is a boolean function of the briefcase variables and the variables of the process that it is currently visiting, and an *action* consists of one or more of the following three operations: (i) modification of its briefcase variables, (ii) modification of the variables of the process that is currently visiting, and (iii) identification of the *next* process to visit. The next node $NEXT$ to be visited is either predefined or computed dynamically. The agent traverses the network along the edges of a spanning tree. Such an algorithm for DFS traversal appears in [5]. By definition, at any node, the visit of an agent is an *atomic event*.

A *reading agent* can only read the local variables of a process for computing the global state. A *writing agent* has the additional ability of resetting the global state to a desired configuration. The number of reading and writing agents present in the system at a certain moment depends on the application and on the agent model chosen. The simplest case is that of a single reading agent, and the most complex is the multi-reader multi-writer case. The primary goal of this paper is to present a protocol, such that even if readers and writers perform their tasks in overlapped time, the snapshots returned by the readers reflect as if the reading and the writing operations have been done atomically.

The *atomicity criterion* can be elaborated as follows. For any execution of the system, there is some way of totally ordering the reads and writes so that the values returned by the reads are the same as if the operations had been performed in that order. Usually, atomicity is discussed with respect a writing operation. We can identify two types of writing operations: *internal* write (belongs to the underlying computation), and *external* write (performed by the reset agent). Let us take an example to illustrate the atomicity criterion. Let W^k and W^{k+1} denote two consecutive write operations (internal or external): W^k updates the local state of every process to 5, and W^{k+1} updates the local state of every process to 6. Let the reading agent take two successive snapshots R^i and R^{i+1} in overlapped time as shown in Fig 1.

1. Each read operation must return a consistent value of the global state, that will correspond to (i) the previous reset state before the read started, or (ii) the state to which the system is being currently set, (iii) or a state reachable from one of these.
2. No read returns a global state that is "older than", i.e. causally ordered before, the global state returned by the previous read.

As a consequence of the second condition, it is okay if both R^i and R^{i+1} return a state $(0,0,0,...)$ or a state reachable from it, but it is not acceptable for R^i to return $(6,6,6,...)$ and R^{i+1} to return $(5,5,5,...)$.

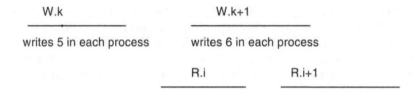

Fig. 1. Atomic behavior when multiple reads overlap a write

We consider the static model of agents, where the number of agents and their homes are known at the beginning of the application, and they remain unchanged throughout the life of the application.

3   The 1-Reader and 1-Writer Cases

3.1   1-Reader Protocol

This protocol directly follows from those in [2] and [3], with the exception that the snapshot is taken by the visiting agent, and collected in its briefcase during the same traversal. The agent starts by taking a snapshot of its home process, and begins a DFS traversal. Thereafter, in each node, it records a snapshot state, which ordinarily is the local state of that node. When the agent returns home after each complete traversal, it computes a consistent global state of the system from the states recorded at the individual nodes. For simplicity, we assume that the channels have zero capacity, so the channel states are irrelevant.

While the reader visits the network to collect a snapshot, a message circulating in the system can be one of the four types (1) from an unvisited node to an unvisited node, (2) from a visited node to a visited node, (3) from a visited node to an unvisited node, and (4) from an unvisited node to a visited node. Of these, when a message m propagates from a visited node i to an unvisited node j, there is the potential for a causal ordering between the recordings of $s(i)$ and

$s(j)$ by the agent. This is because the following causal chain (record $s(i) <$ send $m <$ receive $m <$ record $s(j)$) will exist. To avoid this, we have to ask process j receiving m to save its current state $s(j)$ into a history variable $h(j)$, before receiving m. It is this saved value that the agent will record as the local state of process j. The exact mechanism is explained below:

In order to distinguish between consecutive traversals of the agent, we use a *sequence number*, $SEQ \in \{0, 1, 2\}$, in the briefcase of the agent. Before each traversal, the home increments this value (modulo 3). Each process has two variables seq and $agent\_seq$, both of which are updated to SEQ when the reader visits the process. These two variables will be used to recognize messages from a *visited* to an *unvisited* node. If the values of $agent\_seq$ is appended to the body of every message, then a message m from a visited node i to an unvisited node j is recognized by the condition $agent\_seq(i) = agent\_seq(j) \oplus_3 1$. To receive such a message, node j sets its seq to -1 [1], updates its $agent\_seq(j)$ to $agent\_seq(i)$, and saves its current state $s(j)$ into its history variable. Eventually the agent visits j, records the state of j from this history, and resets $seq(j)$ to $agent\_seq(j)$ (which, in this case is the same as SEQ). The reading agent is responsible for garbage collection by deallocating the history during its visit. So, at the beginning of each new traversal the history is empty. The program is outlined in Fig 2:

Program for the agent while visiting process i
───

agent variables SEQ, S;
process variables seq, s, agent_seq, h (initially h is empty);

if $SEQ = agent\_seq(i) \oplus_3 1 \land seq(i) \neq -1 \rightarrow$
      $seq(i) := SEQ; \, agent\_seq(i) := SEQ; \, S.i := s(i);$
□ $SEQ = agent\_seq(i) \land seq(i) \neq -1 \rightarrow$ skip
□ $seq(i) = -1 \rightarrow seq(i) := SEQ; \, S.i := h(i);$ delete $h(i);$
fi;
$NEXT := DFS$

Program for process i
─────────────────────────

do true $\rightarrow$
if message from j: $agent\_seq(j) = agent\_seq(i) \oplus_3 1 \rightarrow$
      $h(i) := s(i); \, seq(i) = -1; \, agent\_seq(i) := agent\_seq(j);$
      accept the message;
fi;
execute the next instruction of the application program
od

Fig. 2. The 1-reader protocol

───────────────

[1] This signals the agent to record the state from the history of that node.

The global snapshot S consists of the local states recorded at the various nodes.

Theorem 1. *The global state S recorded by the reading agent is consistent.*

Proof. See [12]

Lemma 1. *The read operations performed by a reading agent are atomic with respect to internal write operations.*

Proof. In order to prove that the read operation is atomic we need to show that if two readings are performed one after another, then the second read cannot return a value older than the value returned by the first read. For the proof, see [12]

3.2   The 1-Writer Protocol

During writing, the consistency of the reset operation is preserved by disallowing all messages between the nodes that are reset, and the nodes that are not reset (see [4]). To distinguish between consecutive write operations, we introduce a non-negative integer variable CLOCK with the writing agent. For the purpose of reset only, a binary value of CLOCK will suffice. However, CLOCK will need to have more than two values when we address concurrent reading and writing in the next section. The writer will update the value of $clock(i)$ for every process i that it visits. The spanning trees along which the reading and the writing agents traverse the network can be totally independent. The program for the writer is outlined in Fig 3:

Program for the writing agent while visiting process i

The agent wants to reset the global state to W
agent variables CLOCK, W;
process variables clock, s;

if $(clock(i) < CLOCK) \rightarrow$ $s(i) := W.i;$
                                          $clock(i) := CLOCK$
fi
$NEXT := DFS$

Fig. 3. The 1-writer protocol

When the writer returns home, the resetting is over. The home increments $CLOCK$ before the next traversal begins. The reset operation requires the the cooperation of the individual nodes by requiring them to reject messages that originated from nodes with a different value of the local clock. This requires that messages be stamped with the clock value of the sender.

4   Concurrent Reading and Writing

We now consider the general case when a writing agent and a reading agent perform writing and reading operations in overlapped time on a network of processes. There is no relationship between the speeds at which the writer and the reader traverse the network. The requirements for consistency and atomicity are specified in Section 2.

We will use the value of *clock* at the different nodes as the yardstick of progress. The value of clock is updated by the writing agent in all processes, including the home of the reader process. The reader and the writer agents traverse the network following spanning trees that are not necessarily identical. These are denoted in the algorithm by DFS_R and DFS_W respectively. The writing agent, in addition to updating the local state and the clock, will record the current state of the visited process into the history for that process, that could possible be used by a slower reader. Each entry in the history h is a pair (*clock, local state*). We will designate the entry in the history of process i corresponding to clock j by $h^j(i)$. The saving of the current state becomes unnecessary when *seq* for the visited node is -1, since the state that will be read by the reader has already been saved by the process while updating *seq* to -1. The following two lemmas are relevant to our algorithm:

Lemma 2. $CLOCK(writer) = k \Rightarrow \forall i\ clock(i) \in \{k - 1, k\}$.

When a reader with $CLOCK = k$ assembles a consistent snapshot, it looks for copies of local states that corresponds to $clock = k$. While the writer is writing in round k, it is possible that the reader visits a node whose *clock* has not yet been updated from $k - 1$ to k. In this case, the reader will construct the snapshot from local states recorded at $clock\ k - 1$. All entries in the history corresponding to *clock* lower than $k - 1$ are of no use, and can be deleted by the reader. This leads to the following lemma:

Lemma 3. When $CLOCK(reader) = k$, a consistent snapshot will be assembled from recordings of local states made at clock k only or $k - 1$ only.

We will designate the local snapshots recorded by the reader while visiting process i by $S.i.k$ and $S.i.(k - 1)$. The program is shown in Fig 4. We have identified 3 cases. *Case 1* corresponds to the situation in which both the agent and the visited node have the same clock value. *Case 2* corresponds to the situation in which a node which has not been reset is visited by an agent whose home has been reset at the time the agent was generated. It is clear that the situation in which $CLOCK > clock(i) + 1$ it is not possible, because all the local clocks have been synchronized after a completed reset operation. *Case 3* represents the situation in which a reset node is visited by an agent whose home has not been reset at the time of agent creation. This corresponds to the situation when the reader is slower than the writer. In this scenario, it is possible that a writer had completed several traversals by the time the reader had completed its own visit, and the local clocks as well as the writer's clock havd been incremented several times. These three situations can equally occur, since there is no relationship between the speed of the writing and reading agent and no assumption regarding frequency at which the agents are generated.

Each message is stamped with ($clock$, seq, $agent\_seq$) of the sender. Note that the history in the general case is no longer represented as a single variable that holds the process state, but as a dynamic array that is indexed by $clock$ values, to record the process state at different clock values. A reader never carries more than two entries from the history of any process into its briefcase.

When the reader returns home after collecting various local states and histories, it *assembles* a consistent snapshot from these pieces. The assembly is done as follows: Let C be the largest value of the clock, such that for every process, an entry corresponding to C exists in the reader's briefcase. Then the consistent snapshot consists of all state readings (of local histories) recorded at clock C.

Theorem 2. *The protocol for concurrent reading and writing is correct.*

Proof. The correctness has two parts: consistency of the read and write operations, and atomicity of the read operations with respect to both internal and external write operations, as described in Section 2. The consistency of the read and write operations follows from Theorem 1 and the arguments presented in Section 3.2. We argue about the atomicity only: if R^k and R^{k+1} are two consecutive read operations, then R^{k+1} should not return a value "older" than that returned by R^k.

Case 1. $CLOCK(R^{k+1}) = CLOCK(R^k)$.

This case corresponds to the situation in which no writing agent is present in the system, so it identifies itself with the 1-reader case. Since the reader algorithm is the same, the proof follows from that of Lemma 1.

Case 2. $CLOCK(R^{k+1}) > CLOCK(R^k)$.

Let $CLOCK$ for R^k be C and that for R^{k+1} be $C+1$. The snapshot in R^{k+1} is constructed from states recorded at $C+1$ or C, and the snapshot for R^k is recorded from states collected at C and $C-1$. Atomicity is clearly satisfied if both snapshots are not assembled from readings at clock C. In case both snapshots are assembled from readings at clock C, the situation in Case 1 applies.   □

5   Conclusion

The 1-reader case can be easily extended to multiple readers, since readers do not interact – each process maintains a separate history. The extension to the multiple writer case is under investigation.

The time complexity for a snapshot or a reset operation is determined by the time for one traversal. The space complexity per process is not bounded for this version of the solution. When the writing operation is more frequent than the reading operation, the memory requirement for saving the history can grow indefinitely. Also, CLOCK is an unbounded variable. However, the size of the

Program for the writer while visiting process i
{The writer wants to reset the global state to W}
agent variables CLOCK, W;
process variables clock, s, h;

if $(clock(i) < CLOCK) \rightarrow$
       if $seq(i) \neq -1 \rightarrow h(i) := h(i) \cup (clock(i), s(i));$ **fi**
       $s(i) := W.i;$ $clock(i) := CLOCK$
fi;
$NEXT := DFS_W$

Program for the reader while visiting process i
{The reader is trying to assemble a snapshot S}
agent variables SEQ, CLOCK, S;
process variables seq, agent_seq, s, h;

$\forall j < CLOCK - 1$ delete $h^j(i)$;
{Case 1} **if** $clock(i) = CLOCK \rightarrow$

       if $SEQ = agent\_seq(i) \oplus_3 1 \wedge seq(i) \neq -1 \rightarrow$
          $S.i.CLOCK := s(i);$ $S.i.(CLOCK - 1) := h^{CLOCK-1}(i)$
       □ $SEQ = agent\_seq(i) \wedge seq(i) \neq -1 \rightarrow$ skip
       □ $seq(i) = -1 \rightarrow S.i.CLOCK := h^{CLOCK}(i);$ $S.i.(CLOCK-1) := h^{CLOCK-1}(i)$
       fi;

□ {Case 2} $clock(i) = CLOCK - 1 \rightarrow$

       if $SEQ = agent\_seq(i) \oplus_3 1 \wedge seq(i) \neq -1 \rightarrow$
          $S.i.(CLOCK - 1) := s(i);$ $S.i.CLOCK := null$
       □ $SEQ = agent\_seq(i) \wedge seq(i) \neq -1 \rightarrow$ skip
       □ $seq(i) = -1 \rightarrow S.i.(CLOCK - 1) := h^{CLOCK-1}(i);$ $S.i.CLOCK := null$
       fi;

□ {Case 3} $clock(i) > CLOCK \rightarrow$

       if $SEQ = agent\_seq(i) \oplus_3 1 \rightarrow$
          $S.i.CLOCK := h^{CLOCK}(i);$ $S.i.(CLOCK - 1) := h^{CLOCK-1}(i)$
       □ $SEQ = agent\_seq(i) \rightarrow$ skip
       fi;
fi;
$seq(i) := SEQ;$ $agent\_seq(i) := SEQ;$
$NEXT := DFS_R$

Fig. 4. The concurrent reading and writing protocol

briefcase for both the reader and the writer scales linearly with the size of the network, which is optimal.

Contrary to our original goals, the processes are not passive. The processes could be passive in the 1-reader case, only if we used the dynamic agent model. As soon as a writer is introduced in the scene, the active involvement of the processes becomes unavoidable. Our solutions can be made stabilizing using the method described in [6], thus addressing the situations when the agent might be corrupted.

Further, our agent-based solution can be made truly non-blocking by implementing the technique proposed by Lamport in [8] at each node. In the current version of our algorithm, a node can accommodate only one agent at a time. If two or more agents arrive at a node at the same time, only one will be accommodated by the node, and the rest will have to wait until the chosen agent has finished its program. From the agents' perspective, the state of a node can be viewed as a shared variable. Thus, Lamport's algorithm for concurrent reading and writing on shared registers can be applied to each node to allow the agents true non-blocking read and write access to the process states.

References

1. Araragi, T., Attie, P., Keidar, I., Kogure, K., Luchanugo, V., Lynch, N., Mano, K.: On formal modeling agent computations. LNAI **1871** (2000) 48–62
2. Chandy, K. and Lamport, L.: Distributed snapshots: determining global states of distributed systems. ACM Transactions on Computer Systems **3** (1985) 63–75
3. Mattern F.: Virtual time and global states of distributed systems. In Cosnard M. et al. (EdS) Proceedings of Parallel and Distributed Algorithms. Elsevier Science Publishers (1989) 215–226
4. Arora, A. and Gouda, M.: Distributed reset. IEEE Transactions on Computers **43(9)** 1026–1038
5. Ghosh, S.: Agents, distributed algorithms, and stabilization. LNCS **1858** (2000) 242–251
6. Ghosh, S.: Cooperating mobile agents and stabilization. LNCS **2194** (2001) 1–18
7. Herlihy, M.: Wait-free synchronization. ACM Transactions on Programming Languages and Systems **11(1)** (1991) 124–149
8. Lamport, L.: Concurrent reading and writing. CACM **20(11)** (1977) 806–811
9. Lamport, L.: On interprocess communication. Part II: Algorithms. Distributed Computing **1(2)** (1986) 86–101
10. Tel, G.: Distributed algorithms. Cambridge University Press, Cambridge (1994)
11. Carriero, N. and Gelernter, D.: How to write parallel programs. A *first* course. The MIT Press, Cambridge, Massachusetts, (1990)
12. Bejan, A.: Agent-based approach for concurrent reading and writing on a network of processes. Master thesis, University of Iowa, May 2002.

A Fault-Tolerant Distributed Deadlock Detection Algorithm

R.C. Hansdah, Nilanjan Gantait, and Sandip Dey

Department of Computer Science and Automation, Indian Institute of Science,
Bangalore – 560012, India
{hansdah, sandip}@csa.iisc.ernet.in

Abstract. In this paper, we propose a new fault-tolerant distributed deadlock detection algorithm which can handle loss of any resource release message. It is based on a token-based distributed mutual exclusion algorithm. We have evaluated and compared the performance of the proposed algorithm with two other algorithms which belong to two different classes, using simulation studies. The proposed algorithm is found to be efficient in terms of average number of messages per wait and average deadlock duration compared to the other two algorithms in all situations, and has comparable or better performance in terms of other parameters.

1 Introduction

A distributed system is a collection of several sites or nodes, connected by a communication network. A set of processes is said to be deadlocked if each process in the set waits for a resource to be released by some other process which belongs to the same set. Deadlock detection in distributed systems is harder compared to deadlock detection in centralized systems as each site in a distributed system has only a local view of the whole system.

The distributed deadlock detection algorithms that are found in the literature use one of the following four techniques : *path-pushing, edge-chasing, diffusing computation and global state detection*. In *path-pushing* algorithms, each site sends its local wait-for graph(WFG) to its neighboring sites every time a deadlock detection computation is performed. This is repeated until the complete WFG is constructed. Many path-pushing algorithms have been proposed in the literature[1,2]. In *edge-chasing* algorithms, a cycle is detected by sending probes along each edge of a WFG. When the initiator of a probe gets back the matching probe, it declares a cycle. A few non-priority based edge-chasing algorithms are described in [3,4] and some priority-based algorithms are described in [5,6]. The problem with many path-pushing and edge-chasing algorithms is that they either do not detect valid deadlocks[3,5] or they detect false deadlocks[2,5]. Some of them also suffer from very high system overhead. Algorithms based on *diffusing computation* and *global state detection* are normally used for generalized deadlock detection.

In this paper, we propose a fault-tolerant distributed deadlock detection algorithm which has better performance compared to the existing algorithms in

S.K. Das and S. Bhattacharya (Eds.): IWDC 2002, LNCS 2571, pp. 78–87, 2002.

terms of message overhead and deadlock detection time. In this algorithm, a token carrying a global wait-for graph moves around different sites in a mutually
exclusive fashion. The token movement is guided by the underlying distributed
mutual exclusion algorithm as described in [7]. The global WFG present in the
token is checked for a cycle, and if a cycle is present, a deadlock is declared. The
algorithm is fault-tolerant in the sense that it can handle loss of any resource
release message.

The rest of the paper is organized as follows. Section 2 presents the system model that the algorithm uses. In section 3, different node variables and
messages used by the algorithm are given. A description of the algorithm is presented in section 4. Section 5 gives a sketch of the correctness argument and the
fault-tolerant characteristic of the algorithm. Section 6 presents the simulation
study and results. Finally, section 7 concludes the paper. The detailed algorithm
is given in the appendix.

2   System Model

The algorithm runs on a set of failure-free nodes which are connected by a
complete network. This is an asynchronous distributed environment and nodes
can communicate with each other using message passing only. All message delays
are finite but arbitrary and messages are received in the order sent. Within a
node, there are several processes and resources (or data items). All the resources
in a node are managed by a resource controller. Each process in the system has a
system wide unique process identifier. A process can be in one of two states, viz.,
active or waiting. A process can request for several resources and it can proceed
only if it receives all the requested resources (AND request model). Each resource
has a single instance and is identified by a unique resource identifier. A resource
will be in one of of two states, viz., free or held by some process. There is a
request queue associated with each resource in the system.

3   Variables and Messages

All the node variables and message variables are in *italic* and the message names
are in **bold**. The node states and other constant values are in CAPITAL.

3.1   System Wide Process and Resource Table

Process table is an array of P number of process entries. This table is indexed
by *proc_id*. Each entry in the process table has the following fields : (i)*proc_id*
which holds the identity of the process, (ii)*proc_owner* which is the identity of
the node where the process originated, (iii)*wait_set* that represents the set of
resources for which the process is waiting, and (iv)*hold_set* which is the set of
resources, held by the process.

Resource table is an array of R number of resource entries. This table is indexed by *res_id*. Each entry in the resource table has the following fields : (i)*res_id*

which is the identity of the resource, (ii)*res_owner* which is the identity of the node where the resource is situated, (iii)*holder_proc* that indicates the identity of the process holding the resource, (iv)*holder_owner* which is the identity of the node which owns the holder process, and (v)*res_requestQ* which is a queue of requesting processes, where each entry is a tuple <*proc_id, proc_owner*>.

3.2   Variables at Each Node

Each node has the following variables : (i)*node_id* which holds the identity of the node, (ii)*node_state* that represents the current state of the node and can take any one of the three values, viz., WAITING, INCS, IDLE, (iii)*next_node* which is the identity of the node to which this node had given the token earlier, (iv)*last_node* which holds the identity of the node which had requested earlier for the token and may be having it currently, (v)*token_requestQ* which is a queue of incoming token request messages, (vi)*graph* which is the local wait-for graph and each vertex in this graph is a tuple of <*proc_id, proc_owner*> and each edge is a tuple of <*res_id, res_owner*>, (vii)*proc_table*[P] which is a copy of the system-wide process table, and (viii)*res_table*[R] that is a copy of the system-wide resource table.

3.3   Messages

The following messages are used in the algorithm.
1. Resource Request Message **res_req**(*proc_id, res_id, proc_owner*).
2. Resource Grant Message **res_grant**(*proc_id, res_id*).
3. Resource Release Message **res_rel**(*proc_id, res_id, proc_owner*).
4. Token Request Message **token_req**(*sending_node, timestamp*).
5. Token Message **token**(*graph, token_requestQ*).
6. Edge Verification Message **verify_edge**(*waiting_proc, holder_proc, res_id, holder_owner, receiving_node, sending_node*).
7. Edge Acknowledgment Message **ack_edge**(*still_waiting, waiting_proc, holder_proc, res_id*).
8. Hold Verification Message **verify_hold**(*holder_proc, res_id, sending_node*).
9. Hold Acknowledgment Message **ack_hold**(*still_holding, holder_proc, res_id*).
10. Process Abort Message **abort**(*victim_id*).
11. Resource Clear Message **clear**(*aborted_proc, res_id*).

4   Description of the Algorithm

This section gives a brief description of the algorithm. When a process requests for a resource, it sends a resource request message to a resource controller. If the resource is local, then the resource controller checks whether the resource is free or not. If the resource is free, then it is granted to the process, otherwise the process is placed in the request queue associated with the resource and an edge is added in the local wait-for graph(WFG). If the node has token, then it also updates the global wait-for graph present in the token, and checks for a cycle in the global WFG. Otherwise, the node requests for the token, if it has not already been requested. If the resource request is not local, then the resource controller forwards the request to the corresponding resource controller. When the resource request reaches a remote resource controller, it is handled similarly as in case of local resource request. The token moves around nodes in a mutually exclusive fashion as per algorithm given in [7].

When the token reaches a node, the global wait-for graph present in the token is updated taking help of the local WFG. The algorithm checks whether there exists a cycle in the updated global WFG. If a cycle exists, the controller sends edge verification messages corresponding to each edge in the cycle (a particular resource is still held by a particular process) and waits to receive all edge acknowledgment messages. When a node receives an edge verification message, it checks whether the particular resource is held by the particular process (according to local WFG). If the resource is held by the process, the node sends a hold verification message (this is different from the edge verification message mentioned earlier) to check that the process is actually holding the resource or it has already released the resource. When a node receives a hold verification message, it checks whether the process is still holding the resource or not. If the process still holds the resource, it sends a positive hold acknowledgment to the node from which it received the hold verification message. Otherwise, a negative hold acknowledgment is sent. Depending upon this response, the node which had received the edge verification message, sends an acknowledgment. When a node receives positive acknowledgments for all the edge verification messages it sent, it declares a deadlock. Otherwise, the WFG of the token is updated. When a deadlock is detected, a process from the cycle is chosen as victim and this process is aborted. All the resources held by this victim process are made free. Resource clear messages are sent to all resource controllers where the process is waiting.

5   Correctness and Fault-Tolerance

The correctness of a deadlock detection algorithm depends on two properties, viz.,

- *Progress Property* : Every deadlock must be detected.

- *Safety Property* : If a deadlock is detected, it must indeed exists.

The *progress* property follows from the fact that the algorithm for distributed mutual exclusion[7] is deadlock-free and starvation-free, and single copy of global wait-for graph is used. The *safety* property follows from the fact that the existence of every edge in the deadlock cycle is physically verified. This verification is also able to detect the loss of any resource release messages, and thereby it ensures fault-tolerance to that extent.

Table 1. Simulation Parameters

Parameter	Meaning	Value
N	Number of sites	5, 10
RNO	Number of data items	1000
MPL	Multiprogramming Level	10 - 35
LNO	Number of lock request/transaction	Uniform(LMIN - LMAX)
LMIN	Minimum number of lock requested	5
LMAX	Maximum number of lock requested	20
C_DEL	Communicational delay	Uniform(1 - 10ms) for LAN (100ms - 1sec) for WAN
C_TIME	CPU time of a transaction	5ms
PL	Probability of local request	50%

6   Simulation and Results

We have compared the performance of our algorithm with Ron Obermarck's
Path-Pushing algorithm[2] and Yeung et al.'s Edge-Chasing algorithm[4] using
simulation studies. The simulation model has been adopted from[8]. We have
simulated a distributed database system which consists of N nodes or sites where
each node has some processing power. These nodes are connected by a communication network. Each node contains some part of the distributed database(i.e,
some data items). There are RNO number of data items in the system, and we
assume that these data items are equally distributed among the sites.

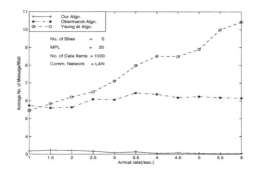

Fig. 1. Average No. of Messages/Wait plot of 5-Node system for LAN

Table 1 shows various simulation parameters. There are a fixed number of
terminals from which transactions originate. The maximum number of active
transactions, at any given time, in the system is the multiprogramming level
(MPL). A transaction requests a data item from a remote site with probability
$(1 - -PL)/(N - 1)$. An extensive simulation study has been carried out for
various arrival rates of transactions beginning with 1.0/sec to 6.0/sec in steps of
0.5.

In addition to throughput and average response time, we have also used the following performance metrics in our simulation study : (i) average number of messages/wait, (ii)average number of messages/deadlock, and (iii)average deadlock duration. Some important graphs illustrating the behaviours of different performance metrics for the three algorithms are given in Fig. 1–3.

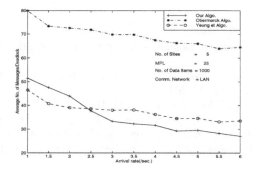

Fig. 2. Average No. of Messages/Deadlock plot of 5-Node system for LAN

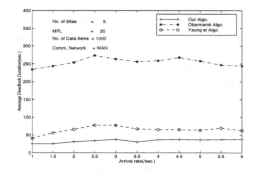

Fig. 3. Average Deadlock Duration plot of 5-Node system for WAN

7   Conclusion

In this paper, we have designed a fault-tolerant distributed deadlock detection algorithm and studied its performance. We have evaluated and compared the performance of our algorithm with Ron Obermarck's path-pushing algorithm and Yeung et al.'s edge-chasing algorithm. As far as the average number of messages per wait and average deadlock duration are concerned, our algorithm turns out to be the best. Average number of messages per deadlock is also minimum for this algorithm. However, average response time and throughput is comparable with Yeung et al.'s algorithm and much better than Obermarck's algorithm. The algorithm is also fault-tolerant in the sense that it can handle loss of any resource release message.

References

1. D. Menasce and R. Muntz. *Locking and Deadlock Detection in Distributed Databases.* IEEE Transactions on Software Engineering, SE-5(3):192–202, March 1979.
2. Ron Obermarck. *Distributed Deadlock Detection Algorithm.* ACM Transactions on Database Systems, 7(2):187–208, June 1982.
3. K. Mani Chandy, J. Misra, and Laura M. Hass. *Distribued Deadlock Detection.* ACM Transactions on Computer Systems, 1(2):144–156, May 1983.
4. C. F. Yeung, S. L. Hung, Kam yiu Lam, and C. H. Law. *A New Distributed Deadlock Detection Algorithm for Distributed Database Systems.* In Proc. of the IEEE TENCON'94, 1994.
5. A. N. Choudhary, W. H. Kohler, J. A. Stankovic, and D. Towsley. *A Modified Priority-Based Probe Algorithm for Distributed Deadlock Detection and Resolution.* IEEE Transactions on Software Engineering, 15(1):10–17, January 1989.
6. A. D. Kshemkalyani and M. Singhal. *Invariant Based Verification of a Distributed Deadlock Detection Algorithm.* IEEE Transactions on Software Engineering, 17(8):789–799, August 1991.
7. R. C. Hansdah and P. K. Dash. *A Fault-Tolerant Token-Based Algorithm for Distributed Mutual Exclusion Using Roughly Synchronized Clocks.* In Proc. of the 6th International Conference on Advanced Computing, Pune, India, pages 7–14, December 14–16, 1998.
8. A. N. Choudhary. *Cost of Distributed Deadlock Detection: A Performance Study.* In Proc. of the 6th International Conference on Data Engineering, pages 174–181, February 1990.

Appendix: Algorithm

The various functions for the resource controller thread at a node are as follows.

handle_res_req()
{
    if((*node_id*==**res_req**.*proc_owner*) and
    (*node_id* == *res_table*[**res_req**.*res_id*].*res_owner*)){
        if(*res_table*[**res_req**.*res_id*].*holder_proc* == NULL){
        res_table[**res_req**.*res_id*].*holder_proc* = **res_req**.*proc_id*;
        res_table[**res_req**.*res_id*].*holder_owner* = **res_req**.*proc_owner*;
        proc_table[**res_req**.*proc_id*].*hold_set*.Insert(**res_req**.*res_id*);
        } else{
        add an edge((**res_req**.*proc_id*, **res_req**.*proc_owner*) $\overset{(\mathbf{res\_req}.res\_id, node\_id)}{\longrightarrow}$
        (*res_table*[**res_req**.*res_id*].*holder_proc*, *res_table*[**res_req**.*res_id*].*holder_owner*))

in *graph*;

proc_table[**res_req**.*proc_id*].*wait_set*.Insert(**res_req**.*res_id*);

res_table[**res_req**.*res_id*].*res_requestQ*.Enqueue(<**res_req**.*proc_id*,

res_req.*proc_owner*>);

check for a cycle in *graph*;

if (a cycle present){

    for all processes in the cycle, which are not local

        send message **verify_hold**(*holder_proc*,*res_id*, *node_id*) to

        proc_table[*holder_proc*].*proc_owner*;

    wait for all **ack_hold** messages;

    if(**ack_hold**.*still_holding* == TRUE) for all **ack_hold** messages

    {

        choose a victim process;

        send message **abort**(*victim_id*) to *proc_table*[*victim_id*].*proc_owner*;

    } else update *graph*;

} /*if (cycle present)*/

if(*last_node* == *node_id*) *handle_token()*;

else{ if(*state* == IDLE) { *state* == WAITING;

    send message **token_req**(*node_id*,*clock()*) to *last_node*;

    activate token handler thread; }

  /* This thread waits for the token & invokes *handle_token()* */

}

}

}

else if((*node_id*==**res_req**.*proc_owner*) and

(*node_id* != *res_table* [**res_req**.*res_id*].*res_owner*)){

    send message **res_req**(**res_req**.*proc_id*, **res_req**.*res_id*,

    res_req.*proc_owner*) to *res_table*[**res_req**.*res_id*].*res_owner*;

    proc_table[**res_req**.*proc_id*].*wait_set*.Insert(**res_req**.*res_id*);

} else{

    if(*res_table*[**res_req**.*res_id*].*holder_proc* == NULL){

    send message **res_grant**(**res_req**.*proc_id*, **res_req**.*res_id*) to

    res_req.*proc_owner*;

    res_table[**res_req**.*res_id*].*holder_proc* = **res_req**.*proc_id*;

    res_table[**res_req**.*res_id*].*holder_owner* = **res_req**.*proc_owner*;

    } else{

    res_table[**res_req**.*res_id*].*res_requestQ*.Enqueue(<**res_req**.*proc_id*,

    res_req.*proc_owner*>);

    add an edge((**res_req**.*proc_id*, **res_req**.*proc_owner*) $\overset{(\textbf{res\_req}.res\_id, node\_id)}{\longrightarrow}$

    (*res_table*[**res_req**.*res_id*].*holder_proc*, *res_table*[**res_req**.*res_id*].*holder_owner*))

    in *graph*;

    if(*last_node* == *node_id*) *handle_token()*;

    else{ if(*state* == IDLE) { *state* == WAITING;

        send message **token_req**(*node_id*, *clock()*) to *last_node*;

        activate token handler thread; }

    }

    }

}

handle_res_grant()
{ *proc_table.*[**res_grant**.*proc_id*].*wait_set*.Delete(**res_grant**.*res_id*);
  proc_table.[**res_grant**.*proc_id*].*hold_set*.Insert(**res_grant**.*res_id*);
}

handle_res_rel()
{ if(*res_table*[**res_rel**.*res_id*].*res_requestQ*!= NULL) {
      <*l, m*> = *res_table*[**res_rel**.*res_id*].*res_requestQ*.Dequeue();
      res_table[**res_rel**.*res_id*].*holder_proc* = *l*;
      res_table[**res_rel**.*res_id*].*holder_owner* = *m*;
      delete an edge((l, m) $\xrightarrow{(\textbf{res\_rel}.res\_id, node\_id)}$
      (**res_rel**.*proc_id*, **res_rel**.*proc_owner*)) in *graph*;
      for all entry <*s, t*> $\in$ *res_table*[**res_rel**.*res_id*].*res_requestQ* {
      delete an edge((s, t) $\xrightarrow{(\textbf{res\_rel}.res\_id, node\_id)}$
      (**res_rel**.*proc_id*, **res_rel**.*proc_owner*)) in *graph*;
      insert an edge((s, t) $\xrightarrow{(\textbf{res\_rel}.res\_id, node\_id)}$ (l, m)) in*graph*; }
      if(m == *node_id*){
         proc_table[*l*].*wait_set*.Delete(**res_rel**.*res_id*);
         proc_table[*l*].*hold_set*.Insert(**res_rel**.*res_id*);
      } else{
         send message **res_grant**(**res_rel**.*proc_id*, **res_rel**.*res_id*) to node *m*;
         if(*last_node* == *node_id*) *handle_token()*;
         else{ if(*state* == IDLE) { *state* == WAITING;
               send message **token_req**(*node_id*,*clock()*) to *last_node*;
               activate token handler thread; }
         }
       }
     }
   }
}

handle_token() { *enter_CS()*; *leave_CS()*; }

enter_CS()
{ *state* = INCS; **token**.*graph* = graph_Merge(**token**.*graph, graph*);
  check for a cycle in **token**.*graph*;
  if(cycle is present){
      for each edge (($a, o1$) $\xrightarrow{(c,w)}$ ($b, o2$)) of the cycle
         send message **verify_edge**(*a, b, c, o2, w, node_id*) to *w*;
      wait to receive all **ack_edge** replies;
      if(**ack_edge**.*still_waiting* == TRUE) in all **ack_edge** messages {
         choose a victim process;
         send message **abort**(*victim_id*) to *proc_table*[*victim_id*].*proc_owner*;
      } else update **token**.*graph*;
   }
}

handle_verify_edge()
{ if(*res_table*[**verify_edge**.*res_id*].*holder_proc* == **verify_edge**.*holder_proc*) {

send message **verify_hold**(**verify_edge**.*holder_proc*, **verify_edge**.*res_id*,
   verify_edge.*receiving_node*) to **verify_edge**.*holder_owner*;
wait for **ack_hold** message;
if(**ack_hold**.*still_holding*)
   send message **ack_edge**(TRUE, **verify_edge**.*waiting_proc*,
      verify_edge.*holder_proc*,**verify_edge**.*res_id*) to **verify_edge**.*sending_node*;
   else{
      send message **ack_edge**(FALSE, **verify_edge**.*waiting_proc*,
         verify_edge.*holder_proc*, **verify_edge**.*res_id*) to **verify_edge**.*sending_node*;
      update *graph*; update *res_table*[**verify_edge**.*res_id*].res_requestQ;
   }
   } else
      send message **ack_edge**(FALSE, **verify_edge**.*waiting_proc*,
         verify_edge.*holder_proc*, **verify_edge**.*res_id*) to **verify_edge**.*sending_node*;
}

handle_verify_hold()
{ if(**verify_hold**.*res_id* ∈ *proc_table*[**verify_hold**.*holder_proc*].*hold_set*)
      send message **ack_hold**(TRUE, **verify_hold**.*holder_proc*, **verify_hold**.*res_id*)
      to **verify_hold**.*sending_node*;
   else send message **ack_hold**(FALSE, **verify_hold**.*holder_proc*, **verify_hold**.*res_id*)
      to **verify_hold**.*sending_node*;
}

leave_CS()
{ *state* = IDLE; if(*token_requestQ* != NULL) {
      next_node = *sending_node* of first entry of *token_requestQ*;
      last_node = *sending_node* of last entry of *token_requestQ*;
      token_requestQ = *token_requestQ* - <first entry in *token_requestQ*>;
      send message **token**(*graph*, *token_requestQ*) to *next_node*; }
   else{ *next_node* = *node_id*; *last_node* = *node_id*; }
}

handle_abort_msg()
{ for all resources *r* ∈ *proc_table*[**abort**.*victim_id*].*hold_set*
send message **res_rel**(*victim_id*, *r*,*res_table*[*r*].*holder_owner*) to *res_table*[*r*].*res_owner*;
   for all resources *r* ∈ *proc_table* [**abort**.*victim_id*].*wait_set*
send message **clear**(*victim_id*, *r*) to *res_table*[*r*].*res_owner*;
}

handle_clear()
{ remove process **clear**.*aborted_proc* from *res_table*[**clear**.*res_id*].*res_requestQ*;
   update *graph*;
}

Performance Evaluation of a Two Level Error Recovery Scheme for Distributed Systems

B.S. Panda[1] and Sajal K. Das[2]

[1] Department of Mathematics
Indian Institute of Technology, Delhi
Hauz Khas, New Delhi, 110 016, INDIA
bspanda@maths.iitd.ernet.in
[2] Department of Computer Science and Engineering
The University of Texas at Arlington
Arlington, TX 76019, USA
das@cse.uta.edu

Abstract. Rollback recovery schemes are used in fault-tolerant distributed systems to minimize the computation loss incurred in the presence of failures. One-level recovery schemes do not consider the different types of failures and their relative frequency of occurrence, thereby tolerating all failures with the same overhead. Two-level recovery schemes aim to provide low overhead protection against more probable failures, providing protection against other failures with possibly higher overhead. In this paper, we have analyzed a two-level recovery scheme due to Vaidya taking **probability of task completion on a system with limited repairs** as the performance metric.

1 Introduction

In the absence of failure recovery scheme, applications in distributed systems must be restarted (from the beginning) whenever a failure occurs. This leads to unacceptable performance overhead for long running applications which are often subject to failures. Therefore, some failure recovery schemes must be incorporated to minimize the performance overhead. Performance overhead of a recovery scheme is the increase in the task execution time when using the recovery scheme. It consists of two components:

- Overhead during failure-free operation (failure-free overhead), e.g., checkpointing and message logging.
- Overhead during recovery (recovery overhead).

One-level recovery schemes do not consider the different types of failures and their relative frequency of occurrence, thereby tolerating all failures with the same overhead. Two-level recovery schemes, on the other hand, aim to provide low overhead protection against more probable failures, providing protection against other failures with, possibly, higher overhead. Vaidya [8] proposed a two-level recovery scheme which considers transient processor failures as more

S.K. Das and S. Bhattacharya (Eds.): IWDC 2002, LNCS 2571, pp. 88–97, 2002.

probable while permanent processor failures and local disk failures being less probable ones.

Although a large number of researchers have analyzed traditional checkpointing and rollback schemes (e.g. see [1,2,5,6,7,9]), work on two-level (or multilevel) recovery schemes is limited [3,4,8]. Vaidya [8] has analyzed the performance of such a scheme taking **average overhead** as the performance metric. It has been shown that under the above metric, the proposed two-level recovery scheme performs better than a traditional one-level recovery scheme for long running applications. In the conclusion of [8] it has also been suggested to evaluate the performance of that two-level recovery scheme using **probability of meeting a given deadline** as a metric.

In this paper, we have analyzed the two-level recovery scheme due to Vaidya [8] by considering **probability of task completion on a system with limited repairs** as the performance metric.

We use Markov chain to model a segment of the task execution. We, then obtain an expression for the performance metric in terms of other system parameters. We then numerically show for certain values of the system parameters that two-level recovery scheme performs better than the one level recovery scheme for long running applications under the new metric. Our result conforms to the result due to Vaidya [8], where he considered **average overhead** as the performance metric.

The rest of the paper is organized as follows. Section 2 discusses the distributed system model used. Section 3 describes the two level recovery scheme to be analyzed. Section 4 presents the performance analysis of this scheme. Section 5 concludes the paper.

2   System Model

Our distributed system consists of a network of N processors (when $N = 1$, it reduces to a uniprocessor system). Each processor has its own volatile memory and local disk. The processors share a stable storage that can be accessed over the network. Each processor executes one process of a distributed application, therefore, a processor failure is synonymous with process failure.

The stable storage is assumed to be always failure-free. A processor is subject to transient as well as permanent failures. Failure of a processor results in the loss of the volatile memory contents; however, it does not cause a failure in the local disk. However, a local disk can also fail, resulting in the loss of information stored in the disk. To be able to access the local disk of a processor, the processor itself must be operational. A permanent failure of the processor makes its local disk inaccessible to other processors. In case of a transient processor failure, the local disk of the faulty processor becomes accessible once the processor comes back up after failure. We assume that a failure of the local disk always crashes the associated processor. This assumption is quite accurate in the case of workstations. The local disk of a workstation often stores swapped out process memory, temporary files accessed by an application, as well as many files that are accessed by the operating system. Failure of a local disk is, therefore, likely to crash the system.

Failures of the N processors are assumed to be independent of each other; similarly, the local disk failures are independent. Let the inter-failure interval for a processor be governed by an exponential distribution with mean $1/\lambda_p$. A failure is detected whenever it occurs. The probability that a processor failure is permanent is denoted by p, thus $(1-p)$ being the probability that a processor failure is transient. Let the time interval between the detection of consecutive local disk failures be governed by an exponential distribution with mean $1/\lambda_l$. Let λ denote $(\lambda_p + \lambda_l)$.

3   Two-Level Recovery Scheme

The recovery scheme exploits the fact that transient failures are more probable than any other failure in many systems. In this section we outline a two-level recovery scheme due to Vaidya [8].

3.1   Failure-Free Operation of the Scheme

The processes periodically takes consistent checkpoints. Every k^{th} consistent checkpoint is stored on the stable storage, all other checkpoints being stored on local disks (e.g., each processor saves its checkpoint on its own local disk). No checkpoint is taken at the completion of a task.

We use the term *local checkpoint* to refer to a consistent checkpoint in which each processor saves its checkpoint on its local disk (the individual processor checkpoints are consistent with each other). A local checkpoint incurs some overhead, denoted by C_l. A consistent checkpoint stored on stable storage is called an *N-checkpoint* and has overhead C_N. Typically, C_l is much smaller than C_N. (The term N-checkpoint alludes to the fact that this checkpoint can be used to recover from any type of failure, including simultaneous failure of all N processors and local disks).

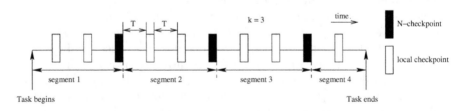

Fig. 1. Local and N-checkpoints: Recovery Scheme

Failure-free execution of a task using this recovery scheme is depicted in Figure 1, assuming $k = 3$. Note that T denotes the duration between two consecutive checkpoints, or the checkpoint interval. The figure illustrates the execution of the task using the single horizontal line. The task consists of N processes, however, as their checkpoints occur at about the same time, the checkpoints are shown on the execution line using a single box. Here we assume that the checkpoint overhead is identical with the checkpoint latency (time required to take checkpoint).

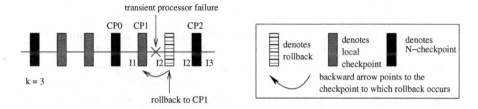

Fig. 2. Rollback: Transient Processor Failure

3.2 Rollback Recovery

Three cases of failures are possible.

1. A processor has a transient failure: In this case, the failure is recovered by rolling back to the most recent checkpoint (which may be a local or N-checkpoint), as shown in Figure 2. Each processor rolls back to its most recent checkpoint, and starts re-execution. When a processor has a transient failure, its local disk contents are not corrupted, therefore, a local checkpoint can be used for recovery.
2. A processor has a permanent failure: In this case, the local disk of the faulty processor is inaccessible. Thus, the task cannot roll back to a local consistent checkpoint, and processors must roll back to the most recent N-checkpoint. This is illustrated in Figure 3. (If no N-checkpoint is taken before the failure, then the task must be restarted from the beginning.)
3. A local disk has a failure: A local disk failure will also crash the corresponding processor, as in case 2, to recover from this failure, the processors must rollback to the most recent N-checkpoint, because a local checkpoint cannot be accessed.

4 Performance Analysis

In this section, we analyze the performance of the two-level recovery scheme. We use Markov chain to model a segment of the task execution. We, then obtain an expression for the performance metric in terms of other system parameters.

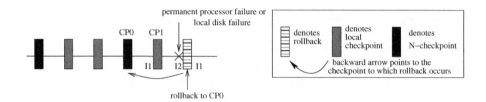

Fig. 3. Rollback: Permanent Failure

Let Y denote the length of the task in the absence of failures and without using any recovery scheme. Let T and μ denote checkpoint interval and the number of checkpoint intervals, respectively. Thus, $Y = \mu T$. We assume that Y is an integral multiple of T. Let k be the frequency of N-checkpoint, i.e., every k^{th} checkpoint is an N-checkpoint. Let R_l and R_N denote the overhead for recovery from a local checkpoint and N-checkpoint, respectively. Let C_l and C_N denote the cost of establishing a local checkpoint and N-checkpoint, respectively.

Let the execution of a task be divided into segments. a segment starts after an N-checkpoint is taken and ends when the next N-checkpoint is taken. Exceptions to this are the first and the last segments, the first segment begins with the beginning of the task and the last segment ends with the completion of the task. No checkpoint is taken at the end of the task.

Thus, $\lceil \mu/k \rceil$ = number of segments.

$\mu - 1$ = Total number of consistent checkpoints taken.

$\lfloor (\mu - 1)/k \rfloor$ = number of N-checkpoints.

When $k = 1$, all checkpoints are N-checkpoints and the two-level scheme reduces to traditional "one level" scheme. When $k = \mu$, all checkpoints are local checkpoints, and the scheme is called the **degenerate two-level scheme**.

4.1 Modelling a Segment by a Markov Chain

The execution of the segment is modelled by a Markov chain, as illustrated in Figure 4. The Markov chain contains $(2k + 1)$ states denoted as $0, 0^*, 1, 1^*, \ldots, i, i^*, \ldots, (k-1), (k-1)^*, k$. Note that there is no state k^*. State 0 is the start state and state k is the sink state. From states i and i^* $(0 \le i \le k-1)$, transitions can occur to states $i^*, i + 1$, and 0^*. State i is reached when the ith checkpoint occurs where 0th checkpoint is equivalent to start of the segment. If a transient processor failure occurs while in state i, then a transition is made to the state i^* because the system rolls back to the ith checkpoint taken since the start of the segment. If a permanent processor failure or a local disk failure occurs while in state i or i^*, then a transition is made to state $i*$, because the system rolls back to the N-checkpoint at the start of the segment. A transient processor failure while in state i^* causes a transition back to state i^* because rollback occurs to the ith checkpoint. If no failure occurs while in state i or i^*, a transition to state $i+1$ occurs when the next checkpoint is taken.

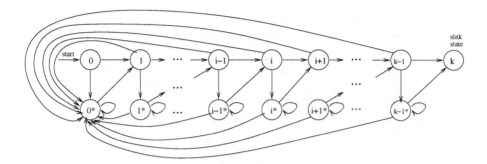

Fig. 4. Markov Chain for a Segment

4.2 Performance Evaluation

Let N_{MAX} be the maximum number of failures that can be tolerated during task execution. Let $P_{N_{MAX}}(Y)$ be the probability of task completion tolerating N_{MAX} number of failures where Y is the task length. Then

$$P_{N_{MAX}}(Y) = \sum_{i=0}^{N_{MAX}} P(Y|N = i) \tag{1}$$

where $P(Y|N = i)$ is the probability of completion of task of length Y, when exactly i failures occur. Let $P(0(n))$ be the probability of going from state 0 to state k, tolerating exactly n failures. This is the probability of successful completion of the segment, i.e., kT units of execution of the task. For all i, $0 \le i \le k - 1$, let us define $P(i^*(n))$ as the probability of going from state i^* to state k tolerating exactly n failures.

Analysis for all but the last segment follows. Let $P = [p_{ij}]_{(2k+1) \times (2k+1)}$, be the state transition probability matrix for the Markov chain of such a segment, where p_{ij} is the probability of reaching state j given that the execution is currently in state i.

4.3 Analysis for the Simple Case of a Segment with Two Intervals

We first consider a simple case for a segment (see Figure 5), that is divided into two intervals, i.e., $k = 2$. Consider that the task successfully executes the segment tolerating exactly n failures. Then, starting from state 0, the task can make the following two transitions corresponding to mutually exclusive events:

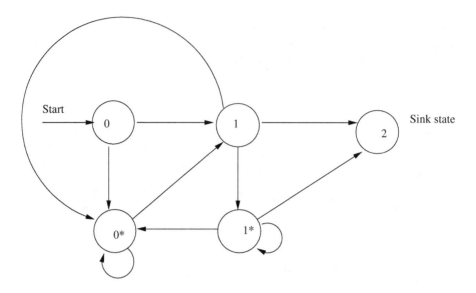

Fig. 5. Markov Model for a Segment with $k = 2$.

1. State 0 to state 1, i.e., no failure within $(T + C_l)$ units of execution.
2. State 0 to state 0*, i.e.,occurrence of a failure within $(T + C_l)$ units of execution.

For case 1 above, the task can be similarly make the following transitions (mutually exclusive events):

1(a) State 1 to state 2 (if n faults have already occurred before coming to state 1).
1(b) State 1 to state 1* (Occurrence of a transient failure within $(T + C_N)$ units of execution).
1(c) State 1 to state 0* (Occurrence of a permanent failure within $(T + C_N)$ units of execution).

For case 2 above, the task is in state 0* and exactly $(n - 1)$ failures are still to happen during the execution of the task in the segment.

Considering cases 1 and 2 as well as cases 1(a),(b),(c) that follow, we get the following recurrence relation:

$$P(0(n)) = P_{00^*} + P_{01}P_{10^*})P(0^*(n - 1)) + P_{01}P_{11^*}P(1^*(n - 1)).$$

Similarly, to compute $P(0^*(n - 1))$ and $P(1^*(n - 1))$, we again consider the possible transitions from these states from Figure 4, and get the following recurrence relations:

$$P(0^*(n)) = P_{0^*0^*} + P_{0^*1}P_{10^*})P(0^*(n - 1)) + P_{0^*1}P_{11^*}P(1^*(n - 1)),$$

$$P(1^*(n)) = P_{1^*1^*}P(1^*(n - 1)) + P_{1^*0^*}P(0^*(n - 1)).$$

4.4   Analysis for a General Segment

Extending the above relations to a general segment, where $1 \leq k \leq \mu$, we get the following recurrence relations:

$$P(0(n)) = [P_{00^*} + P_{01^*}P_{10^*} + P_{01}P_{12} \ldots P_{(k-2)(k-1)}P_{(k-1)0^*}]P(0^*(n-1)) + P_{01}P_{11^*}P(1^*(n-1)) + \ldots + P_{01}P_{12} \ldots P_{(k-2)(k-1)}P_{(k-1)(k-2)^*}P((k-1)^*(n-1)),$$

$$P(0^*(n)) = [P_{0^*0^*} + P_{0^*1}P_{10^*} + \ldots + P_{0^*1}P_{12} \ldots P_{(k-2)(k-1)}P_{(k-1)0^*}]P(0^*(n-1)) + P_{0^*1}P_{11^*}P(1^*(n-1)) + \ldots + P_{0^*1}P_{12} \ldots P_{(k-2)(k-1)}P_{(k-1)(k-1)^*}P((k-1)^*(n-1)),$$

and $\forall i, 1 \leq i \leq k-1,$

$$P(i^*(n)) = [P_{i^*0^*} + P_{i^*(i+1)}P_{(i+1)0^*} + \ldots + P_{i^*(i+1)}P_{(i+1)(i+2)} \cdots P_{(k-2)(k-1)}P_{(k-1)0^*}] P(0^*(n-1)) + P_{i^*i^*}P(i^*(n-1)) + P_{i^*(i+1)}P_{(i+1)(i+1)^*}P((i+1)^*(n-1)) + \ldots + P_{i^*(i+1)}P_{(i+1)(i+2)} \cdots P_{(k-2)(k-1)}P_{(k-1)(k-1)^*}P((k-1)^*(n-1)).$$

In a more compact form, we get the set of recurrences as:

$$P(0(n)) = [P_{00^*} + P_{01} \sum_{i=1}^{k-1} (\prod_{j=1}^{i-1} P_{j(j+1)})P_{i0^*}]P(0^*(n-1)) + \tag{2}$$

$$[P_{01} \sum_{i=1}^{k-1} (\prod_{j=1}^{i-1} P_{j(j+1)})P_{ii^*} P(i^*(n-1))]$$

$$P(0^*(n)) = [P_{0^*0^*} + P_{0^*1} \sum_{i=1}^{k-1} (\prod_{j=1}^{i-1} P_{j(j+1)})P_{i0^*}]P(0^*(n-1)) + \tag{3}$$

$$[P_{0^*1} \sum_{i=1}^{k-1} (\prod_{j=1}^{i-1} P_{j(j+1)})P_{ii^*} P(i^*(n-1))]$$

And for all $i, 1 \leq i \leq k-1,$

$$P(i^*(n)) = [P_{i^*(i+1)} \sum_{m=i+1}^{k-1} (\prod_{j=i+1}^{m-1} P_{j(j+1)})P_{m0^*}]P(0^*(n-1)) + \tag{4}$$

$$P_{i^*i^*} P(i^*(n-1)) +$$

$$[P_{i^*(i+1)} \sum_{m=i+1}^{k-1} (\prod_{j=i+1}^{m-1} P_{j(j+1)})P_{mm^*}P(m^*(n-1))]$$

Now let,

$$P^*(n) = \begin{bmatrix} P(0^*(n)) \\ P(1^*(n)) \\ \vdots \\ P((k-1)^*(n)) \end{bmatrix}_{k \times 1} \tag{5}$$

Expressing Equations (3), (4), and (5) in matrix form, we get

$$P^*(n) = AP^*(n-1) \tag{6}$$

Applying the above equation recursively we get,

$$P^*(n) = A^n P^*(0) \tag{7}$$

where,

$$P^*(0) = \begin{bmatrix} P(0^*(0)) \\ P(1^*(0)) \\ \vdots \\ P((k-1)^*(0)) \end{bmatrix}_{k \times 1} \tag{8}$$

and

$$P(i^*(0)) = P_{i^*(i+1)} \prod_{j=(i+1)}^{k-1} P_{j(j+1)} \tag{9}$$

Let us assume that n_i number of failures occur in segment S_i (where S_i is the ith segment in the execution of the task). Then, $\prod_{i=1}^{\lceil \mu/k \rceil} P(0(n_i))$ gives the probability that the task runs to completion tolerating exactly $\sum n_i$ number of faults. Hence,

$$P(Y|N=n) = \sum_{s \in S} s = (n_1, n_2, \ldots, n_{\lceil \mu/k \rceil}) \prod_{i=1}^{\lceil \mu/k \rceil} P(0(n_i)),$$

where, $S = \{(n_1, n_2, \ldots, n_{\lceil \mu/k \rceil}) | \sum_{i=1}^{\lceil \mu/k \rceil} n_i = n\}$.

Therefore, $P_{N_{MAX}}(Y)$ can be computed with the help of Equation (1).

Due to the complexity of the expressions involved in evaluation of two-level recovery scheme, it seems difficult at this moment to find the optimal value of k analytically (if optimal value of $k \geq 2$, then two-level recovery scheme is better than one level recovery scheme). However, we have numerically evaluated our expressions for certain values of system parameters.

We have assumed that $\lambda_p = 10^{-5}$, $\lambda_l = 10^{-6}$, $N = 256$, $p = 0.05$, $C_N = R_N = 1.0$, and $C_l = R_l = 0.1$. We, then, evaluate the system for $Y = 1000$ and $Y = 50$, signifying a long-running task and a short-running task respectively. Then considering various values of k and μ, we observed that for $Y = 1000$, the two-level scheme performs better than one level scheme. For $Y = 50$, the degenerate two-level scheme, i.e. when $\mu = k$, performs better than the one-level recovery scheme. Thus, our experimental analysis conforms the conclusion obtained by Vaidya [8] for the same two-level recovery scheme taking **average performance overhead** as the performance metric.

5   Conclusions

In this paper we have analyzed a two level recovery scheme due to Vaidya [8] taking probability of task completion on a system with limited repairs as the performance metric. An expression is derived for the performance metric in terms of other system parameters. As shown in [8], it is difficult to find the optimal values of k and μ analytically. We have numerically evaluated our performance expressions for certain values of the system parameters and observed that two-level recovery scheme is better than one lever recovery scheme for long running applications conforming the conclusion of Vaidya [8]. We are currently trying to obtain optimal value of k analytically and through extensive experimentation.

References

1. K.M. Chandy,J.C. Browne, C.W. Dissly, and W.R. Uhrig, Analytic Models for Rollback and Recovery Strategies in Data Base Systems, IEEE Trans. Software Eng, 1 (1975)100–110.
2. S. Garg and K.F. Wong, Analysis of an improved Distributed Checkpointing Algorithm, Technical Report WUCS-93-37, Dept. of Computer Science, Washington Univ., June 1993.
3. E. Gelenbe, A Model for Roll-Back Recovery with Multiple Checkpoints, Proc. Second Int'l Conf. Software Eng., (1976)251–255.
4. E. Gelenbe, Model of Information Recovery Using the Method of Multiple Checkpointing, Automation and Control, 4 (1976)251–255.
5. V.F. Nicola, Checkpointing and the Modeling of Program Execution time, Software fault Tolerance, in: M.R. Lyu Ed. John Wiley & Sons, (1995)167–188.
6. V.F. Nicola and J.M. van Spanje,Comparative Analysis of Different Models of Checkpointing and Recovery, IEEE Trans. Software Eng. 16 (1990)807–821.
7. A.N. Tantawi and m. Ruschitzka, Performance Analysis of Checkpointing Strategies, ACM Trans. Computer Systems, 2 (1984) 123–144.
8. N.H. Vaidya, A case for Two-level Recovery Schemes, IEEE Trans. Computers, 47 (6) (1998) 656–666.
9. J.W. Young, A first Order Approximation to the Optimum Checkpoint Interval, Comm. ACM 17(1974) 530–531.

4-Systolic Broadcasting in a Wrapped Butterfly Network

Ganesh Narayanaswamy[1], Anil M. Shende[2], and Praveen Vipranarayanan[1]

[1] Birla Institute of Technology & Science, Pilani 333031, India
{f1998436,f1998386}@bits-pilani.ac.in
[2] Roanoke College, Salem, VA 24153, USA
shende@roanoke.edu

Abstract. In this paper we present a 4-systolic algorithm for broadcasting, in the one-port model, in an undirected d-dimensional (d even) wrapped butterfly. We prove that the broadcast time for the algorithm is no more than $\frac{5d}{2} - 2$, hence making it the fastest known algorithm of this nature for broadcasting in a wrapped butterfly.

1 Introduction

An important feature characterising the "quality" (suitability) of an interconnection network for parallel computing is the ability to effectively disseminate the information among its processors. This paper deals with the *broadcast problem*, i.e., the problem of broadcasting information from any given node to all the other nodes, in one such interconnection network, namely the wrapped butterfly network, using the single port, half duplex communication model. (See [4, 6] for a comprehensive discussion and literature survey of broadcasting and related notions in various networks.) In the single-port model of communication a node can communicate with only one adjacent node (neighbour) at any given time and a communication takes one unit time or round. In the half duplex model, information can flow in only one direction at a time. We first present, in Section 2, a brief literature survey on the work that has been done on broadcasting, gossiping and systolic protocols on interconnection networks such as butterfly networks, de Bruijn networks etc. In Section 3 we formally define the structure of an undirected wrapped butterfly. Then, in Section 4 we motivate and present a 4-systolic algorithm[1] for broadcasting, using the single-port model of communication, in an undirected wrapped butterfly, and in Section 5, derive the broadcast time of this algorithm.

---

[1] This algorithm was first proposed by Dr. André Raspaud at Université Bordeaux 1, France, conveyed to Dr. Joseph G. Peters at Simon Fraser University, Canada, and subsequently conveyed to us by Dr. Sunil Shende at Rutgers University at Camden, New Jersey, USA.

S.K. Das and S. Bhattacharya (Eds.): IWDC 2002, LNCS 2571, pp. 98–107, 2002.

2   Brief Literature Survey

Broadcasting and gossiping are extensively investigated information dissemination processes. In broadcasting, one node has a message that needs to be sent to all the other nodes in the network. In gossiping, all the nodes have some piece of information which every other node in the network needs to get. The quality of an interconnection network depends on the ability of the network to effectively support these information dissemination processes.

The notion of a systolic communication strategy is similar to the notion of *systolic computations*, i.e., with cheap realization due to a very regular, synchronized periodic behaviour of all processes of the interconnection network during a computation, introduced by Kung [7]. Liestman and Richards [1] studied systolic communication algorithms for broadcasting and gossiping. Their strategies were based on edge colourings of the graph underlying the network and then the periodic (cyclic) execution of communication rounds, each activating the links corresponding to the same colour. [5] presented the more general concept of s-systolic communication algorithms consisting of a repetition of a given sequence of s communication rounds. While broadcasting strategies can be systolized at no cost [5], this in general is not true for gossiping. In this paper we analyze a 4-systolic broadcast protocol on an undirected d-dimensional wrapped butterfly network.

For butterfly and de Bruijn networks, [9] presents lower bounds on broadcasting time obtained by using the structure of these networks; these bounds are improved in [10]. For example, in [10], it has been proved that for a d-dimensional undirected wrapped butterfly, with rows labelled as binary numbers, broadcasting time is at least $1.7621d$. In this paper, we show, constructively, that in a d-dimensional wrapped butterfly network, d even, broadcast time $\leq 5d/2 - 2$.

[2] introduces a technique using the notion of a delay digraph of a dissemination protocol and matrix norm methods to establish lower bounds on systolic gossip protocols. These results imply that the lower bound on the gossiping time of s-systolic protocols decreases as s-increases. Intitively, though, it seems that the lower bound on the broadcasting time of s-systolic protocols increases as s increases; a proof or disproof of this intuition is an open problem. Extending the technique in [2], [3] derives a general lower bound on the broadcasting and gossiping time of *restricted protocols*. A protocol is (i, o) restricted at a given node if every outgoing activation of an arc depends on at most i previous incoming activations, and any incoming activation influences at most o successive outgoing activations. Note that broadcast protocols running on d-bounded degree networks are $(1, d)$ restricted, and s-systolic gossip protocols are (i, o) restricted with $i + o = s$.

The 4-systolic algorithm (see Section 4) that we analyse in this paper has been studied in [8]. They prove that using this algorithm from any node in a d-dimensional (d even) undirected wrapped butterfly, by time unit $2d$ at least one node on each row of the wrapped butterfly receives the broadcast message. We refine the technique used in [8] to prove the exact broadcast time for this algorithm.

3   An Undirected, *d*-Dimensional Wrapped Butterfly

We first formally define an undirected, *d*-dimensional (wrapped) butterfly of degree 2. In the rest of this paper by a *d*-dimensional (wrapped) butterfly we will mean an undirected *d*-dimensional (wrapped) butterfly of degree 2.

Definition 1 *An d-dimensional wrapped butterfly, denoted $WB(d)$, has $d \cdot 2^d$ nodes. Each node is labelled by a unique pair (r, i), where i, the level of the node, is a number such that $0 \leq i < d$, and r, the row of the node, is a d-bit binary number.[2] We will call the rightmost bit of r as the 0th bit, and the leftmost bit as the $(d-1)$th bit. For a row r, r_i denotes the ith bit of r. Two nodes (r, i) and (r', i') are connected by an edge if and only if $i' = (i+1) \mod d$ and either $r = r'$ or r and r' differ in the ith bit. Such edges are called as level i edges. Figure 1 shows a 3-dimensional wrapped butterfly.*

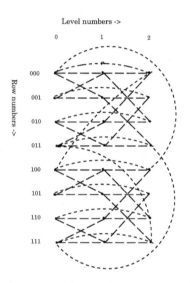

Fig. 1. A 3-dimensional wrapped butterfly

An edge connecting nodes (r, i) and (r', i') is called a straight edge *if $r = r'$; it is called a* forward straight edge *with respect to (r, i) and a* backward straight edge *with respect to (r', i'). The edge connecting nodes (r, i) and (r', i') is called a cross edge *if r and r' are unequal; it is called a* forward cross edge *with respect to node (r, i) and a* backward cross edge *with respect to the node (r', i').*

Definition 2 *The broadcast time, denoted $b(d)$, for $WB(d)$, is the time required to broadcast a message to all the nodes in $WB(d)$ from any node in $WB(d)$.*

---

[2] In a *d*-dimensional wrapped butterfly of *degree* δ, each row is a sequence of *d* symbols, each symbol a member of the set $\{0, \ldots, \delta - 1\}$. For our purposes, we are concerned only with a *d*-dimensional wrapped butterfly of degree 2.

4   The Algorithm and Notation

We now describe an algorithm for completing broadcast in $WB(d)$, where d is even and $d \geq 4$. Henceforth, we will consider only even dimensional wrapped butterflies.

We will order the edges out of a node (r, i) as follows:

1. If i is even, we order the edges as: backward cross, forward straight, backward straight, forward cross. We will use the notation e-BC, e-FS, e-BS and e-FC to denote these edges.
2. If i is odd, we order the edges as: forward cross, backward straight, forward straight, backward cross. We will use the notation o-FC, o-BS, o-FS and o-BC to denote these edges.

The edges are assigned the numbers $0 \ldots 3$ in the ordering above. Without loss of generality, node $(0 \ldots 0, 0)$ is assumed to have the message to be broadcast to all other nodes. We will always refer to the global time in our description of the algorithm below. The node $(0 \ldots 0, 0)$ sends its first message during time unit 1. A node is said to be *active* at the end of the time unit during which it receives the broadcast message for the first time. Suppose a node becomes active at the end of time unit t, it forwards the broadcast message to its neighbours during time units $t + 1$, $t + 2$, $t + 3$ and $t + 4$. Node $(0 \ldots 0, 0)$ is said to be active at the beginning of time unit 1.

The broadcast algorithm is described as:

> During time unit τ, every active node sends a message to its neighbour along the edge numbered $(\tau - 1)$ mod 4. Once an active node has sent four messages, it becomes inactive.

It is easily verified that the above algorithm does obey the single port, half duplex model of communication. It can also be easily seen that the algorithm can be modified to work in the full duplex model of communication.

The following is an immediate consequence of the algorithm above.

Fact 1 *During each time unit τ only two kinds of edges can be active. These sets of edges are given by*

1. $\{e\text{-}BC, o\text{-}FC\} \iff \tau - 1 \bmod 4 = 0$,
2. $\{e\text{-}FS, o\text{-}BS\} \iff \tau - 1 \bmod 4 = 1$,
3. $\{e\text{-}BS, o\text{-}FS\} \iff \tau - 1 \bmod 4 = 2$, and
4. $\{e\text{-}FC, o\text{-}BC\} \iff \tau - 1 \bmod 4 = 3$.

$\square$

Definition 3

1. *For a node $n = (r, i)$ in $WB(d)$, $T(n)$ is the least time t according to the above algorithm so that n is active at the end of time unit t.*

2. For a node $n = (r = (b_{d-1} \ldots b_0), i)$ in $WB(d)$, $n' = (r', i')$ where $r' = (1 - b_{d-1} b_0 b_1 \ldots b_{d-2})$ and $i' = (d - 1 - i)$.
3. For an edge e, $t(e)$ denotes the unique (mod d) time unit when e is active.
4. Given a node $n = (r, i)$ in $WB(d)$, we say that n induces the edge
   a) e-FC if i is even and $r_i = 1$,
   b) e-FS if i is even and $r_i = 0$,
   c) o-FC if i is odd and $r_i = 1$,
   d) o-FS if i is odd and $r_i = 0$,
   e) e-BC if i is even and $r_{i'} = 1$, where $i' = (i - 1) \mod d$,
   f) e-BS if i is even and $r_{i'} = 0$, where $i' = (i - 1) \mod d$,
   g) o-BC if i is odd and $r_{i'} = 1$, where $i' = (i - 1) \mod d$,
   h) o-BS if i is odd and $r_{i'} = 0$, where $i' = (i - 1) \mod d$.
   $\alpha(n)$ will denote the (unique) forward edge induced by n, and $\beta(n)$ will denote the (unique) backward edge induced by n.
5. Given a row r in $WB(d)$, for all $i, j, d - 1 \geq i \geq j \geq 0$, $\mathcal{F}(r, i, j)$, is the sequence of (forward) edges induced by the sequence of nodes (r, j), $(r, (j + 1))$, $\ldots (r, i)$. Thus, such a sequence has $(i - j + 1)$ edges. Note that the node at the end of the sequence of edges is at level $(i + 1) \mod d$.
6. Given a row r in $WB(d)$, for all $i, j, d - 1 \geq i \geq j \geq 0$, $\mathcal{B}(r, i, j)$, is the sequence of (backward) edges induced by the sequence of nodes (r, i), $(r, (i - 1))$, $\ldots (r, j)$. Thus, such a sequence has $(i - j)$ edges. Note that the node at the end of the sequence of edges is at level j.
7. Given a row r in $WB(d)$, for all i,
   a) r_i is a forward 2-skip if $t(\alpha(r, (i + 1) \mod d)) - t(\alpha(r, i)) \mod 4 = 3$,
   b) r_i is a forward 0-skip if $t(\alpha(r, (i + 1) \mod d)) - t(\alpha(r, i)) \mod 4 = 1$.
   c) r_i is a backward 2-skip if $t(\beta(r, (i + 1) \mod d)) - t(\beta(r, i)) \mod 4 = 3$.
   d) r_i is a backward 0-skip if $t(\beta(r, (i + 1) \mod d)) - t(\beta(r, i)) \mod 4 = 1$.
8. Given a row r in $WB(d)$, for all i, j, $(d - 1) < i < j \leq 0$, $f(r, i, j)$ is given by $f(r, i, j) = |\{x | j \leq x < i \text{ and } r_x \text{ is a forward 2-skip}\}|$. For notational convenience, we will write $f(r)$ for $f(r, (d - 1), 0)$.
9. For all $d \geq 0$, $\mathcal{S}_d\langle p, q \rangle$ is given by

$$\mathcal{S}_d\langle p, q \rangle = \{x | \exists r = (b_{d-1}, \ldots b_0), b_{d-1} = p, b_0 = q, \text{ and } f(r) = x\}.$$

5   Broadcast Time

Recall the definition of n' (see Definition 3.2).

Lemma 1. For all even $d \geq 4$, for all n in $WB(d)$, $T(n) = T(n')$.

Proof. Let $S = s_0, s_1, \ldots, s_k$ be the sequence of edges that witnesses that the time required for the broadcast message to reach n is $T(n)$. For an edge e, define e' to be the complementary edge, i.e., the other edge that can be active at the same time unit as the edge e (see Fact 1). Consider the sequence S' defined as follows: if S starts with the edge e-BC, then consider the sequence $S' = s'_1, s'_2, \ldots, s'_k$; if S does not start with the edge e-BC, then consider the sequence $S' = \text{e-BC}, s'_0, \ldots, s'_k$. It can be easily verified that the sequence of edges S' delivers the broadcast message to the node n' by the end of time unit $T(n)$.   □

Lemma 2. *For all $d \geq 4$, where $d = 2k$, and for $i, j \in \{0, 1\}$, each element of $\mathcal{S}_d\langle i, j \rangle$ is different in parity (even or odd) from k iff $i = j$.*

Proof. We prove this by induction on d. It can be easily seen that $\mathcal{S}_2\langle 0, 0 \rangle = \{0\}$, $\mathcal{S}_2\langle 0, 1 \rangle = \{1\}$, $\mathcal{S}_2\langle 1, 0 \rangle = \{1\}$, and $\mathcal{S}_2\langle 1, 1 \rangle = \{0\}$. Thus, the statement of the lemma is true for $d = 2 \cdot 1 = 2$.

Inductive Hypothesis Suppose the statement of the lemma is true for $d = 2 \cdot k$.

We will now show that the statement of the lemma is true for $d + 2 = 2 \cdot (k+1)$.

For a set $X \subseteq N$, and a number δ, we will use the notation $\delta + X$ to mean the set $\{x + \delta | x \in X\}$.

A bit pattern $(b_{d+1}, \ldots, b_0)$ of $d + 2$ bits with p and q as the end bits is one of the sets of bit patterns $(p, 0, \ldots, 0, q)$, $(p, 0, \ldots, 1, q)$, $(p, 1, \ldots, 0, q)$, and $(p, 1, \ldots, 1, q)$. Consider any one of the bit patterns of $d + 2$ bits in the set $r = (0, 0, \ldots, 0, 0)$. r_0 and r_d are both forward 0-skips. Thus any forward 2-skip in r comes from the bits $(b_d, \ldots, b_1)$. Let $r' = (b_d = b'_{d-1}, \ldots, b_1 = b'_0)$. Clearly, then, if r'_i is a forward 0-skip, then r_{i+1} is a forward 2-skip, and if r'_i is a forward 2-skip, then r_{i+1} is a forward 0-skip. Since there are $(d - 1)$ forward skips in all in r', we have,

$$\mathcal{S}_{d+2}\langle 0, 0 \rangle = d - 1 - \mathcal{S}_d\langle 0, 0 \rangle \cup 1 + d - 1 - \mathcal{S}_d\langle 0, 1 \rangle \cup$$
$$1 + d - 1 - \mathcal{S}_d\langle 1, 0 \rangle \cup 2 + d - 1 - \mathcal{S}_d\langle 1, 1 \rangle. \tag{1}$$

Without loss of generality, let k be even. Then, by the induction hypothesis, $\mathcal{S}_d\langle 0, 0 \rangle$ and $\mathcal{S}_d\langle 1, 1 \rangle$ contain odd numbers, and $\mathcal{S}_d\langle 0, 1 \rangle$ and $\mathcal{S}_d\langle 1, 0 \rangle$ contain even numbers. Thus, from Equation 1, it is easily seen that $\mathcal{S}_{d+2}\langle 0, 0 \rangle$ contains only even numbers. The other parts of the lemma can be shown similarly.   □

Lemma 3. *For all rows r in $WB(d)$, for all $i \in \{0, 1, (d-1), (d-2)\}$, $T(n = (r, i)) \leq 2d$.*

Proof. In light of Lemma 1, it is sufficient to show that for all rows r in $WB(d)$, for all $i \in \{0, 1\}$, $T(n = (r, i)) \leq 2d$. Let $r = (b_{d-1}, \ldots, b_1, b_0)$. We first show $T(n = (r, 0)) \leq 2d$ by considering the following exhaustive cases.

Case (1) $b_{d-1} = 0, b_0 = 0$ Consider the following two sequences of edges:

$$s_1 = \text{e-FS}, \mathcal{F}(r, (d-1), 1), \text{ and } s_2 = \text{e-BS}, \mathcal{B}(r, (d-1), 0)$$

Each of the sequence of edges ends in the node $(r, 0)$. By Fact 1, the first time unit during which the edge e-FS is active is 2, and the first time unit during which the edge e-BS is active is 3. Let $f(r) = x$. (See Definition 3.8 for the definition of $f(\cdot)$.) From the definitions of forward and backward 2-skips (see Definition 3.7) it is immediate that r_i is a forward 2-skip iff r_{i+1} is a backward 0-skip. Thus, the total time to complete each of the above two sequences is:

$$t_1 = 2 + 3x + (d - 1 - x), \text{ and } t_2 = 3 + 3(d - 1 - x) + x.$$

It is now easy to verify that

$$x \le \frac{d-2}{2} \implies t_1 \le 2d, \text{ and } x \ge \frac{d}{2} \implies t_2 \le 2d.$$

Note that since d is an even number, and since x is an integer, it is not necessary to consider the quantities $(d-y)/2$ where y is an odd number. In particular, above, it is not necessary to consider the quantity $(d-1)/2$ as a possible value for x, and hence the above two inequalities for x are exhaustive. Thus, we have that $T(n = (r,0)) \le 2d$.

Case (2) $b_{d-1} = 1, b_0 = 0$ Let $f(r) = x$. Consider the following two sequences of edges, ending in the node $(r,0)$, and their respective time for completion:

$$s_1 = \text{e-FS}, \mathcal{F}(r, (d-1), 1), \text{ and } s_2 = \text{e-BC}, \mathcal{B}(r, (d-1), 0)$$

Then, $t_1 = 2 + 3x + (d-1-x)$, and $t_2 = 1 + 3(d-1-x) + x$. Thus, $x \le \frac{d-2}{2} \implies t_1 \le 2d$, and $x \ge \frac{d}{2} \implies t_2 \le 2d - 2$, and we have that $T(n = (r,0)) \le 2d$.

Case (3) $b_{d-1} = 0, b_0 = 1$ Let $f(r) = x$. Consider the following two sequences of edges, ending in the node $(r,0)$, and their respective time for completion:

$$s_1 = \text{e-FC}, \mathcal{F}(r, (d-1), 1), \text{ and } s_2 = \text{e-BS}, \mathcal{B}(r, (d-1), 0).$$

Then, $t_1 = 4 + 3x + (d-1-x)$, and $t_2 = 3 + 3(d-1-x) + x$. Thus, $x \le \frac{d-4}{2} \implies t_1 \le 2d - 1$, and $x \ge \frac{d}{2} \implies t_2 \le 2d$. By Lemma 2 $f(r) \ne \frac{d-2}{2}$, and hence the above two inequalities for x are exhaustive. Hence, we have that $T(n = (r,0)) \le 2d$.

Case (4) $b_{d-1} = 1, b_0 = 1$ Let $f(r) = x$. Consider the following two sequences of edges, ending in the node $(r,0)$, and their respective time for completion:

$$s_1 = \text{e-FC}, \mathcal{F}(r, (d-1), 1), \text{ and } s_2 = \text{e-BC}, \mathcal{B}(r, (d-1), 0).$$

Then, $t_1 = 4 + 3x + (d-1-x)$, and $t_2 = 1 + 3(d-1-x) + x$. Thus, $x \le \frac{d-4}{2} \implies t_1 \le 2d - 1$, and $x \ge \frac{d-2}{2} \implies t_2 \le 2d$, and we have that $T(n = (r,0)) \le 2d$.

We now show that $T(n = (r,1)) \le 2d$.

Case (1) $b_{d-1} = 0, b_1 = 0, b_0 = 0$ Let $f(r, (d-1), 1) = x$. Consider the following two sequences of edges, ending in the node $(r,1)$, and their respective time for completion:

$$s_1 = \text{e-FS}, \text{o-FS}, \mathcal{F}(r, (d-1), 2), \text{e-FS and } s_2 = \text{e-BS}, \mathcal{B}(r, (d-1), 1).$$

Since $f(r, (d-1), 1) \le (d-2)$, $t_1 = 2 + 1 + 3x + (d-2-x) + 3$, and $t_2 = 3 + 3(d-2-x) + x$. Thus, $x \le \frac{d-4}{2} \implies t_1 \le 2d$, and $x \ge \frac{d-2}{2} \implies t_2 \le 2d - 1$, and we have that $T(n = (r,1)) \le 2d$.

Case (2) $b_{d-1} = 0, b_1 = 1, b_0 = 0$ Let $f(r, (d-1), 1) = x$. Consider the following two sequences of edges, ending in the node $(r, 1)$, and their respective time for completion:

$$s_1 = \text{e-FC}, \text{o-FC}, \mathcal{F}(r, (d-1), 2), \text{e-FC} \text{ and } s_2 = \text{e-BS}, \mathcal{B}(r, (d-1), 1).$$

Then, $t_1 = 4 + 1 + 3x + (d - 2 - x) + 1$, and $t_2 = 3 + 3(d - 2 - x) + x$. Thus, $x \le \frac{d-4}{2} \Longrightarrow t_1 \le 2d$, and $x \ge \frac{d-2}{2} \Longrightarrow t_2 \le 2d - 1$, and we have that $T(n = (r, 1)) \le 2d$.

Case (3) $b_{d-1} = 0, b_1 = 0, b_0 = 1$ Let $f(r, (d-1), 1) = x$. Consider the following two sequences of edges, ending in the node $(r, 1)$, and their respective time for completion:

$$s_1 = \text{e-FS}, \text{o-FS}, \mathcal{F}(r, (d-1), 2), \text{e-FC}, \text{ and}$$
$$s_2 = \text{e-BS}, \mathcal{B}(r, (d-1), 1), \text{o-BC}, \text{e-FS}.$$

Then, $t_1 = 2 + 1 + 3x + (d - 2 - x) + 1$, and $t_2 = 3 + 3(d - 2 - x) + x + 1 + 2$. Thus, $x \le \frac{d-2}{2} \Longrightarrow t_1 \le 2d$, and $x \ge \frac{d}{2} \Longrightarrow t_2 \le 2d$, and we have that $T(n = (r, 1)) \le 2d$.

Case (4) $b_{d-1} = 0, b_1 = 1, b_0 = 1$ Let $f(r, (d-1), 1) = x$. Consider the following two sequences of edges, ending in the node $(r, 1)$, and their respective time for completion:

$$s_1 = \text{e-FS}, \text{o-FC}, \mathcal{F}(r, (d-1), 2), \text{e-FC}, \text{ and}$$
$$s_2 = \text{e-BS}, \mathcal{B}(r, (d-1), 1), \text{o-BS}, \text{e-FC}.$$

Then, $t_1 = 2 + 3 + 3x + (d - 2 - x) + 1$, and $t_2 = 3 + 3(d - 2 - x) + x + 1 + 2$. Thus, $x \le \frac{d-4}{2} \Longrightarrow t_1 \le 2d$, and $x \ge \frac{d}{2} \Longrightarrow t_2 \le 2d$. By Lemma 2 $f(r) \ne \frac{d-2}{2}$, and hence the above two inequalities for x are exhaustive. Thus, we have that $T(n = (r, 1)) \le 2d$.

Case (5) $b_{d-1} = 1, b_1 = 0, b_0 = 0$ Let $f(r, (d-1), 1) = x$. Consider the following two sequences of edges, ending in the node $(r, 1)$, and their respective time for completion:

$$s_1 = \text{e-FS}, \text{o-FS}, \mathcal{F}(r, (d-1), 2), \text{e-FS}, \text{ and } s_2 = \text{e-BC}, \mathcal{B}(r, (d-1), 1).$$

Then, $t_1 = 2 + 1 + 3x + (d - 2 - x) + 1$, and $t_2 = 1 + 3(d - 2 - x) + x$. Thus, $x \le \frac{d-2}{2} \Longrightarrow t_1 \le 2d$, and $x \ge \frac{d}{2} \Longrightarrow t_2 \le 2d - 5$, and we have that $T(n = (r, 1)) \le 2d$.

Case (6) $b_{d-1} = 1, b_1 = 1, b_0 = 0$ Let $f(r, (d-1), 1) = x$. Consider the following two sequences of edges, ending in the node $(r, 1)$, and their respective time for completion:

$$s_1 = \text{e-FS}, \text{o-FC}, \mathcal{F}(r, (d-1), 2), \text{e-FS}, \text{ and } s_2 = \text{e-BC}, \mathcal{B}(r, (d-1), 1).$$

Then, $t_1 = 2 + 3 + 3x + (d - 2 - x) + 1$, and $t_2 = 1 + 3(d - 2 - x) + x$. Thus, $x \le \frac{d-4}{2} \Longrightarrow t_1 \le 2d$, and $x \ge \frac{d-2}{2} \Longrightarrow t_2 \le 2d - 3$, and we have that $T(n = (r, 1)) \le 2d$.

Case (7) $b_{d-1} = 1, b_1 = 0, b_0 = 1$ Let $f(r, (d-1), 1) = x$. Consider the following two sequences of edges, ending in the node $(r, 1)$, and their respective time for completion:

$$s_1 = \text{e-FS}, \text{o-FS}, \mathcal{F}(r, (d-1), 2), \text{e-FC}, \text{ and}$$
$$s_2 = \text{e-BC}, \mathcal{B}(r, (d-1), 1), \text{o-BC}, \text{e-FS}.$$

Then, $t_1 = 2 + 1 + 3x + (d - 2 - x) + 3$, and $t_2 = 1 + 3(d - 2 - x) + x + 1 + 2$. Thus, $x \leq \frac{d-4}{2} \implies t_1 \leq 2d$, and $x \geq \frac{d-2}{2} \implies t_2 \leq 2d$, and we have that $T(n = (r, 1)) \leq 2d$.

Case (8) $b_{d-1} = 1, b_1 = 1, b_0 = 1$ Let $f(r, (d-1), 1) = x$. Consider the following two sequences of edges, ending in the node $(r, 1)$, and their respective time for completion:

$$s_1 = \text{e-FC}, \text{o-FC}, \mathcal{F}(r, (d-1), 2), \text{e-FS}, \text{ and}$$
$$s_2 = \text{e-BC}, \mathcal{B}(r, (d-1), 1), \text{o-BS}, \text{e-FC}.$$

Then, $t_1 = 4 + 1 + 3x + (d - 2 - x) + 1$, and $t_2 = 1 + 3(d - 2 - x) + x + 1 + 2$. Thus, $x \leq \frac{d-4}{2} \implies t_1 \leq 2d$, and $x \geq \frac{d-2}{2} \implies t_2 \leq 2d$, and we have that $T(n = (r, 1)) \leq 2d$.

Thus we have that for all rows r in $WB(d)$, for all $i \in \{0, 1\}$, $T(n = (r, i)) \leq 2d$.

Then using Lemma 1, we have that for all rows r in $WB(d)$, for all $i \in \{0, 1, (d-1), (d-2)\}$, $T(n = (r, i)) \leq 2d$.   □

Lemma 4. *If for all rows r in $WB(d)$, for all $i \in \{0, 1, (d-1), (d-2)\}$, $T(n = (r, i)) \leq 2d$, then, for all rows r in $WB(d)$, for all i, $0 \leq i < d$, $T(n = (r, i)) \leq \frac{5d}{2} - 2$.*

Proof. By Lemma 1, it suffices to show that for each row r in $WB(d)$, for each i, $2 \leq i < \frac{d}{2}$, $T(n = (r, i)) \leq \frac{5d}{2} - 2$. Note that for each row r in $WB(d)$, for each i, $2 \leq i < \frac{d}{2}$, the node $n = (r, i)$ is no more than $\frac{d}{2} - 2$ edges away from some node, n_1, at level 1, and can be reached by a sequence of forward edges from n_1.

Consider the node $n = (r, L)$ where $r = (b_{d-1}, b_{d-2}, \ldots, b_1, b_0)$, and $d/2 - 1 \geq L > 1$. Consider the sequence of edges o-FC, e-FS, o-FS, e-FC repeating. Consider the sub-sequence S consisting of the first $L - 1$ edges in the above sequence, i.e. $S(0) = \text{o-FC}, S(1) = \text{e-FS} \ldots$. From Fact 1, S starts at time unit τ such that $\tau - 1 \mod 4 = 0$, and has an edge at every subsequent time unit. In particular then, since d is even, S can start at time unit $2d + 1$ and will finish by the end of time unit $2d + L - 1$. For an edge e, define e' to be the complementary edge, i.e., the other edge that can be active at the same time unit as the edge e (see Fact 1). Now consider the sequence of edges S_r of length $L - 1$ such that for all $i, 0 \leq i < (L-1)$, $S_r(i) = S(L - 2 - i)'$. Let $n^1 = (r^1, L^1)$ be the unique node reached by following the edges in S_r. Since all of the edges in S_r are backward edges, $L^1 = 1$. By the hypothesis of the lemma, n^1 is active by time unit $2d$. Suppose n^1 becomes active at the end of time unit τ such that

$2(d-1)+1 \leq \tau \leq 2d$. Then n^1 is active at time unit $(2d+1)$. (If $\tau \leq 2(d-1)$, then n^1 is active at the time unit $2(d-1)+1$, or $2(d-2)+1$, etc., and does not affect the rest of the analysis.) Then S gets the broadcast message from the node n^1 to the node n. Since consecutive edges in this sequence are active at consecutive time units, $T(n) \leq 2d + L - 1$. Moreover, since $L \leq \frac{d}{2} - 1$, $T(n) \leq \frac{5d}{2} - 2$. $\square$

Lemmas 3 and 4 together give us the following theorem.

Theorem 1. *For all even $d \geq 4$, the time to complete a 4-systolic broadcast in $WB(d)$ is no more than $\frac{5d}{2} - 2$.* $\square$

6   Conclusions and Open Problems

In this paper we have presented a 4-systolic algorithm for broadcasting, in the one-port model, in an undirected d-dimensional (d even) wrapped butterfly. We prove that the broadcast time for the algorithm is no more than $\frac{5d}{2} - 2$. This broadcast time is still over the published lower bound of $1.7621d$. It remains to be shown whether this lower bound can be reached. Based on empirical study of 4-systolic protocols, we believe that the algorithm presented in this paper gives the best broadcast time amongst all 4-systolic protocols. A proof or disproof of this belief may yield more insight into s-systolic protocols for $s > 4$, and perhaps lead to a faster broadcast algorithm.

References

1. A.L. Liestman and D. Richards. Network communication in edge-colored graphs: gossiping. In *IEEE Trans. Par. Distr. Syst.*, pages 4:438–445. 1993.
2. Flammini and Perennes. Lower bounds on systolic gossip. In *IPPS: 11th International Parallel Processing Symposium*. IEEE Computer Society Press, 1997.
3. Michele Flammini and Stephane Perennes. Lower bounds on the broadcasting and gossiping time of restricted protocols. Technical Report RR-3612.
4. Satoshi Fujita, Stephane Perennes, and Joseph G. Peters. Neighbourhood gossiping in hypercubes. Technical report, Simon Fraser University, 1997.
5. J. Hromkovic, R. Klasing, D. Pardubska, W. Unger, and H. Wagener. The complexity of systolic dissemination of information in interconnection networks. In *R.A.I.R.O. Theoretical Informatics and Applications*, pages 28(3–4):303–342. 1994.
6. Juran Hromkovic, Ralf Klasing, Burkhand Monien, and Regine Peine. Dissemination of information in interconnection networks (broadcasting and gossiping). in Combinatorial Network Theory.
7. H.T.Kung. Let's design algorithms for VLSI systems. In *Proc. of the Caltech Conference of VLSI (CL.L. Seifz Ed.)*, pages 65–90, Pasadena, California, 1979.
8. Snehal Joshi and Praveen Vipranarayanan. Broadcasting in a wrapped butterfly network. In *TechFiesta: PSG College of Technology, Coimbatore*, 2001. see citeseer.nj.nec.com/joshi01broadcasting.html.
9. R. Klasing, B. Monien, R. Peine, and E. Stohr. Broadcasting in butterfly and deBruijn networks. In *Discrete Applied Mathematics*, pages 53(1–3):183–197. 1994.
10. S. Perennes. Lower bounds on broadcasting time of deBruijn networks. In *2nd Int. Euro-Par Conference, volume 1123 of Lecture notes in computer Science*, pages 325–332. Springer-Verlag, 1996.

Understanding Wireless Mobile Systems: A Simplified Simulation Approach*

Satish K. Tripathi, J. Jobin, and Michalis Faloutsos

Department of Computer Science and Engineering
University of California, Riverside, CA 92521, USA
{tripathi,jobin,michalis}@cs.ucr.edu

Abstract. Simulation is a widely used technique in understanding and analyzing the properties and behavior of wireless networks. Simulation models abound in the wireless domain. Most of these models suffer from an abundance of parameters. Different models might use different parameters. Moreover, even for common parameters, there are no universally accepted standard values. This makes the task of analyzing simulation results a complicated one.

We propose a framework to address this problem. One component of our framework is based on the reduction of the vast parameter space to a smaller, more compact one that encompasses only a few essential parameters. These parameters try to aggregate other parameters and hide the specifics of the underlying system, thereby easing the task of evaluating simulation results.

The other component is based on a novel concept called steady state utilization which tries to capture the inherent capacity of a network. Using steady state utilization as the maximum potential capacity (without loss) of a network, we show how it can be used in the task of comparing results from different simulation models.

1 Introduction

We propose a methodology that simplifies the task of analyzing results of wireless mobile system simulations. Most simulation models have a large set of parameters and there are no standard values for these parameters. Thus, results from different simulation models can be difficult to compare and interpret. We need a framework that makes the comparison easier. Ideally, we would like as few parameters and metrics in the model as possible.

Consider an example to understand the problem. Assume that we want to compare the performance of two networks A and B. Network A has an arrival rate of 30 users per second, 80% utilization, and 5% loss. Network B has an arrival rate of 40 users per second, 70% utilization, and 2% loss. Clearly, one cannot say much about which system performs better. We cannot compare the offered load in the two systems without knowing their relative sizes. Even if we

---

* This research is partially supported by funds from the Johnson Family Chair.

S.K. Das and S. Bhattacharya (Eds.): IWDC 2002, LNCS 2571, pp. 108–117, 2002.

assume a comparable setup, we still cannot determine whether higher utilization is better than lower loss. Our approach attempts to resolve these problems.

We propose the reduction of the large number of parameters and metrics to a few that capture the essence of the network. Central to our methodology is the novel concept of *steady state utilization* which tries to capture the inherent capacity of the network. We also suggest using *effective utilization* to combine utilization and loss.

The rest of the paper is as follows: In Section 2, we discuss the background. In Section 3, we discuss the main ideas of our paper. We present our simulations and the results in Section 4. In Section 4.3, we demonstrate the use of our methodology through a case study and conclude in Section 5. This paper is based on the material in references [5] and [6].

2   Background and Model

We adopt the commonly used network model [12,1] for cellular wireless networks wherein a geographic region is covered by hexagonal cells with six neighbors each. Each cell has a base station which manages bandwidth amongst the users. A user enters a system if there is bandwidth available, otherwise it is *blocked*. Having entered the system, it spends some time in each cell; this time duration is called the *cell latency*. The user moves from one cell to another (neighboring) cell until either it voluntarily ends its session or is *dropped*.

Most wireless network simulation models have a large number of parameters and realistic values for them are not always obvious. Furthermore, the sensitivity of the results to these parameters is not well established. These issues make it difficult to compare results from different models. While this is a problem with simulations in general, it gets worse in wireless networks.

Research has been done in the direction of simplifying the general simulation environment. Most research that aims for a simple or standardized model attempts to hide as many low level details as possible. The idea of simulation abstraction has been considered in [8], where they try to abstract unnecessary details. Fall [7] suggests decreasing the number of objects in a simulation by aggregating some of them and by coarsening the resolution of some parts of the model. The standard framework as suggested by Bajaj, et al [2] also aims to facilitate easy comparison across models by assuming that everyone is going to use the same framework. We believe that this is not always easy to enforce. Therefore, having parameters that hide system-specific details is important.

Performance metrics can also be improved: consider network utilization as an example. Previous work considers utilization and loss separately [11,10,9]. This can be a problem when comparing two networks as we saw in the example of networks A and B in the introduction section.

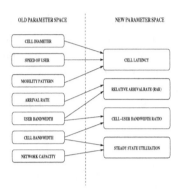

Fig. 1. Reduction of parameter space

3   Description of Our Framework

3.1   System Parameters

First, we describe the system parameters.

Steady State Utilization: *Steady state utilization* gives us an insight into the maximum load a system can support without loss. We start with a fully loaded system (maximum number of users in each cell) and let the users move around in the system. Users are permanent; they do not leave unless they get dropped. In the beginning, as they move, some of them find themselves in cells that are too crowded and hence get dropped. Initially, the drop rate is significant but this slows downs gradually until we reach a point where it is practically zero. We call the utilization at this point the *steady state utilization* of the system.

Steady State Arrival Rate – SSAR: *Steady state arrival rate* is the arrival rate that keeps the system functioning at its steady state utilization. Steady state utilization assumes no arrivals and no departures. However, in a system with finite call durations, there is a corresponding arrival rate to keep the system functioning at the steady state utilization. We define this arrival rate as the (*SSAR*).

$$SSAR = Util_{ssu} * \frac{MaxUsers}{T} \tag{1}$$

$Util_{ssu}$ is the steady state utilization, $MaxUsers$ is the maximum number of users that the system can support, and T is the average call duration.

Relative Arrival Rate - RAR: The *relative arrival rate* is the ratio of the actual arrival rate(λ) over SSAR.

$$RAR = \frac{\lambda}{SSAR} \tag{2}$$

RAR is 1 when the arrival rate equals *SSAR*. It is useful when comparing systems: for example, two different systems with different traffic loads are being equivalently utilized if their RAR values are equal to 1.

Cell-User Bandwidth Ratio: The *cell-user bandwidth ratio* is the ratio of cell bandwidth over user bandwidth. This indicates how many users each cell can accommodate on an average.

3.2 Performance Metrics

We describe the metrics which we use in our framework. Some of them are novel, while some are not.

Observed Utilization: One common metric used for evaluating system performance is *observed utilization*[1]. It reflects the bandwidth used in the system or the number of users in the system. The *observed utilization* is the percentage of the network bandwidth that is actually used. Note that the observed utilization includes all currently active users, even those that might get dropped later.

Wasted Utilization: *Wasted utilization* is the percentage of the network bandwidth at any given instant that is occupied by users that will eventually be dropped. Note that the observed utilization includes the wasted bandwidth. Wasted utilization has a direct negative impact on the utilization of the system because then we have to consider what fraction of the utilized bandwidth is being effectively used.

Effective Utilization: *Effective utilization* tries to incorporate utilization and loss into one metric. A system may seem to be getting utilized at a certain level; in reality, depending upon the wasted bandwidth, the actual utilization (which accounts for the successfully used bandwidth only) is less than the observed utilization. We call this the *effective utilization*. We show how effective utilization instead of observed utilization can provide new insight into our performance analysis. Effective utilization is analogous to the *goodput* often found in literature [3].

3.3 Our Framework

We use our parameters to create an abstract model. Our model has two advantages. First, we have fewer parameters. Second, the parameters hide unnecessary details, and thus, are intuitive and easy to interpret. Figure 1 shows how old parameters map to our parameters. The left side shows some of the commonly used parameters while the right side shows our equivalent parameters. For instance, cell latency is determined by the diameter of the cell, the speed of the user, and

---

[1] Observed utilization is the same as the *utilization* commonly found in the literature.

the mobility pattern of the user. Our steady state utilization concept subsumes both the cell bandwidth and the network capacity. (It also abstracts details such as the the shape of the cell and the moving direction of a user.) The steady state utilization also gives us the steady state arrival rate which helps us define the relative arrival rate.

4   Experimental Results

We assume a cellular wireless network with homogeneous cells. The users have the same bandwidth requirement and unless stated otherwise, they also have the same mean value of cell latency. For changing the cell capacity (in terms of number of users), we change the ratio of the cell bandwidth to the user bandwidth. The simulation programs are written using the C version of CSIM.

4.1   Parameters That Affect Steady State Utilization

First, we conduct some experiments to study the effect of different parameters on the steady state utilization.

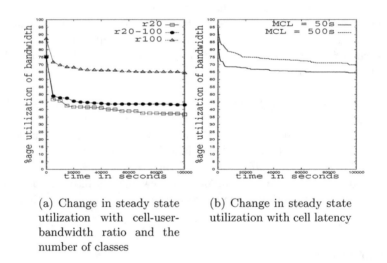

(a) Change in steady state utilization with cell-user-bandwidth ratio and the number of classes

(b) Change in steady state utilization with cell latency

Fig. 2. Steady state utilization

a) **Cell-user-bandwidth ratio:** In Figure 2(a), we plot utilization versus time for three different scenarios. The lowest plot (r20) corresponds to the case where we have a single class of users and the cell-user bandwidth ratio is 20 (i.e., each cell can hold a maximum of 20 users). The steady state utilization level is about 37%. The topmost plot (r100) is for the case where this ratio is

100. Now, the steady state utilization is about 65%. The steady state utilization is more when users have smaller bandwidth requirements. This is because if a higher bandwidth user is dropped, it will affect the effective utilization more. Thus, the experiments suggest that finer granularity of user bandwidth leads to higher steady state utilization.

b) Multiple classes of users: Next, we divide the users equally into two classes with cell-user bandwidth ratio of 100 and 20. The result is seen in the middle plot (r20-100) in Figure 2(a), where the steady state utilization is now about 43%. We see that the combination of two classes leads to a steady state utilization that is in between the steady state utilization of the two individual classes.

c) Cell latency: Here, we consider the effect of cell latency on the steady state utilization level. Figure 2(b) is for two different mean values of cell latency - 50 and 500 seconds. As seen, when the mean cell latency increases from 50 to 500 seconds, the steady state utilization increases from 64% to 70%. Intuitively, as the cell latency increases, the users move slower, there are fewer drops, and hence the steady state utilization increases.

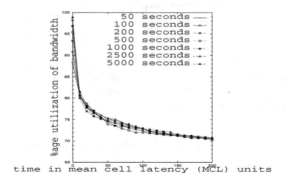

Fig. 3. Variation of utilization with cell latency: 48 hexagonal cells

However, it is interesting to see what happens when we plot time in terms of cell latency units. Figure 3 shows how utilization varies with time. Time is plotted on the x-axis in terms of the mean cell latency. The graph shows seven plots corresponding to different cell latency values. Here, cell latency does not seem to affect the value of steady state utilization for a network; the range of values for the utilization is less than 1%. Indeed, steady state utilization is achieved after a certain number of time units of cell latency. Thus, it is dependent on the number of hops a user makes on an average, as opposed to the actual cell latency. This also indicates an inherent nature of the network to support a particular number of users. An implication is that we can use the steady state utilization without being concerned about the cell latency.

We also studied the effect of cell latency in both hexagon and square cell networks with three different sizes. The range of values for utilization for all cases was less than 2% except in the case of a square cell network with 16 cells where it was less than 3%.

d) Network size: First, we consider a hexagon cell network. Figure 4(a) shows that there is negligible effect of network size on the steady state utilization. The utilization in the 18 cell network is only marginally better - about 0.5%. This implies that if all other factors are constant, there is no dependence on the size.

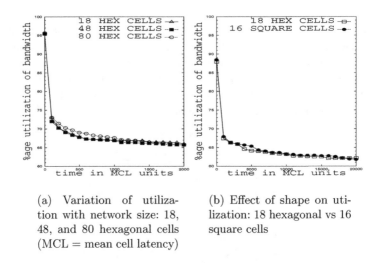

(a) Variation of utilization with network size: 18, 48, and 80 hexagonal cells (MCL = mean cell latency)

(b) Effect of shape on utilization: 18 hexagonal vs 16 square cells

Fig. 4. Effect of network size and cell shape on steady state utilization

Similar results were obtained for a square cell network. We experiment with three sizes (16,49, and 81); the utilization seems to be unaffected by size, except that the 16 cell network is only marginally better - about 0.5%. These results indicate that size is inconsequential except when it is too small. Intuitively, we believe this is because the remainder of the parameters are the same, the users are randomly distributed uniformly throughout the cells, and the cells themselves are all the same. In a smaller network, the correlation between cells is higher and hence, there is a larger margin of error. Indeed, the 18 and 16 cell networks seem to differ a bit from the others.

e) Shape of the cell: We experiment with two kinds of cells - hexagon and square. Hexagon cells are the most commonly found cells in literature ([1,12, 9]). We consider three different network sizes for both types of networks. As we saw earlier, the network size does not seem to affect the steady state utilization.

So, a hexagon cell network can be safely compared to a square cell network of equivalent size without being concerned about any side-effects.

As seen in Figure 4(b), a hexagon cell network of 18 cells has a similar utilization as a square cell network of 16 cells. This suggests that the shape of the individual cells in a network does not play an important role in the final results. We obtained similar results when we compared a 48 hexagon cell network to a 49 square cell network and an 80 hexagon cell network to an 81 square cell network.

4.2   The Significance of Steady State Arrival Rate

As we saw earlier, given the steady state utilization and call duration, we can calculate the steady state arrival rate. Then, we can describe any arrival rate with the relative arrival rate (RAR). For $RAR = 1$, the system is at its steady state utilization. We now examine the behavior for other values of RAR. We vary the RAR, thereby subjecting the system to different loads corresponding to different values of the arrival rates.

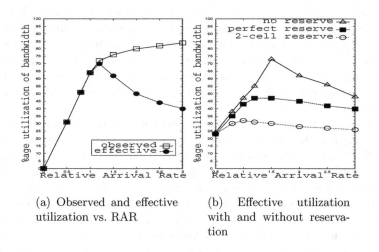

(a) Observed and effective utilization vs. RAR

(b)   Effective   utilization with and without reservation

Fig. 5.

Figure 5(a) shows the comparison between the observed utilization and the effective utilization when the arrival rate is varied. We see that if RAR is below 1, there is no wasted bandwidth but the system is underutilized: the effective utilization is below the steady state utilization.

We have no losses while $RAR \leq 1$ (i.e., $\lambda \leq SSAR$). For $RAR = 1$, we reach the steady state utilization. As RAR increases beyond 1, we start to see wasted bandwidth and a decrease in the effective utilization. Thus, we see that for $RAR = 1$, we have the maximum effective utilization without loss. Above the SSAR, effective utilization increases slightly and then starts to drop.

4.3 Discussion and Applications

Our methodology can be used in the following manner:
1) Given a network and a traffic load, find the steady state utilization[2]. 2) Find the corresponding steady state arrival rate. 3) Plot effective utilization and observed utilization for different values of the relative arrival rate and study the plot to see if the system is near its steady state utilization.

So, given a network and its load characteristics, one can say whether it is being underutilized or over-utilized. Moreover, one can also determine what the arrival rate should be in order to achieve steady state utilization. Thus, $SSAR$ provides us with a reference point using which we can understand how the network is being utilized.

We apply our methodology to a specific problem - to study the benefits of advance reservations in wireless networks. Reservations have been studied as a way of improving the quality of service ([4,1,12]). In brief, the idea is to make reservations in some of the neighboring cells that a user is likely to move into ahead of time. Statistical data like a mobility profile ([4]) can make the advance reservations more accurate. We study how reservations impact the effective utilization.

For reservations, the next cell has to be predicted in advance, before the user moves into it. We consider two cases. (1)We assume we are always able to predict correctly the next cell that the user will move into; this is the *perfect-reservation* case. Here, we need to reserve only one adjacent cell for each user. Perfect-reservation is an ideal scenario but it provides us with a good benchmark. (2)We make reservations in two cells; this is the the 2-cell reservation case. This is a more realistic scenario.

We assume a cellular mobile wireless network for the simulation. For simplicity we assume that all users have the same bandwidth requirements and the same cell latency. First, we follow the steps of our methodology and plot the utilization at different values of the relative arrival rate. Figure 5(b) shows a comparison between the reservation and no-reservation scenarios. The topmost plot corresponds to the no reservation case, the middle one is for the perfect reservation case, and the bottom plot is for the 2-cell reservation case. As the figure shows, under low and medium loads, no reservation is better than having reservations, even if they are perfect. Not having perfect reservations only degrades the performance further. The 2-cell reservation scheme exhibits much lower effective utilization as compared to no reservations. These results indicate that a system might actually perform better without reservation.

5   Conclusions

We proposed a performance evaluation methodology for wireless network simulation models. Our methodology reduces the number of parameters and introduces

---

[2] Our criterion for finding the steady state utilization was a change of less than 5% in the utilization in a time duration of 500 times the mean cell latency.

new metrics that facilitate the evaluation and comparison of system performance across different models.

We introduced the concept of steady state utilization which captures the inherent capacity of a network for a given workload. We defined steady state arrival rate as the arrival rate that will keep the system utilization at the maximum possible level, without losses. Moreover, we proposed *effective utilization* as a more insightful metric which combines both the utilization and the loss.

Finally, we looked at a case study to understand our methodology. As future work, we would like to study in more detail, the interdependencies of our parameters both analytically and with simulations.

References

[1] A.R. Aljadhai and T.F. Znati. A framework for call admission control and qos support in wireless environments. *Proceedings of IEEE INFOCOM '99*, pp. 1019–1026, 1999.

[2] S. Bajaj, L. Breslau, D. Estrin, K. Fall, S. Floyd, P. Haldar, M. Handley, A. Helmy, J. Heidemann, P. Huang, S. Kumar, S. McCanne, and R. Rejaie. Improving simulation for network research. *USC Computer Science Department Technical Report*, March 1999.

[3] H. Balakrishnan, V. N. Padmanabhan, S. Seshan, and R. Katz. A comparison of mechanisms for improving tcp performance over wireless links. *IEEE/ACM Transactions on Networking*, 5(6):756–769, December 1997.

[4] V. Bharghavan and J. P. Mysore. Profile-based next-cell prediction in indoor wireless lans. *IEEE International Conference on Networking*, 1997.

[5] J. Jobin, Michalis Faloutsos, Satish K. Tripathi. Performance Evaluation of Mobile Wireless Networks: A New Perspective. *Fourth ACM International Workshop on Modeling, Analysis, and Simulation of Wireless and Mobile Systems*, 2001.

[6] J. Jobin, Michalis Faloutsos, Satish K. Tripathi. Simplifying the Analysis of Wireless Cellular Network Simulation. *International Symposium on Performance Evaluation of Computer and Telecommunication Systems*, 2002.

[7] T. C. Fall. A framework for the simulation experimentation process. *Proceedings of the 1997 Winter Simulation Conference*.

[8] P. Huang, D. Estrin, and J. Heidemann. Enabling large-scale simulations: Selective abstraction approach to the study of multicast protocols. *Proceedings of the Sixth International Symposium on Modeling, Analysis, and Simulation of Computer and Telecommunications Systems (MASCOTS '98), Montreal, Canada*, July 1998.

[9] Y. Iraqi and R. Boutaba. A novel distributed call admission control for wireless mobile multimedia networks. *Proceedings of the third ACM international workshop on wireless mobile multimedia*, pp. 21–27, 2000.

[10] B. Li, C. Lin, and S. T. Chanson. Analysis of a hybrid cutoff priority scheme for multiple classes of traffic in multimedia wireless networks. *Wireless Networks*, 4:279–290, 1998.

[11] J. R. Moorman, J. W. Lockwood, and S.-M. Kang. Real-time prioritized call admission control in a base station scheduler. *Proceedings of the third ACM international workshop on wireless mobile multimedia*, pp. 28–37, 2000.

[12] S. Singh. Quality of service guarantees in mobile computing. *Journal of Computer Communications*, 19:359–371, 1996.

On the Radiocoloring Problem

Tiziana Calamoneri and Rossella Petreschi

Department of Computer Science, University of Rome "La Sapienza" – Italy
via Salaria 113, 00198 Roma, Italy.
{calamo, petreschi}@dsi.uniroma1.it

Abstract. In this paper a survey on the Radiocoloring Problem is presented. The *Radiocoloring Problem (RCP)* consists of an assignment of colors from the integer set $(0..\lambda)$ to the vertices of a graph, such that vertices at a distance of at most two get different colors and adjacent vertices get colors which are at least two apart. The aim is to minimize λ. The RCP arose in the field of wireless radio networks, and it concerns the problem of frequency assignment. Since its formal definition, the RCP has been widely studied due both to its intrinsic theoretical interest and to the growth of wireless networks.

1 The Problem

A *multihop radio network* is a network consisting of radio transmitters/receivers (hereafter 'radio stations') distributed over a region. Communication takes place by a transmitter broadcasting a signal over a fixed range. The size of the signal is proportional to the power emitted by the transmitter. Any receiver within the range of the transmitter (the radio station's neighbors) receives the signal in a single hop; all other radio stations will receive it in multiple hops.

The *Frequency Assignment Problem (FAP)* in radio networks consists of assigning frequencies to radio stations in order to exploit frequency reuse while keeping signal interference to acceptable levels: this problem is widely studied, due to the growth of wireless networks and to the relatively limited radio spectrum.

Many variants of the frequency assignment problem have been defined and studied (e.g.[1,21,26,29]) but the task of all of them is to assign radio frequencies to radio stations at different locations using limited frequencies and without causing *interference*.

Mathematical approaches to the FAP include graph theory [27], simulated annealing [10], genetic algorithms [11,23], tabu search [8], and neural networks [22,15]. Here, we are interested in a graph algorithmic approach to the problem.

A *Radiocoloring* of a graph $G(V, E)$ is an assignment function $\phi : V \to N$ such that $|\phi(u)-\phi(v)| \geq 2$, when u and v are adjacent in G, and $|\phi(u)-\phi(v)| \geq 1$, when the minimum distance of u and v in G is two. The range of used frequencies is called *span*. The *Radiocoloring Problem (RCP)* consists of determining the minimum span $\lambda(G)$ necessary to radiocolor G.

S.K. Das and S. Bhattacharya (Eds.): IWDC 2002, LNCS 2571, pp. 118–127, 2002.

In the context of the FAP, the first inequality in the definition of radiocoloring avoids a radio station and all its neighbors having different frequencies in order for their signals not to overlap, i.e. it prevents *direct collision*. The second inequality models a radio station being unable to receive signals of the same frequency from any two, or more, of its neighbors, i.e. it avoids *hidden collision*.

The RCP is in general NP-hard [18], so researchers have restricted their attention to special classes of graph: for some classes of graph approximate bounds have been looked for; for other classes tight bounds have been found and algorithms to efficiently radiocolor these graphs have been provided.

In this paper a survey on the Radiocoloring Problem is presented. First some NP-hardness results are described. Then exact results are presented, i.e. classes of graph for which the problem is polynomially solvable; finally, a number of approximate results is listed.

Due to the limit on the number of pages, here we include only a few definitions, those we consider essential for comprehension of the paper. For all the other definitions and properties the reader is referred to the bibliography.

2   The General Bound and NP-Hardness Results

In this section we state NP-hardness of the RCP, both in general and when restricted to some classes of graph. Before doing this, we discuss some results concerning the upper bound on $\lambda(G)$ in terms of Δ, when G is a general graph of maximum degree Δ.

The first of these results is due to Griggs and Yeh, who stated the following theorem:

Theorem 1. *[18] Let G be a graph with maximum degree Δ, then $\lambda(G) \leq \Delta^2 + 2\Delta$.*

The proof of this theorem is based on the fact that a vertex v in G is adjacent to at most Δ vertices and that there are at most $\Delta^2 - \Delta$ vertices which are at distance 2 from v. In the same paper, the authors conjectured that $\lambda(G) \leq \Delta^2$ is a tight upper bound.

Using constructive labeling schemes, Jonas [20] improved the result by showing that $\lambda(G) \leq \Delta^2 + 2\Delta - 4$ if $\Delta \geq 2$ and, successively, Chang and Kuo [9] furtherly decreased the bound to $\Delta^2 + \Delta$. So, Jonas bound is the best one for $\Delta \leq 3$, while Chang and Kuo value is the best one for all the other values of Δ.

Nowadays, it is still an open problem to understand if the conjecture $\lambda(G) \leq \Delta^2$ is true or not.

Griggs and Yeh improved their general upper bound to $\Delta^2 + 2\Delta - 3$ when G is 3-connected and to Δ^2 when G has diameter 2. The proof of this latter result is based on the following lemma, that is also the backbone of the proof of the intractability of the RCP [18,31]:

Lemma 1. *In a graph G with diameter 2, the following two statements are equivalent:*

(1) there exists an injection $\phi : V(G) \to [0, |V| - 1]$ such that $|\phi(u) - \phi(v)| \geq 2$, for all edges (u, v) in G;
(2) the complement graph, G^C, contains an Hamiltonian path.

Indeed, the proof of the complexity of the RCP is done considering a special form of the problem in which the graph G has diameter 2. So the NP-hardness of the RCP follows as an immediate consequence of the well-known NP-hardness of the Hamiltonian Path Problem.

Moreover in [12], it has been proved that the RCP is not fixed parameter tractable: i.e. it is NP-complete to determine if the span is limited by k for every fixed integer $k \geq 4$.

The RCP remains NP-hard also when restricted to planar graphs [13]; this result is proved through a reduction from 3-coloring Planar Problem, i.e. the problem to determine whether the vertices of a planar graph G can be 3-colored.

In [3] it is also shown that the RCP remains NP-hard when restricted to bipartite and split graphs. These proofs are obtained through reduction from the 3-coloring 4-regular Planar Problem and the Hamiltonian Path Problem, respectively. The authors underline that the RCP is NP-hard also for chordal graphs in view of the fact that they are a superclass of split graphs (split graphs = chordal graphs $\cup$ co-chordal graphs).

All the intractability results presented in this section for the RCP have led researchers to focus on special classes of graph and to look for either efficient coloring algorithms or approximate bounds. Next two sections concern these topics and Table 1 collects all the presented results.

3   Exact Results

In this section, we present all the classes of graph for which exact results of λ are known, at the best of our knowledge. We consider first very simple graphs, and then some other classes.

Simple Graphs
    We list a number of exact results concerning not trivial simple graphs, such as paths, cycles, cliques and stars.

Let P_n be a **path** of n vertices. In [31] it has been proven that: $\lambda(P_2) = 2$, $\lambda(P_3) = \lambda(P_4) = 3$, $\lambda(P_n) = 4$ for $n \geq 5$.

A simple extension of this result is an optimal radiocoloring of cycles, since a **cycle** C_n is obtained by joining the first and last vertex of a path. Griggs and Yeh [18] proved that $\lambda(C_n) = 4$, for any n. More precisely, let C_n be defined as a sequence of vertices $v_0, v_1, \ldots, v_{n-1}, v_0$; a feasible and optimal radiocoloring is: $\phi(v_i) = 0$ or 2 or 4 if $i = 0$ or 1 or 2 mod 3, respectively. If n is not multiple of 3, then $\phi(v_i)$ must be defined for the last vertices in the cycle as follows:
- if $n = 1$ mod 3, $\phi(v_i) =$ either 0 or 3 or 1 or 4 according to the value of i ($i =$ eiher $n - 4$ or $n - 3$ or $n - 2$ or $n - 1$, respectively);
- if $n = 2$ mod 3, $\phi(v_{n-2}) = 1$ and $\phi(v_{n-1}) = 3$.

Polynomial results are found by Jonas [20] for classes of cycle-related graphs such as **cacti**, **unicycles** and **bicycles**.

For what concerns **cliques** with n nodes, K_n, their definition implies $|\phi(u) - \phi(v)| \geq 2$, for each pair u, v; hence, it must hold $\lambda(K_n) \geq 2n - 2$. Since a feasible radio coloring can be achieved using all even labels from 0 to $2n - 2$, then $\lambda(K_n) = 2n - 2$.

In a **star** $K_{1,n}$, let us call v_0 the vertex of degree n and $v_1, \ldots, v_n$ the vertices of degree 1. For each $i, j > 0$, v_i and v_j are at distance 2 via v_0, and hence must have different colors. From the other hand $\phi(v_0)$ must be at distance at least 2 from any $\phi(v_i)$, $i > 0$. It follows that $\lambda(K_{1,n}) = n + 1$.

Observe that we considered stars in this subsection for their very simple structure; nevertheless, they are a special case of two classes treated later: trees and complete r-partite graphs.

Trees

For an n-vertex tree T with maximum degree $\Delta \geq 1$, Griggs and Yeh [18] showed that $\lambda(T)$ is either $\Delta + 1$ or $\Delta + 2$. They also conjectured that it is NP-complete to determine if $\lambda(T) = \Delta + 1$. This conjecture was disproved four years later by Chang and Kuo [9], who provided a polynomial time algorithm to determine if $\lambda(T) = \Delta + 1$. This algorithm is based on the property that $\lambda(T) = \Delta + 2$ if there is a vertex x whose neighborhood contains three or more vertices of degree Δ (see Fig. 1.a and 1.b).

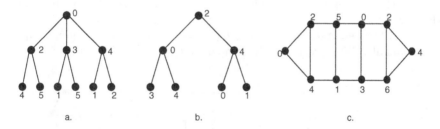

Fig. 1. Optimal radiocolorings of some special graphs.

The algorithm passes through repeated applications of the matching bipartite problem and it requires an overall complexity of $O(|V(G)|(\Delta+1)^2 M(2(\Delta+1)))$, where $M(r)$ is the complexity of solving the bipartite matching problem on r vertices.

Fishburn and Roberts [14] proved that all trees except stars are full colorable, i.e. all colors from 0 to $\lambda(T)$ are used to color some vertex, without holes.

Fiala, Kloks and Fratochvíl [12] showed that the algorithm in [9] can be used to solve the problem for a slightly wider class of graphs: k-**almost trees**. We remind that a k-almost tree is a connected graph with n vertices and $n + k - 1$ edges, k fixed, and can be recognized in linear time [4].

Union and Join of Graphs

Let G and H be two graphs with disjoint vertex sets. The *union* of G and H, $G \cup H$, is the graph whose vertex set is $V(G) \cup V(H)$ and edge set is $E(G) \cup E(H)$. The *join* of G and H, $G + H$, is the graph obtained from $G \cup H$ by adding all edges between vertices in $V(G)$ and vertices in $V(H)$. It holds:
$\lambda(G \cup H) = \max(\lambda(G), \lambda(H))$ [9] and
$\lambda(G + H) = \max(|V(G)| - 1, \lambda(G)) + \max(|V(H)| - 1, \lambda(H)) + 2$ [16].

The results reported in Table 1 for the n-**wheel** W_n and for **complete r-partite graphs**, $K_{n_1,n_2,\ldots,n_r}$ are obtained considering the wheel as the join of C_{n-1} and K_1, and $K_{n_1,n_2,\ldots,n_r}$ as the repeated join of r sets of isolated vertices.

Cographs are graphs not containing P_4 as induced subgraph and are recursively defined in terms of union and join of graphs: namely, if two graphs are cographs, so is both their union and their join. The linear time algorithm [4] to identify whether a graph G is a cograph gives a parsing tree, in case of positive answer. This result, together with the results on λ of the union and the join, leads to a linear time algorithm to compute $\lambda(G)$ for a cograph [9].

Finally, we cite exact results for the RCP of products of complete graphs [17], obtained with a completely different approach (Cayley graphs).

Regular Tilings

The tiling problem consists of covering the plane with copies of the same polygon and it is known that the only regular polygons useful for a tiling are hexagons, squares and triangles.

The RCP of regular tilings has been studied independently by different authors [2,6].

Let Δ be the degree of the tiling T_Δ: $\Delta = 3, 4, 6$ for the hexagonal, squared and triangular tiling, respectively. It holds $\lambda(T_\Delta) = \Delta + 2$ (see Fig. 2).

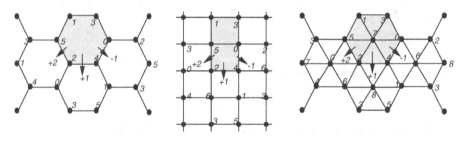

Fig. 2. Optimal radiocoloring of the three regular tilings.

In [2] three different algorithms are provided, one for each tiling, leading to a method for coloring the whole tiling in a distributed fashion in constant time, provided that each vertex knows its relative position in the graph.

In [6] a unique coloring algorithm for the three tilings is presented; it exploits that it is always possible to highlight an hexagon as common basic element in each tiling: the hexagonal tile for $\Delta = 3$, two adjacent squares (an hexagon with a chord) for $\Delta = 4$ and six triangles forming a wheel for $\Delta = 6$ (see Fig. 2).

Threshold Graphs

A graph is threshold if and only if it is a split graph and the vicinal preorder on its vertices is total.

These graphs are very reach in structure and appear in many applications [24]. Exploiting their properties, in [5] threshold graphs are optimally radiocolored with $\lambda \leq 2\Delta + 1$ (the exact values depends on the graph). Since threshold graphs have diameter 2, this result improves the general bound on graphs with diameter 2, when the RCP is restricted to threshold graphs.

4 Some Approximate Results

This section collects most of the results on upper and lower bound for particular classes of graph, listed in alphabetical order.

Bipartite Graphs

Bodlaender, Kloks, Tan and van Leeuwen [3] prove that there exist bipartite graphs requiring $\Omega(\Delta^2)$ colors to be radiocolored. Since $O(\Delta^2)$ is an obvious upper bound for λ, it follows that $\lambda(G) = \Theta(\Delta^2)$ when G is a bipartite graph.

Chordal Graphs

Chordal graphs have been considered by Sakai [28], in order to approach the general conjecture $\lambda(G) \leq \Delta^2$. She proved that chordal graphs satisfy the conjecture and derived the upper bound $\lambda(G) \leq (\Delta(G) + 3)^2/4$ exploiting the property that in a chordal graph there is at least one *simplicial* vertex, i.e. a vertex whose neighbors induce a clique in the graph. Other subclasses of chordal graph (among them **strongly chordal**) have been considered in [9].

Hypercubes

The first result concerning the RCP on the hypercube with $n = 2^k$ vertices, Q_k, is that $k + 3 \leq \lambda(Q_k) \leq 2k + 1$ for all $k \geq 6$ [18,20]. For $k \leq 5$ the same authors give exact values of $\lambda(Q_k)$. Two years later, the upper bound $2k + 1$ has been improved in [30] trough a coding theory method representing vertices of Q_k as binary k-tuples. Namely, the authors prove the existence of a new bound, depending on k, in the range $[\lfloor k + 1 + \log k \rfloor, 2k]$.

Outerplanar Graphs

In [3], the authors prove that at most $\Delta + 9$ colors are sufficient to radiocolor an outerplanar graph with maximum degree Δ. In particular, they leave as open problem to reduce the additive term 9 conjecturing that the tightest bound could be $\Delta + 3$. In [7] the conjecture is proved when outerplanar graph has maximum degree $\Delta \geq 8$, and a linear time algorithm for the RCP in outerplanar graphs is provided. Moreover, for smaller values of Δ, it is guaranteed a number of used colors bounded by 11, improving anyway the bound of $\Delta + 9$. In the special case $\Delta = 3$, it is shown that there exists an infinite class of outerplanar graph needing $\Delta + 4$ colors (a representative graph is depicted in Fig. 1.c) and an algorithm radiocoloring with at most $\Delta + 6$ colors any degree 3 outerplanar graph is presented. It remains an open problem to understand whether $\Delta + 6$ is a tight bound or not for degree 3 outerplanar graphs.

Planar Graphs

Jonas [20] proved that $\lambda(G) \leq 8\Delta - 13$ when G is planar. This bound has been the best one until recently, when van den Heuvel and McGuinnes [19] showed that $\lambda \leq 2\Delta + 25$. Later, in [25], the result has been furtherly improved to $\frac{5}{3}\Delta + 90$. Observe that this latter value is asymptotically better than the previous one when $\Delta \geq 195$. Since for a planar graph G with maximum degree Δ it holds the trivial lower bound $\lambda(G) \geq \Delta + 2$, it remains an open problem to understand which is the tight constant multiplying Δ in the value of $\lambda(G)$.

Split Graphs

Split graphs are the first known class of graph for which λ is neither linear nor quadratic in Δ. Namely, in [3] a bound of $\lambda \leq \Delta^{1.5} + 2\Delta + 2$ is given and it is shown that there exist split graphs having $\lambda = \Omega(\Delta^{1.5})$. It remains an open problem to understand if there exist other classes of graphs whose λ is neither linear nor quadratic in Δ.

Unigraphs

Unigraphs are graphs univocally determined by their own degree sequence up to isomorphism. Taking advantage from the degree sequence's analysis, in [5] a linear time algorithm for radiocoloring these graphs is provided. Upper bounds for specific classes of unigraph are proved, as shown in Table 1. It is to notice that the result for **split matrogenic graphs** improves the result on general split graphs when the RCP is restricted to this subclass.

5   Conclusions

In this paper we noted that the Radiocoloring Problem is in general NP-hard and we have collected exact and approximate results on specific classes of graph.

This survey does not pretend to be exhaustive, but it addresses itself to highlighting the relevance of the Radiocoloring Problem. Due to the large amount of literature on the topic, we have not extended our attention to the numerous variants of the problem. However, just to give a general idea of these variants, we can state that they derive from changing some conditions, either on the frequency distances ($L(h, k)$-Labeling, Coloring of G^2), or on distances between radio stations ($L(2, 1, 1)$-Labeling), or on the constraints of the codomain of ϕ (no-hole Labeling, λ Cyclic Labeling).

During the discussion of the results, some open problems were cited, in particular the conjecture $\lambda(G) \leq \Delta^2$ for graphs with general topology.

It needs to be emphasized that general results may be significant only from a theoretical point of view, because realistic network topologies are sometimes very restricted. For this reason we think that much effort should be put into solving open problems related to planar graphs and particular subclasses of them (e.g. outerplanar graphs).

Table 1. Summary of results. In G, n is the number of vertices and Δ is the maximum degree.

Classes of Graph	Bounds on λ	Complexity
Bipartite	$\lambda = \Theta(\Delta^2)$	NP-hard
Cacti, Unicycles, Bicycles		P
Chordal	$\lambda \leq \frac{1}{4}(\Delta + 3)^2$	NP-hard
Cliques	$\lambda = 2n - 2$	P
Cographs		P
Complete r-partite	$\lambda = n + r - 2$	P
Cycles	$\lambda = 4$	P
Hexagonal Tiling	$\lambda = 5$	P
Hypercube	$\log n + 3 \leq \lambda \leq 2\log n$ exact values of λ if $\log n \leq 5$	
k-Almost Trees		P
Matrogenic	$\lambda \leq 3\Delta$	
Matroidal	$\lambda \leq 3\Delta$	
Outerplanar:	$\lambda \leq \Delta + 2$ if $\Delta \geq 8$ $\lambda \leq 10$ if $4 \leq \Delta \leq 7$	
Paths	$\lambda = 4$ if $n \geq 5$	P
Planar	$\lambda \leq 2\Delta + 25$ $\lambda \leq \frac{5}{3}\Delta + 90$	NP-hard
Squared Tiling	$\lambda = 6$	P
Split	$\lambda = \Theta(\Delta^{1.5})$	NP-hard
Split Matrogenic	$\lambda \leq 3\Delta + 1$	
Star	$\lambda = n + 1$	P
Strongly Chordal	$\lambda \leq 2\Delta$	
Threshold	$\lambda \leq 2\Delta + 1$	P
Trees	$\lambda = \Delta + 1$ or $\Delta + 2$	P
Triangular Tiling	$\lambda = 8$	P
Wheel	$\lambda = n + 2$	P

References

1. K.I. Aardal, S.P.M. van Hoesel, A.M.C.A. Koster, C. Mannino and A. Sassano. Models and Solution Techniques for Frequency Assignment Problems. ZIB-Report 01-40, Konrad-Zuse-Zentrum fur Informationstechnik Berlin, 2001.

2. A.A. Bertossi, C.M. Pinotti and R.B. Tan: Efficient Use of Radio Spectrum in Wireless Networks with Channel separation between Close Stations. *Proc. 4th ACM Int. Workshop on Discrete Algorithms and Methods for Mobile Computing and Communications (DIAL M)*, 2000.

3. H.L. Bodlaender,T. Kloks, R.B. Tan and J. Van Leeuwen. Approximations for λ-Coloring of Graphs. *Tech Rep. UU-CS-2000-25*, 2000. A preliminary version has been published in *Proc. of STACS 2000*.

4. A. Brandstadt,V.B. Le and J.P. Spinrad: Graph Classes: A Survey. *SIAM Monographs on Discrete Mathematics and Applications*, 1999.

5. T. Calamoneri and R. Petreschi. λ-Coloring Unigraphs. Manuscript, submitted to *Journal of Computer and System Sciences*. 2001. A preliminary version has been published in *Proc. of LATIN 02*.

6. T. Calamoneri and R. Petreschi. λ-Coloring of Regular Tiling. *Proc. First Cologne-Twente Workshop (CTW)*. Electronic Notes in Discrete Mathematics, 8, 2001. http://www.elsevier.nl/locate/endmCTW2001.

7. T. Calamoneri and R. Petreschi. $L(2,1)$-Labeling of Planar Graphs (Extended Abstract). *Proc. 5th ACM Int. Workshop on Discrete Algorithms and Methods for Mobile Computing and Communications (DIAL M)*, 2001, pp. 28–33.

8. D. Castelino, S. Hurley and N.M. Stephens. A tabu search algorithm for frequency assignment. *Annals of Operations Research* **63**: 301–319, 1996.

9. G.J. Chang and D. Kuo. The radiocoloring Problem on Graphs. *SIAM J. Disc. Math.*, 9: 309–316, 1996.

10. M. Duque-Anton, D. Kunz and B. Rüber. Channel assignment for cellular radio using simulated annealing. *IEEE Trans. on Vehicular Technology* **42**: 14–21, 1993.

11. W. Crompton, S. Hurley and N.M. Stephen. A parallel genetic algorithm for frequency assignment problems. *Proc. IMACS/IEEE International Symp. on Signal Processing, Robotics and Neural Networks*, pp. 81–84, 1994.

12. J. Fiala, T. Kloks and J. Kratochvíl. Fixed-parameter Complexity of λ-Labelings. *Proc. Graph-Theoretic Concepts of Compu. Sci. (WG99)*, pp. 350–363. Lectures Notes in Computer Science 1665, 1999.

13. D.A. Fotakis, S.E. Nikoletseas, V.G. Papadoulou and P.G. Spirakis. NP-completeness Results and Efficient Approximations for Radiocoloring in Planar Graphs. *Proc. 25th Int.l Symp. on Math. Foundations of Compu. Sci. (MFCS 2000)*, 2000.

14. P. C. Fishburn and F. S. Roberts. Full Color Theorems for $L(2,1)$-Colorings. DIMACS Tech. Rep. 2000-08, 2000.

15. N. Funabiki and Y. Takefuji. A neural network parallel algorithm for channel assignment problem in cellular radio networks. *IEEE Trans. on Vehicular Technology* **41**: pp. 430–437, 1992.

16. J.P.Georges ,D.W.Mauro and M.A.Whittlesey. Relating path coverings to vertex labelings with a condition at distance two. *Discr. Math.* **135**: 103–111, 1994.

17. J. P. Georges, D. W. Mauro and M. I. Stein. Labeling Products of Complete Graphs with a Condition at Distance Two. *SIAM J. Discrete Math.*: 28–35, 2000.

18. J.R. Griggs and R.K. Yeh. Labeling graphs with a Condition at Distance 2. *SIAM J. Disc. Math* **5**:586–595, 1992.
    Graph Labeling and Radio Channel Assignment. *Journal of Graph Theory* **29**: 263–283, 1998.

19. J. van den Heuvel and S. McGuinnes. Colouring the square of a planar graphs. Report LSE-CDAM-99-06, Centre for Discrete and Applicable Mathematics, London School of Economics, London, U.K., 1999.

20. K. Jonas. *Graph Coloring Analogues With a Condition at Distance Two: $L(2,1)$-Labelings and List λ-Labelings*. Ph.D. thesis, University of South Carolina, Columbia, 1993.

21. A.M.C.A. Koster. *Frequency Assignment*. Ph.D. thesis, Universiteit Maastricht, 1999.

22. D. Kunz. Channel assignment for cellular radio using neural networks. *IEEE Trans. on Vehicular Technology* **40**: 188–193, 1991.

23. W.K. Lai and G.G. Coghill. Channel assignment through evolutionary optimization. *IEEE Trans. on Vehicular Technology* **45**: 91–96, 1996.

24. N.V.R. Mahadev and U.N. Peled. Threshold Graphs and Related Topics. *Ann. Discrete Math.* **56**, 1995.

25. M. Molloy and M.R. Salavatipour. *Frequency channel assignment on planar networks. Proc. of 10th Annual European Symposium on Algorithms (ESA 2002)*, pp. 736–747, Lectures Notes in Computer Science 2461, 2002.

26. R.A. Murphey, P.M. Pardalos and M.G.C. Resende. Frequency Assignment Problems. In *Handbook of Combinatorial Optimization*, D.-Z. Du and P.M. Pardalos (Eds.) :295–377, 1999. Kluwer Academic Publishers.

27. F.S. Roberts. T-Colorings of graphs: recent results and open problems. *Discrete Mathematics* **93**: 229–245, 1991.

28. D. Sakai. Labeling Chordal Graphs: Distance Two Condition. SIAM J. Disc. Math **7**:133–140, 1994.

29. M. Shepherd. *Radio Channel Assignment.* Ph.D. thesis, Merton College, Oxford, 1998.

30. M.A. Whittelesey, J.P. Georges and D.W. Mauro. On the λ-Number of Q_n and Related Graphs. *SIAM Journal Disc. Math.* **8(4)**: 499–506, 1995.

31. R. Y. Yeh. *Labeling Graphs with a Condition at Distance Two.* Ph.D. Thesis, Dept. of Mathematics, University of South Carolina, Columbia, SC, 1990.

Efficient Algorithms for Channel Assignment in a Cellular Network

Bhabani P. Sinha

Advanced Computing and Microelectronics Unit, Indian Statistical Institute
203 B. T. Road, Kolkata-700 108, India
bhabani@isical.ac.in

During recent years, the world is experiencing almost an exponential growth in the demand for various mobile communication services. On the other hand, the available bandwidth for such communication is very much limited. As a result, efficient utilization of bandwidth for mobile communication has become more and more critical. When a mobile cellular network is designed, each cell of the network is assigned a set of channels to provide services to the individual calls of the cell. The task of assigning frequency channels to the cells satisfying some frequency separation constraints with a view to avoiding channel interference and using as small bandwidth as possible is known as the *channel assignment problem*. Three types of interference are generally taken into consideration in the form of constraints: i) *co-channel constraint*, due to which the same channel is not allowed to be assigned to certain pairs of cells simultaneously, ii) *adjacent channel constraint*, for which adjacent channels are not allowed to be assigned to certain pairs of cells simultaneously, and iii) *co-site constraint*, which implies that any pair of channels assigned to the same cell must be separated by a certain number. In its most general form, the channel assignment problem (CAP) is equivalent to the generalized graph-coloring problem which is a well-known NP-complete problem.

Here we would discuss about the channel assignment problem in a hexagonal cellular network with 2-band buffering, where the channel interference does not extend beyond two cells. Here, for cellular networks with homogeneous demands, we find some lower bounds on minimum bandwidth required for various relative values of s_0, s_1, and s_2, the minimum frequency separations to avoid interference for calls in the same cell, or in cells at distances one and two respectively. We then describe an algorithm for solving the channel assignment problem in its general form using the Elitist model of Genetic Algorithm (EGA). We next apply this technique to the special case of hexagonal cellular networks with 2-band buffering. For homogeneous demands, we apply EGA for assigning channels to a small subset of nodes and then extend it for the entire cellular network which ensures faster convergence. Moreover, we show that our approach is also applicable to the cases of non-homogeneous demands. Application of our proposed methodology to well-known benchmark problems generates optimal results within a reasonable computing time.

Next we would present a yet improved algorithm for channel assignment so as to further minimize the computation time. For this, we introduce the concept of a *critical block* of the network for a given demand vector and frequency sep-

S.K. Das and S. Bhattacharya (Eds.): IWDC 2002, LNCS 2571, pp. 128–129, 2002.
© Springer-Verlag Berlin Heidelberg 2002

aration constraints. A novel idea of partitioning the critical block into several smaller sub-networks with homogeneous demands has been introduced which provides an elegant way of assigning frequencies to the critical block. This idea of partitioning is then extended for assigning frequencies to the rest of the network. The proposed algorithm provides an optimal assignment for all well-known benchmark instances including the most difficult two. It is shown to be superior to the existing frequency assignment algorithms, reported so far, in terms of both bandwidth requirement and computation time.

Channel Assignment for Wireless Networks Modelled as d-Dimensional Square Grids

Aniket Dubhashi[1], Shashanka MVS[1], Amrita Pati[1], Shashank R.[1], and
Anil M. Shende[2]

[1] Birla Institute of Technology & Science, Pilani 333031, India
{f1999011,f1999154,f1999013,f1999025}@bits-pilani.ac.in
[2] Roanoke College, Salem, VA 24153, USA
shende@roanoke.edu

Abstract. In this paper, we study the problem of channel assignment for wireless networks modelled as d-dimensional grids. In particular, for d-dimensional square grids, we present optimal assignments that achieve a channel separation of 2 for adjacent stations where the reuse distance is 3 or 4. We also introduce the notion of a colouring schema for d-dimensional square grids, and present an algorithm that assigns colours to the vertices of the grid satisfying the schema constraints.

1 Introduction

The enormous growth of wireless networks has made the efficient use of the scarce radio spectrum important. A "Frequency Assignment Problem" (FAP) models the task of assigning frequencies (channels) from a radio spectrum to a set of transmitters and receivers, satisfying certain constraints [8]. The main difficulty in an efficient use of the radio spectrum is the *interference* caused by unconstrained simultaneous transmissions. Interferences can be eliminated (or at least reduced) by means of suitable *channel assignment* techniques, which partition the given radio spectrum into a set of disjoint channels that can be used simultaneously by the stations while maintaining acceptable radio signals. Since radio signals get attenuated over distance, two stations in a network can use the same channel without interferences provided the stations are spaced sufficiently apart. Stations that use the same channel are called *co-channel stations*. The minimum distance at which a channel can be reused with no interferences is called the *co-channel reuse distance* (or simply *reuse distance*) and is denoted by σ.

In a *dense* network – a network where there are a large number of transmitters and receivers in a small area – interference is more likely. Thus, reuse distance needs to be high in such networks. Moreover, channels assigned to nearby stations must be separated in value by at least a gap which is inversely proportional to the distance between the two stations. A minimum *channel separation* δ_i is required between channels assigned to stations at distance i, with $i < \sigma$, such that δ_i decreases when i increases [7]. The purpose of channel assignment algorithms is

S.K. Das and S. Bhattacharya (Eds.): IWDC 2002, LNCS 2571, pp. 130–141, 2002.

to assign channels to transmitters in such a way that (1) the co-channel reuse distance and the channel separation constraints are satisfied, and (2) the *span* of the assignment, defined to be the difference between the highest and the lowest channels assigned, is as small as possible [2].

In this paper, we investigate the channel assignment problem, described informally above, for networks that can be modelled as grids in d dimensions, $d \geq 3$. In Section 3 we define the infinite d-dimensional square and cellular grids, and show that a solution for the channel assignment problem for the d-dimensional square (cellular) grid places an upper bound on solutions for the problem for a suitable d'-dimensional cellular (square) grid. These results partly motivate our study of the channel assignment problem in higher dimensional grids. Another motivation is that when the networks of several service providers overlap geographically, they must use different channels for their clients. The overall network can then be modelled in a suitably higher dimension.

The main focus of the paper is a study of the problem for networks arranged as d-dimensional square grids. We consider the restricted problem requiring a channel separation of 1 for all but adjacent stations, and a larger (than 1) separation for adjacent stations. In Section 4, we present optimal assignments for d-dimensional square grids for $\sigma = 3, 4$ with a channel separation constraint of 2 for adjacent stations. Finally, in Section 4.5, we introduce the notion of a colouring schema for d-dimensional square grids and present an algorithm that assigns colours to the vertices of the grid satisfying the schema constraints.

2   Preliminaries

Formally, the *channel assignment problem with separation* (CAPS) can be modelled as an appropriate colouring problem on an undirected graph $G = (V, E)$ representing the network topology, whose vertices in V correspond to stations, and edges in E correspond to pairs of stations that can hear each other's transmission [2]. For a graph G, we will denote the distance between any two vertices in the graph, i.e., the number of edges in a shortest path between the two vertices, by $d_G(\cdot, \cdot)$. (When the context is clear, we will denote the distance as simply $d(\cdot, \cdot)$.) CAPS is then defined as:

CAPS $(G, \sigma, \boldsymbol{\delta})$
Given an undirected graph G, an integer $\sigma > 1$, and a vector of positive integers $\boldsymbol{\delta} = (\delta_1, \delta_2, \ldots, \delta_{\sigma-1})$, find an integer $g > 0$ so that there is a function $f : V \rightarrow \{0, \ldots, g\}$, such that for all $u, v \in G$, for each i, $1 \leq i \leq \sigma - 1$, if $d(u, v) = i$, then $|f(u) - f(v)| \geq \delta_i$.

This assignment is referred to as a g-$L(\delta_1, \delta_2, \ldots, \delta_{\sigma-1})$ colouring of the graph G [6], and **CAPS** $(G, \sigma, \boldsymbol{\delta})$ is sometimes referred to as the $L(\boldsymbol{\delta})$ colouring problem for G. Note that a g-$L(\delta_1, \delta_2, \ldots, \delta_{\sigma-1})$ uses only the $(g+1)$ colours in the set $\{0, \ldots, g\}$, but does *not* necessarily use all the $(g+1)$ colours. A g-$L(\delta_1, \delta_2, \ldots, \delta_{\sigma-1})$ colouring of G is *optimal* iff g is the smallest number witnessing a solution for **CAPS** $(G, \sigma, \boldsymbol{\delta})$.

Finding the optimal colouring for general graphs has been shown to be NP-complete. The problem remains NP-complete even if the input graphs are restricted to planar graphs, bipartite graphs, chordal graphs, and split graphs [4]. Most of the work on this problem has dealt with specific graphs such as grids and rings, for small reuse distance (σ) values, and for small channel separation (δ_i) values, e.g., optimal $L(1,1)$ colourings for rings and bidimensional grids [1], optimal $L(2,1)$ and $L(2,1,1)$ colourings for hexagonal, bidimensional, and cellular grids [2], etc. Recently, Bertossi et al [3] exhibited optimal $L(\delta_1,1,\ldots,1)$ colourings, for $\delta_1 \leq \lfloor \sigma/2 \rfloor$, for bidimensional grids and rings. (See [3] for a succinct literature survey of this problem.) Below, we refer to $L(\cdot,1,\ldots,1)$ colourings by $L(\cdot,\mathbf{1}_k)$ colourings.

As pointed out in [2], a lower bound for the $L(1,\mathbf{1}_k)$ colouring problem is also a lower bound for the $L(\delta,\mathbf{1}_k)$, $\delta > 1$. Given an instance of **CAPS**, consider the augmented graph obtained from G by adding edges between all those pairs of vertices that are at a distance of at most $\sigma-1$. Clearly, then, the size (number of vertices) of any clique in this augmented graph places a lower bound on an $L(1,\mathbf{1}_{\sigma-1})$ colouring for G; the best such lower bound is given by the size of a maximum clique in the augmented graph.

In each graph, G, for each σ, we identify a canonical sub-graph, $T(G,\sigma)$, of the graph so that the vertices of $T(G,\sigma)$ induce a clique in the augmented graph of the graph. We will refer to $T(G,\sigma)$ as a *tile*. When the context is clear, we will refer to the size of $T(G,\sigma)$ simply as $c(\sigma)$.

Most (but not all) of the assignment schemes described in this paper follow the pattern: for a given graph G, and for a given σ, (1) identify $T(G,\sigma)$, (2) find the number of vertices in $T(G,\sigma)$, and hence a lower bound for the given assignment problem, (3) describe a colouring scheme to colour all the vertices of $T(G,\sigma)$, (4) demonstrate a tiling of the entire graph made up of $T(G,\sigma)$ to show that the colouring scheme described colours the entire graph, and (5) show that the colouring scheme satisfies the given reuse distance and channel separation constraints.

3   Channel Assignments in Higher Dimensional Grids

In this section we relate $L(\delta_1,\delta_2,\ldots,\delta_{\sigma-1})$ colourings for d-dimensional cellular and square grids.

For any d-dimensional lattice, $\mathcal{L}$, the minimal distance in the lattice is denoted by $\mu(\mathcal{L})$. The infinite graph, denoted $\mathcal{G}(\mathcal{L})$, corresponding to the lattice $\mathcal{L}$ consists of the set of lattice points as vertices; each pair of lattice points that are at a distance $\mu(\mathcal{L})$ constitute the edges of $\mathcal{G}(\mathcal{L})$. Henceforth, we will not make a distinction between the lattice points in $\mathcal{L}$ and the corresponding vertices in $\mathcal{G}(\mathcal{L})$. For any lattice $\mathcal{L}$, for any two points u and v in $\mathcal{L}$, $d_{\mathcal{G}(\mathcal{L})}(\cdot,\cdot)$ will denote the distance between vertices u and v in $\mathcal{G}(\mathcal{L})$.

The lattice $\mathbf{Z}^d$ is the set of ordered d-tuples of integers, and $\mathbf{A}_d$ is the hyperplane that is a subset of $\mathbf{Z}^{d+1}$, and is characterised as the set of points in $\mathbf{Z}^{d+1}$ such that the coordinates of each point add up to zero. $\mu(\mathbf{Z}^d) = 1$, and the minimal length vectors in $\mathbf{Z}^d$ are the unit vectors in each dimension. For each $d > 0$, for each $i, j, 0 \leq i, j \leq d, i \neq j$, define $\lambda_{ij}^d = (x_0, \ldots, x_d)$ where $x_i = 1$, $x_j = -1$, and for each $k, 0 \leq k \leq d, k \neq i, j, x_k = 0$. Then, $\mu(\mathbf{A}_d) = \sqrt{2}$, and the set of minimal length vectors in $\mathbf{A}_d$ is $\{\lambda_{ij}^d \mid i, j, 0 \leq i, j \leq d, i \neq j\}$. (See [5,9] for more on these lattices.)

The infinite d-dimensional square grid is, then, $\mathcal{G}(\mathbf{Z}^d)$, and the infinite d-dimensional cellular grid is $\mathcal{G}(\mathbf{A}_d)$.

Theorem 1 *For all $d \geq 2$, if there is a g-$L(\delta_1, \delta_2, \ldots, \delta_{\sigma-1})$ colouring for $\mathbf{Z}^d$, then there is a g-$L(\gamma_1, \gamma_2, \ldots, \gamma_{\lceil \frac{\sigma}{2} \rceil - 1})$ colouring for $\mathbf{A}_{d-1}$ where, for each $i, 1 \leq i \leq \lceil \frac{\sigma}{2} \rceil - 1, \gamma_i = \delta_{2i}$.*

Proof. Consider a point $x = (x_0, \ldots, x_{d-1})$ that is in the intersection of $\mathbf{Z}^d$ and $\mathbf{A}_{d-1}$. Then, $d_{\mathbf{Z}^d}(x, 0) = 2 \cdot d_{\mathbf{A}_{d-1}}(x, 0)$, thus giving us the theorem.   □

Theorem 2 *For all $n \geq 2$, if there is a g-$L(\delta_1, \delta_2, \ldots, \delta_{\sigma-1})$ colouring for $\mathbf{A}_d$, then there is a g-$L(\delta_1, \delta_2, \ldots, \delta_{\sigma-1})$ colouring for $\mathbf{Z}^{\lfloor \frac{d+1}{2} \rfloor}$.*

Proof. Consider the subset of minimal length vectors in $\mathbf{A}_d$ given by $\{\lambda_{i(d-i)}^d \mid 0 \leq i < \lfloor \frac{d+1}{2} \rfloor\}$. Clearly, this subset consists of $\lfloor \frac{d+1}{2} \rfloor$ mutually orthogonal vectors, and hence is a basis for $\mathbf{Z}^{\lfloor \frac{d+1}{2} \rfloor}$. Thus, the infinite graph for $\mathcal{G}(\mathbf{Z}^{\lfloor \frac{d+1}{2} \rfloor})$ is a subgraph of $\mathcal{G}(\mathbf{A}_d)$, and hence the result.   □

4   Colourings for $\mathcal{G}(\mathbf{Z}^d)$

As mentioned in Section (1), we first identify the canonical sub-graph $T(\mathcal{G}(\mathbf{Z}^d), \sigma)$, and then find lower bounds on the colourings of $\mathcal{G}(\mathbf{Z}^d)$. We then present optimal colouring schemes for $\mathcal{G}(\mathbf{Z}^d)$, for $\sigma = 3, 4$, with a separation constraint of 2 for adjacent vertices. We introduce the notion of a colouring schema for $\mathcal{G}(\mathbf{Z}^d)$, and also prove that the colouring schemes presented have running times of $O(d)$.

4.1   Lower Bound

The lower bound on the colouring of $\mathcal{G}(\mathbf{Z}^d)$ is the number of vertices in $T(\mathcal{G}(\mathbf{Z}^d), \sigma)$, denoted by $c(\sigma)$. Henceforth, we will refer to this number by $n(\sigma, d)$. Note that $n(\sigma, 1) = \sigma$. It can be proved that

$$n(\sigma, d) = n(\sigma, d - 1) + 2 \sum_{i=1}^{\lfloor \frac{\sigma}{2} \rfloor} n(\sigma - 2i, d - 1).$$

4.2   Colouring Strategy

Before we present the actual colouring schemes, we present an intuitive discussion of the strategy that we will use to colour $\mathcal{G}(\mathbf{Z}^d)$.

We will use the notation $(x_0, \ldots, x_i, \ldots, x_{d-1})$ to denote the vertex in $\mathcal{G}(\mathbf{Z}^d)$. The strategy used to colour $\mathcal{G}(\mathbf{Z}^d)$ is to identify a *base-segment* on a *baseline*. The baseline is the set of vertices $(x_0, 0, \ldots, 0)$. The base-segment is the set of vertices $(x_0, 0, \ldots, 0)$ with $0 \leq x_0 \leq B(\sigma, d)$, where $B(\sigma, d)$ is the number of colours used to colour $\mathcal{G}(\mathbf{Z}^d)$, with a reuse distance of σ. Note that $B(\sigma, d) \geq n(\sigma, d)$, as $n(\sigma, d)$ is the lower bound on the colouring. This base-segment is *translated* to fill up $\mathcal{G}(\mathbf{Z}^d)$. A translation of the base-segment into the ith dimension is an increase in x_0, and an increment of 1 in the ith dimension. A translation, in other words is to repeat the colouring at some distance. The increase in x_0 is given by the translation function t_i, where $1 \leq i \leq d - 1$.

We thus have a function f that colours vertices on the baseline, and a function C that colours vertices of $\mathcal{G}(\mathbf{Z}^d)$. To prove that our colouring schema work, we will make use of a process called *dimensional collapse*, which is the inverse of the translation process described above. It is the strategy of reducing the colours assigned to arbitrary vertices in $\mathcal{G}(\mathbf{Z}^d)$ to colours assigned to vertices on the baseline. We describe the process here.

Consider two vertices $P = (x_0, x_1, \ldots, x_{d-1})$ and $Q = (x'_0, x'_1, \ldots, x'_{d-1})$ in $\mathcal{G}(\mathbf{Z}^d)$, where $x'_i - x_i = k_i$, $0 \leq i \leq d - 1$. Let t_i be the translation function employed by a colouring scheme C for $\mathcal{G}(\mathbf{Z}^d)$. The colours assigned to P and Q will be:

$$C(P) = C(x_0, x_1, \ldots, x_{d-1}) = C(x_0 - \sum_{i=1}^{d-1} x_i \cdot t_i, 0, \ldots, 0), \text{ and}$$

$$C(Q) = C(x'_0 - \sum_{i=1}^{d-1} x'_i \cdot t_i, 0, \ldots, 0).$$

This means the colours assigned to P and Q are the same as the colours assigned to vertices $u = (x_0 - \sum_{i=1}^{d-1} x_i \cdot t_i, 0, \ldots, 0)$ and $v = (x'_0 - \sum_{i=1}^{d-1} x'_i \cdot t_i, 0, \ldots, 0)$ on the baseline. We call u and v the *collapse points* corresponding to P and Q. Their *collapse positions* are $CP(P)$ and $CP(Q)$ respectively. We define the *collapse distance* as the distance between u and v. We denote it by $CD(P, Q)$.

$$CD(P, Q) = d(u, v) = |k_0 - \sum_{i=1}^{d-1} k_i \cdot t_i|$$

4.3   Optimal Colouring for $\sigma = 3$

Consider the *star* graph S_Δ which consists of a *center* vertex c with degree Δ, and Δ ray vertices of degree 1. We will use the following from [2].

Lemma 1. *[2] Let the center c of S_Δ be already coloured. Then, the largest colour required for a g-L(2, 1)-colouring of S_Δ by the colouring function f is at least:*

$$g = \begin{cases} \Delta + 1, & f(c) = 0 \text{ or } f(c) = \Delta + 1, \\ \Delta + 2, & 0 < f(c) < \Delta + 1. \end{cases}$$

□

Every induced subgraph in $\mathcal{G}(\mathbf{Z}^d)$, with the distance between the vertices $d(u,v) \leq \sigma - 1$ is a *star* graph with a center vertex of degree $2d$ and $2d$ ray vertices, each of degree 1, and hence we have:

Lemma 2. *If there is a g-$L(2,1)$ colouring of $\mathcal{G}(\mathbf{Z}^d)$, then $g \geq 2d + 2$.*   □

Lemma (2) shows that $n(\sigma, d) \geq 2d + 3$. We provide a colouring scheme that uses $B(\sigma, d) = 2d + 3$ colours. The base-segment is coloured using the function:

$$f(x_0) = \begin{cases} 2d - 2x_0 + 1, \ x_0 \bmod (2d+3) \leq d, \\ 4d - 2x_0 + 4, \ d+1 \leq x_0 \bmod (2d+3) \leq 2d+2. \end{cases} \tag{1}$$

We define in Equation (2) the colouring scheme C_3, and later prove that it optimally colours $\mathcal{G}(\mathbf{Z}^d)$:

$$C_3(x_0, x_1, \ldots, x_i, 0, \ldots, 0) = C_3(x_0 - (i+1)x_i, x_1, \ldots, x_{i-1}, 0, \ldots, 0), 1 \leq i < d,$$
$$C_3(x_0, 0, \ldots, 0) = f(x_0). \tag{2}$$

We make the following observations about the colours assigned to the baseline:

Lemma 3. *For colouring the baseline,*

1. *The set of $2d + 3$ colours used by the function f defined in Equation (1) is $\{0, 1, \ldots, 2d + 2\}$.*
2. *Vertices are assigned consecutive colours iff they are $((d+1) \bmod (2d+3))$ or $((d+2) \bmod (2d+3))$ apart.*
3. *For distinct vertices u and v on the baseline, $d(u,v) \neq 2d + 3 \implies f(u) \neq f(v)$.*   □

Theorem 3 *C_3 is an optimal $L(2,1)$ colouring of $\mathcal{G}(\mathbf{Z}^d)$.*

Proof. From Lemma (3.1), the colouring scheme C_3 uses exactly $2d + 3$ colours, with the largest colour being $2d+2$. From Lemma (2), this scheme is optimal if it *works*. To prove that C_3 works, we have to prove that it satisfies the co-channel reuse and the channel separation constraints.

Adherence to the co-channel reuse constraint: Suppose two distinct vertices $P = (x_0, x_1, \ldots, x_{d-1})$ and $Q = (y_0, y_1, \ldots, y_{d-1})$ in $\mathcal{G}(\mathbf{Z}^d)$ are assigned the same colour. Then, the co-channel reuse constraint is satisfied if we prove that $d(P, Q) \geq 3$. Let us assume the contrary, i.e. $d(P, Q) \leq 2$.

Case 1: *P and Q differ in x_0.*

When P and Q differ in x_0, we write P and Q as follows:

$$P = (x_0, x_1, \ldots, x_a, \ldots, x_{d-1}), \text{ and } Q = (x'_0, x_1, \ldots, x'_a, \ldots, x_{d-1}),$$

where $1 \leq a \leq d - 1$, $x'_0 - x_0 = k_0$, and $x'_a - x_a = k_a$, $1 \leq |k_0| + |k_a| \leq 2, |k_0| > 0$.

Performing the *dimensional collapse* on P and Q, we get:

$$CP(P) = (x_0 - dx_{d-1} - \cdots - (a+1)x_a - \cdots - 2x_1, 0, \ldots, 0),$$
$$CP(Q) = (x'_0 - dx_{d-1} - \cdots - (a+1)x'_a - \cdots - 2x_1, 0, \ldots, 0)$$
$$CD(P,Q) = |k_0 - (a+1)k_a|$$

Since the maximum value of a is $d-1$, we have: $0 < |k_0 - (a+1)k_a| \leq d+1$. This means that there are two vertices u and v on the baseline such that $C_3(u) = C_3(P)$ and $C_3(v) = C_3(Q)$, and $0 < d(u,v) \leq d+1$. From Lemma (3.3), $C_3(u) \neq C_3(v)$. Therefore, $C_3(P) \neq C_3(Q)$, giving us a contradiction.

Case 2: *P and Q do not differ in x_0.*
In this case, we write P and Q as follows:

$$P = (x_0, x_1, \ldots, x_a, \ldots, x_b, \ldots, x_{d-1}), \text{ and} \tag{3}$$
$$Q = (x_0, x_1, \ldots, x'_a, \ldots, x'_b, \ldots, x_{d-1}), \text{ where}$$
$$1 \leq a \leq d-1 \text{ and } 1 \leq b \leq d-1, \tag{4}$$
$$x'_a - x_a = k_a \text{ and } x'_b - x_b = k_b, 1 \leq |k_a| + |k_b| \leq 2. \tag{5}$$

Performing the dimensional collapse on P and Q, we get:

$$CD(P,Q) = |-(a+1)k_a - (b+1)k_b|. \tag{6}$$

From Equations (4) and (5), and from the fact that $a \neq b$, we have: $0 < CD(P,Q) \leq 2d$. Therefore we have $0 < d(u,v) \leq 2d$. From Lemma (3.3), $C_3(u) \neq C_3(v)$. Therefore, $C_3(P) \neq C_3(Q)$, giving us a contradiction.

The above two cases thus prove that $d(P,Q) \geq 3$, thereby satisfying the co-channel reuse constraint.

Adherence to the channel separation constraint: To prove the channel separation constraint, we use Lemma (3.2). If P and Q differ in x_0, the argument in Case 1 above applies; otherwise the argument in Case 2 above applies. In either case, P and Q cannot have consecutive colours.   □

4.4   Optimal Colouring for $\sigma = 4$

The lower bound for $L(2,1,1)$ colouring is $n(4,d) = 4d$. Hence, $B(4,d) \geq 4d$. We use the following Lemma, proved in [2], about the span of an $L(\delta_1, 1, \ldots, 1)$ colouring. For the graph $G(V,E)$, [2] also defines $\lambda(G)$ as the largest colour used in an optimal colouring scheme.

Lemma 4. *[2] Consider the $L(\delta_1, 1, \ldots, 1)$-colouring problem, with $\delta_1 \geq 2$, on a graph $G = (V,E)$ such that $d(u,v) < \sigma$ for every pair of vertices u and v in V. Then $\lambda(G) = |V| - 1$ if and only if $\overline{G}$ has a Hamiltonian path.*   □

In [2], Lemma (4) is used to prove the existence of a hole in $L(2,1,1)$ colouring of $\mathcal{G}(\mathbf{Z}^2)$. Lemma (5) extends the proof to $\mathcal{G}(\mathbf{Z}^d)$.

Lemma 5. *If there is a g-$L(2,1,1)$ colouring of $\mathcal{G}(\mathbf{Z}^d)$, then $g \geq 4d$.*

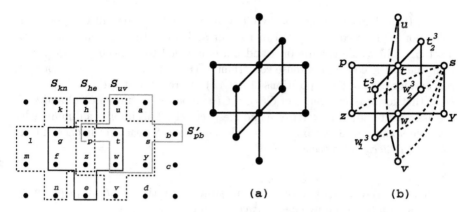

Fig. 1. A plane in $\mathcal{G}(\mathbf{Z}^d)$, (a) Induced subgraph M in $\mathcal{G}(\mathbf{Z}^3)$, and (b) Dummy edges in M

Proof. Consider the plane $\{(x_0, x_1, k_2, k_3, \ldots, k_{d-1})\}$ in $\mathcal{G}(\mathbf{Z}^d)$ where the first two coordinates can vary and k_i's are fixed constants. Such a plane is shown in Figure 1. For any vertex x in this plane, x_1^i and x_0^i denote vertices above the plane of the paper and x_2^i and x_3^i denote vertices below the plane of the paper. The subscripts 1 and 0 denote distances of 1 and 2 above the plane of the paper respectively. Similarly, the subscripts 2 and 3 denote distances of 1 and 2 below the plane of the paper respectively. The superscript i denotes the dimension of the vertex, where $(3 \leq i \leq d)$. Consider the set of vertices which make up the induced subgraph $T(\mathcal{G}(\mathbf{Z}^d), \sigma)$ denoted by M for notational convenience (illustrated in Figure 1a for three dimensions) in $\mathcal{G}(\mathbf{Z}^d)$ with distance between any two vertices less than the reuse distance 4:

$$S_{uv} = \{u, t, w, v, p, z, s, y, t_1^i, t_2^i, w_1^i, w_2^i\}, \text{ and}$$
$$S_{pb}' = \{p, t, s, b, , u, a, w, y, t_1^i, t_2^i, s_1^i, s_2^i\}$$

The points $\{a, b, s_1^i, s_2^i\}$ are adjacent to s. Consider the set of vertices in S_{pb}'. Once S_{uv} has been assigned to all different colours, the vertices $\{a, b, s_1^i, s_2^i\}$ of S_{pb}' must be assigned the colours assigned to the vertices $\{z, v, w_1^i, w_2^i\}$ if only $4d$ colours $\{0, 1, \ldots, 4d - 1\}$ are to be used. Due to the channel separation constraint, colours assigned to $\{a, b, s_1^i, s_2^i\}$ must be at least two apart from the colour assigned to vertex s. This is equivalent to adding dummy edges connecting s to $\{z, v, w_1^i, w_2^i\}$ in M induced by S_{uv}. Figure 1b shows these dummy edges in M in $\mathcal{G}(\mathbf{Z}^3)$. Repeating this argument for vertices y, z and p we get the dummy edges connecting y to $\{p, u, t_1^i, t_2^i\}$, z to $\{u, s, t_1^i, t_2^i\}$ and p to $\{y, v, w_1^i, w_2^i\}$ in S_{uv}. These edges are not shown in the Figure 1b to avoid cluttering.

Four vertices, p, t, w and z, are common between the sets S_{uv} and S_{he}, and their colours are fixed. The remaining vertices $\{h, g, f, e, p_1^i, p_2^i, z_1^i, z_2^i\}$ of S_{he} should be assigned the colours assigned to $\{u, s, y, v, t_1^i, t_2^i, w_1^i, w_2^i\}$ in S_{uv}. We are interested in the vertices u and v in S_{uv}. We want to prove that a colouring of $\mathcal{G}(\mathbf{Z}^d)$ satisfying all constraints implies a dummy edge uv in S_{uv}. For this, we will fix the colour of v (denoted by $C(v)$) in S_{he} and consider all vertices where colour of u (denoted by $C(u)$) can reoccur and prove that we can always find a set $S_{u'v'}$ in which colours of u and v are assigned to adjacent vertices. Note that due to the co-channel reuse constraint, $C(v)$ can reoccur at h, g, p_1^i or p_2^i in S_{he} and for each of these positions of v, $C(u)$ can reoccur at f, e, z_1^i or z_2^i in S_{he}. Note that for any recurrence of $C(v)$, if $C(u)$ reoccurs at e then $C(u)$ and $C(v)$ are assigned to adjacent vertices e and v espectively. This implies a dummy edge between u and v in S_{uv}. Consider the following cases for each recurrence of $C(v)$ when $C(u)$ does not reoccur at e.

Case 1: $C(v)$ reoccurs at h in S_{he}.

Here, $C(u)$ and $C(v)$ are assigned to adjacent vertices u and h respectively. This implies a dummy edge between u and v in S_{uv}.

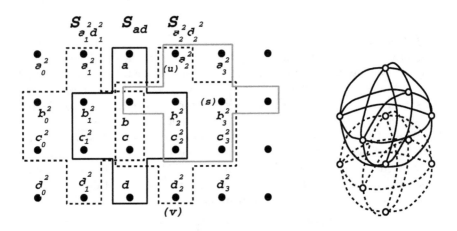

Fig. 2. New nomenclature for vertices in Figure 1, and $\overline{M}$ in $\mathcal{G}(\mathbf{Z}^3)$.

Case 2: $C(v)$ reoccurs at g, p_1^i or p_2^i in S_{he}.

To treat this case conveniently, we introduce a new nomenclature for the vertices in the plane. Figure 2 shows the new nomenclature where the vertices a, d, a_2^2 and d_2^2 correspond to vertices h, e, u and v respectively. As before, the superscripts denote the dimensions, with $i = 2$ for vertices in the plane. This case can be broken down into the following two cases.

Case 2a: $C(v)$ reoccurs at b_1^i and $C(u)$ reoccurs at c_1^i.

Without loss of generality, consider the case when $i = 2$. Here, $C(u)$ and $C(v)$ are assigned to adjacent vertices b_1^2 and c_1^2 respectively. This implies a dummy edge between u and v in S_{uv}.

Case 2b: $C(v)$ reoccurs at b_1^i and $C(u)$ reoccurs at c_1^j, where $i \neq j$ and $2 \leq i, j \leq d$.

Without loss of generality, let $C(v)$ reoccur at b_1^2. Consider the set $S_{a_1^2 d_1^2}$.

In this set, let $b_1^2 = x$ for convenience. Due to co-channel reuse constraint, $C(u)$ at c_1^i can reoccur in $S_{a_1^2 d_1^2}$ at one of b_0^2, a_1^2, x_1^i or x_2^i all of which are adjacent to b_1^2 coloured with $C(v)$.

The above two cases show that no matter where $C(u)$ and $C(v)$ reoccur in S_{he} we can always find a set $S_{u'v'}$ in which $C(u)$ and $C(v)$ are assigned to adjacent vertices. Hence we have a dummy edge connecting u and v in S_{uv} as shown in Figure 1b.

Finally, let us build $\overline{M}$, the complement of M. Figure 2 shows $\overline{M}$ in $\mathcal{G}(\mathbf{Z}^3)$ and Figure 1a shows M in $\mathcal{G}(\mathbf{Z}^3)$. Since $\overline{M}$ consists of two connected components, $\overline{M}$ cannot contain a Hamiltonian path. Hence by Lemma (4), there is no g-$L(2,1,1)$ colouring for $\mathcal{G}(\mathbf{Z}^d)$ with $g = 4d - 1$.   □

We shall use the previous strategy of colouring the base-segment and translating it to fill up $\mathcal{G}(\mathbf{Z}^d)$. Here, for the ith dimension, $t_i = 4i - 1$ and The base-segment is the set of vertices $(x_0, 0, \ldots, 0)$ with $0 \leq x_0 \leq 4d - 1$. The base-segment is coloured using the function:

$$
f(x_0) = \begin{cases} x_0 \text{ div } 4 & x_0 \bmod 4 = 0, \\ d + (x_0 \text{ div } 4) & x_0 \bmod 4 = 2, \\ 2d + 1 + (x_0 \text{ div } 4) & x_0 \bmod 4 = 3, \\ 3d + 1 + (x_0 \text{ div } 4) & x_0 \bmod 4 = 1. \end{cases} \tag{7}
$$

We now define the colouring scheme C_4, and later prove that it optimally colours $\mathcal{G}(\mathbf{Z}^d)$:

$$
C_4(x_0, \ldots, x_i, 0, \ldots, 0) = C_4(x_0 - (4i-1)x_i, \ldots, x_{i-1}, 0, \ldots, 0), 1 \leq i < d
$$
$$
C_4(x_0, 0, \ldots, 0) = f(x_0 \bmod 4d). \tag{8}
$$

We make the following observations about the colouring of the baseline:

Lemma 6. *For colouring the baseline,*

1. *The set of $4d$ colours used by the function f defined in Equation (7) is $\{0, 1, \ldots, 2d-1, 2d+1, \ldots, 4d\}$.*
2. *The difference in colours assigned to consecutive vertices (vertices differing in x_0 by 1) is at least two.*
3. *For distinct vertices u and v in the same base-segment, $f(u) \neq f(v)$.*   □

Lemma 7. *On the baseline, the following is true about vertices that are assigned consecutive colours:*

1. *If they are assigned the colours $2d + 3$ and $2d + 4$, then they are 2 apart.*
2. *If they are not assigned the colours $2d+3$ and $2d+4$, then they are $4k$ apart, where $k \neq 0, k \in I$.*   □

Theorem 4 asserts the optimality of the colouring scheme C_4; the proof for Theorem 4 is similar to the proof of Theorem 3 above.

Theorem 4 *C_4 is an optimal $L(2,1,1)$ colouring of $\mathcal{G}(\mathbf{Z}^d)$.*   □

4.5   Colouring Schema for $\mathbf{Z}^d$

A *colouring schema for* $\mathbf{Z}^d$ is a generalized scheme for $L(\delta_1, 1_{\sigma-2})$ colourings of $\mathcal{G}(\mathbf{Z}^d)$ for all d and odd values of σ. We show the existence of such schema and present a provably-correct algorithm that uses such a colouring schema for $\mathbf{Z}^d$, for colouring $\mathcal{G}(\mathbf{Z}^d)$.

Definition 1 *For* $d \geq 1$, *suppose* $\sigma > 1, N \geq n(\sigma, d)$ *are odd integers, and* $T = \langle t_1, t_2, \ldots, t_{d-1} \rangle$ *is a non-decreasing sequence of* $(d-1)$ *positive, odd integers. Then* (σ, T, N) *is a colouring schema for* $\mathbf{Z}^d$, *denoted* $\mathcal{S}_d$, *iff*

1. *for each* i, $1 \leq i < d$, $\sigma \leq t_i \leq N$, *and*
2. *for all* $X = (x_0, \ldots, x_{d-1}) \in \mathbf{Z}^d$, $X \neq \mathbf{0}$,

$$\sum_{i=0}^{d-1} |x_i| < \sigma \Longrightarrow \left(x_0 + \sum_{i=1}^{d-1} x_i \cdot t_i \right) \ mod \ N \neq 0.$$

Exhaustive verification proves the following proposition that asserts the existence of a colouring schema for $\mathbf{Z}^3$.

Proposition 1 *The triple given by* $\sigma = 5$, $T = \langle 5, 19 \rangle$, *and* $N = 27$ *is a colouring schema for* $\mathbf{Z}^3$.   □

We define in Equation (9) the coloring scheme C_d, based on a colouring schema for $\mathbf{Z}^d$, $\mathcal{S}_d = (\sigma, T = \langle t_1, \ldots, t_{d-1} \rangle, N)$. For each d, define a function $g_d(x, N)$ as:

$$g_d(x, N) = \begin{cases} \frac{x}{2}, & \text{if } x \text{ is even;} \\ \frac{x+N}{2}, & \text{otherwise.} \end{cases}$$

$$C_d(x_0, 0, \ldots, 0) = g_d((x_0 \ mod \ N), N).$$
$$C_d(x_0, x_1, \ldots, x_i, 0, \ldots, 0) = C_d(x_0 - x_i \cdot t_i, x_1, \ldots, x_{i-1}, 0, \ldots, 0). \quad (9)$$

Using properties of the colouring scheme C_d, it is easily verified that:

Theorem 5 *For* $d \geq 1$, *given* $\mathcal{S}_d = (\sigma, T = \langle t_1, \ldots, t_{d-1} \rangle, N)$, *a colouring schema,* C_d *is an* $L(\delta_1, 1_{\sigma-2})$ *colouring of* $\mathbf{Z}^d$ *where* $\delta_1 = \frac{N-t_{d-1}}{2}$. *The span of this colouring is* N.   □

The following is an immediate consequence of Proposition 1 and Theorem 5.

Corollary 1 *The colouring schema for* $\mathbf{Z}^d$ *given in Proposition 1 above witnesses an* $L(4, 1, 1, 1)$ *colouring of* $\mathcal{G}(\mathbf{Z}^3)$. *The span of the colouring is* $N = 27$.   □

We end this section with the following observation about the efficiency of the above assignment algorithms.

Lemma 8. *The running times of the above algorithms for colouring* $\mathcal{G}(\mathbf{Z}^d)$ *are* $O(d)$.

Proof. Consider the general colouring scheme C that uses the translation function t_i to colour a vertex $P = (x_0, x_1, \ldots, x_{d-1})$. The colour assigned to P is given by: $C(P) = C(x_0 - \sum_{i=1}^{d-1} x_i \cdot t_i, 0, \ldots, 0)$. Clearly, the assignment time is $O(d)$.   □

5 Conclusions and Open Problems

We investigated relationships between channel assignments in higher dimensional square and cellular grids, colorings in higher dimensional square grids and presented optimal $L(2,1)$ and $L(2,1,1)$ colourings for square grids in all dimensions $d \geq 1$. We also introduce the notion of a colouring schema for the d-dimensional square grid, and an algorithm that, given the colouring schema, assigns colours to the grid satisfying the schema constraints. Several interesting open questions arise from the work presented here. We list a few of them here: (1) Find optimal, or near-optimal, colourings for higher dimensional cellular grids. (2) Find optimal, or near-optimal, colourings for d-dimensional square grids for reuse distances larger than 4. (3) Find colouring schema $\mathbf{Z}^d$ for various values of reuse distance and dimension.

References

1. R. Battiti, A. A. Bertossi, and M. A. Bonuccelli. Assigning codes in wireless networks: bounds and scaling properties. *Wireless Networks*, 5:195–209, 1999.
2. Alan A. Bertossi, Cristina M. Pinotti, and Richard B. Tan. Efficient use of radio spectrum in wireless networks with channel separation between close stations. In *Proceedings of the DIAL M Workshop*, pages 18–27, 2000.
3. Alan A. Bertossi, Cristina M. Pinotti, and Richard B. Tan. Channel assignment with separation for special classes of wireless networks: grids and rings. In *Proceedings of IPDPS*, 2002.
4. Hans L. Boedlander, Ton Kloks, Richard B. Tan, and Jan van Leeuwen. λ-coloring of graphs. In *Proceedings of STACS*, pages 395–406, 2000.
5. J. Conway and N. Sloane. *Sphere Packings, Lattices and Groups*. Springer Verlag, second edition, 1993.
6. J. R. Griggs and R. K. Yeh. Labeling graphs with a condition at distance 2. *SIAM J. Disc. Math.*, pages 586–595, 1992.
7. W.K. Hale. Frequency assignment: Theory and application. *Proceedings of the IEEE*, 68:1497–1514, 1980.
8. Robert A. Murphey, Panos M. Pardalos, and Mauricio G.C. Resende. Frequency assignment problems. In *Handbook of Combinatorial Optimization*. Kluwer Academic Press, 1999.
9. Dayanand S. Rajan and Anil M. Shende. A characterization of root lattices. *Discrete Mathematics*, 161:309–314, 1996.

Efficient Location Management by Movement Prediction of the Mobile Host

Goutam Chakraborty

Iwate Prefectural University Department of Software & Information Sc.
Takizawa Mura, Iwate, Japan 020-0193
goutam@soft.iwate-pu.ac.jp

Abstract. The mobile host's mobility profile, in a Personal Communication Network (PCN) environment, is modeled. It is argued that, for
a majority of mobile hosts (MHs) for most of the time, the movement
profile repeats on a day-to-day basis. The next movement strongly depends on the present location and the time of the day. Such a pattern
for individual MHs is learned and modeled at the Home Location Register (HLR), and downloaded to the mobile terminal which can verify
its correctness real-time. The model is not static and re-learning is initiated as the behavior of the mobile host changes. The model assumes
that the past patterns will repeat in future, and a past causal relationship (i.e., next state depends on previous state) continue into the future.
This facilitates the system to predict to a high degree of accuracy the
location of the MH. As the model is trained up, the frequency of updates
decreases as well as the probability of success in paging improves. The
movement-pattern model is continuously verified locally, so that any deviation is immediately detected. The validity of the proposed model is
verified through simulations.

1 Introduction

Public communication service (PCS) networks employ a cellular architecture. It
divides its service area, say a large city, into a number contiguous small cells as
shown in Fig. 1. The coverage of a cell, may vary from a few hundred meters
to a few kilometers. Though regular hexagonal cells are drawn, the size and
shape of the cells may vary depending on the situation, e.g., uneven terrain or
buildings in the service area. Communications to or from all the mobile hosts
within a cell are via the base station, installed around the center of the cell.
These communications are by radio channels. Thus communications between
base stations and the mobile hosts use a very costly resource, as the bandwidth
of the radio channel available to a service provider is very limited. Base stations,
and base stations to other stationary telephone switching centers, are connected
by wireline networks. The wireline networks usually have large bandwidths. So
communications at that level is cheaper.

As an incoming call comes to a mobile user, the system has to locate the
receiving host first to get him connected. Thus the network has to send a signal

S.K. Das and S. Bhattacharya (Eds.): IWDC 2002, LNCS 2571, pp. 142–153, 2002.

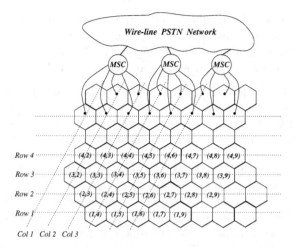

Fig. 1. The cellular architecture of PCS network

to cells, where the user is probably located, and to find where he exactly is. This process is called *terminal paging*, or in short *paging*. If all the cells are *paged* simultaneously, then the user could be located with probability 1 and in the first trial, without any delay. This is called a pure *paging* strategy. In case of PCS networks, as the number of cells is very large, for pure paging an enormous signaling traffic will be involved, even for moderately large networks [14]. In order to avoid such a costly *paging*, the mobile user has to report its location time to time to the system, so that the system knows his whereabouts. This process of reporting is called *location update*. For the system to be always aware of the present location of the mobile host, this update should be done every time the MH crosses the boundary of a cell. But, as in PCS network the cell size is small, if a mobile user has to report its location every time it crosses the boundary of a cell, a lot of channel resource as well as system processing resource will be consumed. In fact, in [18] it is shown by simulation, that if for each cell crossing there is an update message, the signaling traffic due to updating alone would contribute about 70% additional traffic.

To optimize these costs, a compromise between the above two extreme approaches of *paging* and *updating* is done. A number of neighboring cells (base stations) are grouped into what is called *location areas* (LAs). Thus, the whole PCS network is divided into a few number of LAs. Whenever a mobile user crosses the boundary of a LA, it reports (updates). On the other hand, the system pages all the cells of the LA, from where the mobile user had updated last. This simple approach or slight variations of it are prevailing at present.

Personal Communication Network (PCN) environment is characterized by a high density of mobile users moving across very small cells. It will not scale well and will add a huge additional traffic overhead over the costly wireless channels, if the mobile users need to update their locations at a high frequency. With decreasing cell sizes, the number of cells in a LA is becoming large and paging them all is also costly. This update and paging costs together constitute what is called location management cost. During the last decade many research works were reported to reduce this location management cost. Four such schemes are:

1. *Time based* [16]: Here the mobile user updates its location to the system at constant intervals.
2. *Movement based* [6]: Here, every time the mobile user crosses a boundary, a counter is increased by 1. When the count reaches a threshold, the user updates.
3. *Distance based* [13] [10]: Here, the user updates when he moved certain threshold distance from the last updated location.
4. *Zone based* [17] [12]: mobile user updates whenever he crosses a LA boundary. The zone here means LA. A variation of it, called overlay zones is used by NTT DoCoMo in Japan. Here, the zone is redefined with the MH's location at the center, when the MH crosses a zone and updates. In effect, it is same as distance based scheme.

It is easy to see that, except for the *distance based* scheme, fixed duration of time threshold (for *time based* scheme) or same zone size (for *zone based* scheme) for all the users could not achieve optimization of location management cost. This is because the movement profile for different users are considerably different. On the other hand, implementing distance-based scheme calls for some global location information of the cells in the network.

A common paging and updating scheme for all the users would produce unnecessary wireless traffic with respect to most of the mobile users, who are more static or with highly regular movement profile. On the other hand, it could be insufficient for some quickly moving users with changing movement profile. To improve location management cost, Xie et al. [17] proposed a dynamic scheme that determines the LA area by reflecting the call arrival rate and average velocity of each subscriber. An integer programming model was proposed by Kim et al. [11]. Another proposed approach [19] is to use a probabilistic location update scheme. In [20], each mobile user is associated with a set of regions which are derived from the user's movement pattern, and using that information the location management cost is reduced.

In most of the works till date, the mobile host's movement is modeled as a stochastic random walk, based on which the location management strategies are evaluated. Our basic assumption is different. In most of the cases, the mobile user repeats a certain course everyday, like leaving home and traveling to the workplace, goes out during mid-day break to have lunch, in the evening returns home, go to a health club, etc. etc. If this movement pattern could be concisely modeled, the location management cost could be considerably reduced by reducing the frequency of updates as well as the number of simultaneously paged cells. The most notable work in this regard are [8] [7], where they used the algorithm of compression technology [15] to capture the mobility profile. Essentially, they tried to capture the movement pattern, i.e., the sequence of cells visited, by using Markov model, and thereby predicting the next cell. The pattern of the sequence of cells traveled is learned, and stored in a dictionary which is used for paging.

The main contribution of this work is to propose a light-weight model to capture movement profile of the mobile user. A copy of the model is downloaded at the mobile host which facilitates real-time verification of the model. Any deviation of movement from this model could be detected immediately. With the help of this model, the paging is done efficiently, even with sparse updations.

We assume hexagonal cells, which is used in most of the previous works [1], [2], [3], [4], and in many others. A very similar approach could be used for cells with any regular shape. The PCN model and example mobility patterns are explained in section 2. What the mobility-capturing-model should ideally be able to learn, and what possible simplifications we could do to make it a simple concise model, is explained in section 3. The working of the model and its prediction results are also reported in this section. In section 5, we discuss the contributions of the work, the pitfalls of the model, possible extensions, and about necessary simulations to be done to complete evaluation of the model.

2   The PCN Network and the Mobility Model

2.1   Network Model

We assume hexagonal cell structure of the PCN network, as shown in Fig. 2. Inside the cell, we put the corresponding labels, which are duples describing the row and column number of the corresponding cell. The labels now represent the relative location information of the cells too. When the mobile host moves from one cell, it has to enter one of its neighboring cells. By this movement the cell label changes by small integral values +1 or −1, depending on the direction of the movement.

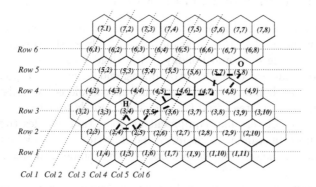

Fig. 2. PCN network with regular hexagonal cells, with an example of the profile

2.2   The User Mobility Pattern

To understand how we should describe the movement, to be able to capture the mobility pattern, let us first examine a typical behavior of a mobile host. In Fig. 2, we show such an example with dashed line. The mobile host's home is at cell $\langle 3, 4 \rangle$, indicated by the letter **H**, and his office is at cell $\langle 5, 8 \rangle$, indicated by the letter **O**. Suppose everyday around 9:00 am he leaves home, and reaches office via cells $\langle 2, 5 \rangle$, $\langle 3, 5 \rangle$, $\langle 3, 6 \rangle$, $\langle 4, 5 \rangle$, $\langle 4, 6 \rangle$, $\langle 4, 7 \rangle$, $\langle 5, 7 \rangle$, $\langle 5, 8 \rangle$. At 12:00 noon, he goes out to lunch at a restaurant in cell $\langle 4, 8 \rangle$. In the evening, around 6:00pm, he retraces the path to home. Sometime goes to play tennis at a club situated in cell $\langle 2, 4 \rangle$, and often dines out at a restaurant in cell $\langle 2, 5 \rangle$. This may be a bit simplistic, but realistic too. Many of the mobile users mobility pattern are as regular and simple as described above during the working days of the week, and building a model to capture this behavior is not difficult. On the other hand, for a salesman for example, there is no such pattern, and a stable model is not possible. Conventional *distance based* scheme is to be used for such users.

We observe that the movement direction depends on the present location, and the time of the day. When the mobile user is in cell $\langle 4, 6 \rangle$ and the time is around 9:00am to 10:00am, we can predict that he is moving towards cell $\langle 4, 7 \rangle$, whereas if the time is in the evening, we can assume that he is moving towards cell $\langle 4, 5 \rangle$. Thus, for every cell location and time of the day, a sequence of movement pattern is there, which is more or less stable. Yet the exact time of crossing the same cell boundary may vary a lot from day to day. For example, if someone leaves office at 5:00 pm on a day, he may take more than an hour to reach home due to traffic. When he leaves office at 9:00pm, it may take just a quarter of an hour. The sequence of cells traveled are same, but the times of crossing cell boundaries are quite different. While modeling, the data should be abstracted such that the essential sequence is retained. How this is done is explained in the next section.

2.3   Movement Data to Train the Model

We consider a mobile host's movement pattern which is repeated over a period of twenty four hours, i.e., the duration of a day. Obviously, this pattern will be different on working days and holidays. We consider the example of a working day movement pattern over the two-dimensional hexagonal topology of cells. For weekends and holidays, when the traffic as a whole is low, existing efficient strategies like overlay area could be used. Each mobile user has an unique identification number or terminal equipment number, that enables the network to identify the user. In standard system, each cell broadcasts a unique identity that all the mobiles in the cell can receive. So, at every moment the mobile knows its location.

When a new user registers, the location management is done using conventional schemes, like *distance-based* strategy. During this period, the mobile host updates its location every time while crossing a cell boundary, and at the end of the day the data for the whole day is available at HLR. Such data for a few consecutive working days are collected. After simple preprocessing, the data to train the model is filtered out. The filtering extracts the core pattern and sheds stray diversions. The data for two consecutive days are shown in the Table. 1. The time is in minutes, where at midnight it is set to 000. On different days, the sequence of cells crossed are same, but times of these crossing are different. Thus, exact times could not be used to train the model. In fact, what is important is the sequence and not the exact times.

Table 1. Data from which the model learn the movement pattern. Here, time = time in minutes where 000 is midnight; loc = Cell location of the MH; BL = Time block; move = Movement direction.

Row	Day 1			Day 2			Train data		
no.	time	loc	move	time	loc	move	BL	loc	move
01	544	34	-1 +1	536	34	-1 +1	1	34	-1 +1
02	551	25	+1 0	548	25	+1 0	1	25	+1 0
03	553	35	0 +1	553	35	0 +1	1	35	0 +1
04	559	36	+1 -1	558	36	+1 -1	1	36	+1 -1
05	564	45	0 +1	562	45	0 +1	1	45	0 +1
06	567	46	0 +1	567	46	0 +1	2	46	0 +1
07	570	47	+1 0	572	47	+1 0	2	47	+1 0

We propose a simple way of abstracting the sequence, which is shown in the last five columns of the Table. 1. The steps are:

1. The whole data is divided into blocks of maximum size *BL_size*, say 5 or 10. In Table. 1, the data is divided into blocks of 5 cells.
2. Two same cell locations with different movement directions should not come in the same block. In case the MH moves within two or three neighbouring cells only, this is difficult to ensure. For such users, *distance based* scheme works best.
3. The user's cell location at the head of each block is matched for data on different days. This is to ensure that a block of cells represent the same region of the movement pattern, when the block number is same.
4. If a MH remains in a cell for a long time, we terminate the block with that location as last entry. Thus a new block starts with a new sequence of movement, e.g., a new block starts when the user leaves home for office, or leaves office for home etc.
5. To keep number of entries in every block equal to *BL_size*, we add dummy entries at the end for smaller blocks. The cell location is kept same as the last entry and the movement is set to $\langle 0, 0 \rangle$.

The data table to train the model is prepared at HLR using the above algorithm, after collecting data for a few days. During processing of the data it is checked if the movement really forms a pattern or not. If yes, the average time of the starting of each block is also recorded. During preparation of the train data, it is also inferred if the movement has a regular pattern or not. For an user, when there is no clear pattern, *distance based* strategy is used for location management.

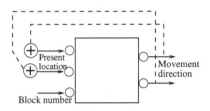

Fig. 3. Mobility Profile Model

2.4   The Model

The important properties, the model should satisfy are:

1. It should learn the regular movement pattern from the train data.
2. Depending on the time of the day, the model should be able to output a set of cells, within which the mobile host should be present with a very high probability. Thus, the model should be able to tell about a zone which the system should page, when there is an incoming call.
3. The model should be able to detect and relearn, if the mobility behavior changes permanently. On the other hand, the model should be able to ignore a short temporary change in movement pattern.

There are several possible ways, with varying complexity, to model the movement pattern. Our model is shown in Fig. 3, where inside the box we used a feed-forward neural network, as shown in Fig. 5. The model has three inputs, two representing the present cell location and one for the block number, which is but an abstraction of the position in the whole sequence of movements. Two output nodes represent the direction of movement.

In the neural network model, the hidden layer consists of 5 units. For this model the total number of connection weight parameters is therefore $(5 \times 3 + 5 \times 2) = 25$. Thus, to download this model to the MH, all that is needed is to transfer only 25 real numbers from the system. The training of the network is done at HLR during lowest traffic hours of the day. The training is very fast, and by experiments it is found that the prediction of the correct movement direction is easily achieved. As unit output functions are used for outputs, the outputs shown in Fig.5 are floating point numbers. It is easy to define simple threshold output functions so that the outputs are 0, +1, and -1, and matches exactly with that of the data table. More details are available in simulation section.

3   The Working Principle of Pattern Based Location Management

As a new MH registers, for a few days all cell-crossing data are collected at the MH and uploaded to the system at intervals. From those data, the system decides if there is a regular movement pattern or not. If there is one, the data is divided into blocks or regions of cells those are visited sequentially by the MH. An artificial neural network, as shown in Fig. 5, is trained with the data, and verified for the correct performance. Two inputs to the neural network are the cell location, and one for the block number. The two outputs are movement directions.

Once the neural network is ready, it is used to predict the set of cells the MH would reside, denoted by Γ_i, during the block i. It is easy to compute Γ_i using the model shown in Fig. 3. The sequence starts at 00:00 hrs, when the MH location is at $\langle \alpha_H, \beta_H \rangle$, its home-cell. The movement directions, obtained as output of the neural network, are fed back and added to the cell location part of the input as shown in Fig. 5. It is carried out for *BL_size* times, after which the block number is to be incremented by 1. Thus a very simple algorithm is used to compute Γ_i set of cells for different values of i. Essentially, different Γ_is are stored concisely in the neural network.

Based on this information of the Movement Pattern, a variety of schemes for location management could be designed. The flow chart of one proposed in this paper is shown in Fig. 4. As the MH knows its present cell location, it can ensure inside which block it is now moving. This information only is updated. After a cell crossing, if the MH is neither in Γ_i nor in $\Gamma_{(i+1)}$, it is concluded that it has either jumped to some other block, or is out of the learned movement pattern. What the case is, is decided at the system. If necessary, the location management is switched to *distance based*.

In normal situation, the communication between MH and the system is required only when the MH verifies that it has moved to the next block of cells. This happens whenever *BL_size* number of cells are crossed. When the MH goes out of the stored movement pattern, and when it returns back to the learned course, we need communication between MH and the system. The first one is initiated by the mobile host, and the second one by the system. These communications, by which the MH and the system are aware of their mutual states, are shown by dashed line in the algorithm flow chart of Fig. 4.

Whenever there is an incoming call, the system pages *BL_size* number of cells. The probability of finding the MH in that set of cells is 1. In *distance based* scheme, all the cells within the radius of the distance has to be paged. This involves a more paging cost, and is necessary as there is no clue to which direction that MH would move. If selective paging [5] is used, the paging delay could be high and ultimately the system may have to page more than *BL_size* number of cells.

For a very punctual person, and in a planned city where the road traffic always move smoothly, the user's movement pattern would be very regular. In that case, the block number of the movement data will have a direct correspondence

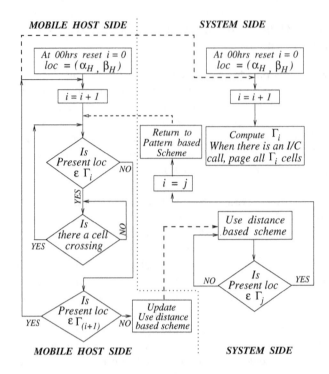

Fig. 4. The Movement Pattern based scheme

with the time of the day. If there is an incoming call for such a user at time t, the system find the corresponding block number τ, and pages the cells belonging to Γ_τ. If the users could not be found in Γ_τ set of cells, next all cells in $\Gamma_{(\tau-1)}$ and $\Gamma_{(\tau+1)}$ are paged, and next all cells in $\Gamma_{(\tau-2)}$ and $\Gamma_{(\tau+2)}$ are paged. This is essentially like selective paging, but exploits the knowledge of the movement pattern of the particular user. In this case, one is needed to page much less number of cells. The algorithm at the MH's side, to check if the actual movement is deviated from the one represented by the neural network, would be the same as described in Fig. 4.

4   Simulation

Till date, in all the reported works related to location management, the movement of the MH is modeled as random walk. We consider the movement to have some purpose, which is more realistic. While creating sample movement patterns, for any user the cell location of its home and working place is fixed first. Cell-sequential paths from home to the working place and back are also fixed. The time of crossing the boundaries of cells varies over a mean value. Thus the time of leaving home could be anything between 8a.m. to 10a.m. and the time of leaving office for home could be anything between 5p.m. to 9p.m. Normal variances are added to the average time of duration from entering a cell and leaving the same on the way of movement.

We created movement data for a user for 5 days and processed it according to the steps mentioned in section 2.3 to have the blocked training data set. The data is used to train a neural network (NN), with 3 input units, 5 hidden layer neurons, and 2 output units, as shown in Fig. 5. The NN is trained with error back-propagation training algorithm. Logistic activation function is used for hidden unit neurons, and tan hyperbolic activation function is used for output layer neurons. This is done because the output could take values +1, 0, and -1. Through simulations it is verified that the NN can be trained and store the movement table correctly. In Fig. 5, the three nodes on the left are input nodes. When the present cell location is $\langle 5, 8 \rangle$, and the *block number* is 5, the movement direction is shown as -0.997 in the x-direction, and 0.1057 in the y-direction. In fact, the actual movement is -1, and 0 respectively. It is easy to modify the output function of the output units using a threshold function to achieve this correct output values.

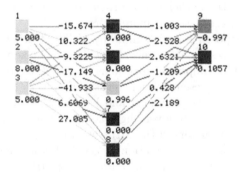

Fig. 5. The neural network model to capture movement pattern

The predictor module is tested by simulation and found to behave correctly. In the next phase, we would model the whole system with a few thousand users. There will be a certain percentage of people with regular movement patterns, and the rest with random movements. Then, the combined updation and paging cost, for the proposed pattern based scheme and other standard strategies like *distance based*, will to be compared. We are yet to do this simulation to evaluate our scheme.

5   Conclusion and Discussion

We have proposed a movement pattern based location management scheme, which learns the regular movement pattern of mobile users to improve update and paging costs. An artificial neural network model is trained to capture the movement pattern, when it is regular. A similar module is communicated to the MH. The MH can easily check the validity of the module in real-time, and in case its movement deviates from that, it switches to conventional location management schemes. The overall improvement in location management cost depends on what percentage of mobile users have regular movement patterns.

The only strong assumption in this work is that, we assume the cells to be forming a mesh or they have regular hexagonal shapes. In fact, in the design stage, the network is always considered having hexagonal cells. Moreover, it is always possible to map any network with cells of irregular shape to hexagonal cell network, if for all the cells in the network the number of neighbouring cells is always 6 or less.

In the algorithm for preparing training data, in section 2.3, we made all the blocks of data of the same size BL_size, if necessary by adding dummy entries. It is also possible to have blocks of variable sizes, when it would be necessary to have the block number appearing at the output of the artificial neural network model. In that case the neural network will have 3 outputs. When the MH will go to the next block is also indicated by the model itself. We tried both options, and have seen that the earlier one is easier to train, and give correct answer. Also, the model representation is more concise.

The scheme proposed here is simple to realize. During low traffic hour, it is possible to preprocess the raw movement data to make the training data for the ANN, and to make important decisions like whether the movement pattern is regular or not. The present model consists of only 25 connection weight parameters, which is easy to download and keep at the MH. The prediction, as explained in section 3, involves very light computation. Thus keeping those few lines of codes and parameters in the MH's working memory is feasible.

If it is observed that the deviation of the MH from the learned pattern is frequent, the collection of movement data by the MH and the training of the NN for the new movement data will be done again to update the model. For more complex mobility pattern, more than one next cell is possible with different probabilities. It is difficult to realize such a situation with neural network model. At present, we are working on a more general statistical prediction model.

References

1. M. Zhang, T. P. Yum, "Comparisons of channel-assignment strategies in cellular mobile telephone systems", IEEE transactions on Vehicular technology, vol. vt-38, No.4, pp. 211–215, November 1989.
2. A. Baiocchi, F. D. Priscolim F. Grilli, and F. Sestini, "The geometric dynamic channel allocation as a practical strategy in mobile networks with bursty user mobility", IEEE transactions on Vehicular technology, vol. vt-44, No.1, pp. 14–23, February 1995.
3. Z. Dong, and Ten H. Lai, "An efficient priority-based dynamic channel allocation strategy for mobile cellular networks", Proceedings of IEEE INFOCOM, pp. 6–13, 1997.

4. H. G. Sandalidis, P. P. Stavroulakis, J. Rodriguez-Tellez, "An efficient evolutionary algorithm for channel resource management in cellular mobile systems", IEEE transactions on Evolutionary Computation, vol. 2, No.4, pp. 125–137, November 1998.
5. I. F. Akyildiz and J. S. M. Ho, "Movement-based location update and selective paging for PCS networks," IEEE/ACM Transactions on Networking, 4(4):629–638, December 1995.
6. A. Bar-Noy, I. Kessler and M. Sidi, "Mobile users: To update or not to update?" Wireless Networks, 1(2):175–185, July 1995.
7. Amiya Bhattacharya, and Sajal K. Das, "LeZi-Update: An Information-Theoretic Approach to Track Mobile Users in PCS Networks," Proc. ACM/IEEE International Conference on Mobile Computing and Networking (MobiCom'99), 1–12, 1999.
8. A. Bhattacharya, and Sajal K. Das, "LeZi-Update: An Information-Theoretic Framework for Personal Mobility Tracking in PCS Networks," ACM/Kluwer Journal on Wireless Networks (Special Issue on selected Mobicom'99 papers, Guest Eds: T. Imilienski and M. Steenstrup), Vol. 8, No. 2–3, pp. 121–135, Mar-May 2002.
9. S. K. Das and S. K. Sen, "A new location update strategy for cellular networks and its implementation using a genetic algorithm," Proc. ACM/IEEE International Conference on Mobile Computing and Networking (MobiCom'97), 185–194, September 1997.
10. J.S.M. Ho and I.F. Akyildiz, "Mobile user location update and paging under delay constraints," Wireless Networks, 1(4):413–425, December 1995.
11. S.J. Kim and C.Y. Lee, "Modeling and analysis of the dynamic location registration and paging in microcellular systems," IEEE Transactions on Vehicular Technology, 45(1):82–90, February 1996.
12. S. Subramanian, S. Madhavapeddy, "System Partitioning in a Cellular Network", Proc. of IEEE Vehicular Technology Conference, 1996.
13. U. Madhow, M.L. Honig and K. Steiglitz, 'Optimization of wireless resources for personal communications mobility tracking,' IEEE/ACM Transactions on Networking, 3(6):698–707, December 1995.
14. D. Plassmann, "Location management strategies for mobile cellular networks of 3rd generation," Proc. 44th IEEE Vehicular Technology Conference, 649–653, June 1994.
15. J. Rissamen and G.G. Langdon, "Universal modeling and coding," IEEE Transactions on Information Theory, 27(1):12–23, January 1981.
16. C. Rose and R. Yates, "Minimizing the average cost of paging under delay constraints," Wireless Networks, 1(2):211–219, July 1995.
17. H. Xie, S. Tabbane and D. Goodman, "Dynamic location area management and performance analysis," Proc. 43rd IEEE Vehicular Technology Conference, 533–539, May, 1993.
18. K.S. Hellstern, E. Alonso, and D. Oniel, "The Use of SS7 and GSM to support high density personal communication," Third Winlab Workshop on Third Generation Wireless Information Networks, pp. 175–186, April 1992.
19. Wha Sook Jeon, and Dong Geun Jeong, "Performance of Improved Probabilistic Location Update Scheme for Cellular Mobile Networks," IEEE Transactions on Vehicular Technology, 49(6):2164–2173, November 2000.
20. Shou-Chih Lo, and Arbee L. P. Chen, "Adaptive Region-Based Location Management for PCS Systems," IEEE Transactions on Vehicular Technology, 51(4):667–676, July 2002.

Multipath Routing to Provide Quality of Service in Mobile Ad Hoc Networks

L.M. Patnaik and Anand Suvernkar

Microprocessor Applications Laboratory
Department of Computer Science and Automation
Indian Institute Of Science, Bangalore-560012
lalit@micro.iisc.ernet.in
sanand@csa.iisc.ernet.in

Abstract. Because of frequent topology changes and node failures, providing quality of service routing in mobile ad hoc networks becomes a very critical issue. The quality of service can be provided by routing the data along multiple paths. Such selection of multiple paths helps to improve reliability and load balancing, reduce delay introduced due to route rediscovery in presence of path failures. There are basically two issues in such a multipath routing .Firstly, the sender node needs to obtain the exact topology information. Since the nodes are continuously roaming, obtaining the exact topology information is a tough task. Here, we propose an algorithm which constructs highly accurate network topology with minimum overhead. The second issue is that the paths in the path set should offer best reliability and network throughput. This is achieved in two ways 1) by choice of a proper metric which is a function of residual power, traffic load on the node and in the surrounding medium 2) by allowing the reliable links to be shared between different paths.

Subject Descriptors
General Terms. Algorithms, Performance, Simulation
Keywords. Mobile ad hoc network, IEEE 802.11 MAC standard, dynamic source routing protocol, network throughput, energy consumption, link sharing, control overhead reduction.

1 Introduction

A mobile ad hoc network is a collection of mobile, roaming, wireless computers forming a temporary network based on radio to radio multi-hopping. Routing in MANET is a non-trivial task because of continuous movement of nodes, changing network topology and hence requires robust and flexible mechanism to discover and maintain the routes.

Mobile ad hoc networks are expected to fulfill a critical role in applications where wired backbone is either not available or not rapidly deployable. These applications span over public, tactical as well as commercial sectors.

S.K. Das and S. Bhattacharya (Eds.): IWDC 2002, LNCS 2571, pp. 154–163, 2002.
© Springer-Verlag Berlin Heidelberg 2002

1.1 Related Work

The single path routing algorithms discover a single path from the source to the destination. However, if the path breaks due to node mobility, again a new path has to be discovered, which is a costly operation adding considerable load on the network and adding considerable delay in the data traffic. One solution to this problem is to use multiple paths for data routing. Due to such multipath routing, even if one path fails, data can still be routed to the destination using the other routes. Thus, the cost of re-discovering new path can be salvaged.

All the multipath routing protocols, use dynamic source routing protocol [6,10]. In this protocol, the complete route to the destination is stored in each data packet which is to be routed. These routes are first obtained in the *route discovery* phase of the dynamic source routing protocol. The *route maintenance* phase takes care of maintaining the routes during the routing of data packets.

An algorithm to choose the most reliable path set is discussed in [1]. The metric used to measure the reliability, is *received signal strength*. However, the received signal strength is not the only reason for the unreliability of a link. There are many other factors like the load on the nodes and the load in the medium surrounding the nodes. Secondly, this algorithm doesn't allow to have shared links. Hence, the reliability of highly reliable links can not be fully exploited. Thirdly, this algorithm doesn't assume a shared medium, which is an unrealistic assumption.

In [2], Wu and Harms assume the existence of a shared medium and consider the correlation factor between two paths as a measurement of interference between the two paths. But the algorithm chooses the paths in the order in which the route requests arrive at the destination. Hence, it chooses paths which are not necessarily reliable. Secondly, the correlation factor which is the number of links joining one node from one path to another node from the second path, fails to capture the load which is already present in the medium surrounding the nodes on the routes.

The route discovery phase is of critical importance in the multipath routing because in order to select multiple paths for routing, the sender node needs to have a very accurate knowledge about the network topology. And this should be achieved with minimum control overhead. The above papers do not give optimized solution for this problem.

1.2 Contributions

In this paper, we give an algorithm for *route discovery* with minimal control overhead. Using this route discovery algorithm, it is possible for the sender node to get better knowledge about the network. It helps in choosing reliable path set.

Selection of a set of paths is in itself a nontrivial task. Due to power and bandwidth constraints, the multipath routing protocol should distribute the load fairly among the mobile nodes. An unbalanced assignment of data traffic results into power depletion on heavily loaded mobile nodes. In addition to power depletion, the unfair distribution also results into reduction in throughput because the data packets routed along heavily loaded mobile nodes take more time to reach the destination.

Even if a route comprising of lightly loaded mobile nodes is chosen, it does not guarantee higher throughput because the traffic in the surrounding medium also affects the throughput offered by the route. Hence the load in the surrounding medium of mobile nodes should also be considered.

While choosing the path set if only disjoint paths are selected, the reliability of a highly reliable link can not be used by more than one path in presence of path failure..

In short, while selecting the path set the following issues should be considered.

- The distribution of load should be even. Mobile nodes with lower traffic load should be preferred to the heavily loaded mobile nodes.
- The traffic load in the medium surrounding the mobile nodes on the routes, should be light
- The paths should comprise of nodes with high residual battery power.
- If a link is highly reliable, it is advantageous to allow it to be shared by more than one path.

Here, we define a metric that can capture the above mentioned conditions and using a K-shortest paths selection algorithm, we find the K best paths that can have shared links. We also provide a method that maintains these routes and distributes the data among these paths.

The paper is organized in the following way. Section 2 describes an algorithm to gather most accurate knowledge about the network topology at the sender node with minimum control overhead in route discovery phase. Section 3 describes the metric that will be used for path set selection. Section 4 describes the methods to compute the values of the parameters used in the metric. Section 5 describes the *K-shortest paths selection algorithm*. Section 6 describes the management of the paths in the path set and how the data traffic is distributed among these paths. Section 7 gives the performance evaluation of the new protocol. Section 8 concludes the paper.

2 Building Network Topology with Minimum Control Overhead

When a node has some data to be routed to some destination, it starts the route discovery phase of the multipath routing protocol. In this phase, it locally broadcasts the *route discovery* packets. Each of *route discovery* packets is uniquely identified by a source identifier and a sequence number. The sequence number distinguishes between two different sessions of route discovery from the same node. Each node maintains a cache of routes called *RoutesSeen,* to other nodes. Using various DSR optimizations like tapping, the nodes keep the cache updated. The new route discovery protocol can be summarized as follows.

- When an intermediate node receives a *route request* packet, it first checks whether the packet has already visited this node. This can be done by looking at the route the packet has taken before visiting this node. If the packet has already visited the current node, then the node ignores the packet.
- Otherwise, it checks whether there are already some paths to the destination in its *RoutesSeen* cache. If so, it returns a *route reply* packet with selected paths.
- If there are no paths to the destination in the *RoutesSeen* cache, then the node checks whether some route request packet with same source-id and sequence number has already visited this node. If so, it adds the route the packet has taken in reaching the current node in *RequestsSeen* cache. If not, it again locally broadcasts the route request packet.

- When the route request packet reaches the destination, it replies with *route reply* packet, copying the path the *route request* packet had taken, into the route reply packet. Now the *route reply* packet is forwarded along this path to the source.
- When an intermediate node receives the *route reply* packet, it checks whether there are some routes in the *RequestsSeen* cache to the destination of the *route reply* packet. For each of such routes, the node sends a route reply packet to the destination of the route reply replacing the prefix P_c of the routes in the route reply packet by the cached route. The prefix P_c of the route in the route reply packet is the reverse of the path the route reply packet would have followed to reach its destination from the current node, if no replacements of subpaths would be done.
- When the route discovery initiator receives the route reply packet, it adds all the links that form these paths into a link cache. This link cache is used further to build the network topology graph and choose the best paths to the destination.

3   Finding Link Cost

The aim here is to define a link metric which can be used to find K paths which are the best in terms of power consumption and throughput they offer. So, such a metric should capture following characteristics

1. **Residual battery power:** Nodes with higher residual battery power should be preferred to nodes with less battery power. This is because an unfair load distribution may result into network partition.
2. **Effect of surrounding objects:** The surrounding objects and medium greatly affect the link error rate.
3. **Surrounding traffic overload:** If there is heavy traffic in the medium around a node, the node will,on an average, have to wait for longer period before its turn to send the data packet comes. This can drastically affect the throughput.
4. **Traffic load on the node:** The traffic load on nodes directly affects the throughput.

Let 'L' be a link. Of the 2 nodes on the link 'L', let 'A' be the one which is further away from the source of the data traffic. Assume,

P_A :Residual power of node A
UR_L: Unreliability of link 'L'
TO_A: Traffic load in the medium surrounding node A
QL_A: Average network output queue length for node A
Then, the cost of this link is given by the following equation

$$LC_L = Log[(a * QL_A * UR_L)/(TO_A * P_A)] \tag{1}$$

where 'a' is a scaling factor
The UR_L value is measured as the inverse of received signal strength. The QL_A value is measured as the weighted average of lengths of the different priority network output queues. The computation of TO_A is done as explained in the following section.

4   IEEE 802.11 MAC Standard and Computation of TO

The IEEE 802.11 standard [4,5] covers the MAC sublayer and the physical layer of the OSI reference model. This standard supports two services, one is *Distributed Co-ordination Function* for contention mode and the other one is *Point Coordination Function* for the contention-free mode. To gain control of the medium, the DCF mode uses the *Carrier Sense Multiple Access with Collision Avoidance (CSMA/CA)*. The CSMA/CA protocol works by having the host that wishes to send a data frame sensing the medium and if no activity is detected in the surrounding medium, it will wait for a random period of time called as *'backoff time'* and if still no activity is found , it will send the packet. In order to avoid the near-far problem or the hidden terminal problem, it optionally uses RTS/CTS mechanism. Any host that wants to send a packet, first sends a RTS packet. When the destination receives the RTS packet, it replies with a CTS packet. After receiving the CTS packet, the sender node sends the data frame. After receiving the data frame, the receiver sends the acknowledgement for the data frame. Due to this RTS/CTS mechanism, all other nodes become aware of the data transmission and do not send any packet. Also, in the RTS, CTS packets, the sender and receiver respectively, give the approximate time by which the data transmission will be completed. Each other listening nodes note this value called as *Network Allocation Vector* (NAV). This helps the other nodes to wait for that amount of time before sensing the medium again. This is called as *virtual carrier sensing*.

Now we discus an algorithm that probabilistically determines the traffic load present around a node. The time axis of the node is divided into variable size time periods. The time period starts at the end of a NAV. Let WAIT_MAX be the maximum possible value of backoff. If no node sends any packet in this duration, it means that no neighboring node has any data to send. So, the time period ends. In case, some node sends a RTS packet or data frame before the WAIT_MAX time, the time period ends when the receiver sends the acknowledgement for the data frame.. Each node records such MAX readings at the most. Let $S_1, S_2...$and S_N be the readings recorded by the node where N is a.positive integer less than or equal to MAX. The traffic load is the average of these readings and is obtained as.

$$TO=(S_1+S_2...S_N)/N \tag{2}$$

The TO value indicates the traffic surrounding the node. This can be explained as follows.

Each node generates a delay between 0 and WAIT_MAX time. Let us assume the random number generator is perfectly random. Hence the probability density function is uniform. Let $S_1, S_2..$ and S_N be the lowest values of random delays generated among all the neighboring nodes. So, larger the number of nodes, the probability of the minimum random delay value being lower will be higher.

The TO value also indicates the traffic around the node. This is because if the traffic is light, many time periods will be idle. In such cases, the time period will be WAIT_MAX. Hence, the value of TO will be larger. Hence, higher value of TO indicate lower traffic and vice-versa.

The value of MAX is changed dynamically. If the number of neighbors sending packets is large, then the value of MAX should be increased because the use of less number of samples will not give an exact estimate of the traffic around the node. So, if the number of active neighbors is large and the number of idle time periods is very less, then the value of MAX is increased linearly. On the other hand, if the number of idle time periods crosses the predefined lower threshold, the value of MAX is reduced.

We will explain the following cases to prove how in each case the value of TO helps to choose the path which gives higher throughput.

- **Few neighbors with heavy traffic load and larger number of neighbors with light traffic**

The TO value will be higher for the first case than that for the second case So, the first path is preferred to the second path. Intuitional explanation behind choosing the first path can be given as: Since there are very few active neighbors in the first case, the probability of the node under consideration getting selected for transmitting a packet is higher than that in the second case. Hence the throughput will be higher if data is routed along this path.

- **Large number of neighbors with light traffic load and larger number of neighbors with heavy traffic load:**

In both of the cases, the value of MAX is increased, because the number of idle periods will be very less for initial value of MAX. For large value of MAX, there will be many more idle time periods in the first case than in the second case. Hence, the value of TO for the first case will be higher. Hence, our algorithm will choose the first path. The intuitional choice for the better path matches with the one selected by our algorithm.

5   Algorithm for Finding K Shortest Paths

At the end of route discovery phase, a set of paths from the source to the destination is available at the source. Using these paths, the source builds a graph. The cost for each link is computed using the equation (1). Now, the aim is to find the set of shortest paths from the source to destination. These paths can have shared links. Finding K-shortest paths is a well-known optimization problem. The algorithm used here, is based on path deletion method.. The algorithm is described bellow.

Let $G(V,E)$ be the graph with V being set of vertices and E being set of edges. The simple logic behind this algorithm is after finding N^{th} shortest path in order to find $(N+1)^{st}$ shortest path, remove some arcs from G_N, so that N^{th} path is no more the shortest path in the graph G_N Here G_N is the graph, after finding N^{th} shortest path. This deletion is done by copying all the nodes in the path and for each node V_i on the path, all arcs except the one from V_{i-1} are copied. This copying and labeling operation is quite costly. One way to make it efficient is to consider only those nodes for which there exists more than one path from the source. This is called as dynamic reverse sorted order.

```
FindKShortest ()

{

            (V₁,E₁)   <-  (V,E) ;
```

```
        Let T_s be the tree of shortest path from the
source to any node i such that i is any node in V.

        Let P_1 be the shortest path from source to
destination in T_s.

        Define (V_1, E_1) in dynamic reverse sorted form

        For (k=2 to N)

        {

            (V_K, E_K) <- After deleting  P_{k-1} from (V_{k-1}, E_{k-1})

            P'_k  <- Shortest path in (V_{k-1}, E_{k-1})

            Map P'_k to P_k .where p_k is a path in (V, E)

        }

}
```

6 Path Set Division and Data Traffic Distribution

The K shortest path selection algorithm finds the K shortest paths from the source to the destination. Let the K paths be $P_1, P_2 \ldots P_k$. These paths can be disjoint or can have some shared links between them. These paths are arranged in the increasing order of their path cost values. Then they are divided into groups each containing all the paths that share some link. The 'group cast' for a group is the value of minimum path cost in that group. Let the groups be $S_1, S_2 \ldots$ and S_N. The group cost of a set S_i is denoted by GC_i.

The load is distributed among the path sets based on the group cost values. We assign weight to each path set. The weight of path set S_i, W_i, is obtained as

$$W_i = (1/GC_i)/(1/GC_1 + 1/GC_2 \ldots 1/GC_N) \tag{3}$$

The traffic routed along routes in a group a is in proportion to the group weight value. If there are more than one paths in the group, again the load is distributed among them based on weight which is assigned in a way similar to the way in which the weights are assigned above.

7 Performance Evaluation

7.1 Simulation Environment

To evaluate the performance of the new multipath routing protocol, we used *Glomosim 2.03 simulator* which is a scalable simulation environment for wired and wireless networks based on *parsec*. Glomosim supports a large number of routing protocols for mobile ad hoc networks including dynamic source routing protocol.

Our evaluations are based on simulation of 100 mobile nodes moving about over a rectangular area of 2000 meters by 2000 meters for 600 seconds of simulation time. A randomly generated seed is used to generate the initial positions of the mobile nodes. We assume that the mobile nodes move randomly according to the random waypoint model. In this model, each node decides a random destination within the area and then moves towards the destination with a randomly chosen speed between the minimum speed (0 m/s) and the maximum speed (10m/s). After reaching the destination, the node pauses for a predefined time and then the repeats the same mobility behavior.

We have assumed the standard radio model which accommodates noise. The packet reception model assumed is *signal to noise ratio bounded*. In this model, if the signal to noise ratio of the received packet is more than some threshold value, then the packet is received without any error. The *Medium Access Control* protocol used is the *IEEE 802.11 Medium Access Control Protocol* with *Distributed Coordination Function*. The energy consumption is measured at the radio layer and the model used for the measurement is IEEE 802.11 compliant *WaveLAN-II* from Lucent. The *Network Interface Card* is kept in promiscuous mode to support the dynamic source routing optimizations.

We used the *Constant Bit Rate (CBR) traffic generator* application to generate the traffic. Each CBR source sends packets of size 512 bytes after every one second to the destination for the whole simulation period.

7.2 Simulation Results

In order to evaluate the performance of the new multipath routing protocol, we executed 20 runs of the simulator with different loads. The load is measured in terms of number of CBR connections. Let us define a parameter *Link Knowledge* (LK) to be the the number of links gathered per single control packet. Let us define *Improvement* as the ratio of LK for the proposed multipath routing protocol to LK for the standard multipath routing protocol.

Hence I*mprovement* is given by

$$\text{Improvement} = LK_M / LK_U \tag{4}$$

where
LK_M is *link knowledge* for modified multipath protocol and
LK_U is the *link knowledge* for standard multipath routing protocol

$$LK_M = L_M / C_M \tag{5}$$

where
L_M = Number of links generated by the modified protocol

C_M= Number of control packets sent by modified multipath routing protocol

And

$$LK_U = L_U/C_U \qquad (6)$$

where
L_U= Number of links generated by the unmodified protocol
C_U= Number of control packets sent by unmodified multipath routing protocol.

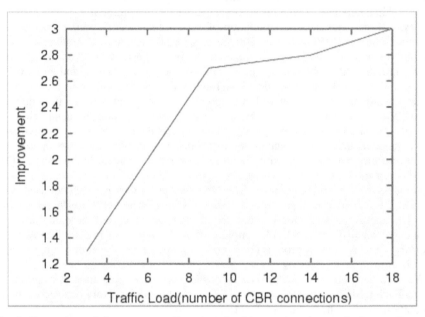

Fig. 1. Comparison of the new route discovery algorithm against the standard route discovery algorithm

The quantity *'Improvement'* shows the work efficiency of the new route discovery protocol. The graph shown in fig. 1, shows that as the traffic load increases, the node that initiates the route discovery can get more accurate knowledge of the network topology with a small additional control overhead. Hence more reliable paths can be selected for multipath routing.

The evaluation of the new multiple path selection algorithm which allows sharing of reliable links, is under progress, The results will be reported later.

8 Conclusions

In this paper, we have proposed an algorithm which gathers highly accurate information about the network topology with minimum control overhead. Then, we define a metric that can capture all four conditions that result into low throughput and less reliability. We define a route selection algorithm that selects routes which can have shared links among them. We, also, propose a way to distribute the data traffic among the routes.

References

[1]   P. Papaadmitratos, Z. J. Hass and E. Gon. "Path set selection in mobile ad hoc networks". *Proceedings of the Third International Symposium on Mobile Ad Hoc Networking and Computing , June 9-11 MOBIHOC , ACM 2002.*

[2]   K. Wu and J. Harms. "On demand multipath routing for mobile ad hoc networks". *21–22 Feb 2001 OVE.*

[3]   D. Eppstain and J.C. Siam. "Finding k-shortest paths". *1998 Society For Industrial and Applied Mathematics vol. 28, No. 2, pp. 652–673.*

[4]   Bob O'Hara and Al Petric. "IEEE 802.11 handbook, A designer's companion". IEEE Press ,1999.

[5]   Bryan P. Crow, Indra Widjaja, Jeong Geun Kim and Prescott T Sakai. "IEEE 802.11 Wireless local area networks", *IEEE Communication magazine, September,1997.*

[6]   J. Broch, D. Johnson and D. Maltz. "Dynamic source routing protocol for mobile ad hoc networks". *http://www.ietf.org/internet-drafts/draft-ietf-manet-dsr-01.txt,Dec 1998, IETF Internet Draft.*

[7]   A. Nasipuri and S. R. Das. "On demand multipath routing for mobile ad hoc networks". *Proceedings of the 8th Int Conf on Computer Communications and Networks, Boston, October, 1999.*

[8]   S. J. Lee and M. Gerla. "Split multipath routing with maximally disjoint paths in ad hoc networks". *Proceedings of ICC 2001, Helsinki, Finland , June 2001.*

[9]   M.R. Pearlman, Z.J. Haas, P. Sholander, and S.S. Tabrizi."On the impact of alternate routing in mobile ad hoc networks". *Proceedings of first workshop on mobile ad hoc networking and computing (Mobihoc 2000), Boston, M.A. Aug. 2000.*

[10]   D.B. Johnson and D.A. Maltz. "Dynamic source routing in ad hoc wireless networks". *Mobile Computing, pages 153–181,1996.*

Energy-Aware On-Demand Routing for Mobile Ad Hoc Networks

Nishant Gupta[1] and Samir R. Das[2]

[1] OPNET Technologies, Inc.
7255 Woodmont Avenue
Bethesda, MD 20814
U.S.A.
[2] Computer Science Department
SUNY at Stony Brook
Stony Brook, NY 11794-4400
U.S.A.

Abstract. We develop a technique to make on-demand routing protocols for ad hoc networks energy-aware. The goal is to increase the operational lifetime of an ad hoc network where nodes are operating on battery power alone. Our techniques uses a new routing cost metric which is a function of the remaining battery level in each node on a route and the number of neighbors of this node. The idea of the cost metric is to be able to route around the nodes that are running low in battery for which alternate routes are available. In addition, rerouting is done proactively when any node *en route* starts running low on battery while the route is being actively used. Further, we save energy by switching off the radio interfaces dynamically during the periods when the nodes are idle. Simulation results using AODV protcol show that combination of these techniques results in a significant improvement of the energy budget of the network as a whole resulting in increased operational life time.

1 Introduction

A mobile ad hoc network (or MANET) [9] is a group of mobile, wireless nodes which cooperatively and spontaneously form a network independent of any fixed infrastructure (e.g., base stations or access points) or centralized administration. A node communicates directly with the nodes within radio range and indirectly with all others using a dynamically-determined multi-hop route. The MANET environment is typically characterized by energy-constrained nodes, variable-capacity, bandwidth-constrained wireless links and dynamic topology, leading to frequent and unpredictable connectivity changes. Many dynamic routing protocols MANET have been proposed and evaluated, some within the IETF MANET Working Group [9]. Of particular interest is the new class of on-demand, source-initiated protocols that set up and maintain routes on an "as needed" basis to reduce routing overheads.

S.K. Das and S. Bhattacharya (Eds.): IWDC 2002, LNCS 2571, pp. 164–173, 2002.
© Springer-Verlag Berlin Heidelberg 2002

The majority of the work reported in the literature focuses on the protocol design and performance evaluation in terms of traditional metrics such as throughput, delay and routing overhead. However, much less attention has been paid in making the routing protocol energy efficient. The challenge in ad hoc networks is that even if a host does not communicate on its own, it still frequently forwards data and routing packets for others, which drains its battery. Switching off a non-communicating node to conserve battery power may not be always a good idea, as it may partition the network.

Conventional on-demand routing protocols such as AODV [10,11] and DSR [8] are energy-unaware. The protocols do not proactively modify routes until they break. A node that lies on several routes will die prematurely and the network may get partitioned. Since recharging or replacing the battery is not feasible in most of the ad hoc network applications, it is imperative to study and design routing protocols which are able to conserve node energy to prevent such premature death.

Our work focuses on augmenting the existing on-demand routing protocols and making them energy conserving. On-demand protocols are more suitable for this study as they typically have lower routing overhead than proactive, distributed shortest path protocols and thus have a low baseline energy consumption. We have used AODV as the base on-demand routing protocol. The techniques implemented are generic in nature and should be applicable to other on-demand routing protocols, such as DSR.

The rest of the paper is organized as follows. In the next section, we briefly describe the AODV protocol. In section 3, we describe our energy aware techniques as an extension of AODV. In section 4 we evaluate the performance of our energy-aware techniques vis-à-vis the baseline AODV via simulations. In section 5 we review related work. We conclude in section 6.

2   AODV Protocol Description

Ad hoc On Demand Distance Vector (AODV)[10,11] is source initiated, reactive protocol. It discovers and maintains routes only if and when necessary. Route discovery works as follows. When the source requires a path to a particular destination, it broadcasts a route request (RREQ) packet in the ad hoc network. Nodes receiving RREQ record a *reverse* route back towards the source, using the node from which the RREQ was received as the next-hop, and then re-broadcasts the RREQ. If the same RREQ is received more than once (via different routes), it is ignored. This way the RREQ packets is flooded to every node in the connected part of the network.

When the RREQ packet reaches the destination, it sends a route reply (RREP) packet back to the source, using the reverse route. If an intermediate node has an up-to-date route to the destination, it may also send a RREP packet back to the source on behalf of the destination. As the RREP packet follows the path back to the source, the corresponding *forward* route is created at each intermediate node towards the destination. Once the RREP packet reaches the source, data traffic can now flow along this forward route.

To prevent routing loops, AODV maintains a sequence number on each node. Any routing information transmitted on routing packets or maintained on a node is tagged with the last known sequence number for the destination of the route. AODV protcol guarantees the invariant that the destination sequence numbers in the routing table entries on the nodes along a valid route are always monotonically increasing. Other than preventing loops, sequence numbers also ensure freshness of routes. Given a choice of multiple routes, the one with a newer sequence number is always chosen.

An important feature of AODV is maintenance of timer based states in each node, regarding utilization of individual routes. A route is "expired" if not used recently. A set of predecessor nodes is maintained for each routing table entry, indicating a set of neighboring nodes that use that entry to route data packets. These nodes are notified with route error (RERR) packets when the next hop link breaks. Each predecessor node, in turn, forwards the RERR to its own set of predecessors, thus effectively erasing all routes using the broken link. This RERR is thus propagated to each source routing traffic through the failed link, causing the route discovery process to be reinitiated if routes are still needed.

3   Energy Aware Routing in AODV

We take a two pronged approach for conserving the power budget of individual nodes. In the first, we modify the routing protocol to route around nodes with lower power budgets. In the second, we strategically turn off the radio interfaces to conserve energy further. The techniques are orthogonal to each other and are described separately in the following subsections.

3.1   Energy Related Cost Metric

The goal of our protocol is routing or re-routing around nodes low on battery power as far as possible. This should be done in such a way that other useful performance metrics (e.g., end-to-end delay and throughput) are not compromised in a significant way. We take a two-step approach to design the adaptive energy-aware protocol. First, the nodes are classified according to their remaining battery energy. Depending on their classification the nodes react differently to the routing protocol dynamics. Second, a new cost function is used as routing metric taking into consideration both the hop-wise distance and the battery levels of the nodes.

The nodes are classified according to the following energy zones.

- **Normal Zone:** Node are in the normal zone if their current energy level is greater that 20% of their initial energy. This signifies that the number of hops should be the deciding factor in determining the cost of routing data packets through these nodes as have ample energy at their disposal.

- **Warning Zone:** Nodes are in the warning zone if their current energy level lies between 10–20% of the initial energy. This signifies that the nodes are running low on energy and the protocol should avoid the use of these nodes if possible.
- **Danger Zone:** Here, the nodes have less than 10% of their initial energy. This means that the nodes are really low on the battery level and should only be used if there is no other cost-effective alternative.

The purpose of assigning zones to nodes with various battery levels is to assign different costs for routing via nodes in different zones. The cost of routing a data packet through nodes in Warning (Danger) Zone is higher than the cost involved with the nodes in the Normal (Warning) Zone. This is to encourage the route discovery mechanism to explore alternate routes with higher battery power.

The total cost of a n-hop route using nodes $x_1, x_2, \ldots, x_n$ is given by $Cost = \Sigma_{i=1}^{n} c(x_i)$, where, the cost function for each node $c(x_i) = C_{normal}$, $C_{warning}$ or C_{danger}, depending on the zone of the node. C_{normal}, $C_{warning}$ or C_{danger} are predefined costs such that $C_{normal} < C_{warning} < C_{danger}$.

As an improvement to the suggested scheme, we keep track of the number of neighbors for each node from the neighborhood information gathered from the routing protocol. If the node lies in the Warning or Danger Zone and has sufficiently large number of neighbors then, we *increase* the cost of routing of data packets through that node by a factor proportional to the number of neighbors. This helps in further avoiding a node with low battery levels if it has nodes in its vicinity that can do the same work. Now the new cost function for each node is $c(x_i) = C_{normal}$, $k_i C_{warning}$ or $k_i C_{danger}$, where k_i is proportional to the number of neighbors of node x_i.

3.2 Protocol Modifications Using Energy Cost

The above cost metric is used in AODV route discovery. Each RREQ packet flooded in the network builds up the cost for the path traversed so far by the packet. Each routing table entry also maintains the cost for that route. In regular AODV any node acts on only the very first RREQ received per route discovery flood. Duplicates of the RREQ received via alternate routes are ignored. However, use of this new cost metric requires that AODV acts on all such duplicates if they carry a lower cost metric. If a RREQ arrives with a lower cost metric (compared the metric in the routing table entry for the source indicating the cost of the reverse path), it is forwarded if the node is not the destination and does not have a route to the destination; otherwise it is replied to.

In AODV routing activity is reactive. It is possible that once a route is set, it remains active for a long period of time. In such cases, it might happen that one or more nodes on the route may move from one energy zone to another as they deplete their battery power in forwarding data packets. If this continues for a long time then some nodes may die. To ensure that the route is recalculated when the battery level depletes sufficiently to move any node on an active route into a different zone, such a node sends a route warning (RWARN) packet back to the source(s) using that route. The warning packet is propagated much like RERR, except that the route is *not* erased. Thus the flow of the data packets is not interrupted. A new route discovery process is initiated at the source on receipt of RWARN.

The new route discovery process do *not* selectively ignore the node(s) that sent RWARN. However, now such nodes incur higher cost using the method above. If a less expensive route is found, the routing tables of the appropriate nodes automatically switch to the new route. If no less expensive route is found, the old route continues to be used.

3.3 Optimizations at the Network Interface

Several studies that performed measurements on network interface indicated that switching off the network interface incurs substantial energy savings. In order to develop a technique to derive energy savings from the network interface we assume that the node is either in *active* or *sleep* state. Generally speaking, a node is in *active* state as long as it has an active route and it has packets in its buffer which needs to be sent, and otherwise it is in *sleep* state. If the node is receiving/transmitting a packet, it waits for a period of T_{active} after it has completed the communication activities. If no more packets are transmitted or received the node switches to the *sleep* state. In sleep state, the radio interface is switched off and the node is unable to transmit or receive any packet. The node switches back to *active* state after a period of T_{sleep} in the sleep state, and remain there for at least T_{active} time. If no packet is transmitted or received it switches back to sleep again. While sleeping, the node can become active earlier than T_{sleep}, if it generates any packet destined for others. Needless to say, the radio interface is switched on when the node is in *active state*.

Note that T_{sleep} cannot be very large, as sleeping nodes cannot participate in any routing activity. T_{sleep} cannot be very small either as from practical perspectives some minimum settling time is needed for the radio interface switching between on and off states. According to the measurements made in [15] using the first generation, 915 MHz WaveLAN radios, around 100 ms must expire from the time the radio is turned on and to the time it is ready to send the first packet. Though much depend on the actual electronics of the radios, we use this measurement as guidance and set the sleep period T_{sleep} at 115 ms. Even with small T_{sleep}, large power savings are possible if both T_{active} and T_{sleep} are small.

4   Performance Evaluation

We simulated our energy-aware routing techniques as an extension to AODV for a mobile ad hoc network. We use the *ns-2* simulator [5] to implement the protocols. The latest version of AODV protocol [11] is used. The energy model used bears similarities to earlier studies [6,15]. It is assumed that that the radio interface, when powered on, consumes 1.15W when listening to the channel for any incoming packet, 1.2W while actually receiving a packet and 1.6W while transmitting a packet. These values correspond to direct measurements on 915 MHz WaveLAN radios as reported in [16]. The physical radio model used in the simulator is very similar to WaveLAN; so these are appropraite numbers to use. The cost functions for nodes in different battery zones chosen as: $C_{normal} = 1$, $C_{warning} = 3$, and $C_{danger} = 4$. Thus, cost of routing via a node in warning (danger) zone is three (four) times the cost of routing through a node in normal zone. The multiplicative factor k_i is chosen as the number of neighbors of node x_i divided by 5. These parameters are some what ad hoc at this point and these values have been found to work well in the scnenarios tested. In our experience, several factors influence their choice including network size and average node density. The values of different timers are chosen as follows: $T_{active} = 100$ ms and $T_{sleep} = 115$ ms.

4.1   Experimental Scenarios and Performance Metrics

In our experiments 50 nodes move around in a rectangular area of 1500m X 300m according to a mobility model (random waypoint, as described in [1]). Each node uses IEEE 802.11 standard [4] MAC layer. The radio model is very similar to the first generation WaveLAN radios with nominal radio range of 250m. The nominal bit rate is 2 Mbps. In this mobility model each node moves towards a random destination and pauses for certain time after reaching the destination before moving again. In our simulations, the nodes move at an average speed of 20m/sec. The pause times are varied to simulate different degrees of mobility. The traffic sources start at random times towards the beginning of the simulation and stay active throughout. The sources are CBR (constant bit rate) and generates UDP packets at 4 packets/sec, each packet being 512 bytes. 30 sources are used in the reported experiments. Note that very similar mobility and traffic models have been used in earlier simulation studies of ad hoc networks [1,7,3]. Each simulation is run for 900 seconds simulated time. Each point in the plotted results represents an average of three simulation runs with different random mobility scenarios.

The following performance metrics are evaluated. The first three metrics are typical metrics usually evaluated for analyze performance of routing protocols with best-effort traffic. The remaining metric are useful for evaluating the efficacy of energy-aware routing.

- *Packet delivery fraction*: measured as the ratio of the number of data packets delivered to the destination and the number of data packets sent by the source.
- *End-to-end delay*: measured as the average end-to-end latency of data packets.
- *Normalized routing load*: measured as the number of routing packets transmitted for each data packet delivered at the destination.
- *Battery energy*: measured as the total amount (in Joules) of remaining battery energy at the end of the experiment.

We also evaluate two more power-related metrics to measure how soon nodes are dying out of power and how many nodes are dead (i.e., have zero energy) at the end of the simulation. These metrics are useful in addition to total battery energy as they indirectly determine connectivity of the network and thus the useful lifetime.

4.2   Simulation Results

We have plotted the performance of the base AODV and energy-aware AODV for various metrics. See Figure 1. Number of traffic sources and pause times are varied to reflect various loads and mobility. Note that pause time = 0 means constant movement and pause time = 900 sec means stationary network. The initial energy for each node in this set of simulations is 1060 Joules, which represent a combined network wide initial energy of 53,000 Joules.

In Figure 1(a), observe that the remaining energy at the end of the simulation is much higher for energy-aware AODV than the base AODV. For the chosen parameter values, the improvement is up to 30 times. Note, however, these factors can be a little deceiving as they depend strongly on the initial energy and the simulation run length. For example, the improvements may not be this substantial if run length is lower. On the other hand, a longer run length may produce a larger factors of improvement of the remaining energy. Very long run lengths will make all nodes die.

The next two figures indicate the regular performance metrics, *viz.* delivery fraction and delay. In Figure 1(b) notice that energy-aware AODV is at per with base AODV. However, we have noticed slightly lower performance here for energy-aware AODV for lower number of sources (not reported here), as here too many nodes sleep sporadically and fail to respond to routing packets. In Figure 1(c), notice lower delay in energy-aware AODV. This is attributed to frequent rerouting which leads to reduced congestion and better load balancing. The improvement is more pronounced for lower mobility as the base AODV hardly changes routes in such cases. Thus congestions do not go away automatically, but they do for energy-aware routing.

From Figure 1(d), we find that routing load increases for energy-aware AODV. The increase is justified as we are allowing more RREQs to be propagated for each route discovery and doing additional route discoveries via the new warning packets. The interesting thing to note is that overall energy savings are still possible even with a higher routing load and somewhat longer routes in energy-aware AODV. This savings are primarily due to the sleep mode introduced at the radio interfaces. Figure 1(e) shows the number of nodes with zero remaining energy at the end of the simulation. Again, energy-aware AODV demonstrates comparatively excellent performance.

5   Related Work

The problem of trying to conserve battery usage within a mobile ad hoc network is not new. Previous other work has gone in different energy conserving strategies

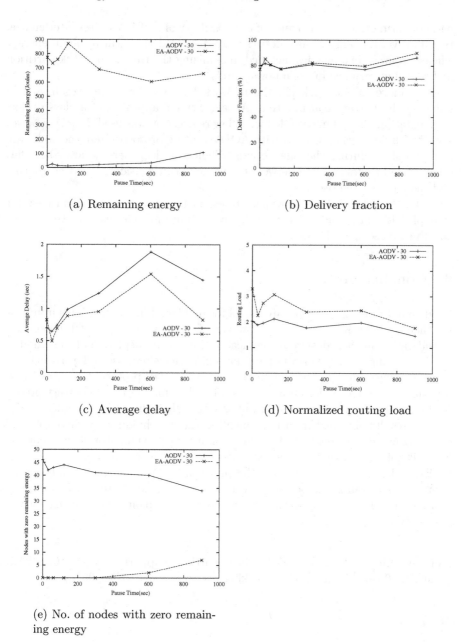

(a) Remaining energy

(b) Delivery fraction

(c) Average delay

(d) Normalized routing load

(e) No. of nodes with zero remaining energy

Fig. 1. Various performance metrics for the 50 node network with 30 sources.

spanning different network layers. In [13] a power-aware multiple access protocol (PAMAS) was proposed. Here, a node turns off its radio interface for a specific duration of time, when it knows that it will not be able to send and receive packets during that time because of the possiblity of multiple access interference. In [14], several energy-aware metrics were discussed that will result in energy-efficient routes. The metrics included maximizing the time to network partition and reducing variance in node power levels.

In a more recent work [2], the network longevity was the overall goal in reducing the battery consumption. An algorithmic approach of a class of flow augmentation algorithms coupled with flow redirection was used. In [17], a power saving technique was proposed with AODV routing protocol. Here the nodes are made to sleep during the idle periods. Choice of sleep periods are somewhat different from ours. Mobile networks have not been considered and no routing cost model has been used.

Also, there has been a growing interest in transmit power control (see, for example, [12]) in the ad hoc networking community for reasons of power savings and to increase spatial reuse.

6   Conclusions

On-demand routing protocols are useful for mobile ad hoc network environment for their low routing overheads. However, if battery energy is not taken into consideration in their design, it may lead to premature depletion of some nodes' battery leading to early network partitioning. We have proposed adaptive energy-aware routing techniques as an extension to the AODV protocol that uses a new routing cost model to discourage the use of nodes running low on battery power. It also saves energy by turning off radios when when the nodes are idle.

The results obtained from implementing these techniques are favorable and encouraging. Performance evaluation using a routing simulator shows that the longevity of the network can be extended by a significant amount.

Even though we implemented the protocol on AODV, the technique used is very generic and can be used with any on-demand protocol. The energy-aware protocol works only in the routing layer and exploits only routing-specific information.

Acknowledgment. This work has been partially supported by NSF CAREER grant ACI-0096186 and NSF networking research grant ANI-0096264.

References

1. J. Broch, D. A. Maltz, D. B. Johnson, Y-C. Hu, and J. Jetcheva. A performance comparison of multi-hop wireless ad hoc network routing protocols. In *Proceedings of the 4th International Conference on Mobile Computing and Networking (ACM MOBICOM'98)*, pages 85–97, October 1998.
2. Jae-Hwan Chang and Leandros Tassiulas. Energy conserving routing in wireless ad-hoc routing. In *Proceedings of the IEEE INFOCOM 2000 Conference*, Tel Aviv, Israel, March 2000.

3. Samir R. Das, Charles E. Perkins, and Elizabeth M. Royer. Performance comparison of two on-demand routing protocols for ad hoc networks. In *Proceedings of the IEEE INFOCOM 2000 Conference*, pages 3–12, March 2000.

4. IEEE Standards Department. Wireless LAN medium access control (MAC) and physical layer (PHY) specifications, IEEE standard 802.11–1997, 1997.

5. Kevin Fall and Kannan Varadhan (Eds.). *ns* notes and documentation, 1999. available from http://www-mash.cs.berkeley.edu/ns/.

6. L.M. Feeney. An energy consumption model for performance analysis of routing protocols for mobile ad hoc networks, July 1999.

7. Per Johansson, Tony Larsson, Nicklas Hedman, and Bartosz Mielczarek. Routing protocols for mobile ad-hoc networks – a comparative performance analysis. In *Proceedings of the 5th International Conference on Mobile Computing and Networking (ACM MOBICOM'99)*, pages 195–206, August 1999.

8. D. Johnson and D. Maltz. Dynamic source routing in ad hoc wireless networks. In T. Imielinski and H. Korth, editors, *Mobile computing*, chapter 5. Kluwer Academic, 1996.

9. J. Macker and S. Corson. Mobile ad hoc networks (MANET). http://www.ietf.org/ html.charters/manet-charter.html, 1997. IETF Working Group Charter.

10. Charles Perkins and Elizabeth Royer. Ad hoc on-demand distance vector routing. In *Proceedings of the 2nd IEEE Workshop on Mobile Computing Systems and Applications*, pages 90–100, Feb 1999.

11. Charles Perkins, Elizabeth Royer, and Samir R. Das. Ad hoc on demand distance vector (AODV) routing. http://www.ietf.org/internet-drafts/ draft-ietf-manet-aodv-11.txt, June 2002. IETF Internet Draft (work in progress).

12. Ram Ramanathan and Regina Rosales-Hain. Topology control in multihop wireless networks using transmit power adjustment. In *Proceedings of the IEEE INFOCOM 2000 Conference*, 2000.

13. S. Singh and C.S. Raghavendra. PAMAS - power aware multi-access protocol with signalling for ad hoc networks. *ACM Computer Communication Review (ACM CCR'98)*, July 1998.

14. S. Singh, M. Woo, and C.S. Raghavendra. Power-aware routing in mobile ad-hoc networks. In *ACM/IEEE International Conference on Mobile Computing and Networking*, pages 181–190, October 1998.

15. Mark Stemm and Randy Katz. Measuring and reducing energy consumption of network interfaces in hand-held devices. Technical report, UC Berkeley, August 1997.

16. Bruce Tuch. Development of WaveLAN, an ISM band wireless LAN. *AT&T Technical Journal*, 72(4):27–33, July/Aug 1993.

17. Ya Xu, John Heidemann, and Deborah Estrin. Adaptive energy-conserving routing for multihop ad hoc networks, October 2000. USC/ISI Research Report 527.

Prospects of Group-Based Communication in Mobile Ad hoc Networks

Prafulla Kumar Behera and Pramod Kumar Meher

Dept. of Computer Science and Application, Utkal University,
Bhubaneswar-751004, Orissa, India
p_behera@hotmail.com, pkmeher@yahoo.com

Abstract. This paper describes the possible prospects of a group-based ad hoc network. It presents the formation of a semi-ad hoc network of mobile hosts termed as a mobile users club. Using a DSR like protocol in such a network simplifies routing protocol selection. Communication through a club improves security in the inherently insecure mobile ad hoc network. Also it sustains variation in node population, node density, and node mobility. Apart from this, DS-CDMA technique used for medium access by the club members ensures better utilization of limited battery power and bandwidth.

1 Introduction

In the recent years, communication among mobile hosts is becoming increasingly popular in everyday business and personal life as well. In the mean while, the network connectivity options for the mobile hosts have increased substantially. Very often, mobile users are expected to meet under circumstances that are not explicitly planned for and in which no connection to a fixed network is available. Under such circumstances, the communication between two users through a wide-area network may not be possible due to lack of facilities or may not be desirable due to time and cost involved for such a connection. Ad hoc network of mobile hosts provides a possible alternative for sharing or exchange of information under such condition. Ad hoc network is a collection of mobile hosts forming a temporary network without the support of any centralized administration or standard support services. In this case, no home agent or foreign agent is required for providing any supporting service. In such a network, when a pair of mobile hosts are not able to communicate directly, they take the help of intermediate hosts coming in between them. A few typical examples of possible users of ad hoc networking include researchers participating in a conference, soldiers relaying information for situational awareness on a battlefield, emergency disaster management group and relief personnel while coordinating efforts after a hurricane or an earthquake. Small vehicular devices equipped with audio sensors and cameras can be deployed at targeted regions to collect important location and environmental information that will be communicated back to a processing node via ad hoc communication. Ship-to-ship ad hoc mobile communication is also desirable since it provides alternate communication paths without reliance on ground or space-based communication infrastructures. Besides, ad hoc networks may work as a useful medium for various civilian forums such as electronic classrooms, convention centers,

S.K. Das and S. Bhattacharya (Eds.): IWDC 2002, LNCS 2571, pp. 174–183, 2002.

construction sites, tourists, journalists, managers for remote conferencing, discussion groups, detective agencies and many more. Presenters can multicast slides and audio to intended recipients. Attendees can ask questions and interact on commonly shared white board. Ad hoc networks have scope to cater to instantaneous and convenient exchange of information among such a large variety of groups of people under different situations.

In a mobile ad hoc network, when a pair of nodes lie within the transmission radius of one another, they can communicate directly with each other. In such cases, there is no need of any routing protocol. However, when no such direct communication is possible, the nodes are required to take the help of a sequence of wireless links through one or more intermediate nodes, where adjacent intermediate nodes lie within the transmission range of each other. Appropriate routing of messages in such cases has been considered as a major task for the researchers due to dynamic topology of mobile ad hoc networks formed by frequently and unpredictably moving hosts. Several routing protocols have, therefore, been suggested in the literature [1-6] during the past few years.

Effective and efficient message communication among the mobile users in an ad hoc network is, however, still confronted by several challenging issues. In this paper, we have discussed some of such issues and their possible solutions through group-based approach to communication among mobile users. The rest of the paper is as follows: The possible prospects of group-based ad hoc network are discussed in the next Section. Section 3 deals with a semi-ad hoc network of mobile users club. Conclusion along with scope of future work has been outlined at the end.

2   Prospects of Group-Based Ad Hoc Network

2.1 Routing Protocol Selection

The proactive or table-driven routing protocols such as DSDV (Destination-Sequenced Distance Vector), WRP (Wireless Routing Protocol), CGSR (Cluster-head Gateway Switch Routing) adopt a connectionless approach for forwarding packets using a routing table. These protocols require updating the underlying routing tables in each of the mobile hosts regularly without any regard to when and how frequent such routes may be used by a node. Regular updating of routing table by flooding technique involves substantial traffic, which consequently suffocates the network if it gets populated with large number of nodes and if the topology changes frequently due to high mobility of nodes. The prominent reactive or on-demand routing protocols include DSR (Dynamic Source Routing), AODV (Ad Hoc On-Demand Distance Vector), and TORA (Temporally Ordered Routing Algorithm). These protocols don't require to maintain a complete routing table, rather hosts establish routes when they need to, i.e., on demand basis. When a host wants to communicate with another host in the network, it invokes route discovery mechanism to find out the path to the destination. A node desiring to communicate with a particular destination will have to wait until such a route is discovered. DSR protocol works satisfactorily only for networks of smaller dimension where mobile nodes move with moderate speed.

Besides, it is not scalable for large networks. AODV and DSR use similar kind of route discovery mechanism. AODV has relatively less control overhead than DSR but involves more bandwidth and power consumption for periodic route advertisement. AODV, moreover, requires symmetric links between nodes and hence can't utilize routes with asymmetric links as do DSR. TORA is a "link reversal" algorithm that is best suited for networks with large and dense population of node.

Ad hoc networks are highly dynamic in nature due to random mobility of the participating hosts. In such a dynamic situation, the mobile users' population, density and the mobility may change very widely during 24 hours of a day and from location to location. However, none of the existing algorithms or class of algorithms is best suited for all scenarios of various node population, network size and node mobility. Each protocol has definite advantages and disadvantages. Therefore, it is difficult to select a routing protocol which can be used efficiently under such varying conditions within a day or when a user changes its location. Moreover, it is not convenient and transparent to switch over from one routing protocol to other depending on density and mobility conditions. Therefore, it is necessary to have a routing scheme that will remain immune to varying density and mobility conditions.

If a group-based ad hoc network can be formed with limited number of users with some common objective. In such a case, only a limited number of nodes that are the members of a particular group mostly communicate with each other. Therefore, in such a case the ad hoc network would not be expected to have large number of nodes. Moreover, the members of the group would be able to know the mobility pattern of the group. Thus, in the group-based ad hoc network, the problem of routing protocol selection may be greatly simplified. Since the density and mobility of users are expected to be moderate within a group, a DSR like protocol can be effectively used for routing information among participating nodes.

2.2 Population Density of Mobile Users

Day by day the number of mobile users is growing enormously due to availability of energy efficient, cheap and portable computers. The trend is towards high computing power, operational convenience, popularity of e-commerce, upcoming dedicated portable machines for using the Internet, and so also the growing popularity of mobile phones for surfing the net using wireless application protocol, 2.5G or 3G wireless. Consequently, at certain places during some specific peak hours of a day the density of mobile hosts is expected to be very large. The existing routing protocols for ad hoc networks are based on the assumption that hosts participating in the network should be willing to forward the packets meant for other hosts along the appropriate path in the network. The functioning of ad hoc network is thus solely dependent on the cooperation of the participating hosts. The cooperative service in ad hoc routing, however, may not be efficient and may lead to chaotic situation under very high density of mobile users due to network congestion, increased chance of packet collision and possibly unpredictable/unreliable behavior of some of the nodes.

In a group-based ad hoc network, the population of nodes is not expected to be very high. Moreover, the group is normally formed with the agreement of its members to provide mutual cooperation for routing as the most basic norm of the group. Also, in such networks, each of the users is supposed to know the fellow participating users. Therefore, the group-based ad hoc network is expected to provide reliable performance for effective communication.

2.3 Security and Authentication

Ad hoc networks [7-9] are more vulnerable to security threats as the transmission media is shared and it does not have any centralized administration. Since each of the mobile hosts in an ad hoc network is an integral part of routing (working as router), there is ample scope for potential intruder to participate in the communication process. The existence of a single malicious node, therefore, can create a great security breach in the ad hoc network. Ad hoc networks are, therefore, inherently insecure due to lack of control over the participating nodes in the wireless medium. Therefore, authentication mechanism is more important in ad hoc network as compared to fixed network or other mobile networks. When the number of users increases substantially, the fundamental security and privacy issues becomes more complex, as well as, important. Ad hoc network can be a reliable and dependable communication medium if it safeguards the basic computer security like confidentiality, integrity, authentication, and non-repudiation.

Operating through a group would significantly enhance security of an ad hoc network and would provide authenticated message communication. Members of the group can exchange secret keys for communication for the purpose of authentication as well as encryption. Besides, DS-CDMA can be used for medium access in such a network. In the CDMA-based communication, an eavesdropper can't identify the source without decoding it by the chip sequence of destination. However, one can listen to a particular destination provided it knows the chip sequence and public key of that destination. But, by resorting to distribution of chip sequences and public keys before the nodes go mobile, eavesdropping by an outsider would be difficult. A sender can encrypt messages by its private key for maintaining confidentiality and such encoding of message would also ensure non-repudiation and authentication. Since the communication is supposed to take place between the members and through the members of the group (who are supposed to be trustworthy), the group-based communication would have fair scope to retain message integrity.

2.4 Bandwidth and Power Considerations

Wireless environment provides a restricted bandwidth. Therefore, the traffic needed for maintenance of a network and for the network connectivity should be kept as minimum as possible, in order to save bandwidth for actual traffic. A large number of mobile users may be present at a particular time and a particular locality, but a specific user need not communicate with all. Whenever possible mobile users in an ad hoc network should ignore messages from unrelated hosts in order to save bandwidth and power. Many hosts may have limited resources in terms of power and memory capacity. So it would be beneficial in terms of power management to allow a host to go to the sleeping mode and not to be obligated to participate in the routing process too frequently. Hosts have to balance between the precision of routing information and resources.

Use of DS-CDMA as medium access technique would lead to better utilization of bandwidth and power. Besides this being an obvious benefit of using DS-CDMA, communication through a group would entitle the members to forward packets only of fellow members. They need not worry about forwarding packets of non-members in the locality. This would save the bandwidth and power consumption to a great extent. Further, the DSR like protocol may be used for routing in a group-based network. It would not require re-invoking of route discovery on failure of a certain link as it caches multiple routes to various destinations. Besides, it would not require regular route advertisements. Therefore, this kind of routing protocol would help to reduce additional traffic resulting in saving of bandwidth and power.

2.5 Node Identification

The ad hoc network environment can be compared with a gathering in a dance party where each participant would be having mask on the face and would be changing his/her place in the hall. One does not know exactly who may be standing or dancing nearby. Such a scenario could lead to various problems in the process of effective message passing. These are i) knowledge of the presence of a specific person with whom one is interested to interact is not known, ii) the identification of actual recipient of the message is difficult. Similar kind of logic is also applicable to ad hoc like networks, where communication will be more effective if it is confined to a group of users who know and trust each other and may have some common objective.

For all practical purposes a mobile user is supposed to communicate usually with another particular user whom he or she knows, or users of some particular profession or business. The identification of fellow participating nodes in ad hoc networks would help in effective interaction or information exchange between the mobile users. It is, therefore, imperative on part of a mobile user to know the presence of a specific mobile user or specific group of users with whom it is interested to interact.

Each of the members participating in a group-based ad hoc network may maintain a node-table containing the MAC addresses and IP addresses of all other participating nodes. Besides, each member of the group may have a permanent member-table containing the member-id, name, home address, public key, and MAC addresses of all the members of the group. Therefore, every participating node of the ad hoc network can easily find out if a particular node with whom it wants to interact is presently available in the network or not.

It is apparent that the in ad hoc networks most of the actual exchange of messages/information would take place among a particular group of nodes having some common objective. Though the mobile nodes on some occasion may be interested to interact with nodes of some other group, but may not be interested or capable enough to participate in co-operative services of ad hoc network in its entirety. Therefore, instead of any arbitrary node participating in an ad hoc network we may think of forming an ad hoc network of group of nodes with some common interest. Moreover, it will be less vulnerable to pass on messages through persons of the same group. Communication will be more secure and effective if it is confined to a group of users who know and trust each other. Persons of the same group will have some knowledge of other members of the group and would not hesitate to provide cooperation in routing of messages.

3   Implementation of Group-Based Ad Hoc Network

Let us suppose that each of the communicating hosts is a member of a group-based ad hoc network termed as "mobile users' club". We may also term such a network as semi-ad hoc network as the mobile hosts would communicate here under the supervision of a club controller though they participate in routing as in case of ad hoc network. Direct-Sequence Code Division Multiple Access (DS-CDMA) [10] be used as medium access technique in this model. Along with medium access control, DS-CDMA will help to identify the presence of a club operating in a region. Also, it will be useful to achieve better utilization of bandwidth and to improve security. DSR is suggested to be a better choice for routing since there will be limited number of users in a mobile users club.

Each member of a club will have its individual member-id and its chip-sequence for CDMA. Besides, each of these club members will maintain a table (say member-table) containing member-id, name, home address, MAC addresses, and public key of all the members of the club. When such nodes participate in an ad hoc network they maintain another table (say a node table) consisting of member-ids and IP addresses of all participating nodes. Such IP address will however, be allocated by the controller when a member joins the club-based ad hoc network.

While sending a message the sender encodes the packets by chip sequence of destination which is available in its member table. To recover the bit stream the destination host decodes the message by computing the normalized inner product of the received stream of chips and its chip sequence. Each of these clubs will have a unique chip sequence that may be called as club sequence or control sequence. This sequence may be used for announcement of the presence of the club and so also for exchange of control messages between club members and the controller. The club controller uses the club sequence for encoding the broadcast message. The member nodes decode the broadcast message of the controller by the club sequence. The control information from the controller is broadcast in down-link control sub-channel that is used for distribution of information among the members. Members of the club functioning at the peripheral areas of transmission range also intermittently broadcast the club sequence in the down-link control sub-channel to indicate the presence of the club to new nodes intending to join the network, but are away from the transmission range of the controller. These peripheral nodes may be termed as relay nodes.

3.1   Initiation of Mobile Users Club

A member node, say A in fig-1 (a) of the club when arrives at a place senses all possible channels and decodes the received signal by club sequence to find the existence of club functioning nearby. If the decoded output is zero in all possible channels then it presumes that their club is yet to be operational in that location. In that case the node assigns itself an IP address, say i=1, and assumes the responsibility of the club controller. The first responsibility of the club controller is to find a free channel available in the region. Thereafter it subdivides the available free channel into two sub-channels. A smaller part is kept as control sub-channel to be used for exchange of control messages, while the major part of the channel as message sub-channel for sending messages. Each of these sub-channels is again separated into up-link and down-link parts. Nodes, in general, will use up-link bands for communicating with the controller, while down-link component is used for sending any message to individual nodes. The bandwidth in each of these sub-channels can be evaluated by a formula pre-determined for the club, so that once a member node gets the estimate of down-link control sub-channel, it can calculate the bandwidth of other channels or sub-channels used for the club. The controller then periodically broadcasts its presence through beacons that consists of all 1s encoded by club sequence in down-link control sub-channel.

3.2   Joining of Members

When the next member node, say B in fig-1 (b), arrives at the same location, it senses the presence of the club. On receiving the club sequence, it comes to know the existence of the club. It then broadcast a join beacon or RIP (request for IP comprised of member-id, public key, and MAC addresses) encoded by club sequence in the up-link control sub-channel. The controller, as a normal authentication procedure, checks the existence of the received member-id, public key, and MAC addresses of the new node in its own member-table to ensure if the requesting node is a member of the club. If a match is found with a club member, the controller registers the new node as a participating node. It allocates and sends the IP address to this new node, say i=2. Besides, it sends its own member-id, public key, and MAC address to the new node by using the MAC address of that node for its self authentication and for favor of updating of node table of the new node. The controller also stores the member-id and IP address of this new node in its node-table. This second member joining the club is taken as standby controller. Whenever controller moves away or goes down standby controller acts as controller with corresponding broadcast to all participating members.

The subsequent node, say C in fig-1 (c), arriving at the location senses the presence of the club and then broadcasts a join beacon. The controller would check the authentication parameters in the beacon in the similar manner as described above. It allocates the IP address, say i=3 and registers the new node after usual authentication procedure. The controller then broadcasts the member-id and IP address of the new node as announcement of registration, so that the other node(s) may update the node-table(s). The controller also sends member-id and IP address of other registered nodes

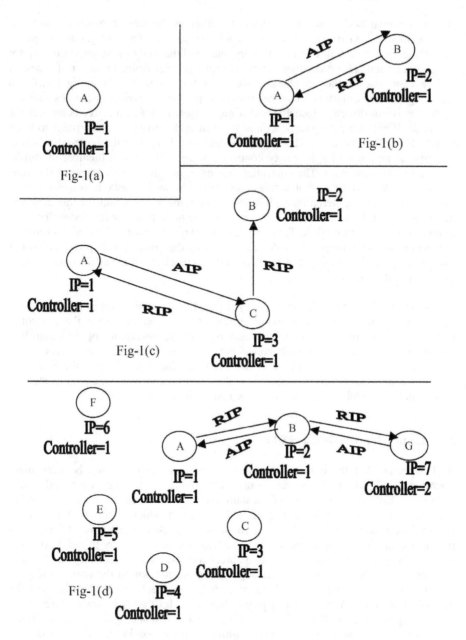

Legends: RIP (Request for IP), AIP (Allocation of IP)
Fig. 1. Ad hoc Network Formation of Mobile Users Club.

in its node-table along with its own member-id, public key, and MAC addresses to the new node.

Any subsequent nodes may be registered further in the similar manner. However, when a node, say G in fig-1 (d), sends a join beacon but does not get any response from the controller it will continue to retry and send the join beacon intermittently for a time-out period. This procedure is repeated for a pre-determined number of times. In such a case, one of the peripheral nodes or relay nodes (say B in fig-1 (d)), on receiving such intermittent join beacons for a prolonged period, presumes that the controller is not directly reachable and decides itself to act as a proxy controller for that node. It will relay the join beacon of the new node towards the controller to fetch an IP address for that node. The fetched IP address along with the node-table is sent towards the new node by the proxy controller along with its own member-id, public key, and MAC addresses. The controller, however, makes announcement of this new registration. The proxy controller relays all control as well as data messages received from the member registered through it and all such messages meant for this member. The proxy controllers are required to store separate node-table for the nodes that have joined the network through it. This very fact of relaying activity of the nodes remains transparent to the unreachable nodes as well as to the controller. If proxy controller moves away and becomes out of reach then the unreachable node again sends beacon to join the network afresh.

In case the controller decides to go away it transfers its responsibility to the standby controller and if the elected standby controller is unavailable, then the controller selects one of its reachable nodes to hand over the responsibility of the controller. When a standby controller node becomes the controller, it immediately selects one of its reachable nodes to act as the next standby controller node. In case the controller goes down accidentally, the standby controller senses the absence of announcement of club from the controller and takes over the responsibility of controller.

3.3   Routing for Mobile Users Club

It is expected that the density of mobile users in a club will not be very high. Therefore, DSR like protocol can be used effectively for routing in a mobile users club. Like DSR protocol, it is based on source routing, in which the sender of a packet determines the complete sequence of nodes through which it has to forward the packet. The sender explicitly lists this route in the packet's header, identifying each forwarding hop to which the packet is to be transmitted on its way to the destination host. This protocol consists of two mechanisms: route discovery and route maintenance. If both the source and target hosts are not within the range, a request may be propagated using some kind of flooding to reach other hosts beyond the transmission range. As the request propagates, each host adds its own address to a route being recorded in the packet. With this kind of scheme, a link or router going down or one or more mobile users moving away would cause the route to mysteriously stop working with no feedback to the sender. The route maintenance protocol would provide the feedback for finding a modified route or a new route to be discovered.

4 Conclusion

We have discussed the possible prospects of a group-based ad hoc network of mobile users. Also, we have presented the formation of a semi ad hoc network that functions as a group under the supervision of a controller and where communication takes place among known and presumably trusted members. It is shown here that the group-based ad hoc network simplifies the problem of routing protocol selection. A simple DSR like protocol may be used for facilitating proper utilization of bandwidth. The DS-CDMA as medium access technique used here not only improves privacy in ad hoc networks, but also facilitates better utilization of bandwidth and power. In the inherently insecure ad hoc wireless network the group-based communication can infuse considerable security.

References

1. Tomasz Imielinski and Henry F. Korth: *Mobile Computing.* Kluwer Academic Publishers, 1996.
2. Charles E. Perkins: *Ad hoc Networking.* Addison Wesley, 2001.
3. Josh Broch, David A. Maltz, David B. Johnson, Yih-Chun Hu, Jorjeta Jetcheva: *A Performance Comparison of Multi-Hop Wireless Ad Hoc Network Routing Protocols.* In Proceedings of the Fourth Annual ACM/IEEE International Conference on Mobile Computing and Networking, October 1998.
4. Elizabeth Royer and C-K Toh: *A Review of Current Routing Protocols for Ad Hoc Mobile Wireless Networks.* IEEE Personal Communications Magazine, April 1999, pp. 46–55.
5. David B. Johnson, David A. Maltz: *Dynamic Source Routing in Ad Hoc Wireless Networks.* In Mobile Computing, edited by Tomasz Imielinski and Hank Korth, chapter 5, pages 153–181. Kluwer Academic Publishers, 1996.
6. Josh Broch, David A. Maltz, and David B. Johnson: *Supporting Hierarchy and Heterogeneous Interfaces in Multi-Hop Wireless Ad Hoc Networks.* In the Proceedings of the IEEE Workshop on Mobile Computing, June 1999.
7. Jim Binkley: *Authenticated Ad Hoc Routing at the Link Layer for Mobile Systems.* Internet Draft, 1999.
8. William Stallings: *Cryptography and Network Security – Principles and Practice.* II Edition, Pearson Education Asia, 2000.
9. Vesa Karpijoki: *Signalling and Routing Security in Mobile and Ad hoc Networks.* MANET, May 2000.
10. Andrew S. Tanenbaum: *Computer Networks*, PHI Publications, 1999.

Multipath Routing in Ad Hoc Wireless Networks with Omni Directional and Directional Antenna: A Comparative Study

Siuli Roy[1], Somprakash Bandyopadhyay[1], Tetsuro Ueda[2], and Kazuo Hasuike[2]

[1]Indian Institute of Management Calcutta, Joka, Calcutta 700104, India
[2]ATR Adaptive Communications Research Laboratories, Kyoto 619-0288, Japan
{siuli, somprakash}@iimcal.ac.in, {teueda, hasuike}@atr.co.jp

Abstract. Several routing schemes have been proposed in the context of mobile ad hoc network. Some of them use multiple paths simultaneously by splitting the information among multitude of paths, as it may help to reduce end-to-end delay and perform load balancing. Multipath routing also diminishes the effects of unreliable wireless links in the constantly changing topology of ad hoc networks to a large extent. *Route coupling*, caused by the interference during the simultaneous communication through multiple paths between a pair of source and destination, severely limits the performance gained by multipath routing. Using *node disjoint* multiple paths to avoid coupling is not at all sufficient to improve the routing performance in this context. Route coupling may be reduced to a great extent if zone disjoint or even partially *zone disjoint* paths are used for data communication. Two paths are said to be *zone disjoint* if data communication through one path does not interfere with other paths. Large path length (number of hops) also contributes to the performance degradation resulting in high end to end delay. So zone disjoint shortest multipath is the best choice under high traffic condition. However, it is difficult to get zone disjoint or even partially zone disjoint multiple routes using omni-directional antenna. This difficulty may be overcome if directional antenna is used with each mobile node. In this paper, we have done a comparative study on the performance of multipath routing using omni-directional and directional antenna. The result of the simulation study clearly shows that directional antenna improves the performance of multipath routing significantly as compared to that with omni-directional antenna.

1 Introduction

The routing schemes for ad hoc networks usually employ single-path routing [1,2]. Multipath routing scheme employs a set of paths from source S to destination D so that total volume of traffic may be divided and communicated via selected multiple paths which would perform load balancing and eventually reduce congestion and end to end delay [3–10]. It also diminishes the effect of unreliable wireless links in the constantly changing topology of mobile ad hoc network [6]. Moreover, the frequency of route discovery is much lower if a node maintains multiple paths to destination. However, *route coupling*, caused by the interference during simultaneous

S.K. Das and S. Bhattacharya (Eds.): IWDC 2002, LNCS 2571, pp. 184–191, 2002.
© Springer-Verlag Berlin Heidelberg 2002

communication through multiple paths, severely limits the performance gained by multipath routing in the context of ad hoc wireless networks. Using node disjoint multipath is not sufficient to improve the routing performance, as this inherent route coupling among those multiple paths may cause congestion. In order to reduce route coupling, directional antenna may be used instead of omni directional antenna. Due to low transmission zone of directional antenna, it is easier to get two physically close paths that may not interfere with each other during data communication. As a result, multipath routing performance will improve with directional antenna as compared to that with omni-directional antenna. To illustrate this point, the remainder of the paper is organized as follows: section 2 reviews related work. In section 3, notion of route coupling and zone disjoint routes is introduced. Section 4 and 5 present an analysis of multipath routing using omni-directional and directional antenna respectively. Section 6 presents a comparative analysis with performance results followed by concluding remarks in section 7.

2   Related Work

Application of multipath routing in ad hoc wireless network has been explored in recent years. An On Demand Multipath Routing scheme is presented in [7] as an extension of DSR [8] which uses one of the alternate routes kept in the source node for data communication if primary one fails. The Split Multipath Routing (SMR) proposed in [10] focuses on using maximally disjoint paths. It was argued in [9] that the performance of Alternate Path Routing depends a great deal on network topology and channel characteristics (Route Coupling). Two node disjoint paths are said to be coupled with each other if they are located physically close enough to interfere with each other during data communication. As a result, nodes on those paths, which are participating in simultaneous active communications, are constantly contending to access the medium and finally end up performing worse than single path protocol. Performance improvement in multipath routing through load balancing is studied in [9] but their work is based on multiple channels that are contention-free but may not be available in normal cases. Selection of node disjoint paths to improve the performance is discussed in [10, 11, 12]. But inherent route coupling degraded the performance gained by using node disjoint multiple paths [9]. So it is intuitive that route coupling should be reduced to achieve good routing performance. The effect of route coupling can be drastically reduced, if we use directional antenna instead of omni-directional antenna with each user-terminal forming an ad hoc network. It has been shown that the use of directional antenna can largely reduce radio interference, thereby improving the utilization of wireless medium and consequently the network throughput [13, 14]. In our earlier work, we have developed the MAC and routing protocol using directional ESPAR antenna [13, 15] and demonstrated the performance improvement. In this paper, we investigate the effect of directional antenna on multipath routing. We have done a comparative study on the performance of multipath routing using omni-directional and directional antenna. The result of the simulation study clearly shows that directional antenna improves the performance of multipath routing significantly as compared to that with omni-directional antenna.

3   Effect of Route Coupling

Suppose there are two node-disjoint paths, S1-x1-y1-D1 and S2-x2-y2-D2, ie. they share no common nodes. Since paths are node-disjoint, it is expected that the end to end delay in each case should be independent of each other. However if x1 and x2 and/or y1 and y2 are neighbors of each other, then two communications can not happen simultaneously because the RTS/CTS exchange during data communication will allow either x1 or x2 to transmit data packet at a time and so on. So end to end delay does not depend only on the congestion characteristics of the nodes, pattern of communication in the neighborhood region also contributes to this delay. This phenomenon is called *route coupling*. As a result, coupled nodes in those two paths are constantly contending to access the medium thereby degrading the performance of multipath protocol. Thus node-disjoint paths are not at all sufficient for improved performance. So we proposed a notion of *zone-disjoint* paths for simultaneous data communication to improve network performance. Two paths are said to be zone disjoint if data communication through one path does not interfere with other paths. But getting zone-disjoint or even partially zone disjoint paths using omni directional antenna is difficult since transmission zone is larger. Transmission zone for each node in case of omni-directional antenna $=\pi R^2$ where beam angle $\theta = 360°$ and transmission range is R. By controlling the beam angle θ ($<360°$) using directional antenna, coverage area of each node may be reduced to $\theta R^2/2$. So a node on a path (x1 on S1-x1-y1-D1), interfering the transmission along other path (S2-x2-y2-D2) due to coupling between x1 and x2 earlier using omni-directional antenna, may not interfere with each other during data communication if directional antenna is used. The effect of route coupling is measured in [12] using a correlation factor η and paths with lower correlation factors are selected for simultaneous communications. We have redefined correlation factor η of a node n in a path P, $\eta^n(P)$, as the number of *active neighbors* of n not belonging to path P, where *active neighbors* of n is defined as those nodes within the transmission zone of n that are actively participating in any communication process at that instant of time. Correlation factor η of path P, $\eta(P)$ is defined as the sum of correlation factor of all nodes in path P (figure 1). Path P is said to be zone disjoint if $\eta(P) = 0$. Paths with lowest $\eta(P)$ values are selected to obtain Zone disjoint / partially zone disjoint paths. But to consider the effect of path length in this context, longer paths with more number of hops are discarded, as they increase end to end delay. To deal with the problem, our route selection criteria is to minimize the product of η and H (=number of hops in path P).

4   Multipath Routing with Omni-directional Antenna

It is difficult to get fully zone-disjoint routes using omni-directional antenna. As in figure 1, since both a and d are within omnidirectional transmission range of S, a RTS from S to node a will also disable node d. Similarly, since both c and f are within omni- directional transmission range of D, a CTS from D will disable both c and f. So, the lowest possible η [$\eta^{min}(omni)$] in case of omni-directional antenna with two multipath between s and d is 2 if two paths have *no common nodes* excepting source and destination. With directional antenna, it is possible to de-couple these two routes, making them fully zone-disjoint. If each node sets their transmission zone towards its target node only, then the communication between S-a-b-c-D will not affect the communication between S-d-e-f-D. Hence $\eta^{min}(omni)=2$ whereas $\eta^{min}(dir)=0$.

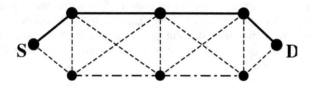

Fig. 1. Two node disjoint paths with $\eta=9$

As a result, even if we get multiple zone-disjoint routes with minimal correlation factor using omni-directional antenna, the best-case packet arrival rate at the destination node will be 1 packet at every $2*t_p$, where t_p is the average delay per hop per packet of a traffic stream on the path p. The best-case assumption is, single traffic stream in the network from S to D with error-free transmission of packets. Let us refer to figure 1 and assume that each node is equipped with omni-directional antenna and two paths having minimal correlation factor i.e. $\eta = 2$ are used for data communication. This implies that nodes{a,b,c} and nodes {d,e,f} are disjoint. Let us denote t_p as a time-tick, and at each time-tick, a packet is getting transmitted from one node to other. Consider table 1. S is sending a data-packet P_1 to node a at time-tick T_0 and node a is sending data-packet P_1 to node b in the next time tick i.e. T_1. With omni-directional antenna, S has to sit idle during T_1, because S has received RTS from node a. So, S can only transmit its second packet P_2 to node d (first node of the second path) at time-tick T_2. The packet transition is shown in Table 1 and destination D will receive packets in alternate time-tick. *Even if we increase the number of paths between s and d beyond 2, the situation will not improve with omni-directional antenna.*

Table 1. Packet arrival rate at D with omni-directional antenna with two paths (s-a-b-c-d and s-d-e-f-d) having minimun η (=2)

	S	a	b	c	d	e	f
T_0	$P_1{>}a$						
T_1		$P_1{>}b$					
T_2	$P_2{>}d$		$P_1{>}c$				
T_3				$P_1{>}D$	$P_2{>}e$		
T_4	$P_3{>}a$					$P_2{>}f$	
T_5		$P_3{>}b$					$P_2{>}D$
T_6	$P_4{>}d$		$P_3{>}c$				
T_7	...	...	...	...	...	...	...

5   Multipath Routing with Directional Antenna

In contrast, if we use directional antenna, best-case packet arrival rate at destination will be one packet at every t_p. Table 2 illustrate this point. With directional antenna, when node a is transmitting a packet to node b, S can transmit a packet to node d simultaneously. Thus, as shown in Table 2, destination D will receive a packet at every time-tick with two zone-disjoint paths using directional antenna. It is to be noted here that *two zone-disjoint paths with directional antenna is sufficient to achieve this best-case scenario.*

Table 2. Packet arrival rate at d with directional antenna with two zone-disjoint paths (s-a-b-c-d and s-d-e-f-d) having $\eta=0$.

	S	a	b	c	d	e	f
T_0	$P_1>a$						
T_1	$P_1>d$	$P_1>b$					
T_2	$P_2>a$		$P_1>c$		$P_2>e$		
T_3	$P_4>d$	$P_3>b$		$P_1>D$		$P_2>f$	
T_4	$P_5>a$		$P_3>c$		$P_4>e$		$P_2>D$
T_5	$P_6>d$	$P_5>b$		$P_3>D$		$P_4>f$	
T_6	$P_7>a$		$P_5>c$		$P_6>a$		$P_5>D$

6   Effect of Directional and Omni Directional Antenna on Multiple Multipath Communications: A Comparative Study

In this study, nodes were randomly placed into an area 1000 X 1500 at a certain density. Sources and destinations were selected such that they are multi hop away from each other. A source and destination were randomly selected and multi-hop (maximum hop = 5) paths are found. Between the selected source and destination, two zone-disjoint routes were found out using fixed range directional antenna. If two zone-disjoint routes were not available for that source-destination pair, another source-destination pair was selected. Then we have assumed that each node is having omni-directional antenna and computed the correlation factor η_{omni} among those two routes that are zone-disjoint with directional antenna. This experiment was repeated for 25 source destination pair. As discussed, in each case, η_{dir} is zero and we compute η_{omni}. Then, the average η_{omni} were found out. Then, we change the node density and repeat this experiment. The results are shown in figure 2. As the number of nodes in the system increases, average η_{omni} increases. However, η_{dir} is zero in all the cases. This indicates that it is possible to get zone-disjoint paths with directional antenna at different node densities but same paths will have high correlation factors, if we use omni-directional antenna instead.

Effect of new coupling factor gamma ($\gamma = \eta*H$) on multiple multipath communications with directional and omni directional antenna is studied in the same simulation environment and it is found that, if the number of simultaneous communications increases in the network, the coupling factor γ increases substantially

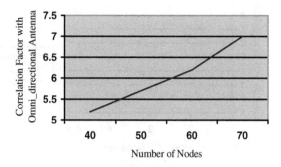

Fig. 2. Average correlation factor η_{omni} at different number of nodes when $\eta_{dir}=0$.

in case of omni directional antenna compared to directional antenna. Average gamma (γ) is calculated by taking two low γ paths for each of the active communications in the system. It is found that average gamma (γ) increases sharply using omni directional antenna if number of simultaneous communications in the system increases. On the other hand if each node is equipped with directional antenna with fixed transmission zone angle $60°$ then increase of average gamma for the system is not so high compared to omni directional case. Figure 3 clearly shows the above result.

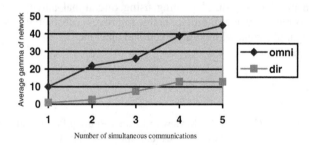

Fig. 3. Increase in route coupling with multiple multipath communications with omni directional and directional antenna

Average end to end delay per packet between a set of selected s-d pairs with increasing number of communication has been shown in figure 4. The result shows that the average end-to-end delay per packet increases much more sharply with omni-directional antenna compared to that with directional antenna. This is an obvious consequence of the phenomenon illustrated with figure 3 and it can be concluded that the routing performance using multiple paths improves substantially with directional antenna compared to that with omni-directional antenna.

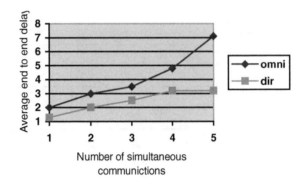

Fig. 4. Increase in average end to end delay with multiple multipath communications using omni- and directional antenna : A sample observation

7   Conclusion

In order to make effective use of multipath routing protocols in the mobile ad hoc network environment, it is imperative that we consider the effects of route coupling. However, high degree of route coupling among multiple routes between any source and destination pair is inevitable, if we use omni-directional antenna. The situation will worsen, if we consider multiple simultaneous communications with multiple active routes. This paper has analysed the problem and proposed a mechanism to alleviate the problem of route coupling using directional antenna. As a result, the routing performance using multiple paths improves substantially with directional antenna compared to that with omni-directional antenna.

References

1. E. M. Royer and C-K Toh, "A Review of Current Routing Protocols for Ad hoc Wireless Networks", IEEE Personal Communication, April 1999, pp. 46–55.
2. J. Broch, D. A. Maltz, D. B. Johnson, Y. C. Hu, and J. Jetcheva, "A Performance Comparison of Multi-Hop Wireless Ad Hoc Network Routing Protocols," *Proc. ACM/IEEE Mobile Comput. and Network*, Dallas, TX, Oct. 1998.
3. Sajal K. Das, A. Mukherjee, Somprakash Bandyopadhyay, Krishna Paul, D. Saha, "Improving Quality-of-Service in Ad hoc Wireless Networks with Adaptive Multi-path Routing, Proc. Of the GLOBECOM 2000, San Francisco, California, Nov. 2000.
4. N.S.V.Rao and S.G. Batsell, QoS Routing via Multiple Paths Using Bandwidth Reservation, Proc. of the IEEE INFOCOM 98.
5. S. Bahk and W. El-Zarki, Dynamic Multi-path Routing and how it Compares with other Dynamic Routing Algorithms for High Speed Wide-area Networks, in Proc. of the ACM SIGCOM, 1992

6. Aristotelis Tsirigos Zygmunt J. Haas, Siamak S. Tabrizi, Multi-path Routing in mobile ad hoc networks or how to route in the presence of frequent topology changes , MILCOM 2001.
7. A. Nasipuri and S.R. Das, "On-Demand Multi-path Routing for Mobile Ad Hoc Networks," Proceedings of IEEE ICCCN'99, Boston, MA, Oct. 1999.
8. B. Johnson and D. A. Maltz, "Dynamic Source Routing in Ad Hoc Wireless Networks," T. Imielinski and H. Korth, editors, *Mobile Computing*, Kluwer, 1996.
9. M. R. Pearlman, Z. J. Haas, P. Sholander, and S. S. Tabrizi, On the Impact of Alternate Path Routing for Load Balancing in Mobile Ad Hoc Networks, MobiHOC 2000.
10. S.J. Lee and M. Gerla, Split Multi-path Routing with Maximally Disjoint Paths in Ad Hoc Networks, ICC 2001.
11. Z. J. Haas and M. R. Pearlman, "Improving the Performance of Query-Based Routing Protocols Through Diversity Injection," *IEEE Wireless Communications and Networking Conference WCNC 1999,* New Orleans, LA, September 1999.
12. Kui Wu and Janelle Harms, On-Demand Multipath Routing for Mobile Ad Hoc Networks EPMCC 2001, Vienna, 20th–22nd February 2001
13. Somprakash Bandyopadhyay, K. Hasuike, S. Horisawa, S. Tawara, "An Adaptive MAC Protocol for Wireless Ad Hoc Community Network (WACNet) Using Electronically Steerable Passive Array Radiator Antenna", Proc of the GLOBECOM 2001, November 25–29, 2001, San Antonio, Texas, USA
14. Y.-B. Ko, V. Shankarkumar and N. H. Vaidya, "Medium access control protocols using directional antennas in ad hoc networks," Proc. Of the IEEE INFOCOM 2000, March 2000.
15. Somprakash Bandyopadhyay, K. Hasuike, S. Horisawa, S. Tawara, "An Adaptive MAC and Directional Routing Protocol for Ad Hoc Wireless Network Using Directional ESPAR Antenna", Proc of the ACM Symposium on Mobile Ad Hoc Networking & Computing 2001 (MOBIHOC 2001), Long Beach, California, USA, 4–5 October 2001.

Performance Modeling of Wireless Voice over IP

Abhishek Roy, Kalyan Basu, and Sajal K. Das*

CReWMaN Lab
Dept of Computer Science and Engineering
University of Texas at Arlington
Arlington, TX 76019-0015, USA
{aroy, basu, das}@cse.uta.edu

Abstract. The recent popularity of voice over IP (VoIP) services in the
Internet world lies in the fact that in VoIP, voice packets are carried
over the shared packet-switched network (the Internet) rather than on
dedicated circuit-switched telephony network. This phenomenon reduces
the cost of carrying the voice packets substantially. We propose that the
concept of VoIP over wireless GPRS (General Packet Radio Service) also
reduces the complexity of the GSM/GPRS architecture. Currently, the
existing GSM (Global System for Mobile Communications) network carries the voice packets in the air link and converts it to circuit-switched
PCM (Pulse Code Modulation) signal by using the voice transcoder.
A 64 Kbps circuit-switched connection is then established through the
existing PSTN (Public Switch Telephone Network). Wireless data packets on the other hand, share the same physical air link, but are carried
through the GPRS packet-switched network. If we carry the voice on the
same packet-switched network rather than on a separate circuit-switched
network, then integration of data and voice would alleviate the necessity
of circuit-switched components. However, maintaining the voice quality
offers significant challenges. In this paper we propose a method of implementing the VoIP in GPRS network using H.323 protocol, and also
identify the additional architecture requirements that will address some
of the performance impediments of current GPRS VoIP implementation. The performance results for control message signals demonstrate
the possibility of maintaining call set-up delay within the current delay
standards. Analytical modeling of the voice traffic shows that significant
improvements in terms of voice traffic capacity is possible with the help
of a silent-detection scheme.

1 Introduction

The wide popularity and high success of mobile voice services are already reflected in the subscription of almost one billion mobile users worldwide. More
than two-third of these mobile phones are of GSM (Global System for Mobile

* This work is partially supported by NSF grants under EIA-0086260, EIA-0115885,
IIS-0121297 and Texas Telecommunication Engineering Consortium (TxTEC).

Communications) standard. GSM supports the business needs for data and messaging by using the circuit-switched data at 9.6 Kbps and SMS (Short Messaging Service). In order to enhance the data capability of the GSM system and provide data services rates of up to 128+ Kbps in GSM Phase2+ [5], new GPRS (General Packet Radio Services) standard has been defined. The introduction of GPRS has created new opportunities for E-business and multimedia services. Many E-business services require integration of mobility, voice and data under one network. Presently in the GSM network this integration is not possible, because voice and data connections are handled through two different network infrastructures. To overcome this complexity and reduce the service cost, the possibility of carrying the voice traffic also on the GPRS network is recently investigated. In order to handle the VoIP and multimedia services on the IP (Internet Protocol) network, ITU (International Telecommunications Union) has already defined the protocol H.323 [8]. The Internet Engineering Task Force (IETF) has also defined SIP (Session Initiation Protocol) [12] to handle VoIP and multimedia with mobility using the Internet.

In this paper we have investigated some major issues and challenges in introduction of VoIP services in the wireless GPRS networks. We first propose the VoIP GPRS architecture, which is capable of supporting the performance of VoIP services close to the ITU voice quality standards. The call set-up delay, burst level media packet blocking and media packet overhead of H.323 protocol are analyzed. The performance efficiency of the architecture is reflected in the reduction of H.323 call set-up delay and GPRS burst level blocking. Results from the analysis confirms the usability of H.323 for control signalling and identifies the opportunity for additional voice capacity of the wireless channel by using a *silent-detection* scheme.

The remaining part of the paper is structured as follows. Section 2 describes the proposed VoIP GPRS architecture. Section 3 analyzes the overhead associated with the voice traffic by providing the selection of low bit rate coding and mapping of the coded frames to GPRS frames. The voice quality issues of GPRS VoIP service, identification of the different impediments contributed by various network segments, and establishment of the preliminary expected performance of the system are discussed in Section 4. In Section 5, the performance of our proposed architecture is evaluated by developing a suitable model. Finally, Section 6 summarizes our results and discusses possible future extensions.

2   VoIP GPRS Architecture

Figure 1 shows the connection of GPRS to a WAN (Wide Area Network) through GGSN/SGSN (Gateway GPRS Support Node/Serving GPRS Support Node). The WAN, in turn, is connected to the H.323 LAN network through GW (Gate-Way) and GK (Gate Keeper). The mobile GPRS terminal can inter-work with H.323 LAN network terminal for voice communications. The protocol considered in this discussion is H.323 using Direct connect mode of operation. As depicted in Figure 2, H.323 is a protocol suite capable of handling session establishment, media connection and different control functions. The functions for session establishment is implemented using the Q.931 messaging on protocol H.225. The H.245 protocol is used for capability verification and synchronization of the terminals. H.225 and H.245 protocols are embedded in the TCP layer. The media control function is implemented through the RTCP (Real-time TCP) to control different media streams. Media transmission occurs using the RTP (Real Time Protocol). One major challenge for wireless VoIP is the high FER (Frame Error Rate) of the wireless links. Although the control message is delay tolerant, it requires very high level of integrity and very low BER (bit error rate) quality. On the other hand, the RTP voice packets are very sensitive to delay, but can tolerate higher FER.

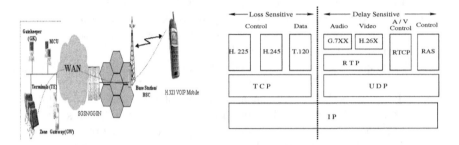

Fig. 1. System-view of VoIP over GPRS   **Fig. 2.** H.323 Protocol Suite

It has been observed in the current wireless network that an FER of 10^{-1}–10^{-3} is suitable for reasonable voice quality. In the wireless air interface, the RLP (Radio Link Protocol) layer brings the attributes needed for the control messages to recover from high FER. For voice packets, RLP will degrade the voice quality due to its delay variations and jitter resulted from ARQ (Automatic Repeat Request) retransmissions. Therefore, we propose to separate these two packet streams and handle them through two different mechanisms of the air-interface.

Table 1. H.323 Messaging Overhead

Messages		Payload (bytes)	
Regular H.323	FastConnect H.323	Regular	FastConnect
Set-Up H.323	Set-up + FastConnect	254	599
Alerting	Alerting	97	97
Connecting H.225	Connect+FastConnect	165	165
TC-Set H.245(2)	–	589 × 2	–
TC-Set ACK H.245(2)	–	71 × 2	–
OC-Set H.245(4)	–	115 × 4	–
OC-Set ACK H.245(4)	–	64 × 4	–
RTCP	RTCP	120	120

The control messages will be routed through the medium access control (MAC) / RLP [6] layer of the air interface. We also propose that RTP voice packets will bypass the RLP stage and be transmitted without any ARQ protection. This capability is supported in H.323 recommendations. Hence, N-PDUs (Packet Data Units) created by the H.323 processing will be classified into two classes by using a classifier as shown in Figure 3. H.323 media streams for interactive traffic (particularly, VoIP) are treated differently from the H.323 control packet streams (e.g., H.225, H.245, RTCP messages). The GPRS protocol will require *transparent* RLP (i.e., no RLP retransmission) for VoIP packets to provide this classification. Also, due to the interactive nature of voice, VoIP packets should get higher priority over any in-band H.323 control packets within the session. The performance of the VoIP call set-up using wireless links is influenced by three factors: (1) the number of messages exchanged to set-up the call, (2) size of the messages, and (3) the number of TCP sessions set-up. Reduction of any of these factors results in shorter call-set up delay. Regular H.323 call set-up uses many TCP messages with varying payload sizes generating about 112 GPRS CS-2 (Coding Scheme-2) message frames. With high FER, the average call set-up delay for the regular H.323 procedure can be as high as about 15–20 secs. This high delay is not acceptable compared to the current call set-up delay (less than 3 secs) of the PSTN (Public Switch Telephone Network) system. To improve the performance, we propose to use the Fast Connect mode in addition to Direct Routing Call in H.323. Table 1 depicts the relatively lower size of Fast Connect messages compared to regular call set-up messages, where TC and OC denotes represent Terminal Capability and Openlogical Connect respectively.

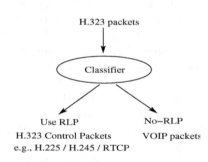

Fig. 3. H.323 Classifier for VoIP

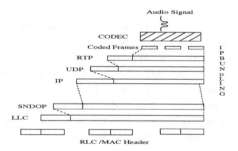

Fig. 4. VoIP Packet Bundling and Mapping over GPRS

3   Voice Packet Overhead Analysis

Before proceeding into the details of the overhead analysis of voice packets, an investigation into the media packet transport design of VoIP reveals that it is composed of three major steps, namely, (i) the selection of the voice codec and the mapping of the coded packets to create the Internet payload, (ii) the selection of Internet protocol (preferably UDP) to transfer the media packets, and (iii) finding out the mechanism for transmission of the voice packets through the wireless access links to the Internet.

The bundling of the voice frames of coder is necessary to reduce overhead. The number of voice frames of coder is grouped together to make one UDP packet as shown in Figure 4. The IP packets are mapped into Link Layer Control (LLC) packets through the SNDOP compression scheme. The LLC packets are then fragmented into Radio Link Control (RLC) frames. This bundling will result additional delay on the voice path. Let r, f, F and β respectively denote the rate, frame-time, frame-size and bundling-factor in voice coding. If H_{ip}, H_{UDP}, H_{RTP} and H_{GPRS} represent the IP, UDP, RTP and GPRS headers respectively, then the resulting GPRS packet size P_{GPRS} and the associated overhead for conversion of voice frames on UDP packets are given by:

$$P_{GPRS} = F.\beta + (H_{ip} + H_{UDP} + H_{RTP} + H_{GPRS}) \qquad (1)$$

$$Overhead = \frac{(H_{ip} + H_{UDP} + H_{RTP} + H_{GPRS})}{P_{GPRS}} \times 100\%.$$

Figure 5 shows the overhead penalty of three different voice coders: AMRC (Adaptive Multi-Rate Codes) at 4.75 Kbps, G.729 at 8 Kbps and GSM voice coder at 13.2 Kbps. With the increase in the number of bundles per frame, the overhead penalty decreases but additional delay results in the system. The codec voice packets, as shown in Figure 4, after being bundled are segmented to fit into the GPRS frame size. The actual transmission of the packets through the GPRS channel in the upstream involves three functions. In the uplink direction, the GPRS traffic channel request is sent to the GPRS base station using uplink random access channel. BSC (Base Station Controller) transmits a notification to MS (Mobile Station) terminal indicating TBF (Temporary Block Flow) allocation. TBF allocation is basically a physical connection used to support the transfer of blocks. Each of this TBF connections is assigned one TFI (Temporary Flow Identifier). This TFI is included in each of the transmitted radio block so that multiplexing of different MS can be done on the same PDCH (Packet Data Channel). The mobile terminal uses TFI to send the voice packet. Since GPRS uses the dynamic bandwidth allocation, when a new user needs bandwidth or an existing user wants more bandwidth, physical connection is established by the interaction between MS and BS (Base Station), thereby allowing the MS to send the data in the uplink direction. Every time when MS wants to send the data, the physical connection with the BS has to be established and at the end of the transmission it needs to be explicitly torn down. This entire procedure of connection establishment and termination is quite time consuming. The PCU (Process Control Unit) of the GPRS performs the allocation of the capacity of the traffic channel for transfer of the voice packets to the base station. Because of the sharing of the multiple GPRS terminals by the same GPRS traffic resources, the VoIP will encounter blocking. This blocking depends upon the number of active GPRS terminals in the cell and the intensity of the voice packets generated by the active voice terminals.

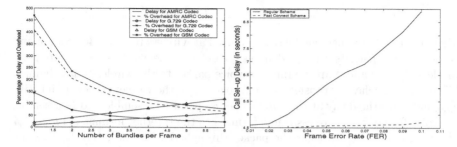

Fig. 5. Overhead vs. Delay for Codec Frame Bundling

Fig. 6. H.323 Call Set-up Delay using GPRS

4   Quality of VoIP Services in GPRS

The support of voice quality in VoIP services using GPRS is a challenging issue. Generally a rating scale of 1 to 5 is used for voice quality specification. This is often termed as MOS (Mean Opinion Score) scale [10]. The wireline voice quality is normally within 4–4.5 MOS. The current wireless voice quality lies within 3.5–4 MOS. In the network the coded voice signals are transmitted through multiple nodes and links as shown in Figure 1. While introducing VoIP, additional delay is introduced due to the selection of coding technology, bundling factor, Internet protocol and allocation of TBF. All these network links and nodes also cause additional impediments to the coded voice signals. The ITU recommendations G.113 and G.114 specify several requirements, including:

1. End-to-end noise accumulation limited to fourteen quantization distortion unit (qdu) where each 'qdu' is equal to the noise of single 64 Kbps PCM (Pulse Coded Modulation) devices;
2. End-to-end transmission delay budget of 300 msecs;
3. G.114 limits the processing delay for codec at each end to 10 msecs.

Among these network requirements, the most important one in the design of VoIP using GPRS link is the end-to-end delay budget of 300 msecs. A hypothetical connection of a wireless voice terminal through wireless and land-line infrastructure would include network components like wireless terminal, air link, access point, wireless gateway, Internet, and Land-line terminal. The wireless terminal includes the codec function and mapping of the frames into the wireless data channel. The delay introduced in the wireless link is caused by the multiple access standards and FER due to propagation and fading characteristics. Once the packet is received at the wireless access point, it is transferred to the terminating media gateway through the Internet. At the media gateway, the coded voice packets are reconverted to the analog voice signals and transferred to the terminating analog voice terminals using copper wire connection. A jitter buffer is used at this stage to eliminate this jitter. The end-to-end delay of the voice packet for this hypothetical connection can be represented by the following equation:

$$D_{end} = d_{wt} + d_{wc} + d_{wl} + d_{wap} + d_{internet} + d_{mgw} + d_{jitter} \qquad (2)$$

where (i) d_{wt} represents the delay introduced at wireless terminal for coding and decoding voice packets, (ii) d_{wc} denotes the delay at the wireless terminal to get a wireless channel and map the Internet voice packet to the wireless data channel, (iii) d_{wl} is the delay to transfer the voice packets to the wireless access point, (iv) d_{wap} indicates the delay at the wireless access point to assemble and re-assemble the voice frame from wireless frame formats to the Internet format, (v) $d_{internet}$ denotes the delay to transfer the packet through the Internet, (vi) d_{mgw} is the delay at the media gateway to convert the Internet voice packets to the analog voice signals and transferred to the analog voice lines and (vii) d_{jitter} denotes delay introduced by the de-jitter buffer. We have considered the AMR coding with 3 frames bundling and CS2 scheme for GPRS. Assuming the average values of d_{jitter}, d_{wt}, d_{wc}, d_{wl}, d_{wap}, $d_{internet}$ and d_{mgw} as 100 msec, 85 msec, 100 msec, 80 msec, 100 msec and 55 msec respectively, assuming negligible delay of d_{wap}, we can make an estimate of the delay as: $D_{end} \approx 100 + 85 + 100 + 80 + 100 + 55 \approx$ 520 msec. The number being more than 300 msec, is not acceptable for the voice quality. Thus the potential areas of improvement are the Internet, TBF allocation, coding, bundling and jitter. Enhancement to all these areas can bring the end-to-end delay close to 300 msec.

The wireless VoIP session hand-off between the two wireless access points is determined by the hand-off mechanism supported by the wireless mobility protocol. The consensus between the different standard bodies is that current Mobile-IP may be suitable for macro-mobility, but new technique is necessary for micro-mobility. GPRS, Cellular-IP [2], HAWAII [11], IDMP [4] are potential candidates for micro-mobility function. The fast registration to the new system in Inter domain hand-off and the continuation of the media packet flow from/to gateway to the new base station are the two major factors in determining the hand-off performance. The concept of Shadow Registration [9] will improve the performance of the registration. The media packet flow scheme from/to Gateway to new base station is yet to be solved. Most of the protocols, in its current form have difficulty to meet the micro mobility requirements of the voice packets.

5   Performance Analysis

The performance analysis of VoIP using GPRS involves three important areas namely, (i) call set-up delay, (ii) blocking of voice packets in GPRS link and (iii) packet transfer delay during hand-off. As the current standards for micro mobility is not mature enough for voice services, we are not addressing this performance issue now.

5.1   Delay Analysis of H.323 Control Signaling over Wireless

The total call set-up delay will be the cumulative delay due to: (a) set-up time for two TCP sessions including exchange of SYN, SYN-ACK, ACK messages;

(b) successful transmission of all H.225 and H.245 messages; and (c) successful reception of an RTCP CNAME message. Here we briefly highlight the salient features of the control-signaling delay. A more detail analysis of this delay is described in our previous paper [3].

Our analysis of RTCP packets is based on mathematical models suggested in [1,13] for CDMA networks. We assume a maximum of 3 trials in our analysis for RLP and restrict the maximum retransmission time for a packet to be much less than the RTCP transmission interval. Let T_2 and T_1 represent the average delay associated with receiving the first RTCP packet containing CNAME item after joining the session with and without RLP respectively. While analyzing the TCP performance a radio channel bandwidth 13.4 Kbps is assumed. The two endpoints are considered to be in close proximity, such that wireline network delay becomes negligible. Furthermore, TCP will not allow infinite number of retransmissions. The TCP packet loss rate is $q = 1 - (1 - p)^\kappa$, where p is the probability of a frame being in error in the air link and κ is the number of air-link frames contained in a TCP segment. Now, if TCP retransmission succeeds after N_m attempts (without loss of generality we assume $N_m = 10$), the probability of successfully transmitting a TCP segment is: $1 - q^{N_m}$. If the average delay for successfully transmitting a TCP segment with no more than N_m retransmission trials is represented by TN, the total call set-up delay is the cumulative addition of the delays for transmitting all the H.323 call set-up messages and the RTCP : CNAME packet. The total delay without RLP is thus

$$T_{noRLP} = \sum_{i=1}^{N_m} TN_i + T_1, \tag{3}$$

where TN_i is the average delay given above for TCP segment. Similarly, if TR represent the average delay to transmit a TCP segment successfully with RLP, the average call set-up delay is represented by

$$T_{RPL} = \sum_{i=1}^{N_m} T_i + T_2, \; where \, T_i = min\{TR_i, TN_i\}. \tag{4}$$

Figure 6 compares the average call set-up delays associated with a regular connect procedure and a Fast Connect procedure for GPRS CS-2, respectively. The call set-up delay for Fast Connect procedure is consistently below 5 seconds for GPRS CS-2 if FER is less than 9%. This is close to the PSTN call set up time of 3 sec.

5.2   Analysis of GPRS Burst-Level Blocking

The channel blocking probabilities are determined by using the two-stage modeling technique. In the first stage the probability of the number of active sources in the system is determined using Markov process with quasi-random arrival. Figure 7 depicts this scenario, where every state represents the number of active VoIP terminals in the cell.

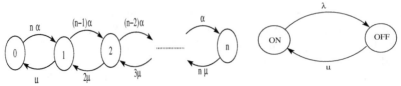

Fig. 7. State-model for VoIP Source

Fig. 8. Two-Stage On-Off Modeling for Voice Traffic

Let n, α, $\frac{1}{\mu}$ and P_k represent the total number of VoIP terminals in the cell coverage area, arrival rate of the *free* VoIP traffic source, mean Service time of one VoIP source, and probability of k VoIP traffic sources active in the system. In equilibrium state the flow must be conserved. Thus from Figure 7, for the k VoIP terminals in the system we have

$$(k - 1)\, \mu P_{k+1} + (n - k + 1)\alpha P_{k-1} = [(n - k)\alpha + k\mu]P_k \tag{5}$$

$$\Rightarrow \quad P_k = P_0 \prod_{j=0}^{k-1} \frac{\alpha(n - j)}{(j + 1)\mu} = P_0 \left(\frac{\alpha}{\mu}\right)^k \binom{n}{k} = P_0 \binom{n}{k}\gamma^k,$$

where $\gamma = \frac{\alpha}{\mu}$. The stationary state probabilities of the above equation is represented by

$$P_k = \frac{\binom{n}{k}\gamma^k}{\sum_{j=0}^m \binom{n}{j}\gamma^j}, \quad \forall k \in [0, m]. \tag{6}$$

The accepted VoIP session will generate the voice traffic bursts depending upon the coding speed and the bundling mechanism used in the system. We assume CS-2 coding scheme, the AMR coding with bundling factor of 3, UDP transport protocol and RTP header compression to model the 'on-off' bursts duration. The probabilities of the simultaneous traffic burst of the active sources are modeled by considering the on/off burst source model of the individual sources as a Bernoulli process. Figure 8 depicts this 'on-off' modeling, where λ and μ' denote the transition probabilities between 'on' and 'off' states. If ρ denotes the probability of being in 'on' state, then $\rho = \frac{\mu'}{\lambda+\mu'}$. Similarly, the probability of being in 'off' state is given by: $1 - \rho = \frac{\lambda}{\lambda+\mu'}$. Hence, among i active users in the system, the probability that k users will be in on-state at any instant is given as follows:

$$P_{ik} = \binom{i}{k}\rho^k(1 - \rho)^{i-k} \tag{7}$$

There are 8 mini slots in the GPRS system with 200 KHz mini spectrum in a cell. We assume VoIP payload from one user can be mapped to one slot of this GPRS channel. The joint probability that i active users in the system and k traffic bursts are generated is $P_i \times P_{ik}$. Hence, the probabilities of blocking of the bursts in the system is given by:

$$B = 1 - \sum_{i=0}^{n} \sum_{k=0}^{Min[i,8]} P_i \times P_{ik} \tag{8}$$

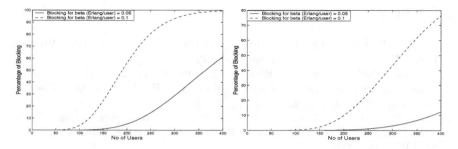

Fig. 9. GPRS Burst Level Blocking

Fig. 10. GPRS Burst Level Blocking With Silent Detection

The blocking performance with respect to the number of users is shown in Figure 9. Here we have assumed that the VoIP terminal generates 50 mili-Erlang and 100 mili-Erlang of traffic per user and the burst occupancy (average on-state duration per second) of 0.5.

In a two way conversation, when codec detects the silent period (*silent detection*), the average number of talk bursts will reduce and bring additional capacity in the radio link. A user normally talks about 50% of the time and listens for remaining 50% of the time. If we use 40% savings on capacity due to the unidirectional flow, more users can be supported in the system as shown in Figure 10. In Figure 10, assuming a very low burst level blocking, the system can support more than 200 users for 50 mili-Erlang/user.

6 Conclusion

In this paper we have discussed the implementation of VoIP using H.323 protocol in the GPRS system. Our analysis indicates that the regular implementation of H.323 using GPRS air-interface would not provide the performance of the system in call set-up delay and voice quality. We proposed the concept of classifier that separates the control packets and VoIP packets into two different air-link protocol stacks. We have also proposed to use Fast-connect method and tunneling to reduce the call-set up delay. Our modeling analysis confirms that this implementation of VoIP on GPRS system will provide the call set-up delay performance close to land-line communications. The burst level blocking probability of the voice packets can be kept low by using appropriate selection of codec type, bundling parameter and TBF allocation activation process. The analytical results of burst level blocking with silent detection indicates considerable subscriber capacity gain by using GPRS VoIP over the current GSM system. The end-to-end delay of the voice packets can be high, if the packet overhead percentage is low. The current TBF allocation mechanism requires enhancement to the delay reduction in allocating resources to the GPRS real-time traffic.

References

1. G. Bao, "Performance Evaluation of TCP/IP Protocol Stack over CDMA Wireless Link", *Wireless Networks*, Vol.3, No. 2, pp. 229–237, 1996.
2. A.T. Campbell, J. Gomez, S. Kim, A. G. Valko, C.-Y. Wan and Z.R. Turáni, "Design, implementation and evaluation of Cellular IP," *IEEE Personal Communications*, vol. 7, no. 4, August 2000, pp. 42–49.
3. S. K. Das, E. Lee, K. Basu, N. Kakani and S. Sen, "Performance Optimization of VoIP Calls Over Wireless Links Using H.323 Protocol", *IEEE INFOCOM*, Vol. 3, pp. 1386–1394, 2002.
4. S. Das, A. McAuley, A. Dutta, A. Misra, K. Chakraborty and S. K. Das, "IDMP: An Intra-domain Mobility Management Protocol for Next Generation Wireless Networks," *IEEE PCS, Spl. Issue on Mobile and Wireless Internet: Architectures and Protocols*, 2002.
5. "GSM 03.60: Digital Cellular Telecommunications Systems (Phase 2+); General Packet Radio Service (GPRS): Service Description Stage-2", *ETSI DTS/SMG-030360Q*, May 1998.
6. "Digital Cellular Telecommunications Systems (Phase 2+); General Packet Radio Service (GPRS): Radio Link Control / Media Access Control (RLC/MAC) protocol," , July, 1998.
7. "One-way transmission time", *ITU-T Recommendation G.114*, February, 1996.
8. "Packet based Multimedia Communication Systems", *ITU Recommendation H.323*, Feb 1998.
9. T. Kwon, M. Gerla, S. Das, and S. K. Das, "Mobility Management for VoIP Service: Mobile IP vs. SIP," *IEEE Wireless Communications (Special Issue on IP Multimedia in Next Generation Mobile Networks*, Guest Eds: S. Apostolis and L. Merakos), Oct 2002.
10. A. Lakaniemi and J. Parantainenj, "On Voice Quality of IP Voice over GPRS", *IEEE International Conference on Multimedia*, ICME, vol. 2, 2000.
11. R. Ramjee, T.F. La Porta, L. Salgarelli, S. Thuel, K. Varadhan and L. Li, "IP-based access network infrastructure for next-generation wireless data networks," *IEEE Personal Communications*, vol. 7, no. 4, August 2000, pp. 34–41.
12. M.Handley et al., "SIP : Session Initiation Protocol", *RFC 2543 Internet Engineering Task Force*, March, 1999.
13. S.K. Sen, J. Jawanda, K. Basu, N. K. Kakani and S.K. Das, "A Call Admission Control Scheme for TCP/IP based CDMA Voice/Data Networks", *ACM International Conference on Mobile Computing and Networking* (MobiCom), pp. 276–283, Dallas, 1998.

Push Less and Pull the Current Highest Demanded Data Item to Decrease the Waiting Time in Asymmetric Communication Environments

Cristina M. Pinotti and Navrati Saxena*

Dept. of Computer Science and Telecommunications, University of Trento,
Via Sommarive 14, Povo (TN), Italy
{pinotti,navrati}@science.unitn.it

Abstract. A hybrid scheduling that effectively combines broadcasting for very popular data (push data) and dissemination upon-request for less popular data (pull data) in asymmetric communication environments is introduced. In this solution, the server continuously broadcasts one push item and disseminates one pull item. The clients send their requests to the server, which queues-up them for the pull items. At any instant of time, the item to be broadcast is designated applying a pure-push scheduling, while the item to be pulled is the one stored in the pull-queue, which has accumulated, so far, the highest number of pending requests. The value of the average expected waiting time spent by a client in the hybrid system is evaluated analytically, and the cut-off point between push and pull items is chosen so that such a waiting time is minimized. It is found out that by doing so the cut off point decreases to a value, which is much less than the total number of items present in the system, improving upon the average waiting time spent by a client in a pure push system and also on that spent in some of the hybrid systems already proposed in literature.

1 Introduction

Day by day the ability to interconnect computers through cable, satellite and wireless networks is increasing and proportionately to this is also increasing a new application based on data dissemination. This application focuses on delivering data to a large population of clients. Often in dissemination-based systems, there exists communications' asymmetry. Basically, there are two approaches to spread data items in such systems: the push-based data scheduling, and the pull-based data scheduling.

A system where the client simply grabs the data being broadcast *without making any requests* is an example of *push-based* system. In such systems, the

---

* This work has been supported by the MIUR under the "REAL-WINE" research grant and by Computer Networks and Distributed Algorithms, DIT Research grant.

S.K. Das and S. Bhattacharya (Eds.): IWDC 2002, LNCS 2571, pp. 203–213, 2002.

clients continuously monitor the broadcast process and retrieve the data items they require. The server, on the other hand, broadcasts data items on scheduled time no matter whether the particular item is being required at that time or not. On the contrary, *pull-based* systems are *on demand* traditional client server systems where clients and server have a request/response style of relationship. In such systems, the clients initiate the data transfer by sending requests and the server then makes a schedule to satisfy the clients' requests.

Both push- and pull- based scheduling have their own advantages and disadvantages; as shown in [3,12] neither push nor pull based scheduling alone can achieve the optimal performance. A better performance is achieved when the two scheduling approaches are used in a combined manner.

In this paper, we divide the data items in two disjoint sets - push-set and pull-set. A push-based scheduling is then used to broadcast the items in the push-set, whereas a pull-based scheduling is used to disseminate those in the pull-set. The system performance metric for our system is the average expected access time experimented by the clients, which depends upon the push scheduling, the pull scheduling and heavily upon the criteria used to partition the items in the push- and pull-sets.

The rest of the paper is organized as follows: Section 2 reviews the past-related work that has been done in this area. Section 3, after introducing some preliminaries, offers motivations behind using our new hybrid system. Section 4 describes the behavior of the server and of the clients in the new hybrid scheduling. Besides, it devises the analytic evaluation of the average expected waiting time based on the push-based and pull-based scheduling adopted. In Section 5, the experimental results are reported. Finally, some discussions on future work are given in Section 6.

2   State of the Art: Past Related Work

Scheduling theory has been studied since decades. Among the research on broadcast scheduling, Acharya et al. [1,4,2] came up with the idea of Broadcast Disks. In such an approach, data items are assigned to several disks of different sizes and speeds, and are then multiplexed on a single broadcast channel. From this channel, the clients can retrieve data items based on their probability of access.

Later, Jain and Werth [15] proved that the optimal expected access time results when the instances of each item to be pushed are equally spaced, while Bennett and Zhang [9] determined which packet from many input queue should be transmitted next in the output channel so that the channel is used in a fair way. The fact that the push broadcast scheduling problem was related to Packet Fair Queuing was brought up by Vaidya and Hameed in [13,14], who also studied scheduling for multiple broadcast channels and the impact of the transmission error on scheduling. For broadcast disks with polynomial cost functions, Bar-Noy et al. [5] presented an asymptotically optimal algorithm for a fluid model, where the bandwidth may be divided to allow for fractional concurrent broadcasting. Mostly all of the above scheduling algorithms assume that the server knew the access probability of all the items in advance, however, in real time this is not the case. This problem was tackled in [16,18]. Precisely, [16] proposed to use broadcast misses to understand the access patterns and Yu, Sakata and Tan [18] presented a statistical estimation model to estimate access probability. Besides, deadline constraints have been integrated into the Broadcast Disks model in [7, 8,10], where, the server tries to compute a periodic schedule that provides worst case guarantees, even in the event of failures and data updates. However, this model is not bidirectional, that is, there is no uplink channel and consequently the server periodically broadcasts items based on a static estimation of the potential user population, not on the actual load. In addition, many researchers, including [2,6,17], realized that caching and prefecthing can save much of the expected access time and thus are important for both push and pull based data dissemination scheduling. In particular, in [17], an efficient gain-based cache replacement policy, called SAIU, is designed for on-demand scheduling that balance individual and overall system needs. SAIU integrates in its performance measure the influence of the data retrieval delays, of the data sizes, of the data access probabilities as well as of the data update frequencies. Clearly, hybrid approaches, that use both the push-based and the pull-based scheduling algorithms in one system, appear to be attractive to meet both the massive data dissemination and the upon-request data delivery. Acharya, Franklin and Zdonik [3] present an asymmetric system with multiple clients and a single server to control the broadcast. In this system, the server pushes all the data items according to some push-based scheduling, but simultaneously the clients are provided with a limited back channel capacity to make requests for the items, which are missing for a time interval greater than a given threshold. In this way, some of the items are both disseminated and also broadcasted, increasing the average waiting time. This happens, however, more frequently in low or medium loaded system since in heavily loaded systems clients' requests on-demand are likely to be dropped/ignored by the server. In [16], a model for assigning the bandwidth to the push- and pull-scheduling in an adaptive way is proposed. To minimize the number of requests arriving at the server, as soon as an item becomes popular it is inserted in the push scheduling. Hence, the cut-off point between the push and the pull items is highly dynamic. Clients listen to the broadcast first, and make a request only if the requested item is not in the push broadcast program. To cope with the dynamism of the push-set, just the flat push scheduling, which sends in round-robin fashion all the items, is adopted. Finally, a hybrid approach is discussed in [12], which divides the data items in two disjoint sets: one for push and one for pull according to their degree of access probability. Roughly speaking, the set of the pull items contains those items which are so rarely requested in the system that no more than one or two requests for all of them are sent by the clients in a single unit of time (i.e., the time necessary to broadcast/disseminate a single data item). All the remaining items belong to the push-set. Repeatedly, the server broadcasts the push item precomputed by the packet fair queuing scheduling applied to the push-set, and after broadcasting, it serves, in first-come-first-serve order, the pending requests arrived for the pull items.

3   Preliminaries and Motivation Behind Our Work

Before discussing the motivation behind our work, which improves on [12], let us introduce some assumptions and terminologies.

First of all, we assume a system with a single server and multiple clients thereby imposing an asymmetry. The database at the server is assumed to be composed of D total number of distinct data items, each of unit length. The *access probability* P_i of item i is a measure of its degree of popularity. It is assumed that the server knows the access probability of each item in advance. The items are numbered from 1 to D in decreasing order of their access probability, thus $P_1 \geq P_2 \geq ... \geq P_D$. Clearly, from time to time, the server recomputed the access probability of the items, renumber them as necessary and eventually make available to all clients the new numbering of the items. It is assumed that one unit of time is the time required to spread an item of unit length.

We say that the client accesses an item if that item is *pushed*, while that an item is *requested* if the item is *pulled*. Moreover, let the *load N* of the system be the number of requests/access in the system for unit of time.

Let the *access time*, $T_{acc,I}$ be the amount of time that a client waits for a data item i to be broadcast after it begins to listen. Moreover, let the *response time*, $T_{res,I}$ be the amount of time between the request of item i by the client and the data transmission. Clearly, the aim of the *push scheduling* is to keep the access time for each push item i as small as possible, while that of the *pull scheduling* is to minimize the response time for each pull item i.

Recalling that the pure push-based systems repeat the same schedule cyclically, let a single repetition of the schedule be termed a *broadcast cycle*. During a broadcast cycle, some items may appear several times. Each appearance is referred to as an *instance* of the item. Indicated with s the space between two consecutive instances of an item, if all instances of item i are equally spaced, then the space between any two instances of item i will be denoted as s_i.

In a push-based system, one of the overall measures of the scheduling performance is called *average expected access time*, $T_{exp-acc}$, which is defined as $T_{exp-acc} = \sum_{i=1}^{D} P_i \cdot \overline{T_{acc,i}}$, where $\overline{T_{acc,i}}$ is the average expected access time for item i. If instances are equally spaced in the broadcast cycle, then $\overline{T_{acc,i}} = \frac{s_i}{2}$

Many scheduling algorithms have been designed to minimize $T_{exp-acc}$. One of them, the *Packet Fair Scheduling* has been widely studied and its performance is well modeled analytically [11]. Such a push scheduling, which was used in [12], is also adopted in our hybrid scheduling as the push scheduling. Therefore, from now on, in this paper, the term *push scheduling* indicates the *cyclic scheduling* derived by the *packet fair scheduling algorithm* applied to the push-set. Similarly, it can be defined the *average expected response time*, denoted $T_{exp-res}$, for the pull scheduling.

In order to explain the rational behind our approach, let us first describe in details the intuition behind the hybrid scheduling in [12] and let us point out some of its drawbacks. Recall that in purely push-based systems, the server alone decides which data items have to be transmitted without interacting with the clients while; in purely pull-based systems, the server is totally guided by the clients' requests. To make the average expected access time of the system smaller, the solution in [12] sends on-demand the less popular items immediately after having broadcast the most popular items. Indeed, let the *push-set* consist of the data items numbered from 1 up to K, termed from now on the *cut-off point*, and let the remaining items from $K + 1$ up to D form the *pull set*. Hence, the average expected waiting time for the hybrid scheduling is defined as:

$$T_{exp-hyb} = T_{exp-acc} + T_{exp-res} = \sum_{i=1}^{K} P_i \cdot \overline{T_{acc,i}} + \sum_{i=K+1}^{D} P_i \cdot \overline{T_{res,i}}.$$

As the push-set becomes smaller, the average expected access time $T_{exp-acc}$ becomes shorter. However, the pull-set size becomes larger, leading to a longer expected response time $T_{exp-res}$. The size of the pull-set might also increase the average access time $\overline{T_{acc,i}}$, for every push item. In fact, if the hybrid scheduling serves, between any two items of the cyclic push scheduling, all the pending requests for pull items in First-Come-First-Served order, it holds for the average expected access time for item i: $\overline{T_{acc,i}} = (s_i + s_i \cdot q)/2$, where q is the average number of distinct pull items for which, arrives, at least one pending request in the pull-queue for unit of time. From now on, we refer to q as the *dilation* factor of the push scheduling.

To limit the growth of the $\overline{T_{acc,i}}$, and therefore that of the $\overline{T_{exp-acc}}$, the push-set is taken in [12] enough large that, in average, no more than 1 request for all the pull items arrives during a single unit time. To guarantee a dilation factor q equal to 1 when the system load is equal to N, [12] introduces the concept of the *build-up point* B. B is the minimum index between 1 and D for which it holds $N(1 - \sum_{i=1}^{B} P_i) \leq 1$, where N is the average access/requests for unit of time. In other words, [12] pushes all the items from 1 up to B to guarantee that no more than 1 item is waiting to be disseminate, and therefore to achieve $q = 1$.

After having bounded the dilation factor to 1, [12] chooses as the cut-off point between the push and pull items the value K, with $K \geq B$, such that K minimizes the *average* expected waiting time for the hybrid system.

Intuitively, the partition between push and pull items found out in [12] is meaningful only when the system load N is small and the access probabilities are much skewed. Under these conditions, indeed, the build-up point B is low. Hence, there may be a cut-off K, such that $B \leq K \leq D$, which improves on the average expected access time of the pure-push system. However, when either the system has a high load N and/or all items have almost the same degree of probability, the distinction between the high and low demand items becomes vague, artificial, hence the value of build-up point B increases, finally leading to the maximum number D of items in the system. Thus, in those cases, the solution proposed in [12] almost always behaves as a pure push-based system.

To corroborate what discussed so far, in Table 1, the relation of the value of the load N of the distribution of the access probabilities θ with the value of the build up point B is illustrated, when the total number of distinct items D is 20.

According to the previous literature, we assume that the access probabilities P_i follow the Zipf's distribution with access *skew-coefficient* θ: $P_i = \frac{(1/i)^\theta}{\sum_{j=1}^{n}(1/j)^\theta}$.

In the remaining of this paper, we present a hybrid scheduling that improves on [12] when the load is high or when the access probabilities are balanced, that is, when the scheduling in [17] reduces to the pure-push scheduling. The solution proposed in this paper again partitions the data items in the push-set and the pull-set, but it chooses the value of the cut-off point K between those two sets independent of the build-up point. Indeed, we let the pull-queue grow in size, and the push-set can contain any number of data items. After each single broadcast, we do not flush out the pull-queue, which may contain several different pending requests. In contrast, we just pull one single item: the item, which has the largest number of pending requests. In contrast we just pull one single item: the item, which has the largest number of pending, requested in the pull-queue. Observe that simultaneously with every push and pull, N more access / requests arrive to the server, thus the pull-queue grows up drastically at the beginning. In particular, if the pull-set consists of the items from $K+1$ up to D, at most $N * \sum_{j=K+1}^{D} P_i$ requests can be inserted in the pull-queue at every instance of time, out of which, only one, the pull item that has accumulated the largest number of requests, is extracted from the queue to be pulled.

The access probabilities $P_1...P_D$ are well balanced for small values of θ, while they become skewed for increasing values of θ.

We are sure, however, that the number of distinct items in thec pull-queue cannot grow uncontrolled since the pull-queue can store at most as many distinct items as those in the pull-set, that is no more than $D - K$ items. So, after a while, the new arriving requests will only increase the number of clients waiting in the queue for some item, leaving unchanged the queue length. From this moment, we say that the system has reached a *steady state*. In other words, the pending requests will start to accumulate behind each pull-item without increasing anymore the queue length. Hence, just pulling the high demanded pull item, the system will not serve just one client but many. Our intuition

Table 1. Build-up point B for several values of N and θ when $D = 20$.

θ \ N	2	4	6	8	10	12	14	16	18	20
0.5	8	14	16	17	18	19	19	19	20	20
0.6	7	13	16	17	18	18	19	19	19	20
0.7	6	12	15	16	17	18	18	19	19	19
0.8	6	11	14	16	17	17	18	18	19	19
0.9	5	10	13	15	16	17	17	18	18	19
1.0	4	9	12	14	15	16	17	17	18	18
1.1	4	8	11	13	14	15	16	17	17	18
1.2	3	7	10	12	13	14	15	16	16	17
1.3	3	7	9	11	12	13	14	15	16	16

is that a pull item cannot be stuck in the pull-queue for more than as many unit of time as the length of the queue. Indeed, in the worst case, when all the pull items have more or less the same access probability, the number of pending requests will be in average the same for all the pull items. Then, the system serves the pull-queue in a *round-robin manner*, and each pull item waits in average half of the length the pull-queue before being pulled. Besides, when the access probability of the pull items vary a lot (i.e., larger than or equal to 1), the expected average response time can only decrease for the high demanded pull items, possibly improving the average expected response time.

In conclusion, the main contribution of our approach is to show that to preserve a constant dilation of the push scheduling is not necessary to avoid that the pull-queue starts to build-up. That is, it is not necessary to choose the cut-off point K larger than the build-up point B. In fact, our approach guarantees a dilation factor q equal to 1 just pulling a single item, and it shows that when K is chosen independent of B, a better tradeoff between the average expected access time and the average expected response time can be found.

4   The New Hybrid Algorithm

We are now in position to describe the behavior of our asymmetric system of communication. As said, we assume that the database of the server contains the D items, indexed from 1 to D according to their decreasing access probabilities. That is, for the items 1 ... D, it holds $P_1 \geq P_2 \geq ... \geq P_D$. Moreover, the clients to designate the data items they are interested in use the same indexes. The server performs several actions simultaneously. From one side, it monitors the access probabilities of the data items and the system load. When those parameters diverge significantly from the assumptions previously made by the system, the server renumber the data items, and recalculates the cut-off point K to separate the push-set from the pull-set, as illustrated in Figure 1. Note that K is selected in such a way that the average expected waiting time of the hybrid scheduling $T_{exp-hyb}$ is minimized. In order to evaluate the cut-off point, recall that it holds:

$$T_{exp-hyb} = T_{exp-acc} + T_{exp-res} = \sum_{i=1}^{K} P_i \cdot \overline{T_{acc,i}} + \sum_{i=K+1}^{D} P_i \cdot \overline{T_{res,i}}.$$

Substituting for $\overline{T_{acc,i}}$ the optimal instance space $S_i = \dfrac{\sum_{j=1}^{K} \sqrt{\hat{P}_j}}{\sqrt{\hat{P}_i}}$, for item i in the pure-push packet fair scheduling obtained by normalizing the access probabilities $\hat{P}_i = \dfrac{P_i}{\sum_{j=1}^{K} P_j}$ of the push items (see [11,15]) and for $\overline{T_{res,i}}$ the maximum length $D - K$ of the pull-queue, K is selected in such a way that

$$T_{exp-hyb}(K) = \sum_{i=1}^{K} S_i P_i + \sum_{i=K+1}^{D} P_i * (D - K)$$

Integer function CUT-OFF POINT $(D, P = P_1, P_2...P_D) : K$

/* D: Total No. Of items in the Database of the server

P: Sorted vector of access probability of items in decreasing order

K: Optimal Cut off Point */

$K := 1; T_{exp-hyb}(0) := T_{exp-hyb}(1) := D;$

while $K \leq D$ **and** $T_{exp-hyb}(K-1) \geq T_{exp-hyb}(K)$ **do**

begin

Set $s_i = \dfrac{\sum_{j=1}^{k} \sqrt{\hat{P}_j}}{\sqrt{\hat{P}_i}}$, **where** $\hat{P}_i = \dfrac{P_i}{\sum_{j=1}^{K} P_j}$,

$T_{exp-hyb}(K) = \sum_{i=1}^{K} S_i P_i + \sum_{i=K+1}^{D} P_i * (D - K); K := K + 1;$

end

return $(K - 1)$

Fig. 1. Algorithm to set the optimal cut-off point K between the push and pull items.

Procedure HYBRID SCHEDULING;

while true **do**

begin

compute an item from the push scheduling and broadcast it;

if the pull-queue is not empty **then**

extract the most requested item from the pull-queue,

clear the number of pending requests for that item, and pull-it

end;

Fig. 2. Algorithm at the server that produces the hybrid scheduling.

is minimized. In addition, the server listens to all the requests of the clients and manages the pull-queue. The pull-queue, implemented by a max-heap, keeps in its root, at any instant, the item with the highest number of pending requests. For any request i, if i is larger than the current cut-off point K, $i \geq K, i$ is inserted in the pull-queue, the number of the pending requests for i increased by one, and the heap information updates accordingly. Vice versa, if i is smaller than or equal to $K, i \leq K$, the server simply drops the request because that item will be broadcast by the push-scheduling sooner or later.

Finally, the server is in charge of deciding at each instant of time which item must be spread. The scheduling is derived as explained in Figure 2, where the details for obtaining the push scheduling are omitted. The interested reader can found them, for example, in [11].

To retrieve a data item, a client performs the following actions (Figure 3).

Note that the behavior of client is independent of the fact that the requested item belongs to the push-set or to the pull-set.

5   Experimental Results

It remains now to evaluate the performance of the new proposed algorithm.

First of all, we compare the simulation results of the new algorithm with those of the hybrid scheduling in [12], with the results of the pure-push scheduling and with the analytic expression used to derive the optimal cut-off point. We run experiments for $D = 100$, for the total number of access / requests in the system $M = 25.000$ and for $N = 10$ or $N = 20$. The results are reported in Table 2 and 3, respectively for $N = 10$ and $N = 20$.

Table 2. Expected hybrid access time for different values of θ (taken in the columns) and different algorithms (taken in the rows) when N=10

	0.50	0.60	0.70	0.80	0.90	1.00	1.10	1.20	1.30
New	40.30	37.78	35.23	32.36	29.38	25.95	22.95	19.90	17.04
[17]	44.54	42.35	40.01	37.31	34.12	29.93	24.38	20.61	17.04
Push	45.03	43.01	40.50	37.47	34.30	30.90	27.75	24.50	20.86
Analytical	36.01	36.21	35.04	33.56	29.94	29.73	27.09	25.19	22.51

Table 3. Expected hybrid access time for different values of θ (taken in the columns) and different algorithms (taken in the rows) when N=20

	0.50	0.60	0.70	0.80	0.90	1.00	1.10	1.20	1.30
New	41.96	39.39	36.59	33.49	30.29	27.20	23.88	21.14	18.26
[17]	44.44	42.45	40.10	37.39	33.78	30.69	27.54	23.23	19.49
Push	44.70	42.61	40.30	37.65	34.12	30.78	27.71	23.94	21.07
Analytical	37.59	35.68	34.53	33.06	29.94	29.73	27.09	34.43	24.24

For both Tables 2 and 3, the value of θ is varied from 0.50 to 1.30, so as to have the access probabilities of the items initially from similar to very skewed. Note that for θ no larger than 1, the analytic average expected access time is close to that measured with the experiments. This confirms that, when the access probabilities are similar, the pull items remain in the pull-queue for a time no larger than to total number of pull items that is $D - K$. For larger values of θ, the experimental measure of the expected response time is smaller that the analytic expected value because due to the fact that the access probabilities are very skew fewer than $D - K$ items can be present simultaneously in the pull-queue. Therefore, the actual waiting time of the client is eventually shorter than $D - K$. Further experimental results have shown that when θ is varied from 0.90 to 1.30; the length of the pull-queue is approximated better by the value $D * \sum_{i=K+1}^{D} P_i$ than by $D - K$. Moreover, as earlier discussed, when the system is highly loaded, the scheduling algorithm in [12], whose cut-off point K must be larger than the

---

Procedure CLIENT-REQUEST (i):
/* i : the item the client is interested in */
begin
send to the server the request for item i;
wait until listen for i on the channel
end

Fig. 3. The algorithm that runs at the client site.

build-up point B, almost reduces to the pure-push scheduling. Contradictory to [12], the new hybrid algorithm, even with very high loaded system, experiments better results than a pure-push based system as illustrated in Figure 4. Besides, in Figure 5, the values of the cut-off point K for our solution, which takes K independent of B, and for the hybrid scheduling proposed in [12] are depicted for $N = 10$ and $N = 20$.

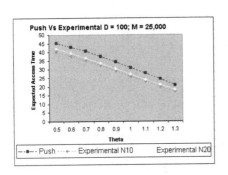

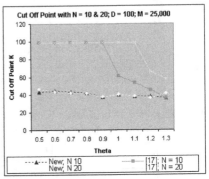

Fig. 4. Pure-Push scheduling Vs new algorithm.

Fig. 5. Cut-Off Point when $N = 10, 20$.

6   Future Work

Several further aspects remain to be investigated to make our system more suitable for real scenario. For example, we assumed that the server knows the access probability of each item in advance, which may not be the case as the demand for an item may change according to time. Thus our future work might try to choose the cut off point in a dynamic way according to the changes in the access probabilities. We also assumed that the server broadcasts and disseminates the items on the same channel. A better performance could be expected if we could use two channels one for broadcasting and the other for disseminating. Our future work could also investigate how the expected access time is related to the cut off point if the items in the database of the server are not of equal length, or if a deadline constraint is associated with each item requested. Even more challenge is the perspective of supporting mobile clients, which pass from a base station to another (possibly broadcasting different flows of information) and which may experience poor transmission conditions.

References

1. S. Acharya, M. Franklin, and S. Zdonik. Dissemination-based data delivery using broadcast disks. *IEEE Personal Communications*, pages 50–60, Dec 1995.

2. S. Acharya, M. Franklin, and S. Zdonik. Prefetching from a broadcast disk. In *Proceedings of 12th International Conference on Data Engineering*, pages 276–285, 1996.

3. S. Acharya, M. Franklin, and S. Zdonik. Balancing push and pull for data broadcast. In *Proceedings of ACM SIGMOD Int. Conference on Management of Data*, pages 183–193. ACM SIGMOD, 1997.

4. S. Acharya and S. Muthukrishnan. Scheduling on-demand broadcasts: New metrics and algorithms. In *Proceedings of the Fourth Annual ACM/IEEE MobiCom*, pages 43–54. ACM MobiCom, 1998.

5. A. Bar-Noy, B. Patt-Shamir, and I. Ziper. Broadcast disks with polynomial cost functions. In *IEEE INFOCOM 2000*, pages 575–584, 2000.

6. D. Barbara and T. Imielinski. Sleepers and workaholics: Caching strategies in mobile environments. In *Proceedings of ACM SIGMOD Int. Conference*, pages 1–12, 1994.

7. S. Baruah and A. Bestavros. Pinwheel scheduling for fault-tolerant broadcast disks in real-time database systems. In *Proceedings of IEEE International Conference on Data Engineering*, 1997.

8. S. Baruah and A. Bestavros. Real-time mutable broadcast disks. In *Proceedings of Second International Workshop on Real-Time Databases, Burlington, VT*, 1997.

9. J.C.R. Bennett and H. Zhang. Hierarchical packet fair queueing algorithms. In *Proceedings of ACM SIGCOMM*, pages 43–56, 1996.

10. A. Bestavros. Aida-based real-time fault-tolerant broadcast disks. In *Proceeding Second IEEE Real-Time Technology and Applications Symposium*, 1996.

11. J. Gecsei. *The architecture of videotex systems*. Prentice-Hall, Englewood Cliffs, NJ, 1983.

12. Y. Guo, S.K. Das, and M.C. Pinotti. A new hybrid broadcast scheduling algorithm for asymmetric communication systems: Push and pull data based on optimal cut-off point. *Mobile Computing and Communications Review (MC2R)*, 5(4), 2001.

13. S. Hameed and N.H. Vaidya. Efficient algorithms for scheduling data broadcast. *Wireless Networks*, 5:183–193, 1999.

14. S. Hameed and N.H. Vaidya. Scheduling data broadcast in asymmetric communication environments. *Wireless Networks*, 5:171–182, 1999.

15. R. Jain and J. Werth. Airdisks and airraid: Modeling and scheduling periodic wireless data broadcast (extended abstract). In *DIMACS Technical Report 95-11, Rutgers University*. DIMACS, 1995.

16. K. Stathatos, N. Roussopoulos, and J.S. Baras. Adaptive data broadcast in hybrid networks. In *Proceedings of 23rd International Conference on Very Large Data Bases, Athens, Greece*, pages 326–335, 1997.

17. J. Xu, Q. Hu, L. Lee, and W. C. Lee. Saiu: An efficient cache replacement policy for wireless on-demand broadcasts. In *Private Communication*.

18. J.X. Yu, T. Sakata, and K. Tan. Statistical estimation of access frequencies in data broadcasting environments. *Wireless Networks*, 6:89–98, 2000.

An Adaptive Resource Reservation and Distributed Admission Control Scheme for Mobile Networks

Hemanta Kumar Pati*, Rajib Mall, and Indranil Sengupta

Department of Computer Science and Engineering
IIT, Kharagpur-721302, INDIA
{hpati,rajib,isg}@cse.iitkgp.ernet.in

Abstract. We propose a resource reservation policy called *Mobility-adaptive Bandwidth Reservation* (MBR) scheme. The scheme performs admission control and is adaptive to changes in traffic caused by user mobility. It involves storing and analyzing information regarding the history of user crossover patterns to predict the future resource requirements. Each of the cell sites does resource prediction and admission control independently with zero traffic/signaling overhead which makes the MBR scheme fully distributed. We have carried out extensive simulation studies to investigate the performance of our scheme and the simulation results appear promising.

Keywords. Resource reservation, admission control, Quality of Service(QoS), handoff, mobile networks.

1 Introduction

The number of mobile devices needing to communicate with each other is increasing rapidly. The general architecture showing connectivity between a cellular system and the wired PSTN for voice communication is discussed in [1-4]. According to the current technology, the heart of the cellular system is the mobile switching center(MSC). The MSC is responsible for providing centralized control and administration of the system. It connects the mobile subscribers to each other and to the PSTN and other networks. The radio link completes the communication process between the mobile host(MH) and the base station(BS). The BS itself is assigned a set of channels and this assignment could be static or dynamic.

Since mobile users are free to go anywhere, the traffic pattern is normally unpredictable. To keep a user communication uninterrupted, it is important to make the required wireless resources available in all the locations to which a mobile user may go. One possible solution to this problem is to keep wireless resources reserved well in advance in all the cell sites. However, determining

---

* The first author is supported by an Infosys scholarship.

S.K. Das and S. Bhattacharya (Eds.): IWDC 2002, LNCS 2571, pp. 214–223, 2002.

an optimal resource reservation policy is a nontrivial problem. To this end, this paper presents an adaptive resource reservation scheme with distributed admission control based on the crossover pattern of mobile users. We consider the expected handoffs during resource reservation and call admission control. Each of the cell sites determines the expected number of handoffs in a fully distributed manner without any transfer of mobility related information among themselves. This proposed scheme reduces the traffic/signaling overhead, in contrast to the earlier schemes [6]. Also our proposed scheme is computationally and spatially more efficient.

The rest of the paper is organized as follows. Section 2 describes our proposed scheme. Our simulation model is discussed in Section 3. The simulation results are presented in Section 4. Section 5 concludes the paper.

2   Mobility-Adaptive Bandwidth Reservation(MBR) Scheme

To reduce resource wastage, we propose to consider the expected handoff arrivals while making bandwidth reservation at a cell. We have named this scheme as *Mobility-adaptive Bandwidth Reservation*(MBR) scheme. In this MBR scheme, we partition the real time into discrete time slots. Each of the base stations determines the expected number of handoff calls for the forthcoming time slot based on recent history. The bandwidth reservation made by each base station is based on the expected number of handoffs obtained for that cell. The amount of bandwidth to be reserved in any cell x to accommodate the handoff calls can be obtained using the following expression.

$$B_{resv}(x) = B_{need} * R_m(x) \tag{1}$$

where $R_m(x)$ is the expected handoff arrivals to any cell x, B_{need} is the bandwidth units requested per call, and $B_{resv}(x)$ is the total bandwidth reserved in cell x.

The resource reservation and admission control schemes for the new calls and handoff calls are described in the following subsections. In the rest of our discussions, we will refer to the cell from which handoff call was initiated as the *old_cell* and the cell to which the handoff call is going to be made as the *new_cell*. The other terminologies used are as follows:

B_{total} : Total bandwidth available in a cell and is assumed to be same for all the cells,
$B_{used}(x)$: Bandwidth used in cell x,
$B_{avail}(x)$: The free bandwidth units in cell x which is neither used by any mobile host or reserved to accommodate the hand-over calls,
C_0 : The cell where a new call is initiated, and
$T(x)$: The threshold value used for admission control in any cell x.

2.1   Admission Control and Bandwidth Allocation to New Calls

Our admission control scheme is as follows. A new call is always admitted, if the bandwidth units currently allocated to the mobile users together with the requested bandwidth in the call initiating cell C_0 does not exceed the threshold value $T(C_0)$ for that cell. Otherwise, the new call is not accepted. When a new call is accepted, the desired bandwidth will be allocated to it to start its communication. The admission control and bandwidth reservation scheme for a new call is given as Algorithm-I.

Algorithm I : Admission Control Scheme
FOR(all cell x) /* Initialization. */
    $B_{used}(x) = 0$;
    $B_{resv}(x) = 0$; /* Assuming that initially $R_m(x)$ is 0. */
    $B_x = B_{resv}(x)$; /* Bandwidth is reserved but currently not in use. */
    $T(x) = B_{total} - B_{resv}(x)$;
    $B_{avail}(x) = T(x)$;
IF a new call THEN
    IF $B_{need} <= B_{avail}(C_0)$ THEN
        $B_{used}(C_0) = B_{used}(C_0) + B_{need}$; /* Allocate the required bandwidth. */
        $B_{avail}(C_0) = B_{avail}(C_0) - B_{need}$;
    ELSE /*Bandwidth is not available in the cell in which the new call was initiated.*/
        Reject connection;

The threshold value used in Algorithm-I is given by the following expression:

$$T(x) = B_{total} - B_{need} * R_m(x) \qquad (2)$$

From equations 1 and 2, we get

$$T(x) = B_{total} - B_{resv}(x) \qquad (3)$$

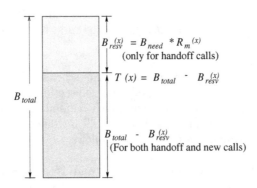

Fig. 1. Resource reservation in any cell x.

The important parameter values for the resource reservation and admission control scheme are depicted graphically in Fig. 1. This figure captures the behavior as described in Algorithm-I that when the bandwidth utilization is lower than the threshold value in a cell, both new and handoff calls are entertained. But, a cell stops admitting new calls when the bandwidth utilization exceeds the threshold value, thus keeping the rest of the resource reserved for the handoff calls.

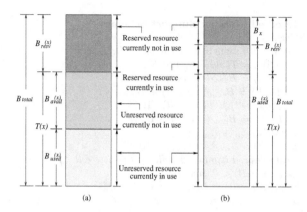

Fig. 2. Two cases of resource reservation in any cell x. (a) Current bandwidth utilization is below threshold $T(x)$, (b) Current bandwidth utilization is above threshold $T(x)$.

2.2   Bandwidth Management to Support User Mobility

The mobility of a mobile host(MH) may cause inter-cell movements necessitating a handoff. In such inter-cell movements, the MH releases the bandwidth units that it was using in the *old_cell* and the desired bandwidth units will be allocated in the *new_cell*. If the current bandwidth utilization is below the threshold $T(new\_cell)$ as shown in Fig. 2(a), the unreserved bandwidth units can be allocated to the handoff call otherwise if the current bandwidth utilization exceeds the threshold $T(new\_cell)$ as shown in Fig. 2(b), it can be allocated the reserved bandwidth units, provided such allocation does not make the total bandwidth utilization for the *new_cell* to exceed its total capacity (B_{total}). This scheme for handling handoff calls is given in Algorithm-II.

2.3   Effective Utilization of Bandwidth

The metric which we use to determine the effective bandwidth utilization for the network as a whole is as follows:

$$B_{eff} = \frac{\sum_i B_{used}(i) * 100}{\sum_i B_{used}(i) + \sum_j B_j} \tag{4}$$

where

B_{eff} - percentage of bandwidth being effectively utilized,
$B_{used}(i)$ - bandwidth used by all the mobile hosts in cell i,
$\sum_i$ - summation to find out the total bandwidth allocated to all the active mobile users in all the cells,
B_j - bandwidth reserved in cell j to accommodate handoff calls, and
$\sum_j$ - summation to get the bandwidth reserved in all the cells.

Algorithm II: Intercell Mobility Support Scheme
IF a handoff call THEN
       /* Release bandwidth units used in the old cell. */
       IF $B_{used}(old\ cell) <= T(old\ cell)$ THEN
           $B_{used}(old\ cell) = B_{used}(old\ cell) - B_{need}$;
           $B_{avail}(old\ cell) = B_{avail}(old\ cell) + B_{need}$;
       ELSE IF $B_{used}(old\ cell) > T(old\ cell)$ THEN
           $B_{used}(old\ cell) = B_{used}(old\ cell) - B_{need}$;
           $B_{old\ cell} = B_{old\ cell} + B_{need}$;
       IF $(B_{used}(new\ cell) + B_{need}) <= B_{total}$ THEN
           /* Allocate desired bandwidth units in the new cell. */
           IF $B_{used}(new\ cell) < T(new\ cell)$ THEN
                $B_{used}(new\ cell) = B_{used}(new\ cell) + B_{need}$;
                $B_{avail}(new\ cell) = B_{avail}(new\ cell) - B_{need}$;
           ELSE IF $B_{used}(new\ cell) >= T(new\ cell)$ THEN
                $B_{used}(new\ cell) = B_{used}(new\ cell) + B_{need}$;
                $B_{new\ cell} = B_{new\ cell} - B_{need}$;
       ELSE IF $(B_{used}(new\ cell) + B_{need}) > B_{total}$ THEN
       /* Bandwidth is not available in the cell to which handoff occurred and so the call is dropped. */
       Drop the connection;

When the current bandwidth utilization is less than the threshold value, the cell site is said to be under loaded and when it is greater than the threshold value, the cell site is said to be overloaded. A resource reservation and admission control scheme showing higher effective utilization of bandwidth will give a lower handoff and new call blocking rate is not always true. An admission control and resource reservation scheme is always considered as better when it shows higher effective utilization of bandwidth with lower blocking rate for new and handoff calls.

2.4 Estimation of Expected Handoffs

We consider two different schemes to approximate the expected handoffs to any cell. The first one is the *sliding window* scheme and the other one is the *exponentially weighted averaging* scheme. We discuss these two schemes in the following.

I. Sliding Window Scheme

In this scheme we assume that the real time is divided into time slots as shown in Fig. 3. To compute the expected handoffs, it is assumed that each of the cell site is able to monitor the number of handoff requests coming to it.

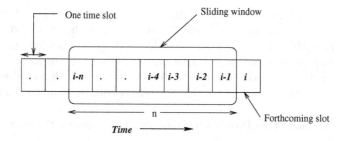

Fig. 3. Virtual time frame with *sliding window*.

This information needs to be time stamped so that the statistical pattern for a sequence of time slots can be obtained for future use. Any cell x is surrounded by six neighbor cells as shown in Fig. 3. The expected number of handoffs for a cell is determined by using the mobility information recorded in n preceding time slots. In other words, a *sliding window* of n slots is considered to determine the number of crossovers. Now the expected number of handoff requests to a cell x from all its neighbors for the next time slot(i.e. i^{th} time slot as shown in Fig. 3) can be expressed as follows:

$$E_i(R_m(x)) = \frac{1}{n} \sum_{j=1}^{m} \sum_{k=1}^{n} R_{i-k,j}(x) \tag{5}$$

where $E_i(R_m(x))$ is the expected handoffs to cell x from all its neighbors for the ith slot,
$R_{i,j}(x)$ is the number of handoff calls requested to cell x from a neighbor cell j in the ith time slot,
m is the number of neighbor cells,
n is the length of the sliding window,
$\sum_{k=1}^{n}$ evaluates the number of crossovers from a particular neighbor during all the time slots covered by the sliding window, and
$\sum_{j=1}^{m}$ finds out the total number of crossovers from all the neighbors during all the time slots covered by the sliding window.

II. Exponentially Weighted Averaging Scheme

In this scheme, the expected handoffs for any cell x in the ith slot is the exponentially weighted average of crossovers from all immediate neighbors to itself in the previous time intervals. The expression that can be used to approximate the expected handoffs for the ith time slot for cell x is as follows.

$$E_i(R_m(x)) = \alpha * (O_{i-1}(R_m(x)) + E_{i-1}(R_m(x))) \tag{6}$$

where $E_{i-1}(R_m(x))$ and $E_i(R_m(x))$ are the approximations for expected handoffs for the $(i-1)^{th}$ and i^{th} slots respectively,
$O_{i-1}(R_m(x))$ is the actual/observed handoffs for the $(i-1)^{th}$ slot, and
α is a weight factor lying in the range (0,1).

This scheme is in contrast to the sliding window scheme, where the slots of the sliding window are weighted linearly to compute the expected handoffs. The actual handoffs for $(i-1)^{th}$ slot (i.e. $O_{i-1}(R_m(x))$ - handoffs in the most recent slot) can be obtained by substituting $n = 1$ in equation 5. The expected handoffs i.e. $E_i(R_m(x))$ will be used to determine the threshold value $T(x)$ of the cell x. $T(x)$ will be used to provide admission control to new calls in cell x.

Algorithm III: Adaptive Bandwidth Reservation Support Scheme
$Temp = T(x)$;
$B_{resv}(x) = B_{need} * R_m(x)$;
$T(x) = B_{total} - B_{resv}(x)$;
IF $((T(x) - Temp) != 0)$ THEN /* A Change in Threshold due to Mobility. */
    IF $((T(x) - B_{used}(x)) > 0)$ THEN
        $B_{avail}(x) = (T(x) - B_{used}(x))$;
        $B_x = B_{resv}(x)$; /* B_x is the reserved bandwidth currently not in use. */
    ELSE IF $((T(x) - B_{used}(x)) <= 0)$ THEN
        $B_{avail}(x) = 0$;
        $B_x = B_{resv}(x) - (B_{used}(x) - T(x))$;

2.5 The Adaptive Bandwidth Reservation Scheme

The expected handoff arrivals for any cell x can be determined in subsequent time intervals using any of the two schemes discussed in section 2.4. Now, any change in the traffic due to mobility of the mobile hosts will change the expected handoff arrivals for the corresponding time slot, and also the threshold to be used to reserve the bandwidth units. This adaptive bandwidth reservation scheme is presented in Algorithm-III. This scheme makes the necessary updates to the available/free and reserve bandwidth units in each of the cell sites.

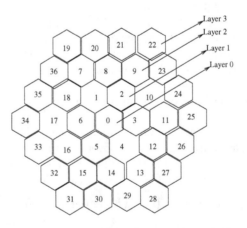

Fig. 4. Cellular network model used in simulation.

3   The Simulation Model

We consider the physical coverage area to be partitioned into a hexagonal mesh structure without any overlapping meshes as shown in Fig. 4. To identify each cell uniquely, we assign a static identification number to each cell. This identification number helps to get the physical address from the logical address of the cell where the mobile host (MH) is actually present. For example, if the MH at, say, cell 2 moves to the neighbor cell on its left, then we have to determine the physical address of the left neighbor cell which is 1. We assume that the new call arrival to any cell is exponentially distributed with mean arrival rate λ. Further, we have considered an uniformly distributed mobility pattern for the mobile user, i.e all possible directions of movement have equal probability. Other assumptions made in our simulation study are as follows:

1. The bandwidth capacity of each cell is 400 units,
2. A call needs 10 bandwidth units for its communication,
3. The traffic is homogeneous, i.e all calls need the same bandwidth,
4. 50% of the total ongoing calls are terminated in each time slot, and
5. 25% of the total ongoing calls undergo handoff after each time slot.

Under the above assumptions, we have carried out simulation experiments to study the performance of our proposed scheme. The simulation results are presented in the next section.

4   Simulation Results

In this section, we present our simulation results investigating the performance of our scheme vis-a-vis a few related schemes. These related schemes include Partitioned cell-based bandwidth reservation(PBR) scheme[7] and non-reservation and reservation-based schemes[5]. Error in approximation in case of the *sliding window scheme* and *exponentially weighted averaging* scheme are given in Fig. 5. Form this Fig. 5 we found that *sliding window* scheme out-performs the *exponentially weighted averaging* scheme for all values of α. Therefore we use the *sliding window* scheme to approximate the expected handoffs.

Simulation results indicating the number of calls being served i.e. the carried traffic vs offered load is shown in Fig. 6(a). Fig. 7(a) depicts new call blocking probabilities (P_B) for the network for different load conditions. Handoff call drop probabilities (P_D) for different load are plotted in Fig. 7(b). Fig. 7 includes results for all the schemes under consideration i.e. non-reservation, reservation, PBR and MBR. From Fig. 7, it can be observed that under low traffic conditions, all these schemes are able to accept nearly all new calls without much rejections and premature call terminations. But as the traffic increases, the MBR scheme accommodates greater number of calls compared to reservation-based scheme and also PBR scheme with relatively lower P_B and P_D. On the other hand, with increase in traffic, the non-reservation based scheme accommodates more calls with a relatively lower blocking probability (P_B), but suffers from a comparatively larger call drop probability (P_D).

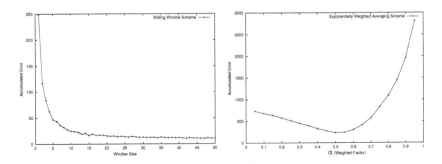

Fig. 5. (a) Error in approximation in the simulation interval for different values of window size, (b) Error in approximation in the simulated interval for different values of α.

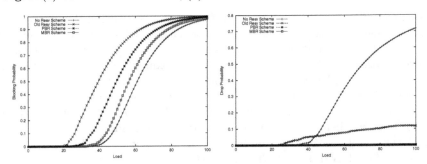

Fig. 6. (a) Carried traffic vs Load, (b) Effective utilization of bandwidth vs Load.

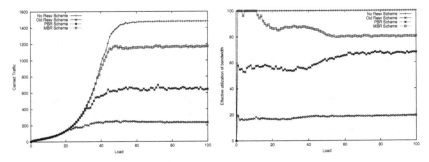

Fig. 7. (a) Blocking probability(P_B) vs Load, (b) Drop probability (P_D) vs Load.

The effective bandwidth utilization achieved for all the schemes studied is shown in Fig. 6(b). For the non-reservation based scheme, the effective bandwidth utilization is always 100%. This is expected since it does not reserve any resource for handoff calls. Effective bandwidth utilization for the old reservation-based scheme is between 14.28% to 25% under all traffic conditions [7]. This highlights the poor utilization of bandwidth by the reservation-based scheme. The MBR scheme shows a poor effective bandwidth utilization in low traffic situations, because in low traffic situations most of the reserved resources remain unused. But, in all traffic conditions, our MBR scheme shows much improved effective utilization of bandwidth compared to PBR scheme and also the old reservation-based scheme. Thus, our MBR scheme shows better effective utilization of bandwidth compared to the reservation-based scheme and also the PBR scheme.

5 Conclusion

Effective utilization of the available bandwidth is essential in wireless communications. To this end, we have proposed a technique for prediction of user mobility from traffic monitoring and statistical observations. Based upon the observed crossovers, our scheme dynamically changes resource reservations for handoff calls. Our scheme applies a threshold depending on the crossover rate to provide a suitable admission control to new calls. We have proposed two schemes in this regard. We have carried out extensive simulations to study the performance of our schemes. The simulation results indicate that our MBR scheme achieves higher bandwidth utilization compared to the reservation-based scheme discussed in [5]. Overall, our MBR scheme enjoys reduced P_B and P_D with higher effective utilization of bandwidth. Moreover, it is able to accommodate larger number of users with lower call rejections for both new as well as handoff calls compared to the reservation-based scheme of [5] and the PBR scheme of [7].

References

1. Moe Rahnema: Overview of the GSM System and Protocol Architecture. IEEE Communications Magazine, 31(4) Apr. (1993) 92–100.
2. W. C. Y. Lee: Mobile Cellular Telecommunication, Analog and Digital Systems. McGraw-Hill (1995).
3. George Edwards and Ravi Sanker: Microcellular Handoff Using Fuzzy Techniques. Wireless Networks. 4(5). Aug. (1998) 401–409.
4. I. Katzela and M. Naghshineh: Channel Assignment Schemes for Cellular Mobile Telecommunication Systems: A Comprehensive Survey. IEEE Personal Communications Jun. (1996) 10–31.
5. Carlos Oliveira and Jaime Bae Kim and Tatsuya Suda: An Adaptive Bandwidth Reservation Scheme for High-Speed Multimedia Wireless Networks. IEEE Journal on Selected Areas in Communications 16(6). Aug. (1998) 858–874.
6. David A. Levine and Ian F. Akyildiz and Mahmoud Naghshineh: A Resource Estimation and Call Admission Algorithm for Wireless Multimedia Networks Using the Shadow Cluster Concept. IEEE/ACM Trans. on Networking. Vol. 5. Feb. (1997) 1–12.
7. H. K. Pati and R. Mall and I. Sengupta: An Efficient Bandwidth Reservation and Call Admission Control Scheme for Wireless Mobile Networks. Elseviers' Computer Communications 25(1) Jan. (2002) 74–83.

On Restructuring Distributed Algorithms for Mobile Computing

R.K. Ghosh[1] and Hrushikesha Mohanty[2]

[1] Department of Computer Science & Engineering,
Indian Institute of Technology, Kanpur
rkg@cse.iitk.ac.in
[2] Department of Computer and Information Sciences,
University of Hyderabad, Hyderabad – 500 053
hmcs@uohyd.ernet.in

Abstract. In this paper we propose a formalization of a subclass of distributed algorithms that can be suitable for execution on mobile environment. In particular, our investigation puts stress on evolving techniques to include the design abstractions of the resources and synchronization typical to a mobile environment with the conventional design of distributed algorithm, so that a greater amount of concurrency can be derived within the available level of resources. To that effect we propose a method to evaluate a *concurrency load* for any abstraction and use it to come up with answer as to which of the abstractions would be better when host mobility is allowed.

1 Introduction

Until recently, distributed algorithms are designed only for a network of static hosts. Such algorithms execute by exchange of messages over the network. Most of the ideal assumptions regarding the unlimited amount of resources availability and the robustness of communication interface in designing normal distributed algorithms can not be extended to a mobile computing environment [1]. Therefore, restructuring the existing distributed algorithms for execution in mobile environment is, indeed, a great challenge. Nevertheless, certain generic observations may, to great extent, help in restructuring the existing distributed algorithms for execution on mobile environment.

1. The distributed algorithms that fragment the problem into smaller parts and attempt to execute those parts independently on many hosts to get benefit of collective computing power of many hosts are ruled out as a mobile host (MH) is resource poor. Performing heavy local computations on an MH is infeasible.
2. Some algorithms may not have any requirement for heavy computation. But may require the hosts to execute operations using globally available resources that require synchronization. This class of algorithms would be ideally suitable for restructuring in a mobile environment; as the mobile host may primarily be used to access services rather than to run services. One of such project is the Wireless Coyote [5].

S.K. Das and S. Bhattacharya (Eds.): IWDC 2002, LNCS 2571, pp. 224–233, 2002.

In this paper, we restrict ourselves the class of distributed algorithms which do not run distributed services but those which access a service from other hosts, and, therefore, require to deal with synchronization issues. A typical example of such a service may be a distributed file system. We examine applicability of Badrinath and Acharya's two-tier approach [2] and also discuss about other generic strategies to restructure such distributed algorithms for mobile computing environment.

2   Bandwidth and Resources

A distributed algorithm comprises of a *communication* component and a *computation* component. The computation component is bound to the individual hosts. From time to time a host might communicate with its neighbours or other nodes to exchange information regarding the state of its own or other's registers, the results of current computations, contacting some hosts for ordering tasks in the algorithm or to get initialization parameters for the next phase of computation, and so on. Thus a distributed system of hosts shows bursts of communication in between periods of local computation. When hosts become mobile not only the cost of computational resources at mobile hosts increase, but two additional cost parameters, namely, *location update* and *lookup* become pronounced. The focus of this section is to examine strategies to minimize communication overheads and resource requirements by ensuring that the computation is largely restricted to the fixed part of the network.

2.1   Two-Tier Approach

The *two-tier principle* [2] states:

Principle 1 *To the extent possible, computation and communication costs of an algorithm is borne by the static part of the network. This attempts to avoid locating a mobile participant and lowers the* search cost *incurred by the algorithm; additionally, the number of operations performed at the mobile hosts is kept to a minimum, and thereby, consumption of battery power, which is a critical resource for mobile hosts, is restricted.*

In order to restrict the costs of location maintenance and lookup, three different strategies, namely, the *search*, *inform* and *proxy* were proposed by Badrinath and Acharya [2] in the context of restructuring the distributed token ring algorithm. These techniques are quite general and can be used in various other classes of distributed algorithms.

Instead of focusing directly on the resource and bandwidth issues, our attempt here is to examine the restructuring problem according to the systemic roles of individual hosts for implementing different distributed algorithms.

2.2   Non-coordinator Systems with All Machines Equivalent

All machines in a non-coordinated system are equivalent. The amount of computational and communication load shared by each machine is same. Such systems can easily be modified to work in a mobile computing environment. We illustrate the method with Lamport's Bakery algorithm [6] for mutual exclusion as an example.

In the Bakery algorithm, a process waiting to enter a critical section chooses a number. This number must be greater than all other numbers currently in use. There is a global shared array of current numbers for each process. The entering process checks all other processes sequentially, and waits for each one which has a lower number. Ties are resolved using process IDs. If no restructuring is done, and the algorithm is directly executed on a collection of N mobile hosts, the overall communication cost (see [4] for details) would be

$$3 * (N - 1) * (2 * C_{wireless} + C_{search}).$$

Now suppose we modify the original algorithm as follows:

1. Time stamping is used only for messages exchanged between the MSSs – which now form the components of bakery algorithm – and not for messages exchanged between the mobile hosts.
2. A mobile host initiates the algorithm by sending an initialization message to its local MSS. The MSS executes the algorithm on behalf of the mobile host. Thus the appropriate request, reply and release messages are marked with the id of the mobile host for which it is sent by the MSS.
3. When the MSS secures mutual exclusion for the MH, it informs the MH. But the mobile host might have changed its location in the meantime. Therefore, a search may potentially be required.
4. The mobile host then accesses the critical section and informs the MSS after need for access is over. A release message is sent to every other MSS.
5. If the mobile host disconnects prior to the requested access to the critical section, then every disconnection has to be informed to the MSS. On receiving the grant for access, the MSS can instantly initiate a release response in this case. Thus, other requests are not delayed.

Those interested to know the correctness of the algorithms may refer to [4] for details. The breakups for the communication cost of this modified algorithm will be as follows:

- Initialization $= C_{wireless}$,
- Granting a request $= C_{wireless} + C_{search}$, and
- Release of lock $= C_{wireless} + C_{fixed}$.

The overall cost along with the cost for executing the algorithm between MSSs is, thus,

$$3 * C_{wireless} + C_{fixed} + C_{search} + 3 * (M - 1) * C_{fixed},$$

where M is the number of MSSs participating in the algorithm execution. Since $C_{search} > C_{fixed}$ and $N \gg M$, the overall communication cost is much cheaper compared to the non-restructured algorithm.

2.3   Non-coordinated Systems with Exception Machines

Non-coordinated systems differ only in the sense that the code executed by one machine (or a few of them) is different than that executed by the most of the other machines. The machines executing different code constitute the set of *exception* machines. An example of this category is Dijkstra's self stabilizing algorithm [3].

Consider a system consisting of a set of n finite state machines connected in the form of a ring, with a circulating *privilege* which denotes the ability of a machine to change its state. when a machine has the privilege, it is able to change its current state which is termed a *move*. Let us now look at Dijkstra's algorithm involving K states, where $K \geq n$, and n is the total number machines. For any machine, we use the symbols S, L, R to denote its own state, the state of its left neighbour, and the state of its right neighbour respectively.

The exception machine, machine 0: if $L = S$ then $S = (S + 1)$ mod K.
Other machines: if $L \neq S$ then $S = L$.

Dijkstra also three proposed a better algorithm involving three state using two exception machines. The three state algorithm is as follows:

The bottom machine, machine 0:
   if $(S + 1)$ mod $3 = R$ then $S = (S - 1)$ mod 3.
The top machine, machine n-1:
   if $L = R$ and $(L + 1)$ mod $3 \neq S$ then $S = (L + 1)$ mod 3.
Other machines:
   if $(S + 1)$ mod $3 = L$ then $S = L$,
   if $(S + 1)$ mod $3 = R$ then $S = R$.

The details of how the self stabilizing systems work are, however, not important so far as restructuring the algorithms to mobile environment is concerned. Instead we need to look at the communication that occurs between any two machines.

In both the algorithms cited above and other self-stabilization algorithms, the essential communication perspective is to access the registers for the left and right neighbours. This class of algorithms are very similar to the previous class of algorithms. The presence of one or more exception machines really does not make much of a difference to the communication costs involved. Since only the neighbour's values are needed, the overhead of wireless communication would be even less, as most *neighbouring* hosts are expected to be under the same MSS except for the two at the edges.

2.4   Fixed Coordinator Based System

Distributed algorithms which involve a coordinator for running the algorithm properly, induce extra communication overhead for the coordinator. The first class of such algorithms the coordinator is the fixed coordinator set of algorithms.

Each member of this class assigns one particular host to act as the coordinator. Thus apart from the normal optimization, the communication pattern for the coordinator has to be specifically optimized.

An example of the fixed coordinator system is encountered in the case of total order atomic broadcast algorithm. Figure 1 illustrates this algorithm with a time-line diagram. The coordinator is always fixed to a particular host, e.g., host 3 in

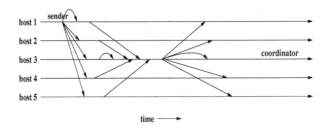

Fig. 1. Total Order Atomic Broadcast using fixed/moving coordinator.

figure 1. To modify such algorithms for execution in a mobile environment, we give special attention to the coordinator. If the algorithm is directly executed on the mobile hosts without any change, the cost incurred for each broadcast will consists of

1. the cost of broadcast: $(N-1) * (C_{search} + C_{wireless})$,
2. the cost of sending to the coordinator: $(N-1) * (C_{search} + C_{wireless})$,
3. the cost of broadcasting the time stamped messages back:

$$(N-1) * (C_{search} + C_{wireless})$$

leading to a overall cost of $3(N-1) * (C_{search} + C_{wireless})$.

This can be improved marginally if the location of the coordinator cached by each MSS. The cost in that case would be

$$2(N-1) * (C_{search} + C_{wireless}) + (N-1) * (C_{fixed} + C_{wireless}).$$

However, if the coordinator is placed on an MSS, the cost gets revised as follows:

1. the cost of broadcast: $C_{wireless} + (M-1) * C_{fixed}$,
2. the cost of sending to coordinator: $(M-1) * C_{fixed}$,
3. the cost of broadcasting back the final timestamped message:

$$(M-1) * C_{fixed} + (N-1) * C_{wireless}.$$

Thus, making it a total cost of $N * C_{wireless} + 3(M-1) * C_{fixed}$.

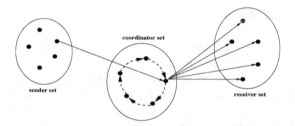

Fig. 2. Conceptual model of a moving coordinator system, the sender, coordinator and receiver sets are the same, that is comprise of the same hosts, but are shown distinctly for the sake of clarity.

2.5   Moving Coordinator Based System

The difference of a moving coordinator system from the afore-mentioned fixed coordinator system is that the role of coordinator can be performed by different mobile hosts at different times. Thus the coordinator is determined by a function of time as shown in figure 2. If the algorithm is executed on mobile hosts without restructuring, the communication cost is $3(N-1) * (C_{search} + C_{wireless})$. We observe that as soon as a mobile host becomes a coordinator the number of accesses to it rises dramatically in a short space of time. Hence, let us modify the system as follows:

- The MH informs its MSS about change of status to coordinator, which in turn broadcasts this information to all MSSs.
- The coordinator MH uses the inform strategy during its tenure as coordinator, while other hosts use the search strategy.

With the suggested modifications,

1. the cost of broadcast: $C_{wireless} + (M-1) * C_{fixed}$,
2. the cost of sending to coordinator: $(M-1) * C_{fixed} + C_{wireless}$,
3. cost of broadcasting back the time stamped message:

$$(M-1) * C_{fixed} + (N-1) * C_{wireless},$$

4. and the additional overhead associated with change of coordinator:

$$C_{wireless} + (M-1) * C_{fixed}.$$

Thus the total cost becomes:

$$(N+1) * C_{wireless} + 3(M-1)C_{fixed} + \alpha(C_{wireless} + (M-1) * C_{fixed}),$$

assuming a change of coordinator occurs after every α broadcasts.

Comparing this with the non-restructured cost the savings are significant.

3   Synchronization

In general, whenever an operation is executed, it holds up the subsequent execution of a subset of operations. It may not be true that this subset contains only or all operations of the same type. The operations may be held up due to non-availability of the parameters to be passed to those operations. The resulting situation can be visualized as acquiring an internal lock or mutex before an operation could be executed. There may be a set of operations which would be trying to acquire the same mutex before proceeding. Hence, exactly one of these operations can proceed at a time. Thus, we may associate a subset of operations to an internal mutex in the algorithm. The concept of internal mutex is introduced only to motivate the formalization, but not included in the formalization itself.

3.1   The State of Synchronization

Generally, a state is associated with anything which has variables and the variables take different values to realize different states of the system. Our interest here is in those states of the object which concerns with synchronization. The subsequent mutexes which would be held depends on operation to be performed and the current state of the object. Also, the current state of the object determines what operations can be performed on the object. The the object itself may have a large number of states, we would like to view them only as the states concerned with the synchronization.

Definition 1. *The state of synchronization is a set of all possible sets of synchronization for that particular state of the object. Given an integer i, let y_i denote the ith state of synchronization. The number of y_is is equal to the number of synchronization states.*

3.2   Operation Frequency Distribution

To evaluate the *goodness* or *performance* of an abstraction an object frequency distribution has to be introduced. We apply our abstractions over this frequency and calculate the number of operations performed per unit time. This number provides an idea about the *load* on the system.

3.3   The Mathematical Modeling

We have an object and concerned with every instance of an object we have an expanded abstraction set. Let us call this set A, i.e.,

$$A = \{x|\ x \text{ is an operation on an instance of the object}\}$$

Now assume that this object has a set of synchronization states. Let this set denoted by Y, i.e., $Y = \{y_1, y_2, \ldots, y_n\}$. Note that y_i itself is composed of many sets of synchronizations. For an integer i let S_i denote sets of synchronizations. Thus, $y_i = \{S_1, S_2, \ldots, S_m\}$ where $S_j \subseteq A$, for $1 \leq j \leq m$. It should be noted that i denotes a state of synchronization.

If an operation $o1$ is required to be performed on an object then another operation $o2$ can not be performed concurrently on the same object if $o1$ and $o2$ are in the same set $S_i(\in y)$, where y is the set of synchronization states for the current state of the object.

Let us move to the operation frequency distribution. We have a function $f(o, y)$ defined for $o \in A$ and for $y \in Y$. We assume further that the function is normalized, i.e., $\Sigma f(o, y) = 1$, where summation runs over all $o \in A$, and for all $y \in Y$. This helps in visualizing the contribution of an operation at a particular state of the object with respect the whole. It may be noticed that occasionally there would be a few operations which cannot be performed when the object is in a particular state. This is captured by setting $f(o, y) = 0$. An operation on the object may or may not change the state of the object.

Applying the frequency distribution we can arrive at computation of concurrency loads. We compute

$$L_{ij} = \Sigma f(o, y), \forall o \in S_j, \text{ where } S_j \in y_i$$

For obvious reasons, $\Sigma_{i,j} L_{ij} \neq 1$. This is because S_i's overlap, thus, the contribution $(f(o, y))$ can be found in multiple L_{ij}'s. In any case, we normalize this again. Thus,

$$L'_{ij} = \frac{L_{ij}}{\Sigma L_{ij}}$$

L'_{ij} represents the sum of the frequency of operations for a set of operations that try to acquire the same mutex. Thus, higher this number means that more operations of this set ($S_j \in y_i$) would be queued together and would have to wait. Also, the maximum of all L_{ij}s would represent a measure of the synchronizing bottleneck for the whole application. As the steps of an application proceeds sequentially at the MH the largest L_{ij} would be the bottleneck for the entire object access. Let us denote this maximum value by CL and call this *concurrency load*. Thus, $CL = max(L'_{ij})$. The advantage of using the normalized L'_{ij} is that it provides a common scale to compare two different abstractions. Each of the abstractions would give a (normalized) concurrency load which can be compared to find which of the two abstraction is better.

Thus the second principle is as follows.

Principle 2 *While making an abstraction for an object try to minimize the concurrency load of the expanded abstraction set.*

It should be noted that the above principle would also improve performance in non mobile environments but the effect would be significantly large in a mobile environment because of the large number of threads that concurrently execute supplemented with the inherent latency of each operation because of poor network resources.

4   Examples

Let us illustrate the proposed abstraction on two simple examples. The first one is concerning the synchronization requirements for updating of cells of a spread sheet. The second deals with read write lock.

4.1   Spreadsheet

Suppose a number of mobile users constantly update a spreadsheet. Let us assume two abstractions for the spreadsheet object. One, a mutex on the entire spreadsheet and another, a mutex over each cell that one wants to edit. Its easy to see that the latter case would be better in high concurrency because more than one user can simultaneously update the spreadsheet if they do not update the same cell. In the former case only one person/process can update the spreadsheet at a time.

Let us examine how two abstractions are captured through our model. In the first instance, there is one set S_1 containing all operations that can be performed on the object. Thus, $L_{11} = 1$ and $CL = 1$. In the second instance, assuming p cells are there in the spreadsheet, there are p internal mutexes, and hence 2^p states of synchronization. As there is no inter-dependence between states, actually the values of S_is in many states would be equivalent. For each state of synchronization we have one S_1 in its set. Thus assuming that $f(o, y)$ is constant for all o and y, we have L_{ij} the same for all i and j. In fact $j = 1$ is the only value. As no Ss overlap, we can safely assume that $\Sigma L_{ij} = 1$ giving $CL = max(L_{ij}) = \frac{1}{2^p}$. Thus gives a straight forward indication that the second abstraction is better.

4.2   Read-Write Lock

Consider an object that supports read and write operations through a read-write lock. The read write lock allows concurrent reads to be performed. But it allows only exclusive writes and while a read is going on, a write cannot take place.

Thus there are two states of synchronization, the read state and the write state. Let us denote the set of synchronization of these by y_r and y_w. There are a number of read operations (many parameters) and similarly many write operations. Assume that there are p entities which can written or read. Let the expanded abstraction set be represented by

$$A = \{or_1, ow_1, or_2, ow_2, or_3, ow_3, \ldots, or_p, ow_p\}$$

where or_i is a read operation and ow_i a write operation.

In state y_r, concurrent reads are supported, whereas in y_w every write operation is exclusive, Thus,

$$y_w = \{\underline{ow_1, ow_2, ow_3, \ldots, ow_p}, or_1, or_2, or_3, \ldots, or_p\}$$
$$y_r = \{\underbrace{or_1}, \underbrace{or_2}, \underbrace{or_3}, \ldots, \underbrace{or_p}, ow_1, ow_2, ow_3, \ldots, ow_p\}$$

The sets of synchronization, are indicated by underbraces. We do not worry about those elements which are not grouped together as these operations cannot be performed in that state of the object. Consequently, in the operation frequency distribution

$$f(ow_i, y_r) = 0 \text{ and } f(or_i, y_w) = 0$$

Hence, the evaluations for these operations would any way cancel out. Assuming $f(o, y)$ to be constant for all o and y, and from the fact that $\Sigma f(o, y) = 1$ we deduce that,

$$f(o, y) = \frac{1}{2p}$$

Now, let us evaluate L_{ij}. Note that $L_{w_i} = \Sigma f(ow_i, y_w)$ for $1 \le i \le p$. Similarly, $L_{r_j} = f(or_j, y_r)$ for $1 \le j \le p$. Thus,

$$L_{w_i} = p\frac{1}{2p} = \frac{1}{2}, \text{ and } L_{r_j} = \frac{1}{2p}$$

Incidentally, no sets of synchronization overlaps. Thus $\Sigma L_{ij} = 1$, and no normalization is required. Thus, the concurrency load $CL = \max\{L_{ij}\} = \frac{1}{2}$. This implies a read write lock is better than a single mutex based lock (in which case $CL = 1$). Note that in typical scenarios, the value of $f(or, y_r)$ is much larger than $f(ow, y_w)$ simply because the number of read operations is much more than the number of write operations. In that case it can be easily seen that the above analysis would give a better value for CL.

References

1. BADRINATH, B. R., ACHARYA, A., AND IMIELINSKI, T. Impact of mobility on distributed computations. *Operating Systems Review 27* (1993), pp. 15–20.
2. BADRINATH, B. R., ACHARYA, A., AND IMIELINSKI, T. Structuring distributed algorithms for mobile hosts. In *Proceedings of ICDCS* (1994), pp. 21–28.
3. DIJKSTRA, E. W. Self stabilizing system in spite of distributed control. *CACM 17* (1974), pp. 643–644.
4. GHOSH, R. K., CHAKRABORTY, A., AND KUMAR, R. Restructuring distributed algorithms for mobile computing environment. Tech. rep., Department of CSE, IIT-Kanpur, April 2002.
5. GRANT, W. C. Wireless coyote: A computer supported field trip. *CACM 36* (1993), pp. 57–59.
6. LAMPORT, L. A new solution of Dijkstra's concurrent programming problem. *CACM 17* (1974), pp. 453–455.

Design of Aliasing Free Space Compressor in BIST with Maximal Compaction Ratio Using Concepts of Strong and Weak Compatibilities of Response Data Outputs and Generalized Sequence Mergeability

Sunil R. Das, Mansour H. Assaf, Emil M. Petriu, and Sujoy Mukherjee

School of Information Technology and Engineering
University of Ottawa, Ottawa, Ontario K1N 6N5, Canada

Abstract. This paper suggests a novel approach to designing aliasing free space compactors with maximal compaction ratio utilizing concepts of strong and weak compatibilities of response data outputs together with conventional switching theory concepts of cover table and frequency ordering for detectable single stuck line faults of the circuit under test (CUT), based on the assumption of generalized sequence mergeability. The advantages of aliasing free space compaction as developed in the paper over earlier techniques are obvious since zero aliasing is achieved here without any modifications of the CUT, while the area overhead and signal propagation delay are relatively less compared to conventional parity tree linear compactors. The approach used works equally well with both deterministic compacted tests and pseudorandom test sets.

1 Introduction

With increasing complexity in digital systems design with increased levels of integration densities, better and more effective methods of testing to ensure reliable operations of chips, mainstay of today's many sophisticated systems, are required. The recent evolution from chip-set philosophy to embedded cores-based system-on-a-chip (SOC) in ASIC design further ushered in a new dimension in the realm of digital circuit testing. Though the concept of testing has a broad applicability, finding highly efficient testing techniques that ensure correct system performance has thus assumed significant importance [1–15]. The conventional testing technique of digital circuits requires application of test patterns generated by a test generator (TPG) to the circuit under test (CUT) and comparing the responses with known correct responses. However, for large circuits, because of higher storage requirements for the fault-free responses, the test procedure becomes rather expensive and thus alternative approaches are sought to minimize the amount of needed storage. Built-in self-testing (BIST) is a design approach that provides the capability of solving many of the problems otherwise encountered in testing digital systems. It combines concepts of both built-in test (BIT) and self-test (ST) in one termed built-in self-test (BIST). In BIST, test generation, test application and response verification are all accomplished

S.K. Das and S. Bhattacharya (Eds.): IWDC 2002, LNCS 2571, pp. 234–245, 2002.
© Springer-Verlag Berlin Heidelberg 2002

through built-in hardware, which allows different parts of a chip to be tested in parallel, reducing the required testing time besides eliminating the need for external test equipments. A typical BIST environment uses a TPG that sends its outputs to a CUT and output streams from the CUT are fed into a test data analyzer. A fault is detected if the circuit response is different from that of the fault-free circuit. The test data analyzer is comprised of a response compaction unit (RCU), a storage for the fault-free response of the CUT, and a comparator.

The extra logic representing the compression circuit must be as simple as possible, to be easily embedded within the CUT, and should not introduce signal delays to affect either the test execution time or the normal functionality of the CUT. Besides, the length of the signature must be as short as possible in order to minimize the amount of memory required to store the fault-free responses. In addition, signatures derived from faulty output responses and their corresponding fault-free signatures should not be the same, which unfortunately is not always the case. A fundamental problem with compression techniques is hence error masking or aliasing [13], which occurs when the signatures from faulty output responses map into fault-free signatures. Aliasing causes loss of information, which in turn affects the test quality of BIST and reduces the fault coverage. Several methods have been proposed in the literature for computing the aliasing probability of which the exact computation is known to be NP-hard.

This paper suggests a novel approach to designing zero-aliasing space compactors using deterministic and pseudorandom testing. The developed approach utilizes switching theory concepts such as those of cover table and frequency ordering [1], together with concepts of strong and weak compatibility of response data outputs in the design, based on detectable single stuck line faults of the CUT. The advantages of aliasing-free space compaction over earlier techniques are evidently clear – zero-aliasing is achieved without any modifications of the CUT, the area overhead and signal propagation delay are relatively less compared to conventional parity tree linear compactors, and the approach used works equally well with both deterministic and pseudorandom test sets. Besides, the approach uses less computation in the design process in successive stages compared to the existing technique [14] that uses an exhaustive approach at every step to decide on the gate to be used for merger of a pair of lines of the CUT to achieve zero-aliasing, if possible. The paper utilizes a mathematically sound selection criterion of merger of a number of lines of the CUT to decide on the gate for zero-aliasing and achieves maximum compaction ratio in the design, as is evident from simulation experiments conducted on ISCAS 85 combinational and ISCAS 89 full scan sequential benchmark circuits.

2   Mathematical Basis

Property 1. Let A and B represent two of the outputs of a CUT. Let these CUT outputs be merged by an AND(NAND) gate and let the AND(NAND) gate output be z_1. Then we can envisage the undernoted scenarios :

Case 1 : Fault-free (FF) outputs = Faulty (F) outputs $\Rightarrow$ Outputs A and B of the CUT do not detect any faults.

Case 2 : Only those faults that occur at A and B are detectable at $z_1 \Rightarrow$ FF $\neq$ F.

Case 3 : Faults occur at A and B but not all or some are detectable at $z_1 \Rightarrow FF \neq F$. That is, these missed faults at z_1 are detected additionally at other outputs of the CUT besides A and B.

Definition 1. Let A, B, C, ... be the different outputs of an n-input m-output CUT. Let the faults detected at the CUT outputs A, B, C, ... be θ where $\theta \leq \beta$, the total number of detectable faults at the CUT output when subjected to a compact set of deterministic tests τ, $\tau \leq 2^n$ (τ might not be a minimal or nonminimal but complete set of tests), or pseudorandom tests. Assume that the fault situation at the outputs A, B conforms to conditions of Cases 1-2 above (but not Case 3). If the CUT outputs A, B are merged by an AND(NAND) gate, we define lines A, B to be **strongly** AND(NAND) compatible, written as

(AB) s-AND(NAND) compatible.

Definition 2. Let A, B, C, ... be the different outputs of an n-input m-output CUT. Let the faults detected at the CUT outputs A, B, C, ... be θ where $\theta \leq \beta$, the total number of detectable faults at the CUT output when subjected to a compact set of deterministic tests τ, $\tau \leq 2^n$ (τ might not be a minimal or nonminimal but complete set of tests), or pseudorandom tests.. Assume that the fault situation at the outputs A, B conforms to conditions of Case 3 above (but not Cases 1-2). If the CUT outputs A, B are merged by an AND(NAND) gate, we define lines A, B to be **weakly** AND(NAND) compatible, written as

(AB) w-AND(NAND) compatible.

Definition 3. Let A, B, C, ... be the different outputs of an n-input m-output CUT. Let the faults detected at the CUT outputs A, B, C, ... be θ where $\theta \leq \beta$, the total number of detectable faults at the CUT output when subjected to a compact set of deterministic tests τ, $\tau \leq 2^n$ (τ might not be a minimal or nonminimal but complete set of tests), or pseudorandom tests. Assume that the fault situation at the outputs A, B conforms to none of the conditions as specified by Cases 1-3 above. If the CUT outputs A, B are merged by an AND(NAND) gate, we define lines A, B to be AND (NAND) incompatible, written as

(AB) AND(NAND) incompatible.

Definition 4. Let A, B, C, ... be the different outputs of an n-input m-output CUT. Let the faults detected at the CUT outputs A, B, C, ... be θ where $\theta \leq \beta$, the total number of detectable faults at the CUT output when subjected to a compact set of deterministic tests τ, $\tau \leq 2^n$ (τ might not be a minimal or nonminimal but complete set of tests), or pseudorandom tests. Assume that the fault situation at the outputs A, B conforms to conditions of Cases 1-2 above (but not Case 3). If the CUT outputs A, B are merged by an OR(NOR) gate, we define lines A, B to be **strongly** OR(NOR) compatible, written as

(AB) s-OR(NOR) compatible.

Definition 5. Let A, B, C, ... be the different outputs of an n-input m-output CUT. Let the faults detected at the CUT outputs A, B, C, ... be θ where $\theta \leq \beta$, the total number of detectable faults at the CUT output when subjected to a compact set of deterministic tests τ, $\tau \leq 2^n$ (τ might not be a minimal or nonminimal but complete set of tests), or pseudorandom tests. Assume that the fault situation at the outputs A, B conforms to conditions of Case 3 above (but not Cases 1-2).). If the CUT outputs A,

B are merged by an OR(NOR) gate, we define lines A, B to be **weakly** OR (NOR) compatible, written as

(AB) w-OR(NOR) compatible.

Definition 6. Let A, B, C, ... be the different outputs of an n-input m-output CUT. Let the faults detected at the CUT outputs A, B, C, ... be θ where $\theta \leq \beta$, the total number of detectable faults at the CUT output when subjected to a compact set of deterministic tests τ, $\tau \leq 2^n$ (τ might not be a minimal or nonminimal but complete set of tests), or pseudorandom tests. Assume that the fault situation at the outputs A, B conforms to none of the conditions as specified by Cases 1-3 above. If the CUT outputs A, B are merged by an OR(NOR) gate, we define lines A, B to be OR(NOR) incompatible, written as

(AB) OR(NOR) incompatible.

Definition 7. Let A, B, C, ... be the different outputs of an n-input m-output CUT. Let the faults detected at the CUT outputs A, B, C, ... be θ where $\theta \leq \beta$, the total number of detectable faults at the CUT output when subjected to a compact set of deterministic tests τ, $\tau \leq 2^n$ (τ might not be a minimal or nonminimal but complete set of tests), or pseudorandom tests. Assume that the fault situation at the outputs A, B conforms to conditions of Cases 1-2 above (but not Case 3). If the CUT outputs A, B are merged by an XOR(XNOR) gate, we define lines A, B to be **strongly** XOR(XNOR) compatible, written as

(AB) s-XOR(XNOR) compatible.

Definition 8. Let A, B, C, ... be the different outputs of an n-input m-output CUT. Let the faults detected at the CUT outputs A, B, C, ... be θ where $\theta \leq \beta$, the total number of detectable faults at the CUT output when subjected to a compact set of deterministic tests τ, $\tau \leq 2^n$ (τ might not be a minimal or nonminimal but complete set of tests), or pseudorandom tests. Assume that the fault situation at the outputs A, B conforms to conditions of Case 3 above (but not Cases 1-2). If the CUT outputs A, B are merged by an XOR(XNOR) gate, we define lines A, B to be **weakly** XOR(XNOR) compatible, written as

(AB) w-XOR(XNOR) compatible.

Definition 9. Let A, B, C, ... be the different outputs of an n-input m-output CUT. Let the faults detected at the CUT outputs A, B, C, ... be θ where $\theta \leq \beta$, the total number of detectable faults at the CUT output when subjected to a compact set of deterministic tests τ, $\tau \leq 2^n$ (τ might not be a minimal or nonminimal but complete set of tests), or pseudorandom tests. Assume that the fault situation at the outputs A, B conforms to none of the conditions as specified by Cases 1-3 above. If the CUT outputs A, B are merged by an XOR(XNOR) gate, we define lines A, B to be XOR(XNOR) incompatible, written as

(AB) XOR(XNOR) incompatible.

Definition 10. Let A, B, C, ... be the different outputs of an n-input m-output CUT. Let the faults detected at the CUT outputs A, B, C, ... be θ where $\theta \leq \beta$, the total number of detectable faults at the CUT output when subjected to a compact set of deterministic tests τ, $\tau \leq 2^n$ (τ might not be a minimal or nonminimal but complete set of tests), or pseudorandom tests. Assume that the fault situation at the outputs A, B conforms to either of the three conditions as specified by Cases 1-3 above, but unknown to us. If the CUT outputs A, B are merged under these conditions by an

AND(NAND), OR(NOR) or XOR(XNOR) gate, then we define lines A, B to be **simply** AND(NAND), OR(NOR) or XOR (XNOR) compatible, written as

(AB) AND(NAND), OR(NOR) or XOR(XNOR) compatible.

Theorem 1. Let A, B, C, ... be the different outputs of an n-input m-output CUT. Let the faults detected at the CUT outputs A, B, C, ... be θ where $\theta \le \beta$, the total number of detectable faults at the CUT output when subjected to a compact set of deterministic tests τ, $\tau \le 2^n$ (τ might not be a minimal or nonminimal but complete set of tests), or pseudorandom tests. Assume that the fault situation at the outputs A, B conforms to conditions of Cases 1-2 above, so that the outputs A, B are s-AND(NAND) compatible. Similarly, let the outputs B, C be s-AND(NAND) compatible, and the outputs A, C be s-AND(NAND) compatible. Then (ABC) is s-AND(NAND) compatible and all faults are detected at z_1.

Proof : The proof follows readily.

Theorem 2. Let A_1, A_2, ... , A_m be the different outputs of an n-input m-output CUT. Let the faults detected at the CUT outputs A_1, A_2, ... , A_m be θ where $\theta \le \beta$, the total number of detectable faults at the CUT output when subjected to a compact set of deterministic tests τ, $\tau \le 2^n$ (τ might not be a minimal or nonminimal but complete set of tests), or pseudorandom tests. Assume that the fault situation at the outputs A_1, A_2, ... , A_m conforms to conditions of Cases 1-2 above, so that the outputs A_1, A_2, ... , A_m are s-AND(NAND) compatible. Then all faults are detected at z_1.

Proof : The proof follows readily.

Theorem 3. Let A, B, C, ... be the different outputs of an n-input m-output CUT. Let the faults detected at the CUT outputs A, B, C, ... be θ where $\theta \le \beta$, the total number of detectable faults at the CUT output when subjected to a compact set of deterministic tests τ, $\tau \le 2^n$ (τ might not be a minimal or nonminimal but complete set of tests), or pseudorandom tests. Assume that the fault situation at the outputs A, B conforms to conditions of Cases 1-2 above, so that the outputs A, B are s-OR(NOR) compatible. Similarly, let the outputs B, C be s-OR(NOR) compatible, and the outputs A, C be s-OR(NOR) compatible. Then (ABC) is s-OR(NOR) compatible and all faults are detected at z_1.

Proof : The proof follows readily.

Theorem 4. Let A_1, A_2, ... , A_m be the different outputs of an n-input m-output CUT. Let the faults detected at the CUT outputs A_1, A_2, ... , A_m be θ where $\theta \le \beta$, the total number of detectable faults at the CUT output when subjected to a compact set of deterministic tests τ, $\tau \le 2^n$ (τ might not be a minimal or nonminimal but complete set of tests), or pseudorandom tests. Assume that the fault situation at the outputs A_1, A_2, ... , A_m conforms to conditions of Cases 1-2 above, so that the outputs A_1, A_2, ... , A_m are s-OR(NOR) compatible. Then all faults are detected at z_1.

Proof : The proof follows readily.

Theorem 5. Let A, B, C, ... be the different outputs of an n-input m-output CUT. Let the faults detected at the CUT outputs A, B, C, ... be θ where $\theta \le \beta$, the total number of detectable faults at the CUT output when subjected to a compact set of deterministic tests τ, $\tau \le 2^n$ (τ might not be a minimal or nonminimal but complete set of tests), or pseudorandom tests. Assume that the fault situation at the outputs A, B conforms to conditions of Cases 1-2 above, so that the outputs A, B are s-XOR(XNOR) compatible. Similarly, let the outputs B, C be s-XOR(XNOR) compatible, and the outputs A, C be s-XOR(XNOR) compatible. Then (ABC) is s-XOR(XNOR) compatible and all faults are detected at z_1.

Proof : The proof follows readily.

Theorem 6. Let A_1, A_2, ... , A_m be the different outputs of an n-input m-output CUT. Let the faults detected at the CUT outputs A_1, A_2, ... , A_m be θ where $\theta \leq \beta$, the total number of detectable faults at the CUT output when subjected to a compact set of deterministic tests τ, $\tau \leq 2^n$ (τ might not be a minimal or nonminimal but complete set of tests), or pseudorandom tests. Assume that the fault situation at the outputs A_1, A_2, ... , A_m conforms to conditions of Cases 1-2 above, so that the outputs A_1, A_2, ... , A_m are s-XOR(XNOR) compatible. Then all faults are detected at z_1.

Proof : The proof follows readily.

Theorem 7. Let A, B, C, ... be the different outputs of an n-input m-output CUT. Let the faults detected at the CUT outputs A, B, C, ... be θ where $\theta \leq \beta$, the total number of detectable faults at the CUT output when subjected to a compact set of deterministic tests τ, $\tau \leq 2^n$ (τ might not be a minimal or nonminimal but complete set of tests), or pseudorandom tests. Assume that the fault situation at the outputs A, B conforms to conditions of Case 3 above, so that the outputs A, B are w-AND(NAND) compatible. Similarly, let the outputs B, C be w-AND(NAND) compatible, and the outputs A, C be w-AND(NAND) compatible. Then (ABC) is w-AND(NAND) compatible and all faults may or may not be detected at z_1.

Proof : The proof follows readily.

Corollary 7.1. Let A_1, A_2, ... , A_m be the different outputs of an n-input m-output CUT. Let the faults detected at the CUT outputs A_1, A_2, ... , A_m be θ where $\theta \leq \beta$, the total number of detectable faults at the CUT output when subjected to a compact set of deterministic tests τ, $\tau \leq 2^n$ (τ might not be a minimal or nonminimal but complete set of tests), or pseudorandom tests. Assume that the fault situation at the outputs A_1, A_2, ... , A_m conforms to conditions of Case 3 above, so that the outputs A_1, A_2, ... , A_m are w-AND(NAND) compatible. Then all faults may or may not be detected at z_1.

Theorem 8. Let A, B, C, ... be the different outputs of an n-input m-output CUT. Let the faults detected at the CUT outputs A, B, C, ... be θ where $\theta \leq \beta$, the total number of detectable faults at the CUT output when subjected to a compact set of deterministic tests τ, $\tau \leq 2^n$ (τ might not be a minimal or nonminimal but complete set of tests), or pseudorandom tests. Assume that the fault situation at the outputs A, B conforms to conditions of Case 3 above, so that the outputs A, B are w-OR(NOR) compatible. Similarly, let the outputs B, C be w-OR(NOR) compatible, and the outputs A, C be w-OR(NOR) compatible. Then (ABC) is w-OR(NOR) compatible and all faults may or may not be detected at z_1.

Proof : The proof follows readily.

Corollary 8.1. Let A_1, A_2, ... , A_m be the different outputs of an n-input m-output CUT. Let the faults detected at the CUT outputs A_1, A_2, ... , A_m be θ where $\theta \leq \beta$, the total number of detectable faults at the CUT output when subjected to a compact set of deterministic tests τ, $\tau \leq 2^n$ (τ might not be a minimal or nonminimal but complete set of tests), or pseudorandom tests. Assume that the fault situation at the outputs A_1, A_2, ... , A_m conforms to conditions of Case 3 above, so that the outputs A_1, A_2, ... , A_m are w-OR(NOR) compatible. Then all faults may or may not be detected at z_1.

Theorem 9. Let A, B, C, ... be the different outputs of an n-input m-output CUT. Let the faults detected at the CUT outputs A, B, C, ... be θ where $\theta \leq \beta$, the total number of detectable faults at the CUT output when subjected to a compact set of deterministic tests τ, $\tau \leq 2^n$ (τ might not be a minimal or nonminimal but complete set of tests), or pseudorandom tests. Assume that the fault situation at the outputs A, B conforms to conditions of Case 3 above, so that the outputs A, B are w-XOR(XNOR) compatible. Similarly, let the outputs B, C be w-XOR(XNOR) compatible, and the outputs A, C be w-XOR(XNOR) compatible. Then (ABC) is w-XOR(XNOR) compatible and all faults may or may not be detected at z_1.

Proof : The proof follows readily.

Corollary 9.1. Let A_1, A_2, ... , A_m be the different outputs of an n-input m-output CUT. Let the faults detected at the CUT outputs A_1, A_2, ... , A_m be θ where $\theta \leq \beta$, the total number of detectable faults at the CUT output when subjected to a compact set of deterministic tests τ, $\tau \leq 2^n$ (τ might not be a minimal or nonminimal but complete set of tests), or pseudorandom tests. Assume that the fault situation at the outputs A_1, A_2, ... , A_m conforms to conditions of Case 3 above, so that the outputs A_1, A_2, ... , A_m are w-XOR(XNOR) compatible. Then all faults may or may not be detected at z_1.

In actual situations we do not know whether the merged outputs conform to the conditions specified by Cases 1-3 as discussed, and as such we have to deal exclusively with the case of **simply** compatible.

3   Experimental Results

A heuristic approach has been adopted and implemented so that we can get the results within an acceptable CPU time. Because of space constraints, the details of the Algorithms and all the simulation results on ISCAS 85 combinational and ISCAS 89 full scan benchmark circuits could not be given. However, some partial results on ISCAS 85 benchmark circuits only are given below in the form of graphs (Figs. 1 through 6), for both deterministic compacted testing and pseudorandom testing. Also, two of the aliasing free compression networks for c432 benchmark circuit are provided in Figs. 7 and 8. The overall compression algorithm includes a **Subalgorithm** for the computation of maximal compatibility classes of the CUT outputs corresponding to possible merger by AND(NAND), OR(NOR) and XOR(XNOR) gates based on knowledge of pairs of incompatibles, using the modified cut-set algorithm by Das [16].

Acknowledgments. This research was supported in part by the Natural Sciences and Engineering Research Council of Canada under Grant A 4750.

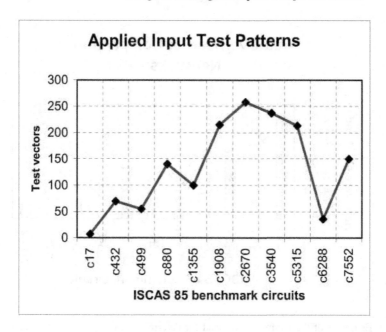

Fig. 1. Input test vectors for deterministic compacted testing of ISCAS 85 benchmark circuits

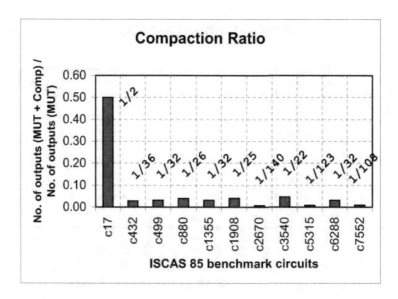

Fig. 2. Compaction ratio for deterministic compacted testing of ISCAS 85 benchmark circuits

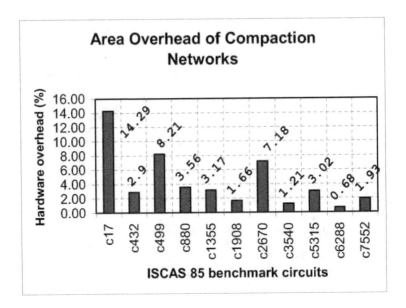

Fig. 3. Estimates of the hardware overhead for deterministic compacted testing of ISCAS 85 benchmark circuits

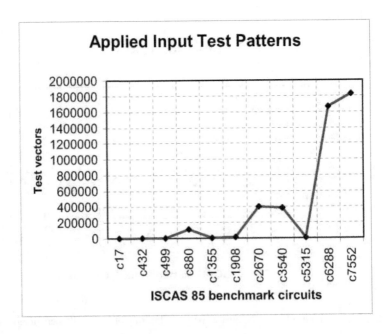

Fig. 4. Input test vectors for pseudorandom testing of ISCAS 85 benchmark circuits

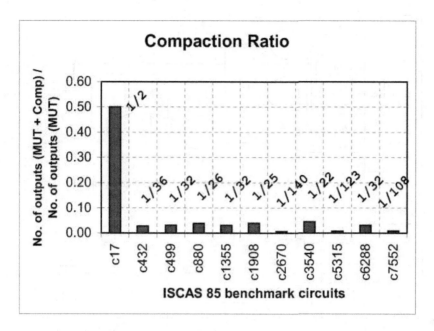

Fig. 5.   Compaction ratio for pseudorandom testing of ISCAS 85 benchmark circuits

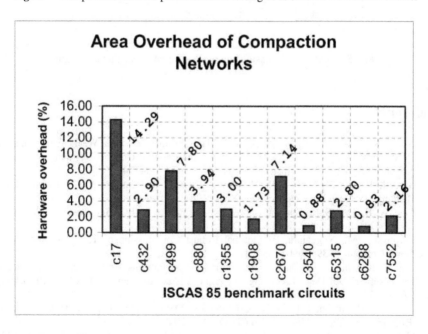

Fig. 6. Estimates of the hardware overhead for pseudorandom testing of ISCAS 85 benchmark circuits

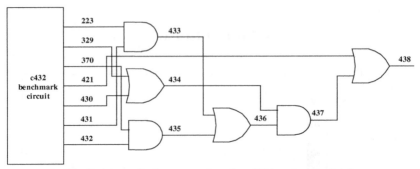

Fig. 7. A zero aliasing compressor for c432 benchmark circuit

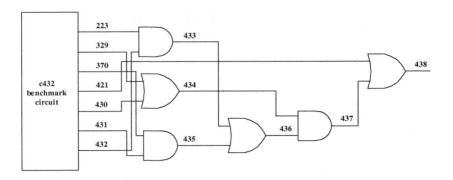

Fig. 8. Another zero aliasing compressor for c432 benchmark circuit

References

1. Das, S. R., Ramamoorthy, C. V., Assaf, M. H., Petriu, E. M., Jone, W. B.: Fault Tolerance in Systems Design in VLSI Using Data Compression Under Constraints of Failure Probabilities. IEEE Trans. Instrum. Meas. **50** (2001) 1725–1747.
2. Bardell, P. H., McAnney, W. H., Savir, J.: Built-In Test for VLSI: Pseudorandom Techniques. Wiley Interscience, New York (1987).
3. Jone, W. B., Das, S. R.: Space Compression Method for Built-In Self-Testing of VLSI Circuits. Int. J. Comput. Aided VLSI Des. **3** (1991) 309–322.
4. Karpovsky, M., Nagvajara, P.: Optimal Robust Compression of Test Responses. IEEE Trans. Comput. **C-39** (1990) 138–141.
5. Lee, H. K., Ha, D. S.: On the Generation of Test Patterns for Combinational Circuits. Tech. Rep. 12-93, Dept. Elec. Eng., Virginia Polytec. Inst. and State Univ., Blacksburg, VA (1993).
6. Li, Y. K., Robinson, J. P.: Space Compression Method with Output Data Modification, IEEE Trans. Comput. Aided Des. **6** (1987) 290–294.
7. McCluskey, E. J.: Built-In Self-Test Techniques. IEEE Des. Test Comput. **2** (1985) 21–28.
8. Pomeranz, I., Reddy, L. N., Reddy, S. M.: COMPACTEST: A Method to Generate Compact Test Sets for Combinational Circuits. Proc. Int. Test Conf. (1991) 194–203.

9. Pradhan, D. K., Gupta, S. K.: A New Framework for Designing and Analyzing BIST Techniques and Zero Aliasing Compression. IEEE Trans. Comput. **C-40** (1991) 743–763.

10. Reddy, S. M., Saluja, K., Karpovsky, M. G.: Data Compression Technique for Test Responses. IEEE Trans. Comput. **C-37** (1988) 1151–1156.

11. Saluja, K.K., Karpovsky, M.: Testing Computer Hardware Through Compression in Space and Time. Proc. Int. Test Conf. (1983) 83–88.

12. Savir, J.: Reducing the MISR Size. IEEE Trans. Comput. **C-45** (1996) 930–938.

13. Chakrabarty, K.: Test Response Compaction for Built-In Self-Testing . Ph.D. Dissertation, Dept. Comp. Sc. Eng., Univ. Michigan, Ann Arbor, MI (1995).

14. Pouya, B. and Touba, N. A.: Synthesis of Zero-Aliasing Elementary-Tree Space Compactors. Proc. VLSI Test Symp. (1998) 70–77.

15. Rajsuman, R.: System-on-a-Chip : Design and Test. Artech House, Boston, MA (2000).

16. Das, S.R.: On a New Approach for Finding All the Modified Cut-Sets in an Incompatibility Graph, IEEE Trans. Comput. **C-22** (1973) 187–193.

A Behavioral Synthesis Tool for Exploiting Fine Grain Parallelism in FPGAs

Prithviraj Banerjee, Malay Haldar, Anshuman Nayak, Victor Kim,
Debabrata Bagchi, Satrajit Pal, and Nikhil Tripathi

AccelChip, Inc.
999 Plaza Drive, Suite 340, Schaumburg, IL-60173
www.accelchip.com

Abstract. This paper describes how fine grain parallelism can be exploited using a behavioral synthesis tool called AccelFPGA which reads in high-level descriptions of DSP applications written in MATLAB, and automatically generates synthesizable RTL models in VHDL or Verilog. The RTL models can be synthesized using commercial logic synthesis tools and place and route tools onto FPGAs. The paper describes how powerful directives are used to provide high-level architectural tradeoffs by exploiting fine grain parallelism, pipelining, memory mapping and tiling for the DSP designer. Experimental results are reported with the AccelFPGA version 1.4 compiler on a set of 8 MATLAB benchmarks that are mapped onto the Xilinx Virtex II FPGAs.

1 Introduction

Applications such as digital cell phones, 3G and 4G wireless receivers, MPEG 4 video, voice over IP, and video over IP, require digital signal processing (DSP) functions that are typically mapped onto general purpose DSP processors such as the Texas Instruments VelociTI C6000 [17], the Phillips Trimedia [18] and the Motorola/Lucent StarCore processor [19]. However, the performance requirements of these applications now exceed the capabilities of these processors. With the introduction of advanced Field-Programmable Gate Array (FPGA) architectures which provide built-in DSP support such as upto 192 embedded multipliers and block RAMs on the Xilinx Virtex-II [14], and upto 48 DSP Blocks and MegaRAMs on the Altera Stratix [2], a new hardware alternative is available for DSP designers who can get even higher levels of performances than those achievable on general purpose DSP processors. This high performance can be achieved by exploiting fine grain parallelism which can use upto 192 embedded multipliers on a Xilinx Virtex2 device, and upto 48 DSP blocks on an Altera Stratix device.

DSP design has traditionally been divided into two types of activities – systems/algorithm development and hardware/software implementation. The majority of DSP system designers and algorithm developers use the MATLAB language [9] for prototyping their DSP algorithm. The first step in this flow is the conversion of the floating point MATLAB algorithm, into a fixed point version using "quantizers" from the Filter Design and Analysis (FDA) Toolbox for MATLAB [9].

S.K. Das and S. Bhattacharya (Eds.): IWDC 2002, LNCS 2571, pp. 246–256, 2002.
© Springer-Verlag Berlin Heidelberg 2002

Algorithmic tradeoffs such as the precision of filter coefficients and the number of taps used in a filter are performed at the MATLAB level. Hardware design teams take the specifications created by the DSP engineers (in the form of a fixed point MATLAB code) and create a physical implementation of the DSP design. If the target is an FPGA, the first task is to create a register transfer level (RTL) model in a hardware description language (HDL) such as VHDL and Verilog. The RTL HDL is synthesized by a logic synthesis tool, and placed and routed onto an FPGA using backend tools. The process of creating an RTL model and a simulation testbench takes about one to two months for average designs with the tools currently used today, hence it is very difficult to perform various area-performance tradeoffs quickly for complex designs.

This paper describes how fine grain parallelism can be exploited using a behavioral synthesis tool called AccelFPGA which reads in high-level descriptions of DSP applications written in MATLAB, and automatically generates synthesizable RTL models in VHDL or Verilog. The RTL models can be synthesized using commercial logic synthesis tools and place and route tools onto FPGAs. Since this automatic generation of VHDL/Verilog from MATLAB takes minutes to run using the AccelFPGA compiler, it is possible to use this tool as a high-level design exploration tool. The paper describes how powerful directives are used to provide high-level architectural tradeoffs by exploiting fine grain parallelism, pipelining, memory mapping and tiling for the DSP designer.

2   Related Work

The problem of translating a high-level or behavioral language description into a register transfer level representation is called high-level synthesis [6]. Synopsys developed one of the first successful commercial behavioral synthesis tools in the industry, the Behavioral Compiler [12], which took behavioral VHDL or Verilog and generated RTL VHDL or Verilog for ASIC design. Recently, there has been a lot of work in the use of the C programming language and other high-level languages to generate synthesizable HDL codes or hardware implementations [7,10]. There have been several commercial efforts to develop compilers taking C/C++ into VHDL or Verilog. Examples are CoWare, Adelante [1], Celoxica [3], C Level Design [4] and Cynapps [5]. SystemC is a new language developed by the SystemC consortium which allows users to write hardware system descriptions in a language similar to C++ [11]. Synopsys has a tool called Cocentric which takes SystemC and generates RTL VHDL/Verilog.

While there have been some research and commercial development of tools that translated from languages such as C or C++ into VHDL and Verilog, this paper describes a compiler that takes behavioral MATLAB descriptions (the default language of DSP design) and generates RTL VHDL and Verilog for FPGA design. The MATCH compiler project [8] at Northwestern University has built a compiler that took applications written in MATLAB, and produced synthesizable RTL VHDL. The technology for the AccelFPGA compiler described in this paper is an outgrowth of the MATCH Compiler project.

Recently, FPGA vendors such as Xilinx and Altera have developed system level tools for DSP applications called the System Generator [15] and the DSP Builder [16] which allow DSP designers to design a DSP system using a SIMULINK graphical user interface. These tools provide a set of pre-designed parameterized building blocks such as adders, multipliers, RAMS, ROMS, FIR filters, FFT units, Viterbi and Reed Solomon decoders. Such tools, though very useful, restrict the user to designing DSP systems using only those specific building blocks provided by the tool, and also restrict the user to map their designs on the specific vendor's FPGA devices. On the other hand, many DSP designers would prefer to develop DSP systems from scratch using the general MATLAB programming language and target any FPGA device. This paper describes how various fine grain parallelism solutions can be explored at the high-level using a behavioral synthesis tool called AccelFPGA which reads in high-level descriptions of DSP applications written in MATLAB, and automatically generates synthesizable RTL models in VHDL or Verilog for a variety of FPGA devices such as the Xilinx Virtex II and the Altera Stratix.

3 An Example Design of an FIR Filter in MATLAB

We will illustrate the use of fine grain parallelism in DSP applications using a 16 tap finite impulse response (FIR) filter example. We will show how various AccelFPGA directives can be used to explore different parallelism solutions.

The first step in this flow is the development of MATLAB algorithm using fixed point precision using "quantizers" from the Filter Design and Analysis (FDA) Toolbox for MATLAB [9]. An example of a 16 tap FIR filter in fixed point precision is shown below.

```
% Example MATLAB code for 16 tap FIR filter with fixed
point quantization
% read input from file
x = load('sines.txt'); % input data
NUMTAPS = 16;  % number of taps
NUMSAMPS = length(x); % number of samples
% define fixed-point parameters
qpath    =    quantizer('fixed','floor','wrap',[8,0]);     %
quantization of inputs in data path
qresults    =    quantizer('fixed','floor','wrap',[16,0]);    %
quantization of operation results
indata = quantize(qpath,x);
% define filter coeffients
% 16-tap low-pass filter; sampling rate 8000 Hz, bandpass
cutoff 2000 Hz; bandstop start 3000 Hz
coeff = quantize(qpath, [-2.4750172265052; -
```

```
3.0362659582556; 3.7764386593039; 4.8119075484636; ...
              -6.3925788455935; -9.1690255759161;
15.5281320470888; 46.9564093514142; ...
              46.9564093514142; 15.5281320470888; -
9.1690255759161; -6.3925788455935; ...
              4.8119075484636; 3.7764386593039; -
3.0362659582556; -2.4750172265052]);
for n = NUMTAPS:NUMSAMPS
  sum = 0;
  % perform sum of products
  for k = 1:16
    mult = quantize(qresults , (indata(n-k+1) *
coeff(k)));
    sum  = quantize(qresults , (sum + mult));
  end
  outdata(n) = quantize(qresults,sum);
end
```

We now apply various AccelFPGA directives to the fixed point MATLAB. AccelFPGA compiler directives are used to bridge the gap between the MATLAB source and the synthesis of the computational structures created by AccelFPGA. Every compiler directive is prefixed by "%!ACCEL". This makes the directives appear as comments to other environments dealing with MATLAB since all comments in MATLAB start with %. The TARGET directive specifies the target FPGA to be mapped to. The BEGIN_HARDWARE and END-HARDWARE directives specify parts of the code that will be mapped onto hardware. The STREAM directive specifies an input data stream.

The resultant FIR filter code with AccelFPGA directives is shown below.

```
% Example MATLAB code for 16 tap FIR filter with basic
AccelFPGA directives
%  Specif\y hardware target Xilinx Virtex2 FPGA
%!ACCEL TARGET XC2V250
% read input from file
x = load('sines.txt'); % input data
NUMTAPS = 16;  % number of taps
NUMSAMPS = length(x); % number of samples
% define fixed-point parameters
qpath = quantizer('fixed','floor','wrap',[8,0]); %
quantization of inputs in data path
qresults = quantizer('fixed','floor','wrap',[16,0]); %
quantization of operation results
indata = quantize(qpath,x);
% define filter coeffients
% 16-tap low-pass filter; sampling rate 8000 Hz, bandpass
cutoff 2000 Hz; bandstop start 3000 Hz
coeff = quantize(qpath, [-2.4750172265052; -
```

```
3.0362659582556;  3.7764386593039;  4.8119075484636;  ...
                -6.3925788455935;          -9.1690255759161;
15.5281320470888;  46.9564093514142;  ...
              46.9564093514142;  15.5281320470888;  -
9.1690255759161;  -6.3925788455935;  ...
              4.8119075484636;  3.7764386593039;  -
3.0362659582556;  -2.4750172265052]);
% apply filter to each input sample
%!ACCEL STREAM n
for n = NUMTAPS:NUMSAMPS
  %!ACCEL BEGIN_HARDWARE indata
  indatabuf = quantize(qpath, indata(n-15:n));
  % initialize sum of products
  sum = quantize(qresults,0);
  % perform sum of products
  for k = quantize(qpath,1:16),
    mult = quantize(qresults , (indatabuf(k) *
coeff(k)));
    sum  = quantize(qresults , (sum + mult));
  end
  outdatabuf = quantize( qresults, sum );
  % store output
  outdata(n) = quantize(qresults,outdatabuf);
  %!ACCEL END_HARDWARE outdata
end
```

The basic MATLAB FIR filter algorithm performs the 16 tap FIR filter operation using 16 iterations using one adder and one multiplier per iteration. This particular design with these AccelFPGA directives when compiled by the AccelFPGA compiler requires 143 LUTs, 75 multiplexers, 1 multiplier, 8 ROMs, runs at 82.9 MHz, and has a latency of 23 cycles, and an initiation rate of 19 cycles (one new data sample every 19 cycles). In terms of DSP filter performance, this design performs FIR filtering at a rate of 82.9/19*1000 = 4363 Kilo-samples per second (KSPS). We will show in the next section how the performance of this filter can be improved.

4   Exploiting Different Parallelism Solutions in the AccelFPGA Compiler

AccelFPGA allows the user to use compiler directives to perform various parallelism solutions. We will now describe the various directives available for the user to perform these explorations.

4.1 UNROLL Directive

The UNROLL directive is a mechanism to expand the source MATLAB to create more copies of loop bodies, thereby increasing performance optimizations as illustrated below.

Let us consider the for loop in the example MATLAB code for the FIR filter.

```
sum = 0;
 for k = 1:16
  mult = quantize(qresults , (indatabuf(k) * coeff(k)));
  sum  = quantize(qresults , (sum + mult));
 end
```

The MATLAB code has one addition and one multiplication operation in the data flow graph of its basic block hence the AccelFPGA compiler will generate an RTL VHDL or Verilog which will use one adder and one multiplier to schedule this computation which will take 16 cycles.

If the code were to be unrolled fully as shown below

```
sum = 0;
%!ACCEL UNROLL 16
for k = 1:16
  mult = quantize(qresults , (indatabuf(k) * coeff(k)));
  sum  = quantize(qresults , (sum + mult));
 end
```

The loop body will be replicated completely 16 times and the for loop will be eliminated.

```
sum=0;
  mult1 = quantize(qresults , (indatabuf(k) * coeff(k)));
  sum1  = quantize(qresults , (sum + mult1));
  mult2 = quantize(qresults , (indatabuf(k+1) * coeff(k+1)));
  sum2  = quantize(qresults , (sum1 + mult2));
...
...
  mult15 = quantize(qresults , (indatabuf(k+14) * coeff(k+14)));
  sum15  = quantize(qresults , (sum14 + mult15));
  mult16 = quantize(qresults , (indatabuf(k+15) * coeff(k+15)));
  sum16  = quantize(qresults , (sum15 + mult16));
end;
```

For this particular choice of UNROLL 16, AccelFPGA produces a design that requires 259 LUTs, 399 multiplexers, 16 multipliers, 8 ROMs. This design has a reduced latency of 5 cycles, and initiation rate of 1 cycle, however, it operates at a frequency of 76.9 MHz owing to a large critical path involving 16 adders and 1 multiplier in one cycle. In terms of FIR filter performance, even though the clock frequency has gone down, the throughput has gone up to 76,900 Kilo-samples per second.

The UNROLL directive is therefore used by the user to generate different area-delay hardware alternatives.

4.2 PIPELINE Directive

Pipelining increases the throughput of a datapath by introducing registers in the datapath. This increase in throughput is particularly important when the datapath is iterated in the overall design. The PIPELINE directive is placed just before the loop, whose body is to be pipelined. For pipelining function bodies the directive is placed just above the function definition. Let us consider the for loop in the example MATLAB for the FIR filter.

```
sum = 0;
 for k = 1:16
   mult = quantize(qresults , (indatabuf(k) * coeff(k)));
   sum  = quantize(qresults , (sum + mult));
 end
```

If the code were to be pipelined as shown below

```
sum = 0;
 %!ACCEL PIPELINE
 for k = 1:16
   mult = quantize(qresults , (indatabuf(k) * coeff(k)));
   sum  = quantize(qresults , (sum + mult));
 end
```

AccelFPGA will now unroll the 16 tap for loop into a data flow graph consisting of 16 multipliers and 16 adders, and breaks off the data flow graph into 16 stages of a pipeline, with each stage having one multiplier and one adder, amnd insert registers between each stage. For our FIR filter example, AccelFPGA now produces a design which improves the frequency of operation of the design to 134.2 MHz, but suffers a large latency of 20 cycles, however, the initiation rate is now at 1 cycle per operation. This design therefore works at 134,200 Kilo-samples per second.

4.3 MEM_MAP Directive

The AccelFPGA compiler by default maps all variables to registers in the hardware implementation. In many cases if the variables are arrays of large size, this may results in large hardware resources in the forms of large multiplexers. The memory map directive indicates that the given array variable should be mapped to a specific memory resource in the target architecture. The MEM_MAP directive can be used to map array variables to embedded RAMs on a Xilinx Virtex II or Virtex-E device or Altera APEX or Stratix device.

Let us consider the MATLAB code for the FIR filter which illustrates the MEM_MAP directive.

```
for n = NUMTAPS:NUMSAMPS
%!ACCEL MEM_MAP indatabuf TO ram_s9_s9(0) AT 0
%!ACCEL BEGIN_HARDWARE indata
  indatabuf = quantize(qpath, indata(n-15:n));
  sum = 0;
  for k = 1,16
    mult = quantize(qresults , (indatabuf(k) * coeff(k)));
    sum  = quantize(qresults , (sum + mult));
  end
  outdatabuf = quantize( qresults, sum );
  outdata(n) = quantize(qresults,outdatabuf);
  %!ACCEL END_HARDWARE outdata
end
```

In this example, the user wants to map the array **indatabuf** to the embedded memory on an Xilinx VirtexII device named "ram_s9_s9" with instance "0" starting at memory location "0" using the following directive:

%!ACCEL MEM_MAP indatabuf TO ram_s9_s9(0) AT 0

For our running design of the 16 tap FIR filter, AccelFPGA produces a design that requires only 126 LUTs, 47 multiplexers, 1 multiplier, 8 ROMs and 1 BlockRAM. However, the latency goes up to 73 cycles, and the throughput goes to 67 cycles between consecutive data streams.   Hence even though the number of multiplexers has gone down from 75 to 47, and the number of LUTS has gone down from 143 to 126, the FIR filter throughput is 115.1/67 = 1717 Kilosamples per second. This is clearly not a good choice of the directive. However, as we will show later on, this will be a good choice if the FIR were a 64 tap filter.

5   Results on Benchmarks

We now report some experimental results on various benchmark MATLAB programs using the AccelFPGA version 1.4 compiler on a Dell Latitude Model C610 laptop with a 1.2GHz Pentium III CPU, 512 MB RAM, and 80 GB hard drive running Windows 2000:

- A 16 tap Finite Impulse Response Filter (fir16tap)
- A 64 tap memory mapped tiled FIR filter (fir64tap)
- A Decimation in Time FIR filter (dec_fir)
- An Infinite Impulse Response Filter of type DF1 (iirdf1)

- An Interpolation FIR filter (int_fir)
- A 64 point Fast Fourier Transform (fft64)
- A Block Matching Algorithm (bma)
- A Digital Subscriber Line (DSL) algorithm (dsl)

We now report on some results of exploring various fine grain parallelism solutions that can be obtained at the system level by the use of the directives. Table 1 shows the results of these explorations for 8 benchmark examples for the Xilinx Virtex2 device. Results are given in terms of resources used, and performance obtained as estimated by the Synplify Pro 7.1 tool executed on the RTL Verilog that was output by AccelFPGA. The resource results are reported in terms of LUTS, Multiplexers, embedded multipliers used. The performance was measured in terms clock frequency of the design as estimated by the internal clock frequency inferred by the Synplify Pro 7.1 tool, and the latency and initiation rate of the design in terms of clock cycles by using the ModelSim 5.5e RTL simulator. We also show the throughput of the design in Kilo-samples per second which is the frequency of the design divided by the initiation rate. For each benchmark, we show the base case on the first row (which is a design with only the information directives like TARGET, BEGIN_HARDWARE, END_HARDWARE, SHAPE and STREAM) included. We next show other designs using various performance directives such as UNROLL, PIPELINE, MEM_MAP and TILE. For example for the 16 tap FIR filter, the second row shows the use of UNROLL 16 directive, the third row shows the use of the PIPELINE directive, the fourth row shows the use of the MEM_MAP directive, and the fifth row shows the use of the MEM_MAP along with the UNROLL directive. It can be seen that it is possible to obtain designs with widely varying resource requirements, latencies and throughputs.

6 Conclusions

With the introduction of advanced Field-Programmable Gate Array (FPGA) architectures such as the Xilinx Virtex-II, and the Altera Stratix, a new hardware alternative is available for DSP designers who can get even higher levels of performances than those achievable on general purpose DSP processors. This paper described how fine grain parallelism can be exploited using a behavioral synthesis tool called AccelFPGA which reads in high-level descriptions of DSP applications written in MATLAB, and automatically generates synthesizable RTL models in VHDL or Verilog. The RTL models can be synthesized using commercial logic synthesis tools and place and route tools onto FPGAs. The paper describes how powerful directives are used to provide high-level architectural tradeoffs by exploiting fine grain parallelism, pipelining, memory mapping and tiling for the DSP designer. Experimental results were reported with the AccelFPGA version 1.4 compiler on a set of 8 MATLAB benchmarks that are mapped onto the Xilinx Virtex II FPGAs.

Table 1. Results of exploration of various fine grain parallelism solutions using directives with the AccelFPGA compiler on a Xilinx Virtex2 XC2V250 device.

	Resources			Performance			
				Freq	Latency	Init rate	Thruput
fir16tap	LUTS	MUX	Mult	(MHz)	(cycles)	(cycles)	(KSPS)
Base	143	75	1	82.9	23	19	4363.2
UNROLL 16	259	399	16	76.9	5	1	76900.0
PIPELINE	373	326	8	134.2	20	1	134200.0
MEMMAP	126	47	1	115.1	73	67	1717.9
PIPE+MEM	1256	565	0	131.2	94	54	2429.6
fir64tap							
Base	894	490	1	50.1	104	100	501.0
UNROLL 16	3172	740	16	58.7	44	40	1467.5
PIPELINE	2066	971	16	83.7	45	41	2041.5
TILE+MEM+PIPE	1654	330	16	79.7	59	55	1449.1
dec_fir							
Base	516	197	1	66.6	74	71	938.0
UNROLL 64	1356	1209	0	61.2	8	5	12240.0
MEM+UNROLL64	3303	1963	0	96.9	207	193	502.1
iirdf1							
Base	119	47	2	107.1	11	7	15300.0
UNROLL 2	41	21	0	134.2	5	1	134200.0
int_fir							
Base	254	49	1	75.3	79	75	1004.0
UNROLL 16	446	231	16	56.8	11	7	8114.3
fft64							
Base	9882	3393	4	30.2	340	64	471.9
MEMMAP	4212	1473	4	66.8	5722	4	16700.0
dsl							
Base	7145	3055	5	38.8	3114	2883	13.5
UNROLL 16	19701	5953	20	29.4	394	227	129.5
bma							
Base	9349	3735	0	40.8	42297	42285	1.0
MEMMAP	929	512	0	72.3	230072	228342	0.3

References

1. Adelante Technologies, AIRT Builder, www.adelantetechnologies.com
2. Altera, Stratix Datasheet, www.altera.com
3. Celoxica Corp, Handle C Design Language, www.celoxica.com
4. C Level Design, System Compiler: Compiling ANSI C/C++ to Synthesis-ready HDL, www.cleveldesign.com
5. CynApps Suite. Cynthesis Applications for Higher Level Design. www.cynapps.com
6. G. DeMicheli, Synthesis and Optimization of Digital Circuits, McGraw Hill, 1994
7. Esterel-C Language (ECL). Cadence website. www.cadence.com
8. M. Haldar, A. Nayak, A. Choudhary, and P. Banerjee, "A System for Synthesizing Optimized FPGA Hardware from MATLAB," Proc. International Conference on Computer Aided Design, San Jose, CA, November 2001, See also www.ece.northwestern.edu/cpdc/Match/Match.html.
9. Mathworks Corp, MATLAB Technical Computing Environment, www.mathworks.com
10. De Micheli, G. Ku D. Mailhot, F. Truong T. The Olympus Synthesis System for Digital Design. IEEE Design & Test of Computers 1990.
11. Overview of the Open SystemC Initiative. SystemC website. www.systemc.org
12. Synopsys Corp, Behavioral Compiler Datasheet, www.synopsys.com
13. Synplicity. Synplify Pro Datasheet, www.synplicity.com.
14. Xilinx, Virtex II Datasheet, www.xilinx.com
15. Xilinx, System Generator Datasheet, www.xilinx.com
16. Altera, DSP Builder Datasheet, www.altera.com
17. Texas Instruments, VelocTI C6000 Architecture Description, www.ti.com
18. Phillips Corporation, Trimedia Architecture Description, www.phillips.com
19. Motorola Corporation, STARCORE Datasheet, www.motorola.com

Performance Driven Routing in Distributed Environment

Arpan Singha and Rajat K. Pal

Department of Computer Science and Engineering
University of Calcutta
92, A. P. C. Road, Kolkata 700 009, INDIA
arpsin@rediffmail.com, rajat@cucc.ernet.in

Abstract. As fabrication technology advances, devices and interconnection wires are placed in closer proximity and circuits operate at higher frequencies. This results in crosstalk between wire segments. Work on routing channels with reduced crosstalk is a very important area of current research [3, 10]. We know that the crosstalk minimization problem in the reserved two-layer Manhattan routing model is NP-complete, even for the channels without any vertical constraints. Since minimizing crosstalk is NP-complete, several polynomial time heuristic algorithms for reducing crosstalk have been developed [8, 9, 15]. All the ideas that are introduced as heuristics are basically sequential in nature. In this paper we have developed two efficient heuristics to compute reduced crosstalk routing solutions in a distributed computing environment. Our proposed heuristics are much better in computational complexity than the existing sequential versions of the algorithms developed in [9, 15].

1 Introduction

In VLSI layout design it is required to realize a specified interconnection among different modules using minimum possible area. This is known as the routing problem. There exist several routing strategies for efficient interconnection among different modules. One of the most important types of routing strategies is *channel routing* [10, 17]. A channel is a rectangular region that has two open ends on two opposite sides, and the other two sides have two rows of fixed terminals. A set of terminals that need to be electrically connected together is called a *net*. The terminals of the same net are assigned the same number. The unconnected terminals are assigned the number zero.

Throughout the paper we consider reserved layer Manhattan routing where only horizontal and vertical wire segments are assigned in respective layers for interconnecting the nets. Consider the case of long overlapping wire segments on adjacent layers. Due to the overlap, there is a possibility of signal interference that may cause electrical hazards. In order to avoid this problem and to achieve feasible routing solutions for most of the channel instances, we assume that a layer has only horizontal wire segments or only vertical wire segments in a reserved layer model. The connection between a horizontal and a vertical wire segment of the same net in

S.K. Das and S. Bhattacharya (Eds.): IWDC 2002, LNCS 2571, pp. 257–267, 2002.
© Springer-Verlag Berlin Heidelberg 2002

adjacent layers is achieved using a *via hole*. This framework for routing a region is known as the *reserved layer Manhattan routing model*.

We all know that the problem of minimizing the routing area is the most important cost optimization criterion in routing a channel. In order to minimize the routing area, the horizontal wire segments of the nets need to be distributed amongst a minimum number of tracks which is guided by two important constraints viz., the horizontal constraints and the vertical constraints. These constraints can be characterized by two graphs viz., the *horizontal constraint graph (HCG)* and the *vertical constraint graph (VCG)* [10, 17]. The *channel density* of a channel is the maximum number of nets passing through a column. We denote the channel density by d_{max}. Through this paper we represent horizontal constraints using the complement of the HCG. We call the complement of the HCG, $HC=(V,E)$, the *horizontal non-constraint graph (HNCG)* and denote it by $HNC=(V,E')$, where V is the set of vertices corresponding to the intervals, and $E'=\{\{v_i,v_j\}|\{v_i,v_j\}\notin E\}$. The notation of the HNCG was introduced in [10, 11] to represent horizontal constraints. Note that a clique of the HNCG corresponds to a set of non-overlapping intervals that may safely be assigned to the same track in a routing solution.

The VCG, $VC=(V,A)$ is constructed to represent the vertical constraints. For an acyclic VCG we denote the *length of the longest path* in the VCG by v_{max}, where v_{max} is equal to the number of vertices belonging to the path.

The *channel routing problem (CRP)* is the problem of assigning the horizontal wire segments of a given set of nets to tracks obeying the horizontal and vertical constraints, so that the number of tracks required (and hence the channel area) is minimized. We say that a problem instance is *feasible* if all the nets can be assigned without any conflict.

In this paper we consider the crosstalk minimization problem as performance driven channel routing. As fabrication technology advances, devices and interconnection wires are placed in closer proximity and circuits operate at higher frequencies. This results in crosstalk between wire segments. Crosstalk between wire segments is proportional to the coupling capacitance, which is in tern proportional to the coupling length (the total length of the overlap between wires). Crosstalk is also proportional to the frequency of operation and inversely proportional to the separating distance between wires. Therefore, it is important that these factors be considered in the design of channel routing algorithms. The aim should be to avoid long overlapping wire segments and/or the wire segments that lie close to each other on the same layer. Work on routing channels with reduced crosstalk is a very important area of current research [3, 10]. It is desirable to design channel routing algorithms that consider this factor. The main objective in performance driven routing is to reduce signal delays due to crosstalk. Note that the crosstalk minimization problem in the reserved two-layer Manhattan routing model is NP-hard, even for the channels without any vertical constraints [8, 9, 15]. Since minimizing crosstalk is NP-hard, several polynomial time heuristic algorithms for reducing crosstalk have been developed [8, 9, 15]. All the ideas that are introduced as heuristics are basically sequential in nature. In this paper we have developed two efficient heuristics to compute reduced crosstalk routing solutions in a distributed computing environment, in the reserved two-layer Manhattan routing model, for the channel instances that are free from any vertical constraint. Our proposed heuristics are much better in computational complexity than the existing sequential algorithms developed for reducing crosstalk in [9, 15].

We know that parallel processing is an efficient style of information processing, which emphasizes the exploitation of concurrent event in the computing process. Concurrency implies parallelism, simultaneity, and pipelining. Parallel event may occur in the resources during the same time instance, simultaneous events may occur at the same time interval, and pipelined events may occur in overlapped time spans. These concurrent events are attainable in a computer system at various processing levels. Parallel processing demands concurrent retrieving and concurrent execution of many programs in the computer. It is in contrast to sequential processing. It is a cost-effective means to improve system performance through concurrent activities in the computer.

Parallel processing and distributed processing are closely related. In some cases, we use certain distributed technique to achieve parallelism. As data communication technology advances, the distance between parallel and distributed processing become closer and closer. So in recent time, we may see distributed processing as a form of parallel processing in a special environment [6]. We use this concept of developing parallel algorithms to execute the same in a distributed environment. We know that most of the problems belonging to VLSI design process are NP-hard in nature, and subsequent heuristics developed to sequentially execute these problems take much amount of time. So, developing parallel heuristic algorithms might be a novel way out to resolve the problems and executing the same using a better computational complexity in a distributed computing environment. In this paper we consider the problem of crosstalk minimization in two-layer channel routing for the instances without any vertical constraint, and develop parallel heuristic algorithms to resolve the same. To design the parallel algorithms for computing reduced crosstalk routing solutions, we consider the sequential algorithms developed in [9, 15] and make them parallel. Analytical results in terms of computational complexity of the algorithms we have developed, are outstanding.

This paper is organized as follows. In Section 2, we discuss the crosstalk minimization problem under consideration. In Section 3, we propose parallel heuristic algorithms for crosstalk minimization, and analyze their computational complexity. In Section 4, we conclude with a few remarks.

2 Computational Complexity of Crosstalk Minimization

Channel routing has been used extensively in the layout of integrated chips in last three decades. The CRP being an NP-complete problem [7, 10, 14, 16], several heuristics have been proposed for routing channels [2, 5, 10, 12, 14, 17]. The CRP is polynomial time solvable if the instances are free from any vertical constraints and we are interested only to resolve horizontal constraints in the two-layer VH routing model [4, 10].

Since the problem of minimizing area for the instances of routing channels without any vertical constraint is polynomial time solvable (using only d_{max} tracks), we define such instances as the *simplest* instances of channel routing. Hashimoto and Stevens [4] proposed a scheme for solving this problem, and according to Schaper [14], it can be implemented in $O(n(\log n + d_{max}))$ time, where d_{max} is the channel density and n is the number of nets belonging to the channel. Later on Pal *et al* [11] developed and analyzed two different algorithms *MCC1* and *MCC2*, based on the Hashimoto and Stevens's scheme. The first algorithm *MCC1* uses a graph theoretic approach and runs in $O(n+e)$ time, where n is the number of nets and e is the size of the HNCG. The second algorithm *MCC2* is achieved using a balanced binary search tree data structure that runs in time $O(n\log n)$, where n is the number of nets. See [10] for the details of the algorithms. Though a routing solution of only d_{max} tracks is guaranteed for the simplest instances of channel specifications in polynomial time in the stated routing model, it may not be a *good* routing solution from the resulting crosstalk point of view.

We now discuss the presence of crosstalk between nets (or intervals) assigned to different tracks in a two-layer channel without any vertical constraint. Note that if two intervals do not overlap, there is no horizontal constraint between the nets. That is, if there is a horizontal constraint between a pair of nets, there is a possibility of having *accountable* crosstalk between them. We measure crosstalk in terms of number of units a pair of nets overlap on adjacent tracks in a feasible routing solution. Consider the problem of minimizing crosstalk in a two-layer VH routing. Suppose we have three intervals a, b, and c as shown in Figure 1, in a feasible routing solution of three tracks only.

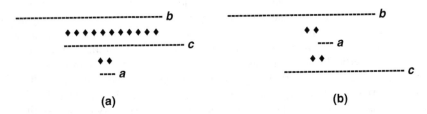

(a)   **(b)**

Fig. 1. (a) A feasible three-track routing solution. (b) A minimized crosstalk routing solution.

Since all the three nets a, b, and c overlap, we are bound to assign them to three different tracks on the same horizontal layer in any feasible routing solution. But the most interesting feature we can point out is that in Figure 1(a), nets b and c that are assigned to two adjacent tracks share 11 units of horizontal span in the channel and nets c and a share 2 units, whereas in Figure 1(b), we have a net sharing of 4 units of horizontal span in total just by reassigning the nets to tracks. It is inevitable that the assignment of nets to tracks in Figure 1(b) produces a reduced crosstalk routing solution; in fact it is the minimum crosstalk three-track routing solution for this instance. In this context we are interested to pose the following problem.

Problem: Crosstalk minimization in two-layer VH channel routing.
Instance: A simplest channel specification and a positive integer k.
Question: Is there a two-layer VH routing solution with the total crosstalk k or less?

Note that the problem of area minimization for the simplest instances of channel specifications is polynomial time solvable, and there are algorithms that compute routing solution for such an instance using exactly d_{max} tracks [4, 10, 11]. The noticeable feature is that the crosstalk minimization problem in two-layer channel routing for such instances of channel specifications is NP-hard. The detail of the proof is available in [8, 9, 15]. So, eagerly we wish to point out the following: The crosstalk minimization problem is not only important from its practical aspects of computing performance driven routing solutions point of view, it is equally interesting to view the same as a combinatorial optimization problem.

As the problem of interest is NP-hard, researchers have developed several polynomial time heuristic algorithms for computing reduced crosstalk routing solutions for the simplest instances of channel specifications [9, 15]. In this paper, in the following section, we have developed two parallel algorithms based on the algorithms developed in [9, 15], to compute reduced crosstalk routing solutions for the existing routing solutions of minimum area for the simplest instances of the CRP. While analyzing the algorithms developed in this paper are encouraging enough in comparison to their sequential counterparts.

3   Algorithms for Crosstalk Minimization

Pal *et al* [8, 9, 15] proved that the crosstalk minimization problem in two-layer channel routing is NP-hard even for the simplest instances of channel specifications. Whatsoever, for any feasible two-layer VH routing solution S we can compute another routing solution $S*$ with the total amount of crosstalk equals to zero. Suppose we have a two-layer feasible routing solution S of t tracks. In computing $S*$ we just introduce $t-1$ blank tracks into the routing solution S, where between each pair of adjacent tracks in S a blank track is introduced. As a result we must not have any crosstalk in $S*$, following the process of accounting crosstalk we have made and the geometry of the routing model we have assumed. So, $S*$ is a valid routing solution of near about $2t$ tracks without any crosstalk in it. Here the main thing we wish to emphasize is the following. If we provide sufficient space between the wires assigned to adjacent tracks (and layers), the amount of crosstalk will eventually be reduced. But we all know that the area minimization problem is the most important cost optimization problem in VLSI physical design. Therefore, we must not encourage in computing such a routing solution $S*$ that takes almost twice the area of S. So it's a trade-off between routing area and the resulting crosstalk in routing a channel. That is why instead of computing $S*$, we start with S of t tracks, compute another feasible routing solution S' of the same t tracks with reduced total crosstalk. To do that we consider the routing solutions S, that are computed using *MCC1* [10, 11] for the simplest instances of channel specifications, as the problem of two-layer crosstalk minimization is NP-hard for such instances of routing channels.

3.1   Algorithm 1: *Parallel Track Change*

The *Parallel Track Change* algorithm is naturally evolved from the theory of reducing crosstalk; see Figure 1, for example. The algorithm starts with a t-track two-layer feasible routing solution S that is computed using *MCC1* [10, 11] for a simplest instance of channel specification and compute another t-track two-layer feasible routing solution S' with reduced total crosstalk. In the algorithm, we first compute in parallel the effective spans of intervals of all the tracks in S. The *effective span of intervals* of track i is obtained by adding the actual spans of intervals of all the nets assigned to track i in S. Then for the t-track routing solution S, we sort the tracks in descending order according to their effective spans of intervals. In this algorithm, we sandwich the track with the minimum effective span of intervals into the tracks with the maximum and the next to maximum effective spans of intervals. Then we sandwich the track with the next to minimum effective span of intervals into the tracks with the second and the third maximum effective spans of intervals, and so on. The flanked assignment of a track with less effective span of intervals by a pair of tracks with more effective spans of intervals is absolutely motivated by the geometry of the channel and the initial routing solution provided as input to execute the algorithm. In other words, in order to compute S', we reassign the tracks of intervals from the computed sorted sequence as the following. Suppose Π is the sorted sequence of tracks in descending order in their effective spans of intervals, and the sequence $\Pi = \{\Pi_1, \Pi_2, \Pi_3, ..., \Pi_{t-2}, \Pi_{t-1}, \Pi_t\}$. Here our desired sequence of effective spans of intervals is $\Pi' = \{\Pi_1, \Pi_t, \Pi_2, \Pi_{t-1}, \Pi_3, \Pi_{t-2}, ...\}$ to assign the nets from top to bottom in t different tracks, and hence the resulting solution S' is obtained. Note that any pair of nets that are assigned to the ith track in S are assigned to the jth track in S', where i and j may or may not be the same.

One more clarification in our *Parallel Track Change* algorithm is required when we have two or more tracks with the same effective span of intervals. In this case in sorting those tracks of the same effective span of intervals, we compute the total span of intervals of each such track. The *total span of intervals* of the nets assigned to a track in S is the separation of columns between the starting column of the first net and the terminating column of the last net i.e., the span of the track used. Here we sort such tracks with the same effective span of intervals in ascending order based on their total spans of intervals in computing Π, as stated above. This is done in ascending order being motivated that the nets belonging to a track with more total span of intervals are more distributed over the track, and its reassignment to a track will eventually result in reducing long overlapping (i.e., less crosstalk) between the nets assigned to its adjacent tracks. If there are two or more tracks with the same total span of intervals, we sort them arbitrarily. Hence Π is computed from the given routing solution S, Π' is computed from Π as stated above, and following the sequence of tracks in Π' we assign the nets to tracks from top to bottom of the channel, and a routing solution S' with reduced total crosstalk is obtained. This completes the presentation of the heuristic algorithm *Parallel Track Change*. We now analyze the computational complexity of the algorithm.

Computational Complexity of Algorithm *Parallel Track Change*

Now we analyze the time complexity of the algorithm *Parallel Track Change*. In order to do that we consider an *Exclusive Read Concurrent Write (ERCW) Parallel Random Access Machine (PRAM)* in a *Single Instruction stream Multiple Data stream (SIMD)* parallel computing environment, where a control unit issues an instruction to be executed simultaneously by all processors on their respective data. In our algorithm we primarily perform three sorts of computation, as the following: (1) Trackwise computation of effective span of intervals (and total span of intervals, whenever required), (2) Trackwise sorting of nets based on their effective spans of intervals (and total spans of intervals, whenever required), and (3) Trackwise reassignment of nets to tracks in computing S'. Initially, we keep all the information (i.e., starting column position, terminating column position, span of interval, etc.) related to each of the n nets belonging to a simplest channel specification in $O(n)$ shared memory locations of the PRAM. An *Exclusive Read (ER)* instruction is executed by $O(n)$ processors, where processors gain access to memory locations for the purpose of reading in a one-to-one fashion. Thus when this instruction is executed, p processors simultaneously read the contents of p distinct memory locations such that each of the p processors involved reads from exactly one memory location and each of the p memory locations involved is read by exactly one processor. Then a *Concurrent Write (CW)* instruction is executed in the form of *COMBINED SUM* CW (and *COMBINED DEDUCT* CW, whenever required) by $O(n)$ processors, where two or more processors can write into the same memory location at the same time. Moreover, when this instruction is executed, $O(n)$ processors simultaneously write into $O(d_{max})$ distinct memory locations, where $d_{max} \leq n$, such that each of the $O(n)$ processors involved writes in exactly one memory location, whereas each of the $O(d_{max})$ memory locations involved can be written into by more than one processor. Specifically, in computing d_{max} effective spans of intervals (and total spans of intervals, whenever required), sum of the spans of the nets in track i (and the total span of the nets in track i, whenever required), $1 \leq i \leq d_{max}$, are simultaneously computed and written into the ith memory location of the shared memory of the PRAM. Now it is very clear that the d_{max} effective spans of intervals (and the d_{max} total spans of intervals, whenever required) of a given d_{max}-track routing solution S are computable in constant time using the stated parallel computing environment.

Sorting of trackwise non-overlapping sets of nets based on their effective spans of intervals (and total spans of intervals, whenever available) of a given routing solution S of d_{max} tracks can be computed in time $\Theta(\log^2 d_{max})$ time. Batcher's *bitonic merge* algorithm is the basis for the sorting algorithm used in processor arrays organized as shuffle-exchange networks and hypercubes, as well as multicomputer models. This sorting can be performed in $\Theta(\log^2 n)$ time on the shuffle-exchange and hypercube processor array models, given $O(n)$ processing elements [13]. Bitonic merge takes a bitonic sequence and transforms it into a sorted list that can be thought of as half a bitonic sequence of twice the length. A *bitonic sequence* is a sequence of values a_0, ..., a_{n-1}, with the property that (1) there exists an index i, $0 \leq i \leq n-1$, such that a_0 through a_i is monotonically increasing and a_i through a_{n-1} is monotonically decreasing, or (2) there exists a cyclic shift of indices so that the first condition is satisfied [13]. If a bitonic sequence of length 2^m is sorted into ascending order, while an adjacent sequence of length 2^m is sorted into descending order, then after m compare-exchange steps the combined sequence of length 2^{m+1} is a bitonic sequence. A list of n elements to be sorted can be viewed as a set of n unsorted sequences of length 1 or as $n/2$ bitonic sequences of length 2. Hence we can sort any sequence of elements by successively merging larger and larger bitonic sequences. Given $n = 2^k$ unsorted elements, a network with $k(k+1)/2$ levels suffices. Each level contains $n/2 = 2^{k-1}$ comparators. Hence the total number of comparators is $2^{k-2}k(k+1)$. The parallel execution of each level requires constant time. Note that $k(k+1)/2 = \log n(\log n+1)/2$. Hence the algorithm has complexity $\Theta(\log^2 n)$ [1]. So, in our problem of trackwise sorting of nets based on their effective spans of intervals (and total spans of intervals, whenever available) in a routing solution S of d_{max} tracks, we require $\Theta(\log^2 d_{max})$ time in the worst case, using the Batcher's *bitonic merge* algorithm as stated above.

Now we trackwise reassign the nets based on the sorted sequence obtained in the previous step, and compute S'. A more succinct formulation of this part of the algorithm is given next as algorithm PRAM REASSIGNMENT.

```
Algorithm PRAM REASSIGNMENT
        for i = 1 to dmax do in parallel
                if i ≤ ⌈dmax/2⌉
                then i ← 2i-1
                else i ← 2(dmax-i+1)
                end if
        end for
```

In algorithm PRAM REASSIGNMENT, the statement

```
for i = 1 to dmax do in parallel
```

means that all processors P_i, $1 \leq i \leq d_{max}$, perform the step simultaneously. Clearly, this PRAM step takes $O(1)$ time. So, trackwise reassignment of nets takes constant time using a PRAM machine.

Now we compute the overall computational complexity of the algorithm *Parallel Track Change*. Without loss of generality we can assume that the memory access time τ_a and the computation time τ_c are of the same order, either in the absolute terms or relative to an algorithm for another model. Hence the overall running time $t(n)$ of our algorithm is $\tau_a + \tau_c = \Theta(\log^2 d_{max})$.

3.2 Algorithm 2: *Parallel Net Change*

The heuristic algorithm *Parallel Track Change* we have designed in the previous section is simple but efficient enough to reduce the maximum amount of crosstalk belonging to a given routing solution where the channel is free from any vertical constraint, by just reassigning the nets trackwise. In this heuristic algorithm *Parallel Net Change*, our objective is to interchange a pair of nets only when (i) the nets are horizontally constraint to each other, (ii) the interchange do not introduce any horizontal constraint violation due to overlapping with some other nets, and (iii) the resulting crosstalk after interchanging the nets is reduced. This is not an easy task at all, since we do not know a priory the sequence of interchanging pairs of nets so that a maximum amount of crosstalk is reduced. Furthermore, a particular net can be interchanged $O(d_{max})$ times (where d_{max} is $O(n)$) over the tracks without giving any remarkable gain in overall crosstalk, and that might increase the problem of minimizing crosstalk drastically cost expensive. As a consequence, in this algorithm, without interchanging a pair of nets we do interchange a net with a blank space in some other track if this interchanging reduces overall crosstalk. For some net x if several such interchanging is possible, we accept the interchange that maximizes the crosstalk reduction.

We define a net, in a given routing solution S of d_{max} tracks, which is interchangeable with a blank space in some other track as an *interchangeable net*, and otherwise, as a *non-interchangeable net*. Note that each of the non-interchangeable nets p_i, $1 \le i \le n$, assigned to a track s, $1 \le s \le d_{max}$, in S is also assigned to the sth track in S', and each of the interchangeable nets q_i, $1 \le i \le n$, assigned to a track t, $1 \le t \le d_{max}$, in S may be assigned to a possibly different track t' in S'. It might be so happen that an interchangeable net cannot be interchanged though there is a blank space in some other track in S, as there is no gain in crosstalk out of that interchange. Clearly, there are $O(n)$ such interchangeable nets in S of n nets in total. Now the algorithm searches a blank space for net q_i in some other track, if q_i is an interchangeable net, where its interchange reduces a maximum amount of crosstalk. Three cases may arise for a set of r nets, $1 < r < d_{max}$, that are horizontally constrained to each other and assigned to r different tracks in S. (1) Simultaneous interchanging of tracks of all these nets to the same track t, where the corresponding zone of columns in S contains a blank space in t. (2) Pairwise interchanging of the nets to two adjacent blank tracks. (3) Pairwise interchanging of the nets to two blank tracks that are not adjacent. Obviously, Case 3 is straightway acceptable, because in this case the interchangeable nets themselves must not introduce any crosstalk. Case 2 is acceptable only when these interchanges render a routing solution S' with most reduced amount of crosstalk; otherwise, the victimized interchangeable net for which the amount of crosstalk increases, is kept in its track in S. In Case 1, we allow interchanging for that net which renders a least amount of crosstalk in S'. Needless to mention that this algorithm can subsequently be executed in constant times considering S' as S for a successive computation; otherwise we terminate if S' is not a better solution in terms of total crosstalk than the amount of total crosstalk in S. In this way, following this algorithm, a most reduced crosstalk routing solution S' is computed. This completes the presentation of the heuristic algorithm *Parallel Net Change*. We now analyze the computational complexity of the algorithm.

Computational Complexity of Algorithm *Parallel Net Change*

In our heuristic algorithm *Parallel Net Change*, we involve $O(n)$ processors for each of the nets in S. In addition, for each processor P_i, $1 \le i \le n$, we have the information of blank spaces in all the tracks in S in the form of a balanced binary search tree data structure of the blank spaces sorted on their starting column numbers. Moreover, each vertex of the search tree consists of the interval information of the corresponding blank space. Note that the size of this tree is $O(n)$ and its height is $O(\log n)$. An *Concurrent Read (CR)* instruction is executed by $O(n)$ processors, where processors gain access to $O(d_{max})$ shared memory locations, corresponding to the given d_{max}-track n-net routing solution S. So, each memory location s, $1 \le s \le d_{max}$, contains a super-value, rather a combined information of net numbers that are assigned to the sth track in S. Now processor P_i, corresponding to net q_i, searches a blank space in some other track, if q_i is an interchangeable net, so that this interchange reduces maximum amount of crosstalk. This can easily be achieved by executing a *Concurrent Write (CW)* instruction in the form of *COMBINED* CW by $O(n)$ processors, where *all* the values, rather net numbers, that a set of processors wishes to write simultaneously into a memory location are combined into a single super-value, corresponding to a set of non-overlapping intervals, which is then stored in that location. Clearly, searching of a blank space in some other track in S takes time $O(\log n)$ in the worst case, and crosstalk computation is a matter of constant time. Without loss of generality we can assume that the memory access time τ_a and the computation time τ_c are of the same order, either in the absolute terms or relative to an algorithm for another model. Hence the overall running time $t(n)$ of this algorithm is $\tau_a + \tau_c = O(\log n)$.

Now we provide a better computational complexity result of our *Parallel Net Change* algorithm from its implementation point of view. For each of the $O(n)$ processors P_i, our previous implementation considered the complete information of blank spaces in S in the form of a balanced binary search tree data structure. Any way, this complete information is good but overburdens processor P_i as its associated net q_i can only be reassigned to some other track containing a suitable blank space in its zone of columns that is determined by the span of q_i. More specifically, information related to all the remaining blank spaces other than the zone of columns spanned by q_i renders redundant to P_i. Clearly, it suffices if processor P_i keeps all the blank space information that is related to net q_i only. Note that S is a routing solution of d_{max} tracks, and $d_{max} \ll n$ though $d_{max} = O(n)$. Hence the size of the said tree associated to processor P_i is $O(d_{max})$ and its height is $O(\log d_{max})$. So, the overall computational complexity of this algorithm becomes $O(\log d_{max})$.

4 Conclusion

In this paper we have developed two parallel heuristic algorithms for the problem of computing reduced crosstalk routing solutions in two-layer channel routing for the simplest instances of channel specifications, where there is no vertical constraint in the channel. The first algorithm *Parallel Track Change* runs in time $\Theta(\log^2 d_{max})$ whereas the second algorithm *Parallel Net Change* runs in $O(\log d_{max})$ time, where d_{max} is the channel density. The sequential counterparts of these algorithms take time $O(d_{max} \log d_{max})$ and $O(n \log d_{max})$, respectively, where n is the number of nets belonging to the channel and d_{max} is the channel density [9, 15]. If a distributed computing environment is available, we have a plan to implement our algorithms developed in this paper and execute the same on several simplest instances of channel specifications. From performance point of view, logically we are convinced that our algorithm *Parallel Track Change* would never perform worse and algorithm *Parallel Net Change* would perform better in computing the routing solutions than their respective sequential counterparts. This is because during the CW SIMD instruction executed in the latter algorithm, the possibility of selecting a *proper* net for its assignment to a blank space in some other track is too high, while this selection in the sequential algorithm is a matter of chance.

Here we wish to point out a few possible extensions of our algorithms and/or open problems as the following. (i) Our algorithms may also be worthwhile for the general instances of channel specifications with multi-terminal nets where both the horizontal as well as vertical constraints are present. (ii) A generalized version of the algorithm *Parallel Net Change* may produce better routing solutions in terms of reduction in crosstalk when two overlapping nets interchange their tracks. (iii) Researchers may also be interested in computing much-reduced crosstalk routing solutions in expense of negligibly more channel area. (iv) Instead of starting from a given routing solution researchers may also compute *good* routing solutions directly optimizing crosstalk and some other cost optimization factor(s) of CRP. (v) Minimized crosstalk routing solutions in the case of three- and multi-layer channel routing might draw the current interest of research. Also doglegging may be introduced in all these cases.

References

1. Batcher, K.E.: Sorting Networks and their Applications, Proc. of the AFIPS Spring Joint Computer Conf., Vol. 32, AFIPS Press, Reston, VA (1968) 307-314. Reprinted in: Wu, C.L. and Feng, T.S. (eds.): Interconnection Networks for Parallel and Distributed Processing, IEEE Computer Society (1984) 576–583.
2. Chen, Y.K., Liu, M.L.: Three-Layer Channel Routing, IEEE Trans. on CAD of Integrated Circuits and Systems **3** (1984) 156–163.
3. Gao, T., Liu, C.L.: Minimum Crosstalk Channel Routing, Proc. of IEEE Int. Conf. on Computer-Aided Design (1993) 692–696.
4. Hashimoto, A., Stevens, J.: Wire Routing by Optimizing Channel Assignment within Large Apertures, Proc. of 8th ACM Design Automation Workshop (1971) 155–169.
5. Ho, T.-T., Iyengar, S.S., Zheng, S.-Q.: A General Greedy Channel Routing Algorithm, IEEE Trans. on CAD of Integrated Circuits and Systems **10** (1991) 204–211.
6. Hwang, K.: Advanced Computer Architecture: Parallelism, Scalability, Programmability, McGraw-Hill, Inc., New York (1993).
7. LaPaugh, A.S.: Algorithms for Integrated Circuit Layout: An Analytic Approach, Ph.D. thesis, Lab. for Computer Sc., MIT, Cambridge (1980).
8. Pal, A., Dam, B., Sadhu, S., Pal, R.K.: Performance Driven Physical Synthesis, Communicated to an International VLSI Journal (2002).
9. Pal, A., Singha, A., Ghosh, S., Pal, R.K.: Crosstalk Minimization in Two-Layer Channel Routing, Accepted in 17th IEEE Region 10 Int. Conf. on "Computers, Communications, Control and Power Engineering" (TENCON'02), to be held in Beijing, China (2002).
10. Pal, R.K.: Multi-Layer Channel Routing: Complexity and Algorithms, Narosa Publishing House, New Delhi (2000). Also published from CRC Press, Boca Raton, USA (2000) and Alpha Sc. Int. Ltd., UK (2000).
11. Pal, R.K., Datta, A.K., Pal, S.P., Pal, A.: Resolving Horizontal Constraints and Minimizing Net Wire Length for Multi-Layer Channel Routing, Proc. of IEEE Region 10's 8th Annual Int. Conf. on "Computer, Communication, Control and Engineering" (TENCON'93) **1** (1993) 569–573.
12. Pal, R.K., Datta, A.K., Pal, S.P., Das, M.M., Pal, A.: A general Graph Theoretic Framework for Multi-Layer Channel Routing, Proc. of 8th VSI/IEEE Int. Conf. on VLSI Design (1995) 202–207.
13. Quinn, M.J.: Parallel Computing: Theory and Practice, Second Edition, McGraw-Hill, Inc., New York, USA (1994).
14. Schaper, G.A.: Multi-Layer Channel Routing, Ph.D. thesis, Dept. of Computer Sc., Univ. of Central Florida, Orlando (1989).
15. Singha, A., Ghosh, S., Pal, A., Pal, R.K.: High Performance Routing for VLSI Circuit Synthesis, Proc. of 6th VLSI Design and Test Workshops (VDAT'02) (2002) 348–351.
16. Szymanski, T.G.: Dogleg Channel Routing is NP-Complete, IEEE Trans. on CAD of Integrated Circuits and Systems **4** (1985) 31–41.
17. Yoshimura, T., Kuh, E.S.: Efficient Algorithms for Channel Routing, IEEE Trans. on CAD of Integrated Circuits and Systems **1** (1982) 25–35.

Performance Prediction Methodology for Parallel Programs with MPI in NOW Environments

Li Kuan Ching [1], Jean-Luc Gaudiot [1], and Liria Matsumoto Sato [2]

[1] Dept. of Electrical and Computer Engineering (ECE)
University of California – Irvine, Irvine CA92697-2625 USA
likuan@aardvark.ece.uci.edu, gaudiot@uci.edu
[2] Dept. of Computer Engineering and Digital Systems (PCS)
University of São Paulo, Sao Paulo SP05508-900 Brazil
liria.sato@poli.usp.br

Abstract. We present a methodology for parallel programming, along with MPI performance measurement and prediction in a class of a distributed computing environments, namely networks of workstations. Our approach is based on a two-level model where, at the top, a new parallel version of timing graph representation is used to make explicit the parallel communication and code segments of a given parallel program, while at the bottom level, analytical models are developed to represent execution behavior of parallel communications and code segments. Execution time results obtained from execution, together with problem size and number of nodes, are input to the model, which allows us to predict the performance of similar cluster computing systems with a different number of nodes. The analytical model is validated by performing experiments over a homogeneous cluster of workstations. Final results show that our approach produces accurate predictions, within 5% of actual results.

1 Introduction

Distributed processing has been widely used to improve the performance of applications with intensive demands for computational power. Different architectures and topologies have been the goal of studies in search for high performance, to provide the resources for the parallelism exploitation present in the applications.

In recent years, a new class of distributed computing system has gained great popularity, namely NOW (Network of Workstations) or PC-based clusters. They are easy to build, cost effective and highly scalable. Workstations are interconnected through a high speed network, such as Gigabit Ethernet, SCI or Myrinet, and they run commodity operating systems, such as NT or Linux. Parallel applications for distributed systems are mostly developed using low-level communication mechanisms, such as Active Messages or Fast Messages, or message passing libraries, such as MPI or PVM. This class of system is well suited for communication intensive applications.

Therefore, several applications and software systems have been developed, aiming at the integration of distributed components in order to benefit from the aggregation

S.K. Das and S. Bhattacharya (Eds.): IWDC 2002, LNCS 2571, pp. 268–279, 2002.

of their processing power. Unfortunately, the major drawback is the programming of these systems, which is usually complex and difficult, given that it is necessary to identify the existing parallelism in these applications, verify the existence of data distribution, and also manage communications between the nodes. All must be explicitly specified and implemented, which often requires significant code and sometimes even algorithm changes when parallelizing a sequential program code.

Parallel programs can behave in a number of unexpected ways, because of their complex structure, the parallel system on which they run, the number of nodes used in a network of workstations, the parallel code's input, and the program execution time. Moreover, effective partitioning, allocation, and scheduling of application programs on a network of workstations is crucial to obtain good performance.

In a performance prediction methodology, a high-level abstraction of an application plays an important role. Based on the distributed programming paradigm used in MPI and other programming systems, we define a new class of timing graph, which we call Distributed Processing Graph (*DP*Graph*). We use it to describe the execution as well as the communication and synchronization relationships of the parallel computation at hand. To separately quantify the effects of the program structure and those of the system, the communication and synchronization points are independently identified in the graph of the application.

In this paper, we introduce a methodology for the performance measurement and prediction of parallel programs with MPI for the network of workstations computing environment. Our methodology provides an integrated interface which binds performance and analysis back to the original source code, allowing users to estimate the execution time of the execution under excellent bounds. This tool should afford a better understanding and investigation of parallel program structure, performance and behavior.

The remainder of this paper is organized as follows. Some related work is briefly discussed in section 2, followed by the description of the methodology in section 3. In section 4, we present experiments and results of performance measurements and prediction. Finally, we give some remarks and conclusions in section 5.

2   Related Work

A number of performance evaluation and prediction research projects are known. These include algorithms, techniques and projects, and can be recognized as iterative algorithms [12], analytical approaches [4], trace transformation [9], symbolic performance modeling [3], or adaptive sampling statistics techniques [6]. However, these techniques and algorithmic approaches are not well suited for general studies of interactions between PC-based cluster systems performance and parallel programming with MPI.

H.W. Cain, B.P. Miller and B.J.Wylie [2] have introduced strategies for performance diagnosis, G. Karypis and V. Kumar [5] introduced analysis techniques for multilevel graph partitioning, while P. Puschner and A. Schedl [11] introduced an analytical technique to analyze program execution times. Timing graphs are used to describe the sequence of execution of a program code. The computation of MAXTs (maximum execution times) is mapped to a graph problem, a generalization of maximum cost circulation calculus of a directed graph.

One question appears frequently: if we execute a parallel application with eight processing nodes of a cluster computing system, and obtain X as its execution time, what would be the result of this same application if we execute in a sixteen node cluster computing system, with the same system characteristics? The ideal result in this case, is half of X. Unfortunately, due to overhead, interconnection network contention, synchronization and other factors, this result is significantly different [12]. What is then the approximate value for the execution time ?

3   Methodology

Writing a parallel program is quite a difficult task, particularly when the programmer plans to describe the parallel algorithm efficiently. Yet, the execution of a parallel program depends on several factors which interact in complex ways. To identify and understand which would be the best structure to be used when writing a parallel program, it is important to understand which factors can affect this program's performance.

The methodology introduced by Li in [7] eases performance analysis and prediction of parallel programs implemented with message passing interface (MPI), executed in a network of workstations environment. The methodology basically entails the definition of an extension for *T-graphs* (timing graphs), which we name *DP*graphs*, a class of graphs from which we can represent not only serial programs, but also parallel programs instrumented with communication and synchronization. Moreover, new strategies are defined for the performance measurement and prediction of parallel applications described by a parallel programming language, for this class of distributed computing system [7].

Once we obtain the graph representation of the parallel program and its analytical model, it is possible to proceed with experimental evaluations and studies of the performance prediction, based on the experimental data obtained previously.

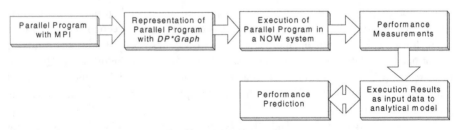

Fig. 1. Methodology scheme.

3.1 DP*Graph Definition

In distributed processing, synchronization and communication operations among processing nodes are fundamental operations. Using a message passing interface in a parallel program, these can be performed explicitly with MPI functions such as *send*, *receive*, *broadcast*, *reduce*, *scatter*, among others.

Figure 2 shows *DP*Graph* elements used to represent parallel programs.

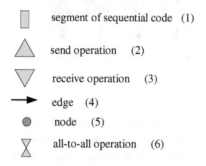

segment of sequential code   (1)

send operation   (2)

receive operation   (3)

edge   (4)

node   (5)

all-to-all operation   (6)

Fig. 2. Graph elements for representation of parallel programs.

3.2 Program Representation

The representation of parallel programs with MPI (or any other message passing interface) can be worked out as follows. Figure 3 shows a sample code and a graph representation using *DP*Graph*.

Note that ▽ n means that the processing node is receiving a message sent by node n. At the same time, ▲n means that the current processing node sends a message to processing node n.

```
if (rank == 0){          {                          MPI_Recv(buf4,3,2);
for                          buf2[x] = x + 7;      }
(x=0;x<BUF888;x++)       }
{                                                  if (rank == 3){
   buf1[x] = x + 99;     MPI_Recv(buf1,0,1);       for
}                          }                       (x=0;x<BUF999;x++)
                                                   {
MPI_send(buf1,1,0);      if (rank == 2){              buf4[x] = x + 99;
}                        for                       }
                         (x=0;x<BUF999;x++)
if (rank == 1){          {                         MPI_Send(buf4,2,3);
for                         buf3[x] = x + 89;
(x=0;x<BUF888;x++)       }
```

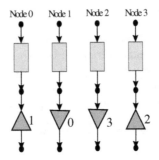

Fig. 3. Parallel code listing and its graph representation.

3.3 Communication Model

The Message Passing Interface (MPI) was defined as a standard for parallel applications in distributed memory computing systems. It provides a flexible environment, a widely portable and efficient programming library for developing high performance parallel applications. The MPI standard has several implementations, but if compared on the same computing system, all of these versions have similar performance [10]. In this work, all analysis and performance measurements were done on the LAM implementation of MPI.

MPI provides several primitives to specify point-to-point and collective communication. A point-to-point operation can be blocking or non-blocking with the following modes: standard, buffered, synchronous and ready. More details will be shown in subsection 3.5.

3.4 Execution Time Calculus

To obtain the execution time of a parallel application, it is needed to evaluate the execution time of all running processes in each processing node of a parallel computer system. The process of calculating the total execution time of a parallel program with MPI is shown in figure 4.

The execution time of a parallel program is taken as the maximum execution time among all processing nodes, each of them obtained through the sum of the partial execution times t_i.

$$T_{\text{execution time parallel application}} = \max \left(\sum t_i^1, \sum t_j^2, \sum t_k^3, \ldots, \sum t_t^n \right),$$

where $\sum t_t^n$ stands for: sum of all partial times t_t of the n-th processing node.

Figure 4 shows the graph representations of a parallel application; figure 4(a) is the graph representation of a parallel application, in execution process view, while figure 4(b) shows in detail the execution of the parallel application, in the execution of each process in each processing node. The total execution time for this parallel application can be given as:

$$T_{\text{execution time parallel application}} = \max \left(t'_1 + t'_2 + t'_3, t''_1 + t''_2 + t''_3 \right)$$

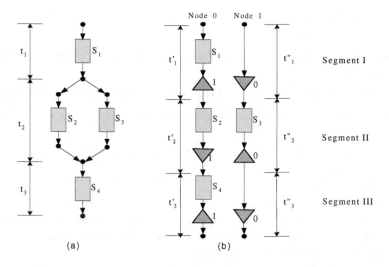

Fig. 4. Example of calculating execution time process.

3.5 Communication Operation Modeling

The time spent in communication is an important factor to be considered in the study and analysis of parallel applications designed to run on clusters of workstations. Considering a message with n elements, this time can be decomposed into the following components [7]:

- $t_e(n)$ = time spent to transfer the message from memory to network buffer;
- $t_t(n)$ = time spent to transfer the message by the network between two nodes;
- $t_r(n)$ = time spent to receive the message from the network buffer.

These components can be best viewed in the conceptual model presented in Figure 5.

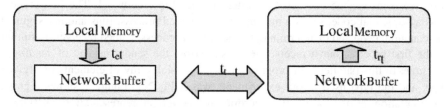

Fig. 5. The communication time components involved in a message transfer.

In order to construct a proper and consistent model, it is important to identify the factors which may influence the communication performance. Among many factors which may influence the time spent in the communication, this work considers two of them represented by the following constants [7]:

- k_l the network latency;
- k_b its bandwidth.

Thus, the components of communication time viewed above can be represented by these equations:

$$t_e(n) = n * c_1 \qquad t_t(n) = k_b * n + k_l \qquad t_r(n) = n * c_2 \text{, where } c_1 \text{ and } c_2 \text{ are constants.}$$

>From these considerations, the communication time of a message with n elements is given by:

$$t_c(n) = t_e(n) + t_t(n) + t_r(n) \qquad\qquad t_c(n) = n*c_1 + k_b*n + k_l + n*c_2$$

$$t_c(n) = (c_1 + k_b + c_2)*n + k_l \qquad\qquad t_c(n) = c*n + k_l \text{, where c is a constant.}$$

Martin *et al* [8] have presented a study of the impact of the communication performance on parallel applications on a cluster of workstations. Some factors such as network latency, overhead and bandwidth were analyzed and among others things the tests performed indicated the following:

- overhead strongly determines the ultimate application performance;
- applications were least sensitive to network latency;
- decreasing of bandwidth affected only applications which sent very large messages.

The overhead mentioned in [8] indicates the length of time that a processor is engaged in transferring a message from memory to network buffer or from network buffer to memory. Therefore, this overhead is addressed by the components $t_e(n)$ and $t_r(n)$.

4   Experiments

The example program used to perform the tests was implemented in C with some communication primitives of the message passing interface library. This program was designed to run with exactly two processes: a *sender* and a *receiver*. Each of these processes runs on one node of the cluster described in section 4.1. The first process runs a sequential code, sends a message to the second process, runs another segment of sequential code and then terminates. The second process, named receiver, is similar to the first process, but it receives a message from the sender instead of *sending a message*. In this parallel MPI program, a message is an array of elements of a given type, and the type used in our experiments was MPI_INT. Figure 6 shows a graph representation of the program, according to the graph representation DP*Graph introduced in the previous section.

4.1   Experimental Setup

Tests have been done on a cluster of workstations, consisting of 16 nodes connected by a switch 3COM SuperStack3300 in a Fast-Ethernet network. This computer system was isolated from the network, so there were not any other user processes running on this system. Each processing node consists of an Intel Celeron processor

433 MHz, 128 Mb of SDRAM (66 Mhz), a 100 Mb/s INTEL Ether-Express Pro network interface card. Moreover, the workstations run Linux Red Hat 6.2 and LAM 6.4.

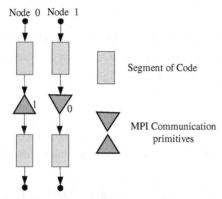

Fig. 6. Representation of the program used in this experiment.

4.2 Experimental Results

This section presents the results of the tests performed on the homogeneous PC-based cluster described previously. The tests with the four *send* modes presented in section 3.5 were executed, considering the following message lengths: 100,000, 250,000, 400,000, 550,000, 700,000, 850,000 and 1,000,000. The average times (in seconds) of these experiments are presented in Figure 7, where *tsender* and *treceiver* represent the time spent respectively by the process sender and process receiver.

Thousands of integers		100	250	400	550	700	850	1000
Standard	Tsender	0.03854	0.09897	0.16112	0.22229	0.28388	0.34633	0.40756
	Treceiver	0.04840	0.1178	0.18810	0.25878	0.32936	0.40073	0.47226
Buffered	Tsender	0.00671	0.01676	0.02664	0.03754	0.04846	0.05781	0.06900
	Treceiver	0.04840	0.11780	0.18762	0.25919	0.33077	0.39885	0.47068
Ready	Tsender	0.04007	0.10249	0.16604	0.22880	0.2918	0.35514	0.41741
	Treceiver	0.04993	0.12132	0.19259	0.26394	0.33510	0.40620	0.47774
Synchronous	Tsender	0.03974	0.10166	0.16486	0.22721	0.28982	0.35292	0.41478
	Treceiver	0.05032	0.12341	0.19637	0.26889	0.3414	0.41480	0.48900

Fig. 7. Average times obtained as the execution time of the experiments.

Some analysis indicates that all processes present an almost linear increase in their communication time. For instance, considering the synchronous mode, the average time for the sender process presented an increase by approximately 0.062 at each new message length introduced. In fact, this behavior can be best observed in Figure 8.

As noted in section 3, the communication time can be expressed by $t_c(n) = c*n + k_1$. From the average time of the tests presented in Figure 7, some equations were developed to represent the behavior of the *send* modes analyzed. An interpolation method was used to construct these equations which form the analytical model to estimate the communication time:

1. Standard send

$t_{ss}(n) = 4.10604E-07*n - 0.00315782$ $t_r(n) = 4.7111E-07*n + 0.000242238$

where $t_{ss}(n)$ is the time spent to send a message with n elements with a standard *send* and $t_r(n)$ is the time to receive a message with n elements. For all *send* modes, $t_r(n)$ has the same semantics.

2. Buffered send

$t_{bs}(n) = 6.92293E-08*n - 0.000512821$ $t_r(n) = 4.69539E-07*n + 0.00080281$

where $t_{bs}(n)$ is the time spent to send a message with n elements with a buffered *send*.

3. Synchronous send

$t_{ys}(n) = 4.17289E-07*n - 0.00222082$ $t_r(n) = 4.86643E-07*n + 0.00152971$

where $t_{ys}(n)$ is the time spent to send a message with n elements with a synchronous *send*.

4. Ready send

$t_{rs}(n) = 4.1978E-07*n - 0.00205469$ $t_r(n) = 4.75167E-07*n + 0.00249505$

where $t_{rs}(n)$ is the time spent to send a message with n elements with a ready *send*.

Figure 8 shows the communication time in relation to the message length, considering each send mode. The lines *tpre_sender* and *tpre_receiver* represent an interpolation of the points which correspond to the sender and receiver communication times respectively. Despite the almost linear behavior presented by *tpre_sender* and *tpre_receiver*, the results point the performance of the send modes considering message lengths. When other lengths much bigger or smaller than these values are used, some factors such as operating system overhead or bandwidth may highly influence the performance communication. It may therefore lead to erratic communication times.

4.3 Performance Prediction

Let us now test the analytical models described in the previous section. The tests were re-executed with new message length: 40,000, 60,000, 1,600,000 and 1,700,000. The obtained results to each send modes are presented in Figure 9. The results show that the methodology produced very accurate models: the error of the prediction studies change from 0,06% to 16%.

The benchmark program IS / NPB (NASA Parallel Benchmarks) can be described as its main goal to sort a given set of numbers in parallel. All experiments were done using problem sizes A and B, with 64^3 and 102^3 elements, respectively. More information about this and other NAS benchmark programs can be found at [1].

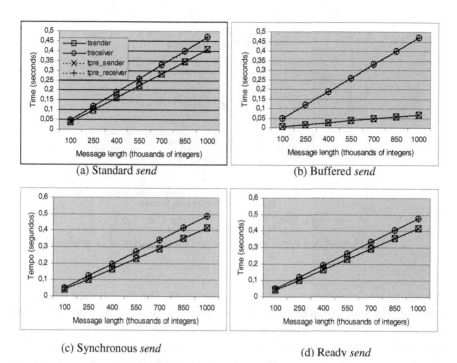

(a) Standard *send*

(b) Buffered *send*

(c) Synchronous *send*

(d) Ready *send*

Fig. 8. Communication time variation related to message length.

Size	Standard			Buffered		
(10^3)	Meas	Pred	% error	measure	predict	% error
40	0.01242	0.0133	6.846	0.00269	0.0023	16.009
60	0.0224	0.0215	4.0179	0.0042	0.0036	14.286
1600	0.65206	0.6538	0.2684	0.109	0.1103	1.1494
1700	0.6927	0.6949	0.3129	0.11616	0.1172	0.8741
	Synchronous			Ready		
	measure	predict	% error	measure	predict	% error
	0.01295	0.0145	11.704	0.01314	0.0147	12.135
	0.0224	0.0215	4.0179	0.0235	0.0231	1.7021
	0.66586	0.6654	0.0631	0.66926	0.6696	0.0496
	0.70741	0.7072	0.0341	0.71098	0.7116	0.0831

Fig. 9. Predicted results versus measured results.

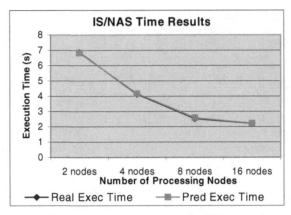

Fig. 10. Predicted versus measured results for IS benchmark program.

Figure 10 shows execution results of the program IS. The curve named Real Exec Time brings us results from experimental executions of the benchmark program in the computer system described in section 4.1. A second curve, named Pred Exec Time, shows results obtained from modeling techniques, applied to IS parallel program. After analyzing these results, the largest difference among the data checked for same points was less than 4%.

5   Conclusions

In this paper, a methodology for the performance analysis and prediction of parallel programs is introduced. A new graph representation for parallel programs was defined, mainly issues regarding communication operations. Concurrently, analytical models are constructed to represent the behavior of the communication operations. During the development of these models, some more important factors that contribute to the reduction of the overhead were considered, such as network latency and bandwidth. The accuracy of the methodology introduced was confirmed by numerous tests and verified with the predicted and measured results.

There is a high demand for parallel program analysis tools and, at the same time, a need for tools to study and analyze those applications that demand high performance. Nowadays, in the cost/benefit point of view, PC-based cluster systems are an excellent way to access supercomputing.

As a next step in this research, new studies about performance analysis and prediction about factors that may contribute to improve communication overhead will be done. Also, studies will be done on other interconnection networks, such as Gigabit Ethernet, SCI, Myrinet and ATM.

Heterogeneous cluster systems are more popular today than ever, since it is easy to connect a computer system into an existing cluster computing system. In our research investigation, once a graph representation of a parallel application is mapped, load balancing can be applied for task distribution, to minimize the total execution time.

Acknowledgements. The material reported in this paper is based upon work supported in part by the National Science Foundation under Grants No. CSA-0073527 and INT-9815742. Any opinions, findings, and conclusions or recommendations expressed in this material are those of the authors and do not necessarily reflect the views of the National Science Foundation.

References

[1]   D.H. Bailey, J. T. Barton, T.A. Lasinski and H. D. Simon. The NAS parallel benchmarks. Tech. Report NASA memorandum 103863, NASA Ames Research Center, July 1993.
[2]   H.W. Cain, B.P. Miller and B.J.Wylie. A callgraph-based search strategy for automated performance diagnosis. In: Proceedings of the Euro-Par 2000, Munich, Germany, 2000.
[3]   A.J.C. van Gemund. Performance modeling of parallel systems. PhD thesis, Delft University of Technology, Delft University Press, ISBN 90-407-1326-X, 1996.
[4]   P.G. Harrison, N.M. Patel. Performance modeling of communication networks and computer architectures. Addison-Wesley, 1993.
[5]   G. Karypis, V. Kumar. Analysis of multilevel graph partitioning. Technical report 98-037, University of Minnesota, 1998.
[6]   J. Landrum, J. Hardwick and Q.F. Stout. Predicting algorithm performance. Computing Science and Statistics 30, pages 309–314, 1998.
[7]   K.C. Li. Performance analysis and prediction of parallel programs on network of workstations. Ph.D. thesis, Department of Computer Engineering and Digital Systems, University of São Paulo, 2001.
[8]   R. P. Martin et al. Effects of Communication Latency, Overhead, and Bandwidth in a Cluster Architecture. In: Proceedings of the 24th Annual International Symposium on Computer Architecture, pages 85–97, Denver, 1997.
[9]   C.L. Mendes, D.A. Reed. Performance prediction by trace transformation. In: V SBAC-PAD Brazilian Symposium on Computer Architecture – High Performance Computing, São Paulo, 1993.
[10]   N. Nupairoj, L. Ni. Performance Evaluation of Some MPI Implementations. Technical Report MSU-CPS-ACS-94, Department of Computer Science, Michigan State University, Sept. 1994.
[11]   P. Puschner, A. Schedl. Computing Maximum Task Execution Times – a graph-Based Approach. In: Journal of Real-Time Systems, vol. 13, no.1, pages 67–91, 1997.
[12]   D. F. Vrsalovic, D.P. Siewiorek, Z.Z. Segall and E.F. Gehringer. Performance prediction and calibration for a class of multiprocessors. IEEE Transactions on Computers, v. 37, n. 11, pages 1353–1364, 1988.

New Scheme for Design of Static Virtual Topology in Wide Area Optical Networks

Raja Datta, Sujoy Ghose, and Indranil Sengupta

Dept. of Computer Science and Engineering,
Indian Institute of Technology, Kharagpur-721302,
INDIA.
{raja,sujoy,isg}@cse.iitkgp.ernet.in

Abstract. In this paper, we present a new improved scheme to establish lightpaths in a physical topology for the formation of a static WDM optical connection graph. One of the major design issues in these networks is the assignment of the limited number of wavelengths among network stations so that greater capacity can be achieved. Many researchers have tackled the problem of *routing and wavelength assignment* (RWA) with a number of efficient heuristic algorithms. Our paper proposes a scheme to generate connection requests to connect physical nodes optically in an efficient way to form an improved virtual topology. To better the wavelength utilization we also propose a wavelength assignment algorithm which uses the best alternate physical path while establishing lightpaths. We have simulated about six thousand random graphs of various sizes and densities to show that our algorithm gives a better virtual topology compared to the existing ones.

Keywords. Optical connection graph, Lightpath, WDM, Routing and Wavelength Assignment algorithms(RWA), WAN.

1 Introduction

There has been a considerable progress in the area of all-optical Wavelength Division Multiplexed(WDM) networks. As the demand for the bandwidth in today's Internet is increasing every day, more and more people believe that optical WDM is the most promising solution for setting up next generation networks. Wavelength-selective and Wavelength-interchangeable are the two important types of wavelength routed networks that can be used in Wide Area Networks(WAN). In a Wavelength-selective network, a lightpath can be established if the same wavelength is available on all the links between a pair of source-destination nodes. If the same wavelength is not available in any one of the links in the path, the connection request will be blocked. This blocking probability can be reduced by allowing the optical connection to switch from one wavelength to another during its course to the destination node. The network employing this technique is known as Wavelength-interchangeable network. It has been shown that wavelength selective networks are less complex and does

S.K. Das and S. Bhattacharya (Eds.): IWDC 2002, LNCS 2571, pp. 280–289, 2002.
© Springer-Verlag Berlin Heidelberg 2002

not suffer much performance degradation as compared to the complex wavelength interchangeable networks [4]. The optical connection in which there is no wavelength conversion is known as a *lightpath*[1], [5], [6].

The virtual topology is the network topology in which a link represents a lightpath that has been established between two physical nodes. The virtual topology is also sometimes called the optical connection graph or the logical topology [Figure 1]. We will use the terms interchangeably. The virtual topologies can fall into two categories: (1) *Static*: which is formed with the help of static lightpath establishment(SLE). Here the relative traffic between node pairs are available from a pre-assumed traffic matrix [2]. (2) *Reconfigurable*: where the lightpath establishment is dynamic(DLE) and the lightpaths in the logical topology are setup according to some connection requests at regular intervals and torn down after its holding time elapses [7]. This is done to accommodate the varying traffic pattern between the nodes of the network. Our focus here will be on static virtual topology in which the lightpaths once established are fixed till the virtual topology is entirely changed due to the change in traffic matrix. In the static case the traffic in the network is known a priori with the help of a

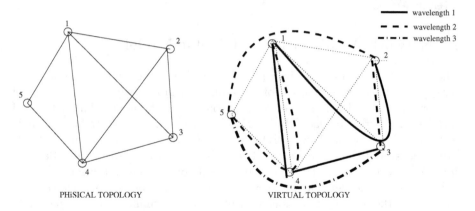

PHiSICAL TOPOLOGY   VIRTUAL TOPOLOGY

Fig. 1. Optical Connection graph formed over a 5 node physical network

traffic matrix. The source-destination pair for setting up lightpath can be chosen in a particular order to establish an efficient virtual topology with the limited number of available wavelengths. Researchers have given various schemes to line up the connection requests while setting up the lightpaths for the static virtual topology [1], [2], [8]. The performance of these existing policies heavily depend upon the physical topology of the networks.

Here in this paper, we present an algorithm where the complete connection request set is not known in the beginning. Instead, the request for connecting two nodes with a lightpath is sent out one by one after iteratively evaluating the changing(increasing) virtual connections on the physical network. The topology of the network is taken into consideration at every step while designing the virtual topology. As the indirect traffic shuffles between the optical domain and the electronic domain in the intermediate nodes the buffer sizes of these nodes also needs a special mention. With extensive simulation we show that our algorithm helps in designing a virtual topology where the traffic handled by these intermediate nodes are much less compared to a popular existing algorithm.

The problem of setting up of a lightpath by routing and assigning a wavelength between a source destination pair is known as *Routing and Wavelength Assignment* (RWA) problem. The path used while setting up a lightpath between two nodes is usually the shortest path. But due to the wavelength constraints alternative paths are required for the full utilization of the wavelengths. In most of the earlier algorithms we find that the complexity for searching an alternate route of connection is high. We also propose here an wavelength assignment algorithm which gives better utilization of wavelength with less complexity.

The rest of the paper is organized as follows: In section 2 we discuss the network architecture and traffic model used in our work along with the problem formulation. In section 3 we give a brief review of the existing algorithms for the establishment of virtual topology. We present our new policy of issuing connection request in section 4. Section 5 presents our new wavelength assignment algorithm. Simulation results are reported in section 6 and the conclusions are given in section 7.

2   Network Architecture and Traffic Model

The network structure is a given physical topology (fiber interconnection pattern) $G = (V, E)$ which consist of an undirected graph, where V is the set of network nodes, and E is the set of links connecting the nodes. The number of wavelengths carried by each fiber is P. The long term average (relative) traffic demand is given by an $N \times N$ traffic matrix T, where N is the number of network nodes, and the $(i, j)th$ element, t_{ij} the long term average traffic demand from *Node i* to *Node j*. The diagonal elements of the matrix are zero. Though the average traffic demand between any two nodes may be *asymmetric*, i.e., $t_{ij} \neq t_{ji}$, in the remaining sections we will assume a symmetric traffic matrix by considering the larger traffic from either side.

We have to determine a virtual topology $G_v = (V, E_v)$, in which each node corresponds to the node of the physical topology, and each link in the virtual topology corresponds to the direct all-optical *lightpath* between a pair of nodes in the physical topology.

3   Previous Work

Many researchers have studied the problem of building an efficient virtual topology over physical networks [1], [2], [8]. The virtual graph established in static case is fixed and is usually based on a long time relative traffic assumptions between the nodes of a network [2]. Whereas, in the dynamic virtual topology, the lightpaths are setup as per demand and are torn down when the requirement is over [7]. One of the popular heuristic algorithms for generating virtual topology was introduced by Acampora and Ganz in [2]. They formulated the problem as an optimization problem which can select a virtual topology subject to the transceiver and wavelength constraints. The largest-traffic-first scheme was used to line up the connection requests for setting up the lightpaths. The authors introduced a connection-link indication matrix, generated in decreasing order of traffic demand, to check if two or more connections uses a common link. Identical wavelengths are then assigned to the connections not using common links to as many paths as possible. The algorithm is repeated for all the available wavelengths. For a physical topology of N nodes, in the worst case one has to check all the N^4 elements which makes the complexity of the algorithm as $O(N^4)$.

In [1] the connection requests for lightpaths are sorted according to their respective lengths, and then the wavelengths are allocated to the longest lightpath first. This is done because a long lightpath is harder to establish since an unallocated identical wavelength is required in more links and thereby utilizing the wavelengths in a better way. The other two main schemes for the logical topology design are traffic independent logical topology design algorithm (TILDA) and random logical topology design algorithm (RLDA), both introduced in [8].

There exists many wavelength assignment proposals in the literature [2], [7], [9]. The firstfit assignment schemes attempts to assign wavelengths in a numerical order [9]. The most-used schemes attempt to allocate the most utilized wavelength first and then in decreasing order of utilization [7], [9], [10]. The least-used schemes attempt to allocate the least utilized wavelength first and then in non-decreasing order of utilization [7], [9]. The random schemes attempt to allocate a wavelength randomly [7], [9]. The path used while setting up a lightpath between two nodes is usually the shortest path. But due to the wavelength constraints it may not be possible to allocate wavelengths in all the shortest paths. As such alternative paths are required for better utilization of the wavelengths. In case of reconfigurable virtual topology the path selection for a lightpath was done in an adaptive way in [7]. The unconstrained path is then searched with the help of dynamic shortest algorithm. In [10] several heuristic algorithms were presented that will efficiently operate the network under dynamic traffic loading.

4   Request Generation

We propose here a heuristic algorithm to generate *connection request* for lightpaths. The input to this algorithm is the traffic matrix introduced in section 2 and the physical topology on which the virtual topology is to be designed. These requests will be given as an input to the wavelength assignment algorithm presented in section 5 to establish the respective lightpath.

We take the maximum value of t_{ij} and t_{ji} from the traffic matrix and generate a symmetric matrix T_{max}. The elements of this new matrix will be $\tau_{ij} = max(t_{ij}, t_{ji})$. This is because, if a lightpath is assigned between any two nodes, it is expected to carry traffic for both the ways.

From the symmetric traffic matrix T_{max} we next make the undirected traffic graph, G_t, whose nodes are equal to the network nodes N, and the edges have weights equal to τ_{ij}. We assume that G_t is a connected graph.

Next we introduce a factor which we call the *wh-factor* of the network:

$$(weight_{ab})(no.\ of\ hops_{ab})$$

where $(weight_{ab})$ is the traffic between the two nodes a and b, and $(no.\ of\ hops_{ab})$ is the no. of logical hops required for that traffic to reach from node a to node b through the logical paths of the network at that stage.

The algorithm is described as follows:

4.1 The Request Generation Algorithm

Step 1. A maximum weight spanning tree is generated from the traffic graph, G_t and stored in a matrix L_{req}. The edges of the spanning tree in L_{req}, forms the initial requests for the lightpaths. The *connection requests* are given out for wavelength assignment, one by one in decreasing order of the weight of the edges. The edges in L_{req} are removed from the traffic graph, G_t. We store the edges for which the wavelength assignment algorithm(section 5) is unable to assign a wavelength, in a matrix called B_t and remove it from L_{req}. IF in case a spanning tree as above is not possible due to wavelength constraints then restore G_t, delete all the edges of L_{req} and go to step 2. ELSE, go to step 3.

Step 2. Assign some weight arbitrarily to the edges of the physical network. Make a minimum weight spanning tree with the newly assigned weights. Send out *connection requests* for the edges of the spanning tree one by one by deleting the corresponding edge from G_t and adding them to L_{req}.

Step 3. Compute

$$\frac{\sum_{all\ node\ pair(x,y)} (weight_{xy})(no.\ of\ hops_{xy})}{\sum (weight)}$$

of the network when the whole traffic from the traffic matrix is routed through the edges of L_{req} only.

Here the $\sum_{all\ node\ pair(x,y)} (weight_{xy})(no.\ of\ hops_{xy})$ is the summation of the product of the traffic between every node pair (x, y) and the number of hops required for the traffic to reach from node x to node y. $\sum (weight)$ is the summation of the whole traffic from the traffic matrix of the network.

Step 4. Check whether the value of step 3 is equal to one. If yes, then STOP.

Step 5. Find an edge from the reduced G_t, that has the maximum *wh-factor* $[(weight_{ab})(no.\ of\ hops_{ab})$ value] and send it for wavelength assignment. Remove it from G_t. If it is possible to assign a wavelength add it to L_{req}, else add it to B_t.

Step 6. Go to step 3.

It can be seen that our algorithm makes a maximum weight spanning tree initially to ensure that the logical topology is connected. Intuitively, a long lightpath is harder to establish and as such our algorithm orders the request in such a way that both the magnitude of traffic and optical hops required for carrying the traffic from one node to another are considered when the traffic is routed through the already established lightpaths. The initial *connection requests* for lightpaths are the edges of the maximum spanning tree in decreasing order of weight as the tree gets formed. This is because, we initially have the minimum number of lightpaths established which will try to serve the traffic of all the nodes in the network.

The algorithm next calculates the product of the traffic demand and the optical hops required to route the said traffic through the already established lightpath between all the node pairs not given a direct optical path so far. And then sends out *connection request* for the node pair with maximum value of the said product. This heuristic choice of lightpath request also reduces the maximum possible load from the already established lightpaths. In case it is not possible to make a maximum spanning tree as discussed above(which happens if the network density is very less or if there are very few available wavelengths per link), the proposed algorithm first spans the physical network with lightpaths assuming some arbitrary weights in the links and then proceeds as usual. The virtual topology thus created is guaranteed to be connected.

5   Wavelength Assignment

We present a wavelength assignment algorithm which searches for a suitable connection path if available and allocates the wavelength offering the shortest path.

Initially a $L \times M$ matrix U is formed where L is the number of wavelengths available per link and M is the total number of the connected node pairs in the physical topology. We call this matrix the *Utilization matrix* since the elements of this matrix u_{lm} shows the utilization of the wavelength between every pair of connected node pairs.

5.1   The Wavelength Assignment Algorithm

Step 1. When a connection request (from our proposed algorithm in section 4) arrives, search all the rows of the Utilization matrix U for zero elements corresponding to the links on the shortest path. Allocate the wavelength to the request corresponding to the first row in which all such elements are found to be zero. Change the same elements from zero to one. If it is not possible to allocate any wavelength go to step 2, ELSE go to step 5.

Step 2. A *Graph set* $S_G = (G_{l1},\ G_{l2},\ G_{l3}, \ldots)$ is formed, where the elements are the physical graphs with modifications in their link sets $E_{l1},\ E_{l2},\ E_{l3}, \ldots$ as follows: The link set E_{ln} of G_{ln} will contain only the links corresponding to the zero elements of row ln.

Step 3. Find the shortest path for the connection (if at all a path is available) in all the elements of S_G in step 2 and form a *path set* $P = (p_{l1},\ p_{l2},\ p_{l3}, \ldots)$ in which the elements are the number of links in the respective shortest paths.

If no path is available due to the connected graph converting into forest, the corresponding elements are made ∞.

Step 4. If all the elements of the path set P is ∞, go to step 5. ELSE, the wavelength li corresponding to the smallest element (p_{li}) is allocated to the lightpath, STOP.

Step 5. It is not possible to allocate any wavelength. The request remains unassigned, STOP.

In this algorithm, the path set P gives all the alternate paths available for a connection in case it is not possible to allocate a wavelength through the shortest path. As an example, we show below the utilization matrix U with three wavelengths for the virtual topology of figure 1, where the links 1-2, 1-3, 1-4, 1-5, 2-3, 2-4, 3-4, 4-5 are represented in the columns 0, 1, 2, 3, 4 ... serially. The *Graph set* S_G in this case, will have three elements (G_{l1}, G_{l2}, G_{l3}) as shown in figure 2.

$$U = \begin{pmatrix} 0\,1\,1\,0\,1\,0\,1\,0 \\ 1\,0\,1\,1\,1\,0\,0\,1 \\ 0\,0\,0\,0\,0\,0\,1\,1 \end{pmatrix}$$

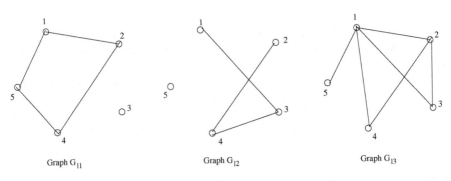

Graph G_{l1} Graph G_{l2} Graph G_{l3}

Fig. 2. The elements of the Graph set S_G

The path set is obtained from these graphs(elements of S_G) and a wavelength is allocated as shown in the algorithm.

6   Experimental Results

We evaluate the performances of our proposed connection request and wavelength assignment algorithms by simulating approximately six thousand random networks of various shapes, sizes and densities. Our density gradation of the random graphs is as follows: graph density, $\delta = 1$ when the graph is a spanning tree constructed with random edge weights. The graphs with $\delta = 2$, $\delta = 3$ and $\delta = 4$ will have edges equal to twice, thrice and four times respectively, the number of edges of the graph with $\delta = 1$, placed randomly all over the network. In the simulation results shown in Table 1 through Table 3, column 1 shows the algorithm numbers as follows:

Algo(1): Our proposed connection request scheme with new wavelength assignment algorithm.

Algo(2): The algorithm presented by Zang and Acampora in [2].

From column 2 to column 8 the value of the following parameters are shown that evaluates the performance of the algorithms:

NRA *No. of requests arrived:* The number of connection requests according to the respective traffic matrix and is same for the cases with similar sizes.

NUR *No. of unassigned requests:* The number of connection requests the algorithm is not able to assign a wavelength.

MHop *Maximum-hop:* The maximum number of logical hops between any two nodes in a network.

MIB *Maximum intermediate buffer size:* The maximum size of the buffer required by the intermediate nodes in terms of relative traffic to handle the indirect traffic.

AIT *Average Intermediate traffic:* Average relative traffic handled by the intermediate nodes of the network.

WH/W Average value of $\sum (weight)(no.\ of\ hops)/\sum (weight)$ of the networks as introduced in section 4. Here this expression is computed taking into consideration the blocked connection requests after the design of the virtual topology is complete. The minimum value of this expression is 1 when all the connection requests are allocated a separate lightpath.

SpW *Spare wavelength(SpW):* The average of the un-utilitized wavelength per link of the physical network.

We have done extensive simulation taking many combinations of the random network and number of available wavelengths. Due to space constraint we show here some typical cases each from 20–node, 30–node and 40–node random networks. The results shown below are the averages of 25 networks in each of the cases. In Table 1 the results are shown for a 20 node network graph density $\delta = 3$ with no. of wavelengths available(wl) equal to 4, 8 and 12 respectively. The results justify that the virtual topology designed with our request generation scheme gives much better performance i.e. smaller intermediate buffer sizes, less indirect traffic and lesser value of $\sum (weight)(no.\ of\ hops)/\sum weight$. The parameters in 3rd, 4th and 8th column are supporting parameters that gives an idea about (a) the number of node-pairs that cannot be assigned a lightpath, (b) The maximum number of lightpaths that needs to be traversed and (c) the wavelengths remaining un-utilized, in a network. Barring a few cases, we find that the values of these parameters are also better(less) when evaluated with our proposed algorithms. In Table 2 the results are shown for 30 node random networks with $\delta = 3$ for 8, 12 and 16 wavelengths. For all the parameters in Table 2, our proposed algorithm [Algo(1)] gives better result.

Table 1. No. of Nodes = 20, graph density(δ) = 3

	NRA	NUR	MHop	MIB	AIT	WH/W	SpW
wl=4							
Algo(1)	190	74.91	2.04	591	86	1.278	0.17
Algo(2)	190	77.87	2.04	618	103	1.332	0.81
wl=8							
Algo(1)	190	5.24	1.88	76	3	1.013	1.93
Algo(2)	190	26.68	2.00	311	27	1.090	3.00
wl=12							
Algo(1)	190	0.88	1.16	13	0	1.002	5.97
Algo(2)	190	6.20	2.00	79	4	1.016	6.21

Table 2. No. of Nodes = 30, graph density(δ) = 3

	NRA	NUR	MHop	MIB	AIT	WH/W	SpW
wl=8							
Algo(1)	435	133.88	2.00	1162	93	1.196	0.60
Algo(2)	435	152.39	2.00	1162	127	1.267	1.89
wl=12							
Algo(1)	435	31.68	2.00	367	17	1.036	1.99
Algo(2)	435	84.76	2.00	844	62	1.131	4.13
wl=16							
Algo(1)	435	6.00	1.64	99	3	1.007	5.69
Algo(2)	435	43.40	2.00	499	28	1.059	6.99

Table 3. No. of Nodes = 40, graph density(δ) = 4

	NRA	NUR	MHop	MIB	AIT	WH/W	SpW
wl=8							
Algo(1)	780	212.39	2.00	1813	100	1.157	0.41
Algo(2)	780	258.23	2.00	1900	159	1.250	1.91
wl=12							
Algo(1)	780	20.00	2.00	266	7	1.012	1.98
Algo(2)	780	138.32	2.00	1467	75	1.118	4.24
wl=16							
Algo(1)	780	4.20	1.32	81	1	1.003	6.13
Algo(2)	780	68.08	2.00	858	32	1.051	7.22

Lastly, in Table 3 we show the results obtained by simulating a 40–node random
network with $\delta = 4$ for 8, 12, and 16 wavelengths. It can be seen that the gains
obtained with our proposed algorithm are significant compared to the existing
algorithm.

7   Conclusion

We presented a new scheme for designing virtual topology in wavelength routed optical networks. Unlike earlier algorithms, our proposed algorithm takes the topology under construction at every stage while deciding the next lightpath to be inserted in the network. We also propose a new wavelength assignment algorithm that uses alternate paths, if required, for assigning wavelengths in minimum computation time. Our results show that the virtual topology designed with our algorithm gives better performance as compared to a popular existing scheme.

References

1. I.Chlamtac, A.Ganz, and G.Karmi, "Lightpath communication: a novel approach to high bandwidth optical WDN's." *IEEE Transactions on Communications*, 40(7), July 1992, 1171–1182.
2. Z.Zang and A.Acampora, "A heuristic wavelength assignment algorithm for multi-hop wdm networks with wavelength routing and wavelength re-use", *IEEE/ACM Transactions on Networking*, 3(3), June 1995, 281–288.
3. R.Ramaswami and K.N.Sivarajan, "Optical Networks: A practical perspective", Morgan Kaufmann Publishers, 1998.
4. E.Karasan and E.Ayanoglu, "Effects of wavelength routing and selection algorithms on wavelength conversion gain in WDM optical networks", *IEEE/ACM Transactions on Networking*, 6(2), April 1998, 186–196.
5. I.Chlamtac, A.Ganz and G.Karmi, "Lightnets: Topologies for high speed optical networks", *IEEE/OSA Journal of Lightwave Technology*, 11(5/6), May/June 1993, 951–961.
6. I.Chlamtac, A.Farago and T.Zang, "Lightpath (wavelength) routing in large WDM networks", *IEEE Journal of Selected areas of communications*, 14(5), June 1996, 909–913 .
7. A.Mokhtar and M.Azizoglu, "Adaptive Wavelength Routing in All-Optical networks", *IEEE/ACM Trans. Networking*, 6(2), April 1998, 197–206.
8. R.Ramaswami and K.N.Sivarajan, "Design of logical topologies for wavelength-routed optical networks", *IEEE Journal of Selected areas of communications*, 14(5), June 1996, 840–851.
9. J.S.Choi and D.Su, "A functional classification of RWA schemes in DWDM networks: Static case", *NRC 2000, New Jersey, U.S.A.* April 14–15, 2000.
10. G.Shen, S.K.Bose, T.H.Cheng, C.Lu, T.Y.Chai, "Efficient heuristic algorithms for light-path routing and wavelength assignment in WDM networks under dynamically varying loads", *Elsevier Computer Communications*, 24(2001), 2001, 364–373.

A Fast Technique for Assigning Wavelengths in WDM All-Optical Networks (AONs)[*]

Sahadeb Jana[1], Debashis Saha[2], Amitava Mukherjee[3], and Pranay Chaudhuri[4]

[1] Department of Science, Maheshtala College, 24 Paraganas(S), India
{sahadeb_jana@rediffmail.com}
[2] Indian Institute of Management (IIM)-Calcutta,
Joka, D. H. Road, Kolkata 700104, India
{ds@iimcal.ac.in}
[3] IBM Global Services, Kolkata, India
{amitava.mukherjee@in.ibm.com}
[4] Dept of Computer Science, Mathematics & Physics,
University of the West Indies, Barbados, West Indies
{pchaudhuri@uwichill.edu.bb}

Abstract. This paper presents a fast algorithm for effectively assigning wavelengths to requested ligthpaths in a wavelength division multiplexed (WDM) optical network. The physical medium of the network consists of optical fiber segments interconnected by wavelength selective optical switches. WDM permits a limited number of wavelengths to be re-used among various fiber links, thereby offering a very high aggregate capacity. Here we have followed a technique, which can assign wavelengths to the lightpath without making any auxiliary graphs. The algorithm is proved to be correct, and its complexity is analyzed. The performance of the algorithm is tested on several networks for various lightpath demands through extensive simulations. The timing efficiency is studied and compared with the existing best-known wavelength assignment heuristic. It is found that, for a wide range of lightpath requests, the proposed algorithm performs considerably better than the existing one.

1 Introduction

Fiber optic technology [1] holds out the promise of catering to the ever-increasing demand for bandwidth intensive end-user applications of future. The technique of Wavelength Division Multiplexing (WDM) [2], due to its efficient use of bandwidth, has emerged as the most promising transmission technology for optical networks. It divides the huge bandwidth of an optical fiber into a number of channels, where each channel corresponds to a different wavelength. A WDM optical network consists of optical wavelength routers interconnected by pairs of point-to-point fiber links (Figure

---

[*] This work is partially supported by the UGC funded major research project (SWOPNET) grant no. F.14-24/2001 (SR – I) and AICTE funded R&D project (OPTIMAN) grant No. 8088/RDII/BOR/R&D(189)/99-2000 of Govt. of India.

S.K. Das and S. Bhattacharya (Eds.): IWDC 2002, LNCS 2571, pp. 290–299, 2002.

1). A wavelength router receives a message at some wavelength from an input fiber and redirects it to any one of the output fibers at the same wavelength. Hence, a message can be transmitted from one routing node to another through a wavelength continuous path by configuring the intermediate routing nodes on that path. Such a wavelength continuous path is known as a *lightpath* [3]. The requirement, that the same wavelength must be used on all the links along the selected path, is known as the *wavelength continuity* constraint. This constraint is unique to WDM networks. Due to this constraint, wavelength channels may not always be utilized efficiently. Usually, a lightpath LP_i is uniquely identified by a tuple $<\lambda_i, P_i>$, where λ_i is the wavelength used in the lightpath and P_i represents the physical path corresponding to LP_i. Two lightpaths LP_1 $<\lambda_1, P_1>$ and LP_2 $<\lambda_2, P_2>$ can share the same fiber, if and only if they use different wavelengths i.e., $\lambda_1 \neq \lambda_2$. The problem of establishing lightpaths, with the objective of minimization of the required number of wavelengths or minimization of the lightpath blocking probability, for a fixed number of wavelengths, is termed as the *lightpath establishment problem* (LEP) [4]. Usually, lightpath establishment is of two types. One is *static* (SLEP) or proactive [4], where a set of lightpaths and their wavelengths are identified a priori. Another is *dynamic* (DLEP) [4], where lightpath management is done on-demand, i.e., they are established and terminated on the fly. A good survey of the existing formulations for LEP can be found in [3]. A number of heuristic algorithms for assigning wavelengths in WDM optical networks are available in the literature [4]-[7]. An overall review of these algorithms is also available in [4].

The static lightpath establishment problem (SLEP) can be formulated as a mixed-integer linear program, which is NP complete [4]. In order to make the problem more tractable, SLEP is normally partitioned into *two* sub-problems: *routing*, and *wavelength assignment*. Each sub-problem can be solved separately. In this paper, we assume that routes of the lightpaths are known i.e., routing is done prior to wavelength assignment and concentrate only on the *wavelength assignment problem* (WAP) [5]. This work improves upon our previous effort on WAP, which is to be presented elsewhere [8] in the terms of execution efficiency.

2 Network Architecture

The network architecture, considered in this work is based on the use of: a) high-density WDM, b) wavelength to route each signal to its intended destination in the network (wavelength routing) and c) multihop switching and multiplexing/ demultiplexing. These three principles are used to build a virtual network [3]-[5] in which the number of nodes is essentially unlimited and is independent of the number of wavelengths available. The network 1) consists of: a) an all-optical inner portion which contains the wavelength routing cross-connection (or switching) elements, each capable of independently routing an incident wavelength, and b) an outer portion which contains user access stations which attach to the optical medium. The WDM core permits a limited number of wavelengths available to each link to enable full virtual connectivity, if desired, among all users.

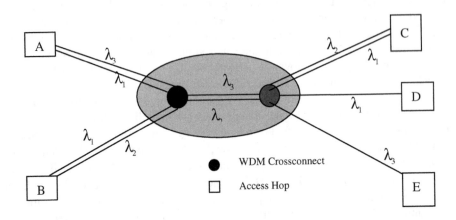

Fig. 1. An example WDM optical network showing access nodes and the core network

In Figure 1, WDM cross connects are shown within the circle constituting the optical portion, and the squares represent the network access stations. Wavelength λ_3 carries a one-optical-hop signal (no intermediate detection or *wavelength translation*) from node A to node E, while a signal from node A to node C is carried in two optical hops: A to B on λ_1 and B to C on λ_2. Wavelength λ_1 is reused to carry a signal from C to D. Since the number of receivers and transmitters per access station is limited, the optical connectivity among the stations is not full. Thus, most of the end-to-end connections will require multiple hops, through a sequence of optical channels or lightpaths. These connections are referred to *virtual connections*. The full virtual connectivity is possible by using intermediate stations cooperating as relay nodes. When a new virtual connection request is generated, the job of the admission controller is to decide whether to admit or block the request by finding a path capable of handling the virtual connection. A virtual connection request is blocked, if the controller is unable to find or create a path, without unacceptably degrading the quality of service enjoyed by other virtual connections.

For a given fiber topology which consists of some nodes, a long term average traffic demand matrix (t_{ij}), and number of wavelength available, K, an objective is to find a wavelength assignment algorithm and a routing scheme such that the call blocking probability is minimized, subject to following physical constraint: *on each fiber link no two virtual connection use the same wavelength*. The problem, being conjectured to be NP–hard [4], is usually decomposed into two separate sub-problems [5] stated below.

Sub-problem 1: Find a wavelength assignment algorithm, which tends to favor the one-optical-hop traffic (i.e., pair of stations exhibiting large traffic flow receive optical links from the resulting optical connection graph; heavy traffic flow is thereby handled in one hop, reducing the burden on the other optical links).

Sub-problem 2: For the resulting optical connection graph, develop routing schemes, which produce low call blocking probability.

As pointed out in section 1, we consider only the sub-problem 1, namely wavelength assignment problem (WAP) [5] such that the one-optical-hop traffic is maximized, subject to the following physical layer constraint: *on each optical link, two connections can not use a common wavelength.* Because of the constraint, the mathematical formulation of the problem is difficult, and a mixed linear integer program results [5] shown below.

Let us define a connection-link indication matrix m = $(m_{(p\,q),(l\,m)})$, where

$m_{(pq),(lm)}$ = 1, if connection (p, q) and connection (l, m) use a common link

$\qquad\qquad$ = 0, otherwise $\qquad\qquad\qquad\qquad\qquad\qquad\qquad\qquad\qquad\qquad$ (1)

It is also assumed that

z_{pq} (w) = 1, if node p and node q are connected through wavelength w

$\qquad\qquad$ = 0, otherwise.

Let the capacity of each wavelength be C and the maximum capacity of the optical channel between i and j be $\Sigma^{K}_{w=1} z_{pq}$ (w)C. If $\Sigma^{K}_{w=1} z_{pq}$(w)C = 0, no optical channel is set up between p and q. The maximum one-optical-hop traffic carried on the optical channel between p and q is $min(t_{pq}, \Sigma^{K}_{w=1}z_{pq}$(w)C). Hence, WAP can be formulated as follows [5]:

$$max\ \Sigma_{pq}\ min\ (\ t_{pq}\ ,\ \Sigma^{K}_{w=1}z_{pq}(w)C)$$

subject to:

$\qquad\Sigma^{N}_{m=1}\ z_{pm}(w) \leq 1 \qquad$ and $\qquad \Sigma^{N}_{m=1}\ z_{mq}(w) \leq 1$

$\qquad\qquad\qquad\qquad\qquad$ w = 1,2,...,K and p,q = 1,2,..,N $\qquad\qquad$ (2)

$m_{(p,q),(l,m)}(z_{pq}(w) + z_{lm}(w)) \leq 1,$

$\qquad\qquad\qquad\qquad$ w = 1,2,...,K for all distinct pairs (p,q) and (l,m) $\qquad$ (3)

$z_{pq}(w) = 0$ or 1,

$\qquad\qquad\qquad\qquad$ w = 1,2,...,K and i,j = 1,2,..,N $\qquad\qquad\qquad$ (4)

For each wavelength, constraint (2) states that there should be at most one connection starting from node p and at most one connection terminating at q, respectively. Constraint (3) indicates that, if connections (p, q) and (l, m) use a common link, z_{pq}(w) and z_{lm}(w) can not be equal to 1 at the same time, i.e., connections (p, q) and (l, m) can not use the same wavelength w at the same time. Constraint 4 indicates that, if z_{pq} (w) = 1, then nodes p and q are connected through the wavelength w.

3 Wavelength Assignment Algorithm

Given the physical topology and lightpath requests of a WDM optical network, we try to assign wavelength to the lightpaths at one go using this algorithm. The wavelength assignment is done in such a way that a lightpath LP_i in the system gets a wavelength (say, λ_i) which is not used by any of the links of P_i. For example, Figure 2(a) shows the physical topology of an example optical network with eight lightpaths (solid lines numbered 1 through 8) requested upon it. Throughout the paper, dotted lines indicate the fiber links among network nodes. Say, during assignment, we get that route of lightpath_1 as F-A-B and that of lightpath-4 as A-B-C (Figure 2(a)). When wavelength assignment is considered, these two lightpaths cannot use the same wavelength as they share a common link viz. (A-B) (remember that $\lambda_i \neq \lambda_j$, if $P_i \cap P_j \neq \phi$).

Let us now introduce a few related notations before we discuss the algorithm:

LP: Set of lightpaths in the WDM optical network = {LP_i, i = 1, 2, 3...........M}

$WU_{m,n}$: A bit array of size K for link (m-n), where each bit indicates whether the wavelength is currently in use. A bit 0 indicates that wavelength is in use and 1 indicates that it is free now. (m,n = 1, 2,   ,N). N is the number of nodes in the physical network.

wavlength_set : Set of wavelengths needed to assign, { λ_j | 1≤j ≤K }

wavelength(LP_i) : Wavelength assigned to LP_i

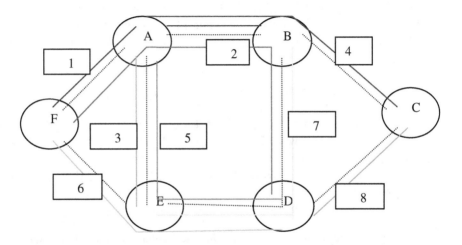

Fig. 2 (a). Physical topology of an optical network (different colors represent different lightpaths)

The proposed algorithm, PROBE 'N' ASSIGN assigns wavelength to it in two passes. In the first pass, it takes a lightpath, finds out the corresponding route (we assume predetermined static routing) and probes the lowest order non-used wavelength on its rout. In the second pass, it assigns that wavelength to the current lightpath and updates the link/links in the routed path about the assignment. Individual information about the used wavelengths of all the links avoids reassigning of the same wavelength to any future lightpath sharing the same link(s). Thus at the termination of the algorithm, each lightpath is assigned with a different wavelength. Avoiding the construction of auxiliary graph and assigning wavelengths at one go are the novelties of the algorithm. Here, it has been assumed that sufficient number of wavelengths has been supplied in the given wavelength_set to assign all the lightpaths.

3.1 *Algorithm* **PROBE 'N' ASSIGN**

> *Input:*   *A set of lightpaths LP for a given WDM optical network.*
> *Output:* *At the termination of the algorithm, each lightpath is assigned with a permanent wavelength, wavelength(i).*

Step 1: Set $WU_{m,n} = \{\phi\}$, (m,n = 1, 2, 3, ..., N)
Step 2: wavelength(LP_1)= wavelength _set(0).
Step 3: Inform the wavelength usage to all the links of LP_1 setting the corresponding bits in $WU_{m,n}$ as 0.
Step 4: for each $LP_i \in [LP - LP_1]$ do

  wavelength(LP_i) = Probe the lowest order wavelength yet to be used by all the links of LP_i taking interdsection of all $WU_{m,n}$

  Inform the wavelength usage to all the links of LP_i setting corresponding bits in $WU_{m,n}$ as 0.

  od
Step 5: End .

Now, we will describe how this algorithm PROBE 'N' ASSIGN works with the example network shown in Figure 2(a). In step 1, all WUs (i.e., wavelength usage information on all links) are set to be null to indicate any of the wavelengths are not being used in any link. In step2, LP_1 is assigned the first available wavelength in the wavelength_set (here λ_0). Now this information is used to update WUs on all the links involved in P_1. So, for the links F-A and A-B, the bits of $WU_{F,A}$ and $WU_{A,B}$, corresponding to λ_0 is set to zero. Then, in step 3, when the turn of LP_2 comes, first of all, it checks all the links in the routed path (F-A-B-D). At the time of checking, it probes that the links F-A and A-B have already used λ_0 and the link B-D is yet to use any available wavelength. So it finds that λ_1 is lowest order wavelength yet to be used by any of the links of LP_2 and assigns λ_1 to it. Accordingly, it updates the corresponding bits of $WU_{F,A}$, $WU_{A,B}$ and $WU_{B,D}$. In this way, all the demanded lightpaths are assigned a particular wavelength as shown in the final auxiliary graph of Figure 2(b), corresponding to 8 lightpaths of Figure 2(a). In Figure 2(b), nodes represent lightpaths [8] and an edge between two nodes indicates that they are sharing some common link/links.

4 Correctness Proof

The correctness of algorithm PROBE 'N' ASSIGN can be established through the following lemmas.

Lemma 1.1: At the termination of algorithm PROBE 'N' ASSIGN, every lightpath is assigned with a wavelength.

Proof. As wavelength_set is assumed to consist of enough number of wavelengths and steps 2 and 4 considers all lightpaths one by one, it is obvious that all the lightpaths will be assigned wavelength at the termination of the algorithm.

Lemma 1.2: Any two lightpaths will have distinct wavelengths at the termination of algorithm PROBE 'N' ASSIGN.

Proof. Let us prove it by contradiction. Say, LP_i and LP_j (j>i) have identical wavelengths at the end of the execution of algorithm and they share some common link/links. Now, we will prove that wavelength(i) and wavelength(j) cannot be same. Let us consider the stage at which the wavelength of the LP_i is fixed to have wavelength(i). Now, whenever LP_i will be assigned wavelength(i) that information will immediately be informed to all the links in the route P_i of that very lightpath. When turn of LP_j will come, first of all it will probe which wavelengths are currently unused by all the links in P_j. At the time of probing, it is obvious that LP_j must not get wavelength(i) as the non-used one (as all links in P_i are already previously informed about its usage). Thus, probe will get some other wavelength as non-used one, wavelength(j) $\neq$ wavelength(i) and will assign that to LP_j.

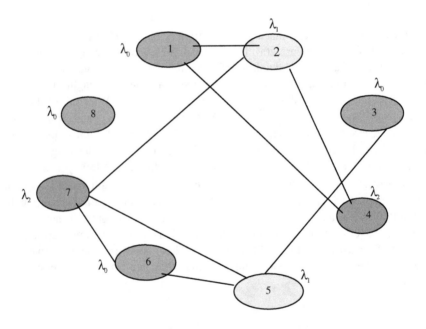

Fig. 2(b). The auxiliary graph with final wavelength assignment

Lemma 1.3: Algorithm PROBE 'N' ASSIGN eventually terminates.

Proof. Due to the presence of the deterministic 'for each' loop, the algorithm requires a finite amount of time to complete the wavelength assignment. More specifically, it always requires exactly (|LP|-1) i.e., of the order of M iterations to be terminated.

Theorem 1: Algorithm PROBE 'N' ASSIGN is correct.
Proof. Follows from Lemmas 1.1, 1.2 and 1.3.

Now we examine the complexity of the algorithm minutely. Step 1 takes time in the order of (N^2*K), where K is the number of wavelengths. Step 2 does $(N*K)$ operations and step 3 N operations. In Step 4, there is a "for each" loop. This "for" loop performs two things within it. First, wavelength to be used is probed and it does $(N*K)$ operations and then this information is sent to all the links that does N operations. Thus, Step 4 does total $(M-1)(N*K +N)$ operations. Therefore, the overall (worst case) complexity of algorithm PROBE 'N' ASSIGN comes as $O(N*M*K + N*M + N^2*K)$ i.e., $O(N^3*K)$.

This completes the analysis.

5   Results

The algorithm has been tested with a number of synthetically generated networks of varying node sizes and lightpath demands. In the simulation, we first generate a network graph and then create a number of lightpath requests, randomly from a small value to a considerably large one, for the network. Routes of the lightpaths have been fixed using shortest path algorithm. Taking those lightpath requests as input, we apply them to our proposed algorithm to obtain the assignment scheme. The results are found to be satisfactory in all cases. However, in order to rate the performance of the algorithm PROBE 'N' ASSIGN (called as PNA in short) against the best-known algorithm by Zhang and Acampora [5] (called as Z-A in short), we calculate the number of wavelengths required and computational time taken by each algorithm for several networks. In all cases, the number of wavelengths is found to be the same for both the algorithms.

Table 1. Total number of nodes in physical network: 30 (Connectivity: 0.3)

LP Requests	PNA Algorithm.		Z-A Algorithm.		Speed-Up (t2/t1)
	No. of Wave-lengths (K)	Execution Time (t1)	No of Wave-lengths (K)	Execution Time (t2)	
30	3	0.062	3	0.066	1.06
60	4	0.14	4	0.19	1.35
90	6	0.188	6	0.5	2.67
120	6	0.25	6	0.828	3.31
150	8	0.313	8	1.312	4.19
180	11	0.36	11	1.922	5.34
210	10	0.421	10	2.641	6.27

Interestingly, our algorithm always takes much less time than that taken by its competitor. Two such comparative results are given in Table 1 (for a 30-node network) and in Figures 3 (for a 50-node network). Here, the unit of time is taken as: 1unit = 1 msec., when run on a P4 Intel PC under Borland C++ compiler. Connectivity signifies the ratio of links among the nodes, which is actually present in the network, to the total possible links among the nodes (i.e., N^2/2). For comparing the time efficiencies of the algorithms, we consider the speed-up factor = t2/t1, where t1 = time taken by PNA and t2 = time taken by Z-A. Both Table 1and Figure 3 indicate that the speed-up is considerable for larger networks.

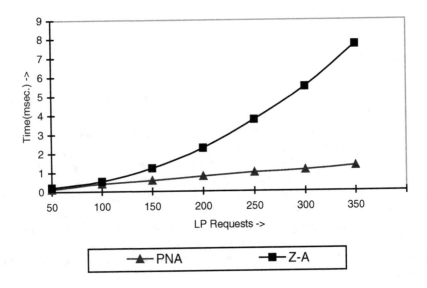

Fig. 3. Execution time comparison for a 50-node Network (Connectivity: 0.3)

6 Conclusion

In this paper, we have presented an efficient algorithm for wavelength assignment, which can be employed for assigning wavelengths in WDM optical networks. Given the physical topology and lightpath requests of a WDM network, we assign wavelength to the lightpaths using the above algorithm. The algorithm is applicable to SLEP only i.e., it can assign wavelengths to the lightpaths in a static WDM optical network environment. The algorithm has been tested, and the coloring and timing efficiencies are studied through extensive simulation studies. When compared with the existing wavelength assignment algorithm, we find that, for a wide range of lightpath requests, the proposed algorithm performs better.

Acknowledgements. This work is partially supported by the UGC funded major research project (SWOPNET) grant No. F.14-24/2001 (SR – I) and AICTE funded R&D project (OPTIMAN) grant No. 8088/RDII/BOR/R&D(189)/99-2000 in the department of Computer Science & Engg. Of Jadavpur University, Kolkata and Indian Institute of Management(IIM) – Calcutta, India.

References

1. P. E. Green, "Progress in Optical Networking", IEEE Communications Magazine, pp. 54–61, January 2001.
2. B. Mukherjee, "WDM Optical Communication Networks: Progress and Challenges", IEEE Journal on Selected Areas in Communications, Vol. 18, No. 10, pp. 1810–1824, October 2000.
3. R. Dutta, G. N. Rouskas, "A Survey of Virtual Topology Design Algorithms for Wavelength Routed Optical Networks", Optical Networks Magazine, pp. 73-89, January 2000.
4. H. Zang, J. P. Jue and B. Mukherjee, "A Review of Routing and Wavelength Assignment Approaches for Wavelength Routed Optical WDM Networks", Optical Networks Magazine, pp.47–60, January 2000.
5. Z. Zhang and A. S. Acampora, "A Heuristic Wavelength Assignment Algorithm for Multihop WDM Networks with Wavelength Routing and Wavelength Re-Use", IEEE/ACM Transactions on Networking, Vol.3, No.3, pp. 281–288, June 1995.
6. S. Banerjee, J. Yoo and C. Chen, "Design of Wavelength – Routed Optical Networks for Packet Switched Traffic", Journal of Lightwave Technology, Vol.15, No. 9, pp. 1636–1646, September 1997.
7. R. Ramaswami and K. N. Sivarajan, "Routing and Wavelength Assignment in All-Optical Networks", IEEE/ACM Transactions on Networking, Vol.3, No.5, pp. 489–500, October 1995.
8. S. Jana, S. Chowdhury, D. Saha, A. Mukherjee and P. Chaudhuri, "Assigning Wavelengths in WDM Optical Networks: A Novel Dynamic Approach" Proc. 6th International Conference HPC Asia, Bangalore, India, Dec, 2002.

Design of 1-FT Communication Network under Budget Constraint[1]

Loknath Ghosh[1], Amitava Mukherjee[2], and Debashis Saha[3]

[1]Haldia Institute of Technology, Haldia, India
loka_ghosh@yahoo.com
[2]IBM Global Services, Calcutta 700 091, India
amitava.mukherjee@in.ibm.com (Author for correspondence)
[3]Indian Institute of Management Calcutta, Joka, Calcutta 700 104, India
ds@iimcal.ac.in

Abstract. This paper considers the design of reliable backbone networks under certain real-life constraints of cost and fault tolerance. The constraints are: keeping the cost of the links with in a predefined budget; and keeping the topology 1-FT (fault-tolerant) to 1-link failure. A network topology is said to be 1-FT iff every pair of nodes is reachable from all other nodes for 1 link failure. i.e., the graph remains connected. Formally, a graph G is 1-FT iff all the graphs, which have one less link than graph G, are connected. That is, 1-FT network can survive 1-link failure in the network. Therefore, the problem is to find a reliable network topology for a set of nodes whose total link cost is minimized subject to constraints that the backbone network can accommodate a 1-link failure under a given budget. The problem is NP-hard i.e. there exists no polynomial time algorithm to solve this problem. In this paper we have proposed an efficient method based on genetic algorithm to solve the problem. In our method we have represented a backbone layout by means of an upper triangular matrix by concatenating a row with its previous rows. The genetic operators iteratively attempt to find a more cost-effective and reliable network layout. Through the extensive simulation we show that our proposed genetic algorithmic approach can efficiently find a sub-optimal solution for most of the cases.

1   Introduction

An important design-constraint for any reliable backbone network is that the network must remain connected even on failure of one or more links. Usually the design of backbone layout is subjected to the budget constraints as well as the reliability requirements to cope with the fault occurred in the network. A number of approaches to topological network optimization have been developed [5–9]. The optimal solutions as well as approximate solutions are established. In [5–6], the authors have considered topological optimization for maximizing the network reliability subject to

---

[1] This work is partially supported by the UGC funded major research project (SWOPNET) grant No. F.14-24/2001 (SR – I) and AICTE funded R&D project (OPTIMAN) grant No. 8088/RDII/BOR/R&D(189)/99-2000

S.K. Das and S. Bhattacharya (Eds.): IWDC 2002, LNCS 2571, pp. 300–311, 2002.
© Springer-Verlag Berlin Heidelberg 2002

a cost constraint. Jan, et al [10] has considered the topological optimization of communication networks subject to reliability constraints. All these papers find an approximate solution due to the intractability of the problems. In [11], author presents a decomposition approach to the problem in which the total link-cost subject to the reliability constraint.

This problem has addressed two constraints, namely cost and fault tolerance, to obtain a backbone layout of a network with a minimum cost. For simplicity we have assumed that all the links are equally reliable i.e., the reliability for all links is equal to 1. Though in practical this range is between $0 < r_{ij} < 1$ where r_{ij} = reliability of the link between node i and node j. Cheng, *et al* [1] has proposed a method for optimizing the total cost of a backbone layout with fault-tolerance as one of its constraints. Our proposed solution methodology has performed better than the methodology discussed in [1]. In this paper, we have designed an efficient algorithm based on genetic algorithmic approach for designing a backbone network layout. Through simulation we have shown that our proposed algorithm can efficiently find out an optimal (or sub-optimal) solution for the above problem.

The paper is organized as follows. The Section 2 states the problem. The Section 3 gives the overview of Genetic algorithm. In Section 4 we explain the proposed algorithm. In Section 5, we give an example how the proposed algorithm can find out an optimal solution and we also show the simulation results obtained through simulations.

2 Problem Statement

Assumptions:
The link costs are known and given for every pair of nodes
The set of nodes is given and known
All links are bi-directional; $l_{ij} = l_{ji}$ for all i, j∈ L
The network layout does not contain any redundant links; no two links connect to the same two nodes

Definitions:
A network topology is 1-FT iff every pair of nodes is reachable for any 1 link-failure in the network. In the simpler sense we can say that A network topology is 1-FT iff a node of the graph is reachable from all other nodes of the graph even on the failure of a single link.

Connected graph: Every node is reachable from all other nodes.

A graph is 1-FT iff all the graphs, which have one less, link than graph G in connected. Degree of a node is the number of links incident on it.

The problem is to find a back-bone layout for the given set of nodes such that the link cost minimized, subjected to the condition that the layout is 1-FT. Given N and C_{ij} for all i, j then find a 1-FT network topology such that the total link cost is minimized. The formal description of the problem is given below:
Minimize

$$[\Sigma_{i,j\in L} x_{ij}(C_{ij}/r_{ij})]^{\alpha} \tag{1}$$

where α is the computational complexity
Subject to :

$$\Sigma_{i,j\in L.}\, x_{ij}C_{ij}\leq B \tag{2}$$

$$0\leq x_{ij}\leq 1 \tag{3}$$

$$K[G(N,L-\{x_{ij}\}]=1,\ \forall\ x_{ij}\ \text{and}\ i,j\in L \tag{4}$$

The objective function (1) determines the reliable minimum cost graph. The constraint (2) ensures that the cost of the links must not exceed the given budget. The constraint (3) assures that when the link exists then value must be greater than 0.The constraint equation (4) ensures that the resulting graph must be connected and satisfy 1-FT.

3   Overview of Genetic Algorithm

Genetic Algorithm proposed by Holland [4] has been successfully applied to many problems. The basic idea of GA is to begin with some initial solutions [2-4]. Each initial solution is then evaluated to see whether it is a good solution or not. According to the objective function a fitness value is assigned to each solution. The recombination (crossover) of pair of solutions generates offspring. More fit solutions are selected for more number of times for crossover to produce new population, as they produce more fit solutions. And the least fit solution is deleted from matting population. All offsprings could be mutated with some probability. The offsprings are then evaluated to see how good they fit into the mating population, thus replacing their parents to create the next population. The process is repeated until the termination criteria are reached. The design of a GA consists mainly of 6 tasks:

1. Formulation of the fitness function.
2. Representation of a solution point
3. Generation of the initial population
4. Design of genetic operators
5. Determination of the probabilities for the genetic operators
6. Definition of the termination criterion

4   Genetic Algorithmic Approach

As in any optimization based on GA, the method never deals with the actual solution rather this is concerned with a coded form of the solution point. The encoded form of the solution is known as *chromosome* in GA. In the whole optimization *process*, initially a population of solution points is generated randomly, with maintaining the constraints (i.e. the cost-constraint and the FT- constraint). Now all the solution points in the initial population are valid solutions. After that using the solution points and applying the genetic operators generate the solution points for the next population.

This process of generating next-population is continued until an optimal solution is found out.

Lemma 1: In a 1-FT backbone layout, the degree of all nodes must be at least 2 [1].

4.1 Representation of a Solution Point

As we are presently dealing with only 1-FT topologies, our solution point at any point of time is basically a ring topology or graph (which is an optimal graph for any 1-FT topology). We represent the graph as a bit stream, which is the chromosome of the corresponding graph. This approach leads to a generalization of the representation of a solution point for any GA based approach.

Any Graph or topology can be represented in two ways: by *Adjacency List* and by *Adjacency Matrix*. In our algorithm, the encoding technique is based on the upper triangular part of the corresponding *Adjacency Matrix* of that layout or topology. By this approach we can also represent a topology with a K-FT constraint i.e. the topology will remain connected even on the failure of K links.

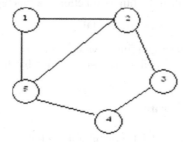

Fig. 1. A Graph for which the bit string will be generated

Let us take an example, the Adjacency Matrix for the graph or topology shown in figure1 is:

$$\begin{pmatrix} 0 & 1 & 0 & 0 & 1 \\ 1 & 0 & 1 & 0 & 1 \\ 0 & 1 & 0 & 1 & 0 \\ 0 & 0 & 1 & 0 & 1 \\ 1 & 1 & 0 & 0 & 0 \end{pmatrix}$$

Now the upper triangular part of the above Adjacency Matrix is (excluding the diagonal): 1001101101. In our entire GA method we consider each row of the above upper triangular matrix as a sub-string of the string representing the chromosome. The algorithm for the generation of a chromosome is as follows.

Procedure: ChromFromGraph

Step I: allocate a bit string with space N (N-1)/2 where N is the number of nodes in the corresponding graph.

Step II: set bitPositionCnt to 0.

Step III: for node i, 1 to N-1

Step IV: for node j, i+1 to N
           if edge exists between i and j
                set ChromRep [bitPositionCnt ++] to 1
      else
                ChromRep [bitPositionCnt ++] to 0
    End for
  End for
Step V. end procedure
We are representing the upper-triangular matrix of the graph in the chromosome thus reducing redundancy and increasing efficiency in space management.

4.2 Fitness Assignment

We have used a rank-based fitness assignment scheme, which sorts the population of chromosomes according to the cost of the topology. A linear ranking is used where ranks are assigned from 1 to n, where the chromosome with the highest cost is assigned the lowest rank and so on. Let the number of solution points in a single population be MAX_POP, then the fitness function is a function of rank position

$$f(r)=(r-1/N-1)F \tag{5}$$

where F is a pre-defined maximum fitness value.
The best-fit solution has f(r)=F and the least-fit solution has f(r)=0

4.3 Initial Population Generation

As we are dealing here with 1-FT graphs, our initial population is a set of ring topologies. And in any ring topology the number of links is $|N|$ (which in minimum). The algorithm for construction of a ring is given as follows.
Procedure: GenerateInitialPopulation
1. Randomly select a node from the node set N
2. Check the selected node in an array of nodes representing the already selected nodes to see if it has been pre-selected
    If yes, go to step 1
    Else go to step 3
3. Store the selected node as the next element of the array
4. Repeat until all the nodes are selected
5. Make the last element of the array same as the first element
6. Then convert the array-represented graph to the chromosome format
7. end Procedure

4.4 Selection of Matting Population

In any GA Roulette-wheel selection is the most widely used selection criterion. The algorithms are as follows.

Procedure: MakeRouletteWheel
1. Prepare a Roulette-wheel with Σr f(r)*(MAX_POP-1)
2. For each solution p with rank position r, allocate f(r)*(MAX_POP-1) slices for it
3. End Procedure

Procedure: SelectMatingPopulation
1. Call MakeRouletteWheel to create a Roulette-wheel
2. Randomly select (MAX_POP) slices from the Roulette-wheel. Use the index of these slices to find the corresponding solution points; add these into matting population. Always add the solution with the highest fitness value into the matting population
3. End Procedure

4.5 Crossover

In our method, the chromosome consists of (N-1) sub-strings where each sub-string represents each row of the corresponding upper-triangular adjacency matrix for the graph. The length of the ith sub string is (N-i). The ith substring represents the link between the ith node and the remaining nodes (i+1 to N). So length of the chromosome is N(N-1)/2. Then we proceed to do crossover. In the algorithm of optimization we require problem specific crossover technique. Any topology which is a ring must have minimal number of links i.e. |N|, where |N| is the number of nodes in the topology. The crossover technique we have used is based on the selection of two sub-strings (i.e., i^{th}) from two chromosomes those have equal numbers of 1s but not all in same positions. Then we swapped them (i.e., the sub-strings). This approach helps us for maintaining the 1-FT constraint. In any ring topology the minimal number of link is established among all nodes of the topology that the degrees of all nodes are exactly 2. After crossover the number of links are also minimal (as we are swapping equal number of 1s between two chromosomes) in the child population but their orientation may be in such a way that the degrees of all the nodes may not be equal to 2 i.e., the topology may not be a 1-FT (rather a ring). To make it 1-FT we may require calling the routine Make_1FT for child chromosomes. Another routine Check_1FT is used to checking for a chromosome to determine whether it is a 1-FT layout or not. The algorithm for crossover is as follows.

Procedure: DoCrossover
1. Select 2 chromosomes from the mating population
2. Leave the last sub string of both the chromosomes (which is of length 1)
3. Starting from the right cruise to left for each chromosome- searching for the ith sub-string pairs (1 from each chromosome) which have equal number of 1s but all not in same position
4. Swap these sub-strings to give the child chromosome, which becomes the part of the new population
5. end procedure

4.6 Check 1-FT and Make 1-FT

In order to maintain the 1-FT constraint, each new chromosome which contends to be the part of the new population has to be checked for 1-FT, and if not found to satisfy the constraint, has to be made into 1-FT.

Algorithm for checking 1-FT: *Procedure: Check_1FT*
1. Let the number of nodes be N
2. Initialize an array of node_values to 0
3. for i 1 to N-1
        for j 1 to N-i
            if link exists between i and i+j nodes
                (i.e., the bit in the jth position of the
                i^{th} sub-string is set in the chromosome)
            then increment node_value[i] and node_value[i+j] by 1;
        end for
    end for
4. The graph is 1-FT if all the node values are at least 2
5. End Procedure

This algorithm can also be used for checking K-FT graph where all the node values must be at least K+1. If the chromosome is not in 1-FT then we have to make it so in order to conform to the closure property. The algorithm for Make_1FT is as follows.

Procedure: Make_1FT
1. Pass chromosome thorough the previous algorithm to find degrees of the nodes, where the array node_value represents the degree of each node
2. If node i has degree < 2
        search for node k with highest degree greater than 2
        redirect an edge from k to the node i
3. If degree of i ≥2
        goto step 4
  Else
        goto step 2
4.end procedure

4.7 Closure Property

The crossover operation we have applied has the closure property: the resulted graphs after applying crossover (including Check_1FT and Make_1FT) are always 1_FT.The crossover takes input from the legal search space and generates output in the legal search space. A crossover function does not have the closure property, would generate invalid solutions. Extra efforts would require checking and removing these solutions from the population. Consequently, much computation time is wasted in handling the illegal solutions and the performance degrades [1].

4.8 Complete Algorithm

The complete algorithm for topological optimization is given as follows.

Procedure: GAForTopologicalOptimization
1. Call GenerateInitialPopulation MAX_POP numbers of times to generate the initial population
2. Compute the link costs and fitness values of all the solution points and keep the best-fit solution as the BestSolution
3. Do until the termination criterion is met
      3.1. Call SelectMatingPopulation to select MAX_POP mating solution
      3.2. Do until MAX_POP number of new solution is generated for next population
          Call DoCrossover
                Check for budget-constraint of the new population
                    If budget-constraint is not met
                          Return to do do_crossover
                Compute the fitness values of all solution points in the new population
                Take the best-fit solution point from it as the BestSolution
      End Do
4. Output best solution
5. End procedure

5   Example

This example illustrates the problem formulation and one iteration of the GA we have used. The example network topology consists of 5 nodes. The link cost matrix is:

$$\begin{pmatrix} 0 & 79 & 92 & 81 & 67 \\ 79 & 0 & 71 & 42 & 92 \\ 92 & 71 & 0 & 69 & 92 \\ 81 & 42 & 69 & 0 & 73 \\ 67 & 92 & 92 & 73 & 0 \end{pmatrix}$$

Let the number of solution points in a population i.e. MAX_POP=3. Therefore, our initial population is as follows:

Chromosome	Cost	Rank	Fitness value
$S_1^1 \equiv 0011101100$	380	1	0.000000
$S_2^1 \equiv 0011110010$	353	3	10.000000
$S_3^1 \equiv 1001100101$	359	2	3.000000

BestSolution is solution no 2 and its cost = 353. The corresponding graph for all the 3 solution points is given in Figure 5.

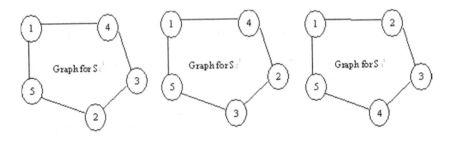

Fig. 2. 1-FT graph generated by GenerateInitialPopulation() in the Initial Population

The total link cost for $S_1^1 = 380, S_2^1 = 359, S_3^1 = 353$, and the BestSolution is set to S_3^1. For crossover we selected two solution points S_2^1 and S_3^1, and according to the algorithm of DoCrossover the sub-string selected for crossover is the 3rd one. So after crossover the chromosomes will be: $S_1^2 \equiv 0011110001$ and $\overline{S}_2^2 \equiv 1001100011$. By checking both chromosomes through the procedure Check_1FT we found that both the graphs are not 1-FT, so we have pass them to Make_1FT.The corresponding graph for the chromosomes are shown in Figure 3.

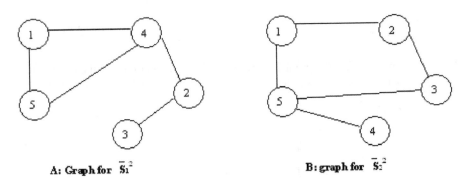

A: Graph for $\overline{S}_1^2$ B: graph for $\overline{S}_2^2$

Fig. 3. The graph after Crossover

In Make_1FT procedure, in the graph $\overline{S}_1^2$ the link (1,4) is selected as the changing link, and in graph $\overline{S}_2^2$, (1,2) link is selected. By redirecting the link (1,4) to (3,4) we get a 1-FT graph, and same for graph $\overline{S}_2^2$ the link(1,2)is redirected as (1,4) resulting a 1-FT graph. Thus, the graphs S_1^2 and S_2^2 after invoke of Make_1FT is shown in Fig-4.

It is clear from the Figure 4 that both the graph is 1-FT. And the corresponding chromosomes are: 0101110001 and 1010100011.The costs are 334 and 409 respectively. Therefore the solutions are: $S_1^2 \equiv 0101110001$ 334 and $S_2^2 \equiv 1010100011$ 409. These two solution points are added to the new population. It is clear that in the 1st iteration the cost has been reduced and the 1-FT constraints have also been

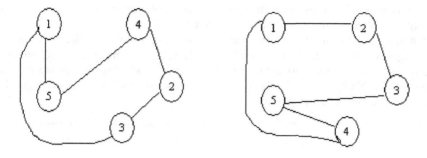

Fig. 4. Graph by the procedure Make_1FT() after making it 1-FT

maintained. Another solution point is: $S_2^3 \equiv 0011110010$ 353. Therefore the next population is:

Chromosome	Cost	Rank	Fitness value
$S_1^2 \equiv 0101110001$	334	3	10.000000
$S_2^2 \equiv 1010100011$	409	1	0.000000
$S_3^2 \equiv 0011110010$	353	2	3.000000

Hence, the BestSolution = S_1^2.This is not the final solution, but the BestSolution in iteration 1.Through the higher iteration better solution points can be find out easily.

6 Simulation Results

The reliable backbone layout we have obtained is entirely by simulation. The simulation program generates various network backbone layout problems; each is characterized by |N|, and the link-cost matrix. The simulation parameters are:
Population size: 50 (for 21≤|N|≤50), 100 (for |N|= 100)
Range of fitness-value = 10
Maximum number of Iteration for termination =300
Maximum link cost =100
Minimum link cost = 30
Set of possible values for |N| = {5,6, 8,10,20,50,100}
Link costs are randomly generated in between 30 to 100 with uniform distribution. The crossover technique we have used never increases the number of links in the whole network. The thing we have done is changed the orientation of the links in such a way that the 1-FT constraint is maintained. Since, the total number of links in the whole network is minimum thus we need not require the Genetic operator mutation. But we can select the link, whose direction is to be changed for making the backbone layout 1-FT, is the link with the minimum cost among all the links we can select for re-direction. The termination criterion is when the algorithm stays on a local optimum

for a certain number of iteration (It means no better solution can be found out and the algorithm converges, in our simulations we set this parameter as 120). The number of iteration is set by simulation parameter. According to the simulation results, it converges within 100 iterations (for |N|≤100). But for confirming that the solution is converges to an optimum, we set maximum iteration as 300. Figure 5 shows the total link-cost for N=50 and N=100 explicitly, and also shows how fast the algorithm converges to a local optimum.

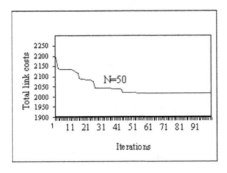 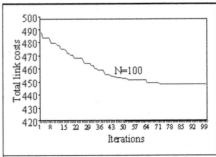

Fig. 5. Cost Optimization found by our algorithm

Our optimization converges quite fast, because of following reasons:
- The crossover technique we have used searches solution with more efficient fitness values at each iteration
- The population sizes, we have set in the simulations are quite large; so in each iteration it was possible to find out more solution points. Thus, reducing the number of iterations required converging to an optimum
- The crossover technique, used in the optimization algorithm satisfies the closure property. Hence, there is no need for rejecting any solution point

7   Conclusion

The optimization algorithm, based on Genetic Algorithm can be extended to solve the topological optimization problem subjected K-fault tolerances. The Genetic operator crossover does not require any changes for the application of K-fault tolerance problem. The operators like Check_FT and Make_1FT will require small changes to make them Check_KFT and Make_KFT. In Check_1FT the value against which we are checking the degrees of each node are changed from 2 (for 1-FT) to K+1 (for K-FT, as the degree of each node in any K-FT graph must be greater than equal to K+1).But a systematic way of randomly generating initial K-FT solutions is essential. Through extensive simulation we have shown that the algorithm for this design of backbone layout can produce a sub-optimal solution in a time-effective way. And the convergence criterion is also very simple.

Notations

G a Graph
1-FT Fault Tolerant to 1 link failure.
I Index Set
N set of nodes
L set of links
B total budgets
|N| number of nodes in N
C_{ij} cost of link i,j where i,j $\in$ L
x_{ij} link between i,j where i,j$\in$ L
x_{ij} = 1   when link exists between i and j
   = 0 otherwise
r_{ij} reliability of link i,j$\in$ L
G(N,L) graph with N and L
1[.] 1[True]=1, 1[False]=0
k[G(N,L)] 1[G(N,L)is connected]
MAX_POP number of solution points in one population
r rank of a solution point
f(r) fitness value of a solution point

References

1. Sheng-Tzong Cheng, "Topological Optimization of a Reliable Communication Network", IEEE Transactions on Reliability, vol-47, no-3, 1998.
2. J.E. Baker, "Adaptive selection method for genetic algorithm", Proc. Int'l Conf. Genetic Algorithm, 1985, pp. 101–111.
3. D.E. Goldberg, Genetic Algorithms in Search, Optimization and Machine Learning, 1989; Addison-Wesley.
4. J.H. Holland, "Adaptation in natural and artificial systems", 1975, Univ. Michigan Press.
5. K.K. Aggarwal, et.al., "Topological layout of links for optimization the s-t reliability in a computer communication system", Microelectronics and Reliability 1982, pp 341–45
6. K.K. Aggarwal, et.al., "Topological layout of links for optimization the overall reliability in a computer communication system, Microelectronics and Reliability 1982, pp 347–351
7. Y.C Chhopra, et. al., "Network topology for maximizing the terminal reliability in a computer communication network", Microelectronics and Reliability 1984, pp 911–13
8. S. Klu, D.F. McAllister, "Reliability optimization of computer communication networks", IEEE Trans Reliability 1988, pp 475–83
9. IM Soi, KK Aggarwal, "Reliability indices for topological design of computer communication networks", IEEE Trans Reliability 1981
10. RH Jan, et. al., "Topological optimization of a communication network subject to a reliability constraint", IEEE Trans Reliability 1993, pp 63–70
11. A N Venetsanopoulos, et. al, " Topological optimization of communication networks subject to reliability constraints", Problem of Control and Information Theory 1986, pp 63–78

Approximating the Range Sum of a Graph on CREW PRAM

Saurabh Srivastava and Phalguni Gupta

Department of Computer Science & Engineering,
Indian Institute of Technology Kanpur,
Kanpur 208 016, INDIA
{srivs,pg}@iitk.ac.in

Abstract. In this paper we have studied the problem of finding the range sum of a graph $G = < V, E >$ which is to color the vertices of a graph with ranges from a specified set in such a way that adjacent vertices are colored with non-overlapping ranges and the sum of the lengths of the ranges is the maximum possible. The problem of finding a good approximation to the range sum is often encountered in many engineering problems. We have presented an efficient parallel algorithm for computing an approximate solution to the range sum problem of a graph on CREW PRAM.

1 Introduction

The problem of graph coloring is a well studied problem and is to assign colors to vertices in a graph $G = < V, E >$ such that adjacent vertices have different colors. Perhaps it was originally encountered in relation to map-coloring and has been found of much interest due to its applicability in numerous other problem domains. Some important instances where the problem has been encountered are time tabling and scheduling [3], frequency assignment [4], register allocation [5] etc. There exist various other modified versions of this problem. With regard to code assignment problem in next generation wireless networks, we have encountered a new variant of this problem termed as the *range sum* of a graph. To compute the range coloring of a graph, we color the vertices with ranges, taken from a specified set in such a way that adjacent vertices do not have any overlap in their assignment. The range sum problem is to find a coloring with the maximum possible sum. It is found that this problem has numerous other applications in domains where spatial location determines the way of assignments to be done.

In [6] it has been shown that finding the range sum of a general graph is an NP-Complete problem. Further, for large graphs it is computationally intensive and requires a large amount of resources. Therefore it is worth-while to design an efficient parallel algorithm for finding a good approximation to the range sum and to analyse its complexity.

In this paper we have proposed an approach to parallelize the sequential greedy algorithm into a scalable parallel range coloring algorithm for general

S.K. Das and S. Bhattacharya (Eds.): IWDC 2002, LNCS 2571, pp. 312–318, 2002.
© Springer-Verlag Berlin Heidelberg 2002

graphs. The basic approach behind the parallelization is to reduce the problem size in such a way that each individual sub-problem can be solved efficiently in parallel. But doing so results in a coloring which might not be proper and hence we may need to process the solution obtained further to yield a proper range coloring. An analysis on the CREW PRAM yields a time complexity which is a linear speedup to the sequential algorithm when the number of processors is upper bounded by $\frac{|V|}{\sqrt{2|E|}}$, which holds in practical situations when the input graphs are relatively sparse.

The rest of the paper is organized as follows. Preliminary material and various notations used in the paper are discussed in Section 2. The parallel algorithm along with its analysis has been proposed in Section 3. Conclusions are given in the last section.

2   Preliminaries & Notations

A coloring of a graph is called *proper* if no two adjacent vertices share the same color. The *chromatic number* of a graph is defined to be be the minimum number of colors which are required to achieve a proper coloring of the graph from the set of natural numbers. The *chromatic sum* [7] of a graph is the minimum sum of the colors of the vertices over all colorings of the graph with natural numbers.

The order of an undirected graph $G =< V, E >$ with the set of V vertices and E edges is the number of vertices, $|V|$ while the size of the graph is the number of edges, $|E|$, in the graph G. Further, let Δ and $\bar{\delta}$ denote the maximum and average degree of the graph.

Consider the problem of finding the range sum of a graph as introduced in [6]. Instead of coloring the nodes with colors from the set of natural numbers as is the case in the chromatic number and chromatic sum problem, the vertices are colored with ranges which are obtained by equally subdividing the line segment $[0, 1)$ recursively into σ equal parts in such a way that no two adjacent nodes are colored with ranges having a non zero intersection. More formally, the sets $R_\sigma(k)$ with parameters σ, k may be defined recursively as follows

$$R_\sigma(k + 1) = \left\{ \left[l(r) + (t - 1) * \frac{|r|}{\sigma}, \ l(r) + t * \frac{|r|}{\sigma} \right) \mid 1 \leq t \leq \sigma, \ \forall r \in R_\sigma(k) \right\}$$

with $R_\sigma(0) = \{[0, 1)\}$ where $l(r)$ denotes the left end of the range r. The ith element of $R_\sigma(k)$ is referred as $R_\sigma(k, i)$ and the set of $R_\sigma(k)$'s is denoted by $\Re_\sigma$ i.e. $\Re_\sigma = \lim_{k \to \infty} \bigcup_{i=0}^{k} R_\sigma(k)$.

Figure 1 illustrates graphically the hierarchical organization of the range set $\Re_2$. Overlapping ranges are connected to form a complete binary tree. The set $R(i)$ corresponds to the ith level in this *range tree*. The parameter σ which is 2 in this case may be considered as the degree of branching of this range tree.

A proper *range coloring* of a graph $G =< V, E >$ with vertex set V and edge set E is a coloring of the nodes such that adjacent nodes are being colored with non-intersecting ranges from $\Re_\sigma$; i.e. define $r : V \to \Re_\sigma$ such that $r(u) \cap r(v) = \phi$ whenever $(u, v) \in E$. Further, the *Range Sum* of the graph G, $\Gamma_\sigma(G)$, is defined

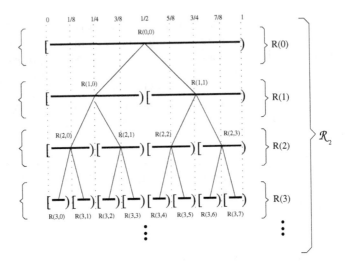

Fig. 1. The range tree for $\sigma = 2$

to be the maximum sum of the lengths of ranges over all proper range colorings of G.

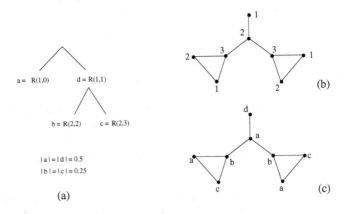

Fig. 2. (a) Part of the range tree for $\sigma = 2$ (b) An example graph and its chromatic sum coloring (c) The range sum coloring requires 4 ranges.

Consider for instance the problem of finding the range sum for the graph in Figure 2. It can be easily seen that the chromatic number of the graph is 3 and the chromatic sum is 15 which is obtained by the coloring shown in Figure 2(b). But for achieving the range sum of 3.0 we require an additional range (labelled as 'd' in the figure) and the coloring is shown in Figure 2(c).

For the family of sparse graphs with average degree $\bar{\delta}$ there exists a greedy algorithm in [6] which generates a proper range coloring $r : V \rightarrow \Re_\sigma$ for an undirected graph $G =< V, E >$ having σ ranges. For each node $v \in V$ the algorithm computes $r(v)$, the range (*color*) to be assigned to the vertex v and *Unused(v)*, the subset of $[0, 1)$ not being used to color any node u adjacent to v; or more formally, $Unused(v) = [0, 1) - \bigcup_{\forall u;(u,v) \in E} r(u)$. For the ith range in the lexicographic ordering on the index, let $Range_\sigma(i)$ be used to denote (k, t), of the ranges in $\Re_\sigma$. For the vertex v the algorithm first finds the least value of t satisfying the following

1. $Range_\sigma(t) \cap Unused(v) = Range_\sigma(t)$
2. $Unused(u) - Range_\sigma(t) \neq \phi, \quad \forall u$ and
3. $(u, v) \in E$ and $r(u) = \phi$

Then it colors v with $Range_\sigma(t)$, i.e $r(v) = Range_\sigma(t)$ and then updates $Unused(u)$ to $Unused(u) - r(v_r) \forall u, (u, v_r) \in E$. The algorithm continues the above process until all the vertices are assigned with some color. It is shown that the algorithm finds a $\sigma^{\frac{\sigma+d}{\sigma-1}}$-approximation to the range sum of G. For the special case of $\sigma = 2$ we can get a better bound of $2^{1+\bar{d}}$.

3   Approximate Parallel Range Sum Algorithm

In this section we present a parallel algorithm for finding an approximate solution to the range sum problem and analyse its performance on the CREW PRAM. The underlying principle used here is that of block partitioning the problem instance into subproblems which is equal to the number of processors available for computation and solving the ensuing subproblems. We arbitrarily partition the set of vertices into equal blocks (at most one block containing less vertices than the others) and color each of these blocks in parallel. Since the partitioning is arbitrary there may be edges between vertices in different blocks and hence the subproblems defined by each block may not be independant and the solutions computed by this trivial parallelization may have to be processed further to obtain a valid range coloring for the graph.

The algorithm consists of three major stages. In the first stage, the input vertex set V of the input graph $G =< V, E >$ is partitioned into p blocks where p is the number of processors, as $\{V_1, \ldots V_p\}$ such that $|V_i| = \left\lceil \frac{n}{p} \right\rceil, 1 \leq i \leq p-1$ and $|V_p| = n - (p-1) \left\lceil \frac{n}{p} \right\rceil$. The vertices in each block are then colored in parallel using the available p processors. The parallel range coloring comprises of $\left\lceil \frac{n}{p} \right\rceil$ parallel steps and proceeds with synchronization which is achieved via barriers at the end of each step. When coloring a vertex *all* its neighbors, both the ones in the local block and the ones in other blocks, are taken into account. This may result in two processors accessing and trying to find a range for a pair of vertices that are adjacent. Such vertices may be colored with ranges which are overlapping and hence we call the range coloring obtained after this first stage a *partial range coloring*. To produce a valid coloring from this partial range coloring we construct a table, called the *Conflict-Table*, of the vertices that need to be colored again. This is done in parallel in Stage 2 of the algorithm in which all the processors examine in $\left\lceil \frac{n}{p} \right\rceil$ parallel steps each of the vertices colored in the corresponding step in the previous stage. Then at the final stage the vertices in the conflict table are recolored using the sequential greedy algorithm. The complete pseudo code for the parallel coloring procedure is given below.

Stage 0:

For each vertex v,

Maintain unused(v), portions of the segment $(0,1]$

that cannot be used by it, i.e., the union of

all ranges being used by its neighbors

Partition the vertex set V into p equal blocks $V_1 \ldots$

V_p such that $|V_i| = \left\lceil \frac{n}{p} \right\rceil$, $1 \le i \le p-1$ and

$|V_p| = n - (p-1) \left\lceil \frac{n}{p} \right\rceil$

Stage 1:

for $i = 1$ to p do in parallel

for each $v_j \in V_i$ do

Assign the largest range, r, such that

unused(v) $\cap$ r $=$ r and

unused(u) $-$ r $\ne \phi$ for any neighbor u

Update unused(u) for all neighbors u

Barrier synchronize

endfor

endfor

Stage 2:

for $i = 1$ to p do in parallel

for each $v \in V_i$ do

for each pair of neighbors u and v that are colored

in the same parallel step in Stage 1 do

if range(u) $\cap$ range(v) $\ne \phi$ then

Store min(u,v) in Conflict-Table

endfor

endfor

endfor

Stage 3:

Proper color the vertices in Conflict-Table using

the sequential greedy range color algorithm.

Algorithm 1: Computing the range sum of a graph in parallel

3.1   Analysis

Without loss of generality we assume that n/p, the number vertices per processors, is an integer. Let the vertices on each processor be numbered from 1 to n/p and the parallel time used for coloring in Stage 1 of the algorithm be divided into n/p time slots. We call the number of pairs of vertices which are colored with overlapping ranges as the number of collisions generated by Stage 1 of the algorithm. Since it is entirely possible that the number of collisions to be the maximum possible, i.e. n/p, hence we do not look at the worst case scenario and instead concentrate on the expected number of collisions.

Assuming that the number of neighbors of v are randomly distributed, the expected number of neighbors that are simultaneously colored at time unit t is $\frac{p-1}{n-1} degree(v)$. To get an upper bound on the number of total collisions we sum over all vertices in the input graph. But doing so we count each collision twice, once for each end of the pair. Moreover each term of the sum will only be a real collision only if the processors choose the same range, hence the sum is an upper bound on the expected number of collisions. Evaluating the sum, we have

$$E[\# of collisions] = \frac{1}{2} \sum \frac{p-1}{n-1} degree(v) = \frac{1}{2} \times \frac{p-1}{n-1} \times 2|E|$$

Since the average degree of the graph, $\bar{\delta}$ and the degree of each vertex, is $2|E|/n$, therefore the above sum can be approximately be written as $0.5\bar{\delta}(p-1)$.

The time complexity of the algorithm is computed by summing the time required by each stage. Both the first two parallel stages consists of n/p steps, with each step in the worst case requiring time proportional to the maximum possible number of neighbors of a vertex, i.e. Δ. The running time of the last stage of the algorithm depends upon the number of collisions created by the first stage and hence the *expected* time required by it is $O(\Delta \frac{p-1}{n-1}|E|)$, which can be approximated to $O(\Delta p \bar{\delta})$ when n is large and $n \approx n-1$. Hence, the overall expected time complexity of the algorithm is $O(\Delta n/p) + O(\Delta n/p) + O(\Delta p \bar{\delta}) = O(\Delta(n/p + p\bar{\delta}))$.

A simple analysis of the the term $(n/p + p\bar{\delta})$ leads us to observe that for $p \leq \frac{n}{\sqrt{2|E|}}$ the term n/p dominates and the expected time complexity of the algorithm is $O(\Delta n/p)$ which is a linear speedup to the sequential algorithm. This condition can be seen to be satisfied for most graphs that are reasonably sparse, which the case for most real-life scenarios.

Since in our algorithm a vertex is never colored simultaneously by different processors and hence we do not require concurrent write capabilities in our model of parallel computation. But each vertex might be accessed by multiple processors simutaneously since it might be adjacent to many vertices which are being colored in some time step. Hence, our algorithm works on a CREW PRAM.

4 Conclusions

We have presented an approximate parallel algorithm for the range sum problem of a general graph on a CREW PRAM. The algorithm runs in $O(\Delta n/p)$ expected time when the number of processors is bounded above by $\frac{|V|}{\sqrt{2|E|}}$.

References

1. L. V. Kale, Ben Richards, and Terry Allen. Efficient parallel graph coloring with prioritization. Lecture Notes in Computer Science, 1996.
2. Gary Lewandowski and Anne Condon, Experiments with parallel graph coloring heuristics and applications of graph coloring, Cliques, Coloring, and Satisfiability: Second {DIMACS} Implementation Challenge, pp. 309–334, 1993.
3. Gary Lewandowski. Practical Implementations and Applications of Graph Coloring. PhD thesis, University of Wisconsin-Madison, August 1994.
4. Andreas Gamst. Some lower bounds for a class of frequency assignment problems. IEEE Transactions on Vehicular Technology, 35(1):8–14, 1986.
5. G.J. Chaitin, M. Auslander, A. K. Chandra, J. Cocke, M.E. Hopkins and P. Markstein. Register Allocation via coloring. Computer Languages, 6:47–57, 1981.
6. S. Srivastava, S. Tripathi. Resource Optimization in CDMA based Wireless Ad Hoc Networks. BTP Report 2001–2002, Department of Computer Science and Engineering, IIT Kanpur.
7. Ewa Kubicka and A. J. Schwenk, An Introduction to Chromatic Sums, Proc. of ACM Computer Science Conference, pp. 39–45, 1989.
8. Assefaw Hadish Gebremedhin and Fredrik Manne. Scalable Parallel Graph Coloring Algorithms, Concurrency: Pract. Exper. 2000, 12:1131–1146.
9. Gjertsen, R. K., Jr., M. T. Jones, P. E. Plassmann. 1996. Parallel Heuristics for Improved, Balanced Graph Colorings. Journal of Parallel and Distributed Computing 37:171–186.
10. Magnús M. Halldórsson. Parallel and on-line graph coloring. Journal of Algorithms, 23(2):265–280, May 1997.

Design and Implementation of a Soft Real Time Fault Tolerant System

Surajit Dutta[1], Sudip Dutta[2], Riddhi Burman[3], Mridul Sankar Barik[4],
and Chandan Mazumdar[4]

[1] Cognizant Technologies Solutions, Kolkata, India
surajit_dutta@rediffmail.com
[2] Tata Consultancy Services, Thiruvananthpuram, India
sudipju@yahoo.com
[3] Indian Institute of Management, Ahmedabad, India
[4] Department of Computer Science and Engineering, Jadavpur University, Kolkata, India
b_mridul@hotmail.com, chandanm@vsnl.com

Abstract. The increasing trend in use of computer systems in safety critical applications has driven the researchers to develop techniques to achieve high degree of fault tolerance. In mission critical applications like banking, satellite launching etc. a single failure may incur huge monitory loss. So far numerous techniques have been developed to impart fault tolerance in computer systems. Dual redundant systems are widely used in applications where fault tolerance is required. Although there are commercially available dual redundant fault tolerant systems, high cost and lack of customizability of those systems render them unusable in some cases. In this paper we present an implementation of a dual redundant system using low cost off-the-shelf personal computers.

1 Introduction

Computer systems are increasingly becoming an integral part of every information-processing system. Such systems may range from multimedia applications to computer systems performing mission-critical tasks. In many cases, loss of information or incorrect information, or hardware failures cannot be tolerated during operational lifetime. Some examples of such areas are banking systems, flight control systems, monitoring systems in hospitals, missile launching and control systems, air traffic control systems etc.

Systems that require a pipeline of processing modules interlinked with each other for data exchange are prone to link failures and device failures. Failures in such systems can lead to catastrophe in terms of money, property or human life. Hence in such areas, highly dependable systems are needed. Once deployed such systems should be able to tolerate foreseeable faults, and maintain a minimum performance level throughout its working lifetime. In case of failure, such systems should fail in a predictable manner, which is deemed safe in the operating environment.

S.K. Das and S. Bhattacharya (Eds.): IWDC 2002, LNCS 2571, pp. 319–328, 2002.

One way of achieving high degree of reliability for mission-critical systems is to design the system to be fault tolerant. Such a system would be able to function correctly even when some of its hardware/software components malfunction or fail. This is achieved using redundant hardware and/or software components in the system.

In this paper we present the design and implementation of a dual redundant fault tolerant system on the Linux platform using off-the-shelf PCs.

2   Fault Tolerant Systems

A *fault tolerant system* is one that can continue the correct performance of its specified tasks in the presence of hardware and/or software systems [1,2].

Fault tolerance is used to increase the system reliability and availability by introducing redundancy in a system in terms of hardware, software, information or time.

The concept of fault tolerance implies the presence of redundant components that come into play when a fault occurs. This requires addition of information, resources, or time beyond what is needed for normal system operation. The redundancy can take one of the several forms, including hardware redundancy, software redundancy, information redundancy and time redundancy. We will be primarily focusing on hardware redundancy.

Hardware redundancy is achieved by physical replication of hardware. There are three basic forms of hardware redundancy [2].

Active Redundancy: Active techniques use the concept of fault masking to hide the occurrence of faults and prevent faults from resulting in errors. Active approaches are designed to achieve fault tolerance without requiring any action on the system or an operator. They usually do not provide for detection of faults but simply mask faults.

Passive Redundancy: The second form of redundancy is the passive approach. Passive methods achieve fault tolerance by detecting the existence of faults and performing some action to remove the faulty hardware component from the system. Passive redundancy uses fault detection, fault location, and fault recovery in an attempt to achieve fault tolerance.

Hybrid Redundancy: The final form of hardware redundancy is the hybrid approach. Hybrid techniques combine the attractive features of both passive and active approaches. Fault masking is used in hybrid systems to prevent erroneous results from being generated. Fault detection, fault location, fault recovery are also used to improve fault tolerance, by removing faulty hardware and replacing them with spares. Hybrid methods are most often used in critical-computation applications where fault masking is required to prevent momentary errors, and high reliability must be achieved. This form of redundancy is usually very expensive form of redundancy to implement.

In the next section we discuss about a dual redundant fault tolerant system that uses active redundancy.

3 Dual Redundant Fault Tolerant System

In many real-life/practical situations, there is a need for a command chain consisting of various decision-making computer systems. A conventional command/decision chain layout is shown in Figure 1.

Here R_a, R_b, R_c are successive nodes in a command/decision chain hierarchy. However if any one device or link in the command chain fails the entire command chain may be affected leading to systems failure. In critical applications or command systems such failures are undesirable and the system should be able to continue with one or more links or devices failing [6].

For situations mentioned above, we propose a *fault tolerant soft real-time command chain*, using hardware redundancy. At each level in the hierarchy of the command/decision chain, the failure of at least one link, or device should not affect the system performance and the system should have a high degree of reliability.

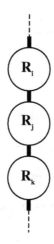

Fig. 1. Conventional Command Chain

A fault detection mechanism used in active redundancy is the duplication with comparison method. The basic concept of duplication with comparison scheme is to develop two identical pieces of hardware, have them perform the same computations in parallel, compare the results of these computations. In the event of a disagreement, an error message is generated. In its most basic form, the duplication concept cannot tolerate faults but can only detect them because there is no method for determining which of the two modules is faulty.

In our implementation we have introduced hardware redundancy to each node in the command chain. Each node consists of two computer systems that are replicas of each other. The proposed layout is shown in Figure 2. We now term each node in the command chain as fault tolerant dual redundant node. Replicas of one such node are connected to replicas of the other node in the command chain. Also there is a connection between replicas within the same node.

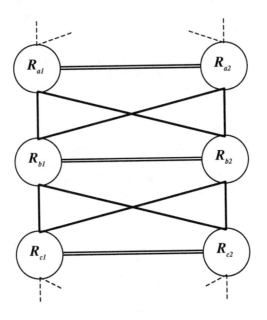

Fig. 2. Dual redundant command chain

This fault tolerant command chain achieves two goals, which are

1. The system continues to function even when one link fails at each command level.
2. The system continues to function even when one device fails at each command level.

At each level each of the two systems can exchange messages with each other as well as send receive messages to each of the nodes both above and below them in the command chain. The peer level communication should also be in a redundant manner, however for demonstration purposes only one communication link is provided.

Thus even if one link fails or one system or node fails, the system can function according to its specification, since there are alternative paths for data exchange, via the healthy links (in case of link failure) or the healthy node (in case of node failure).

4 Implementation

The two replicas at each level of the command chain is an off-the-shelf personal computer running Linux operating system. Each replica has its own keyboard, mouse as input devices and VDU as output device, and communicates with nodes of other level via serial links. Each replica within a level also has a 10/100Mbps Ethernet card for communicating with its peer.

4.1 Software Architecture

In order to make the development of application software independent of the fault tolerance aspects, the total software has been developed using a layered approach. The software in each of the nodes is divided into four layers as shown in Fig 3.

Presentation Layer: This layer consists of a GUI (Graphical User Interface) server process and a keyboard handler process. This layer serves the requests from the application layer. It also captures the keyboard/mouse data and sends them as messages to the application layer.

Presentation Layer
Application Layer
Fault Tolerant Layer
Communication Layer

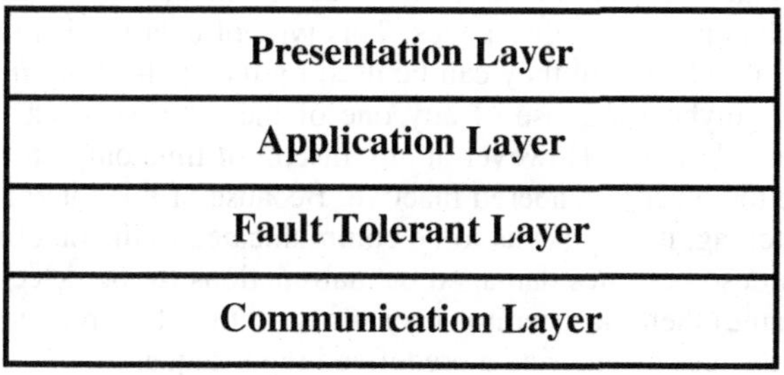

Fig. 3. Software architecture

Application Layer: In each level in the command chain, identical copies of an application process run on both the replicas. This application process directly communicates with the GUI server for user interaction. When the application receives some command from a higher-level node or requires sending some computed data to other level, it does so via the fault tolerant layer.

Fault Tolerant Layer: This layer is responsible for providing fault tolerance services to the application layer. Functioning of this layer is detailed in the next section.

Communication Layer: This layer consists of processes those are responsible for the data communication through serial links (between two levels in the command chain) and the Ethernet link (between the two replicas within a level).

4.2 Design of the Fault Tolerant Layer

The fault tolerant layer consists of the processes for the fault tolerant transmission and reception of data between two levels in the command chain. The present design uses a two-phase fault tolerant protocol.

During reception of data, replicas within a node receive data from replicas of other node and compare them locally in the first phase. The results of this comparison are exchanged between the replicas. In the second phase, the results of this local match are compared by each of replicas. This phase ensures that the applications at the two replicas move to similar states.

During transmission of data from one node to another, the data from the two replicas within the source node are compared and are sent to the replicas of the destination node if they match. In the second phase, the results of the transmission attempts are compared and the application process is notified about the status of the transmission. This second phase ensures that the applications at the two replicas move to the similar states.

4.2.1 Input Agreement

The data that come to a dual redundant node can be of two types. *External input* data are those, which come from other nodes. This type of data needs to be agreed by the two replicas of a node before they can be used by the application. *Internal input* data comes from the keyboard/mouse of any one of the replicas. Both the replicas have their own keyboard/mouse. However at any instant of time only one keyboard/mouse is active, while the other is rendered inactive. Because of this internal input data does not require matching, it only needs to be communicated to the other replica. If one of the keyboard/mouse becomes damaged or malfunctions (to be detected by the operator using the same) then the operator may move to the other replica and activate the replica's input devices by entering a predefined input sequence.

Table 1. Generation of local match message

Local Match Status	Description
m0	Messages are valid, data contents match
m1	Messages are valid, data contents do not match
m$	One or both messages do not arrive or are not valid

External input data agreement is done in two phases.

Phase I: Each replica of a node receives data from replicas of the other node. Then each replica generates a local match status after validating and comparing the content of the received data. The replicas then exchange the two local match status.

The local match status is generated as given in Table1.

Phase II: Now each replica has two local match status. One generated by itself (LMS$_{own}$) and another from its replica (LMS$_{replica}$). These two local match status are then compared. The application receives the final mesage along with the match result according to Table 2.

The application treats results **m0, m$** as success and others as failures.

Table 2. Generation of final status during reception

LMS$_{own}$	LMS$_{replica}$	Final Match Status
	m0	
m0	m1	m0 for all cases
	m$	
	m0	m0
m1	m1	mx
	m$	m$
	m0	m0
	m1	m$
m$	m$	m$ or mx[*]

[*]Final match status is m$ if data from both replicas match or only one copy of data available, mx data from both replicas do not match.

4.2.2 Output Match

The application processes on each of the replicas processes the agreed input data identically and hence produce identical output data. The output data may be of two types. The VDU output data is restricted to the local display and since the same graphical actions using the same libraries are requested, the display on both the replicas should be identical. Hence this type of output does not require any matching. The external output data are those which application processes send to other nodes. The data to be sent should be matched upon and then transmitted. Also the status of the transmission should be sent back to the application. This is achieved in two phases.

Phase I: The two replicas exchange the data to be transmitted. If they do not match an error status message is generated. If they do match then the message is transmitted over the serial ports and the local transmission status is prepared as shown in Table 3.

Table 3. Generation of local transmission status

Local Transmission Status	Description
E0	The transmission data of two replicas match and both the serial port writes succeed.
E1	The transmission data of two replicas match but the serial port write fails on both ports.
E2	The transmission data of two replicas match but the serial port write fails on one port (say port1).
E3	The transmission data of two replicas match but the serial port write fails on the other port (say port 2).
E4	The transmission data of two replicas do not match.
E5	The Local Transmission Status message from other replica does not arrive.

The replicas then exchange local transmission status.

Phase II: Now each replica has two transmission status messages. LTS_{own} is the local transmission status of the replica itself and $LTS_{replica}$ is that of the other replica. Two replicas prepare the final status of transmission as shown in Table 4.

Table 4. Generation of final status during transmission

LTS_{own}	$LTS_{replica}$	Final Status
E0	E0	R0
E0	E1/E2/E3	R1
E1/E2/E3	E0	R2
E1/E2/E3	E1/E2/E3	R3
E0	E5	R4
E2/E3	E2/E3	R5
E4	E4	R6

The final status during transmission is generated as follows.

R0: Indicating that both the replicas transmitted successfully.

R1: Indicating that local node transmitted successfully, whereas the other replica reported a transmission failure.

R2: Indicating that the local node failed to transmit whereas it replica has transmitted successfully.

R3: Indicating that both the replicas failed to transmit the message.

R4: Indicating that the transmit data from the replica was not received but the local system was successful to send.

R5: Indicating that both replicas could transmit one copy of the message only.

R6: Indicating that transmission data in both the replicas did not match and no message was transmitted.

The application may treat the result messages **R0**, **R1**, **R4** and **R5** as a success and other result messages as failure.

5 Performance Issues

The dual redundant system aims to achieve fault tolerance in the following areas

1. If one or more serial links fail then the system should still function properly
2. If one of the nodes fail the system should still function with the remaining node.
3. If the system cannot perform it should fail safely.

Also, the system must not unduly slow down operations, i.e. there should be an upper limit on the turnaround time. It is assumed that the Ethernet link is in perfect health. This assumption is crucial for the proper functioning of the system.

Our system achieves fault tolerance in different failure conditions assuming permanent failures only.

6 Conclusion

The dual redundant command system as described in the previous sections continues to operate even when one node fails or when one, two or even three serial links fail. The only link that needs to be working properly all the time is the Ethernet link. This is essential for the working of the entire system.

The current implementation of the dual modular redundant system costs much less compared to commercially available fault tolerant computer systems, since it is built up using off-the-shelf personal computers and other readily available components, which are quite inexpensive.

One major drawback of the system is its dependency on the Ethernet link. However two Ethernet links may be used by the system in future to reduce chances of failure.

328   S. Dutta et al.

Acknowledgement. This work has been supported by funds from, DRDO, Govt of
India.

References

1. Jalote, P., "Fault Tolerance in Distributed Systems," Chapter 1, Englewood Cliffs, New
   Jercy, 1994.
2. Pradhan, D. K., "Fault Tolerant Computer System Design," Chapter 1, Prentice Hall, New
   Jercy, 1996.
3. Das, P. K., "Distributed Computing – Real Time Fault-Tolerant Applications," National
   Workshop on Distributed Computing, Jadavpur University, Jan 7–8, 1999.
4. Muller, G., Banatre, M., Hue, M., Peyrouze, N., Rochat, B., "Lessons from FTM: an Experiment in the Design and Implementation of a Low Cost Fault Tolerant System," Technical Report, INRIA, February 1995.
5. Coulouris, G., Dollimore, J., Kindberg, T., "Distributed Systems Concepts and Design",
   Second Edition, Addison Wesley, 1994.
6. Brasileiro, F. V., Ezhilchelvan, P. D., Shrivastava, S. K., Speirs, N. A., Tao, S., "Implementing Fail-Silent Nodes for Distributed Systems," Technical Report, Department of Computer Science, University of Newcastle upon Tyne, January, 1996.

Expressing Constraint Models in Object Oriented Data Using UML and ODL

Samiran Chattopadhyay[1], Chhanda Roy[2], and Matangini Chattopadhyay[3]

[1]Department of Information TechnologyJadavpur University, Salt Lake Campus,
Kolkata – 700 098, INDIA
chttpdhs@yahoo.com
[2] R.C.C Institute of Information Technology, South Canal Road, Beliaghata,
Kolkata – 700 015, INDIA
chhandaray@hotmail.com
[3]School of Education Technology, Department of Electrical Engineering, Jadavpur University,
Kolkata – 700 032, INDIA
chttpdhy@yahoo.com

Abstract. Modeling of constraints in Object Oriented Data Model has been the focus of attention of many researchers in recent times [1, 2, 8, 13, 14]. In this paper, we attempt to further formalize the constraint model described in [3]. First, necessary extensions of UML meta-model is examined to express the constraint-model of [3]. The motivation behind expressing constraint models in UML is formalization. It is expected that such formalization effort would lead to the development of sound software tools for analysis and synthesis. The second objective is to establish the correspondence between the extended model and a standard Object database model developed by ODMG. This correspondence is established in ODL by extending the standard specified by ODMG. Such formalizations not only shows the expressive power of the model but these correspondences do also enhance the portability of the schema of object oriented databases across different vendors.

1 Introduction

The Unified Modeling Language (UML) [11, 15, 16, 17, 18] is the result of an effort in developing a single standardized language for object oriented modeling. In the process of object oriented analysis and design, a model and a number of diagrams in UML are produced. The model contains all underlying elements of information about a system under consideration, while diagrams capture different perspectives or views of the system being modeled. In UML, class diagrams are used to specify static structure of a system, such as classes, types and various kinds of static relationship among them. Objects of the persistent classes are stored in object oriented databases. Hence, UML class diagrams are also used for specification of a conceptual design of object oriented databases. This conceptual model, then, is transformed to a database design (represented by a database schema definition) which can be implemented in an object oriented database (OODB) system.

Database integrity is enforced by integrity rules or constraints. A constraint specifies a condition and a proposition that must be maintained as true. Certain kinds of constraints are predefined; others may be user-defined. A user defined constraint is

S.K. Das and S. Bhattacharya (Eds.): IWDC 2002, LNCS 2571, pp. 329–338, 2002.

described in words in a given language, whose syntax and interpretation is a tool responsibility.

Design and implementation of "Object Oriented Model" of Database systems has been the focus of many research efforts [4, 5, 6, 9]. Jasmine, a full-fledged implementation of OODB, has been reported in [7]. [10, 12] deal with other advanced object modeling environments. In [2], constraints have been modeled by means of exceptions in an object oriented database. Other constraint models have also been described in [1, 8]. Ou deals with the specification of integrity constraints such as key, uniqueness using UML class diagrams [13, 14]. Ou's work proposes two ways to specify integrity constraints in a class. One is to use a property string to specify attribute constraints and the other is to add a compartment to specify class constraints.

Our work [3] differs from Ou in a major way. In [3], we have proposed a model to incorporate constraints in an Object Oriented data model. In that model, a constraint is specified as a boolean method of a class. For the sake of elegance, we considered constraints of three categories: constraints involving single attributes, constraints involving multiple attributes and class constraints. Class constraints can be enforced only after checking all objects belonging to a class. The model in [3] is also used to develop a pre-processor for generating code checking constraints in user defined classes and methods.

The layout of the paper is as follows. Section 2 presents a brief description of the constraint model proposed in [3]. Section 3 describes the extension of UML meta model for accommodation of integrity constraints in line of [3]. Section 4 proposes an extension of ODMG object model to accommodate constraint specifications. In section 5, we conclude.

2   Brief Description of the Constraint Model

We attempt to model each constraint as a boolean method, which returns either true value or false value. If the predicate within a method is satisfied by a model element then the method will return true; otherwise the method returns false. These methods are clearly distinguished from the usual methods of a class by their usage and therefore, the constraint methods are accommodated differently than usual methods in object–oriented data model.

We have considered three different types of constraints present in an object oriented data model. Single Attribute Constraints, Multiple Attributes Constraints & Class Constraints.

Single attribute constraints are applicable to individual attributes of a class; multiple attributes constraints involve more than one attributes of a class and class constraints are applicable to individual classes of an object oriented database system. For example, suppose that there is a class "Employee" with usual attributes and methods as shown in Figure 1(a).

A constraint on the attribute "age" of any "Employee" object may be described as "age of an employee must between 20 & 60". Similarly a constraint on "id" may be described as "id must be greater than "0". These constraints involve only one attribute of the class and they are called single attribute constraints. Similarly, there could be a constraint described as "if experience of an employee is less than 5 years then the salary of that employee can not be more than $2500". This constraint is an example of a multiple attribute constraint. A constraint, which can be checked by considering all objects of a class, is called a class constraint. A typical example of a class constraint in the "Employee" class may be described as "id of an employee must be unique". This constraint implies that whenever "id" field of an "Employee" object is modified, uniqueness of the updated "id" value must be guaranteed by checking "id" values of all other "Employee" objects.

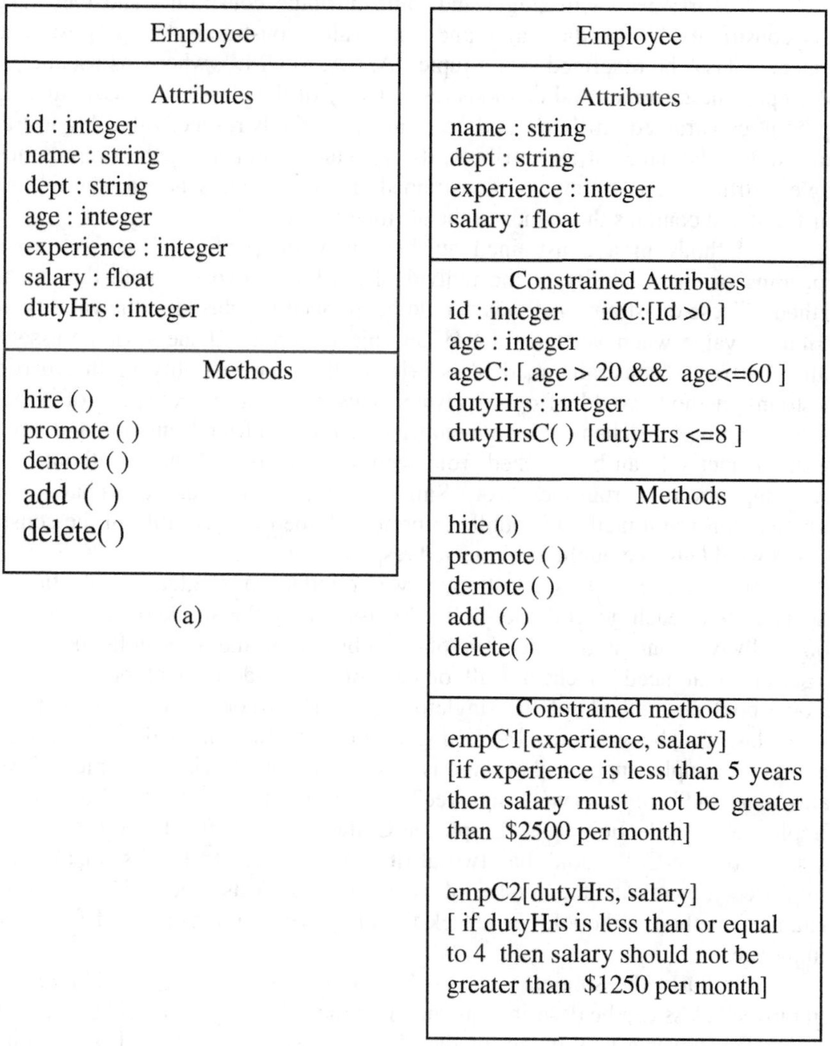

Employee
Attributes
id : integer
name : string
dept : string
age : integer
experience : integer
salary : float
dutyHrs : integer
Methods
hire ( )
promote ( )
demote ( )
add ( )
delete( )

(a)

Employee
Attributes
name : string
dept : string
experience : integer
salary : float
Constrained Attributes
id : integer   idC:[Id >0]
age : integer
ageC: [age > 20 && age<=60]
dutyHrs : integer
dutyHrsC( ) [dutyHrs <=8]
Methods
hire ( )
promote ( )
demote ( )
add ( )
delete( )
Constrained methods
empC1[experience, salary]
[if experience is less than 5 years then salary must not be greater than $2500 per month]
empC2[dutyHrs, salary]
[if dutyHrs is less than or equal to 4 then salary should not be greater than $1250 per month]

(b)

Fig. 1. (a) Class "Employee" (b) Class "Employee" with constraints

The methods for the constraints idC and empC1 are shown in the following.

```
Boolean idC( )    {
                  if (empid <= 0)  return (false);
                  return(true);
    }
Boolean empC1( )          {
                  if  ((salary > 2500) && (experience < 5)) return (false);
                  return(true);

}
```

We first deal with single and multi attribute constraints and then take up class constraints. To handle single and multi-value constraints, we propose that the element "Class" be redefined as a 4-tuple <A, CA, M,CM> , where, as usual , "A" & "M" represent attributes and methods respectively of the class. And "CA" and "CM" represent constrained attributes and constrained methods respectively. A constrained attribute has the name of the attribute, its type and a boolean method representing a single attribute constraint. A constrained method represents a multi-attribute constraint and contains the names of the attributes involved.

Methods in a constrained attribute may be public, private or protected depending on the visibility of the individual attributes involved with the constraint methods. These constraint methods would be invoked for checking the validity of the attribute's value whenever the value of an object changes. If the attribute associated with a particular constraint method is private, then the visibility of that particular constraint method would also be private. This is because the value of a private attribute can only be changed by a member function or a friend function and a private constraint method can be invoked from within members or friends without causing any compilation or runtime error. Similarly, if the attribute associated with a particular constraint method is public or protected, then the visibility of the constraint method would also be public or protected respectively.

To represent class constraints, we introduce a singleton collection class associated with each general user-defined class, where the singleton collection class would always contain a collection of all objects of the user-defined class. All constraints that need to check all objects of a user-defined class for validation become boolean methods of the singleton class. Thus, constraints on objects of the user's class can be validated by calling a corresponding method of the collection class. For example, suppose that there is a constraint on the class "Employee" which states that "id" of every "Employee" object must be unique. For the class "Employee", a collection class "Employee-Collection" is defined (see Figure 2). The class "Employee-Collection" has two attributes, a pointer to the list of all existing "Employee" objects and the number of "Employee" objects. The collection class also contains a method "uniqueId" to check the class constraint mentioned for the class "Employee".

Similarly the singleton class which is the collection of all objects of the "Employee" class can be described as shown in the following figure (Figure 2).

Whenever a new object of the class "Employee" is created, a reference to that object is added to the list "allElements" and the integer "noOfElements" is incremented. Similarly, whenever, an "Employee" object is deleted then the reference of that object is deleted from the list "allElements" and the integer "noOfElements" is decremented. Whenever the "id" of an object is modified by a statement in the user's program, the system must call the class constraint method "uniqueId( )" of the collection class to check whether the "id" remains unique for all object of the "Employee" class even after the modification.

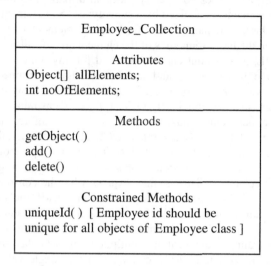

Employee_Collection
Attributes Object[] allElements; int noOfElements;
Methods getObject( ) add() delete()
Constrained Methods uniqueId( ) [Employee id should be unique for all objects of Employee class]

Fig. 2. The class "Employee_Collection"

For linking the only instance of the class "Employee_Collection " with the class an "Employee" object, the system first calls the class level method getobject( ) of the collection class. After getting the object of the singleton class it would call the constraint method of "Employee_Collection" class on that single object.

In [3], we have shown that the model is sound even when inheritance is considered. We have also explored the feasibility of using the semantics of our constraint model to construct a preprocessor that would add constraint validation code to user's programs.

3   Extension of UML Meta Model

UML is a third generation object oriented modeling language for specifying, constructing, visualizing, and documenting software systems. The UML meta model defines the constructs that designers can use in modeling software systems. The meta model is represented by a Foundation Package that contains all of the constructs provided by UML for modeling software systems. The UML Foundation Package is the infrastructure for UML. It is made up of three sub packages; the core, the Extension Mechanisms, and the Data types. The core package defines the basic abstract and concrete constructs needed for the development of the object models. The extension Mechanism package specifies how the model elements can be customized and extended. It defines the semantics for stereotypes, constraints and tagged value. A stereotypes extends an existing model element by introducing additional values, constraints and graphical representations. It shares the attributes, associations and operations of its base class and cannot add others. Creating stereotypes allows users to customize model elements for a particular application. A tagged values allows arbitrary information to be attached to a model element. Tagged values are often associated with stereotypes to specify extra information required by the specific application. An element specialized by a stereotypes "S" is semantically equivalent to a new model class, also named "S". Each model element may have one or more stereotypes when the basic semantics of the element are not sufficient.

In UML, a constraint can be specified for any model element by putting a text string inside braces ({ }) and attached to the constrained element. Such a constraint is of very general purpose, it can be written in natural language or in a formal language such as the UML OCL (Object Constraint Language). OCL is designed to augment class diagrams with additional information that cannot be otherwise expressed by UML diagrams. OCL allows the definition of both meta model constraints and user-level constraints. The main purpose of OCL is to specify restrictions on the possible system states with respect to a given model. OCL constraints are declarative. That is, they express what the constraint is, but does not specify how it should be maintained. According to the UML meta model , any kind of model element can be associated with a constraint. A constraint can be a note or a comment also. The UML meta model offers mechanism to specify integrity constraints. For example, the attribute multiplicity of meta class attribute can be used to define if the attribute is optional or mandatory or single valued or multi-valued. The properties of an associationEnd such as aggregation, isNavigable , multiplicity and qualifier can also be used to specify integrity constraints.

The following are the brief descriptions of the classes of the core package that have been extended.

(a) Class: A class is a description of a set of objects that share the same attributes, operations, methods, relationship and semantics. In the metamodel a *Class* describes a set of *Objects* sharing a collection of *Features*, including *operations, Attributes* and *Methods*, that are common to the set of objects. Each object that instantiates a class contain its own set of values corresponding to the *StructuralFeature (Attributes, Methods, Operations)* in the class. In the metamodel, *Class* is a child of *Classifier*. A *classifier* is a model element that describes behavioral and structural features. It declares a collection of features such as *Attributes, Methods, Operations*. Thus every class also has these features associated with it.

(b) Attribute: An *attribute* is a named piece of the declared state of a *Classifier*. It specifies the range of values that the classifier may hold. An *Attribute* can specify an initial value that it will hold upon initialization. Each class can be associated with several attributes, that together describe that state of the objects defined by the class.

(c) Method : An *Operation* is a *BehaviouralFeature* that can be applied to the instances of a *Classifier*. It represents service provided to change that state of an instance of a *Classifier*. The *Operation* has a signature that specifies the format of the parameters along with possible return values. A *Method* is a conceptual construct, a *Method* is the implementation of an operation. The *Method* specifies the algorithms and techniques required to implement the *Operation* specified in the signature.

To accommodate the specification of integrity constraints, we introduced four new model elements to the core package of UML meta model :

ConstrainedAttribute: ConstrainedAttribute class is introduced as a subclass of *Attribute* class, which is also a subclass of *StructuralFeature* class. *Constrained Attribute* class can contains a number of methods. So, this new model element *Constrained Attribute* class is connected with the UML meta model class *Method*, which is a subclass of *BehaviouralFeature* class. In UML metamodel, *Class* class is a subclass of *Classifier* class which describes behavioral and structural features and thus, each *Constrained Attribute* class is associated with *Class* class.

The detailed description of new model elements which have been introduced into UML meta model are as follows.

ConstrainedAttribute: The *ConstrainedAttribute* class extends the UML meta model *Attribute* class. By the virtue of inheritance all the attributes of the *Attribute* class, such as *Changeable, frozen, addOnly, initialValue, multiplicity* etc. will be inherited into this class. In addition, it has three new attributes *name, attributeNames, methodCount* which specifies the name of the constraint, the names of the attributes associated with the constraint and the total number of constraints.

ConstrainedMethod : The *ConstrainedMethod* class extends the *Method* class of the UML meta model. In addition to all attributes of the *Method* class of UML meta model, it has four extra attributes *name, attributeName, methodCount* and *attributeCount. Name* attribute indicates the name of the constraint, *attributeName* is an array of name of the attributes associated with a constraint, *methodCount* represent the total number of constrained methods and *attributeCount* represent the number of attributes associated with a constraint. The *attributeCount* attribute represents the number of elements within the *attributeName* array.

CollectionClass: The *CollectionClass* class is introduced as a subclass of *Classifier* class of the UML meta model. In addition to all attributes of *Classifier* class, it has three new attributes *className, objectTotal and constraintCount* which represent the name of the *MyClass* class associated with the *CollectionClass* class, the total number of objects within the *MyClass* class and the total number of constraints of the *MyClass* class respectively.

MyClass: *MyClass* is introduced as a subclass of *Class* class in UML meta model. By the virtue of object orientation, all the attributes of *Class* class will be inherited into *MyClass* class. In addition, it has one new attribute *cclassName* which represents the name of the *CollectionClass* class associated with the *MyClass* class.

4   Extending the ODMG Object Model for Constraint Specification

In line with relational data model, there is an independent group of industry representatives, known as the Object Database Management Group (ODMG), who has been working to prepare for object oriented data model.

The specification language used to define the specification of object types for the ODMG/OM is called Object Definition language (ODL). In ODL, a type can be specified by its interface or its class. A class can be instantiated, while an interface can not be instantiated. Interfaces and classes may inherit from other interfaces. A class may EXTEND another class. A class may have attributes and relationships describing the state of its instance and operations describing the behaviors of its instance. An object is an instance of a class and a literal can be an attribute of a class. A database schema contains a set of class definitions. Extensions to the ODMG/OM to accommodate constraint are discussed in the following.

(i) **Single attribute constraints & multiple attribute constraints** – We regard these constraints definition as a part of class definition and extend the class declaration accordingly.

        <class> :: = <class header>{<interface_body>[<cons_dcl>]}

        < cons_dcl>::=   <cons_spec><attributes_lists>:<action>

        <cons_spec>::= constrainedattribute|constrainedmethod

        <attribute_lists>::={attr1, attr2,.....attrn}

        <action>::= <user_defined_procedure>

(ii) **class constraints** - To show the connection between a general purpose class and the corresponding collection class we use a *relationship* with in the class definition of the general purpose class. To include the integrity definitions in the ODMG ODL, the BNF for relationship declaration is extended accordingly.

<rel_dcl>:= relationship<collection_type><class_name><relationship_name>

                    inverse <inverse_class_name>

<collection_type>:= set|bag|list|array|dictionary

To declare the constrained methods in collection class the corresponding BNF is as follows.

        <class> :: = <class header>{<interface_body>[<cons_dcl>]}

        < cons_dcl>::=   <cons_spec><subclass attributes_lists>:<action>

        <cons_spec>::= constrainedmethod

        <subclassattribute_lists>::={subclassname.attr1,subclassname.attr2,....,

                                    subclassname..attrn }

        <action>::= <user_defined_procedure>

ODMG Database Design from UML Class Diagram

The derivation of an ODMG schema begins from a package. Within a package, the following steps are needed to map a UML class diagram to an ODMG-ODL schema:

For each class in UML, create a class definition in ODMG-ODL with the same class name. Then examine the UML class specification:

(i) if the **isAbstract** attribute is false, then add an **extent** definition to the ODMG class. The name of the extent is the plural name of the class name.

(ii) For each attribute in the UML class with cardinality of the form m..1 (m>=0), define the attribute as single value; otherwise, define the attribute as a set.

(iii) For each operation in the UML class , make a correspondent operation definition in the ODL class.

(iv) For each constraint of the UML class:

•   If the name of the constraint is constrainedattribute, then first make a correspondent attribute definition in the ODL class and with this definition define a operation with unique name. The return type of the operation is boolean and the input parameters of the operation is the name of the attribute.

• If the name of the constraint is constrainedmethod, then make a correspondent operation definition in the ODL class. The return type of the opeartion is boolean and the input parameters are the names of the attributes associated with the constraint.

• If the name of the constraint is class constraint, then create a correspondent relationship definition in the ODMG-ODL class. For example,

relationship set<Employee> contained_in inverse
Employee :: Employee_Collection;

The related collection class would be define by using the similar class definition as general purpose class.

(v) For each interface in UML, create an interface definition in ODMG-ODL with the same interface name.

(vi) For each generalization between a supertype stype and one or more subtype type1, type2, ...

• If stype is a class, then add the EXTENDS relationship from type1, type2, ... to stype.

type1 extends stype
type2 extends stype

• If stype is an interface, then add the ISA relationship from type1, type2,.. to stype

type1:stype
type2:stype

....

5   Conclusion

In this paper, we have further formalized the model as described in [3]. The meta model of UML is extended so that schema in object-oriented data bases involving constraints may be expressed in the extended language. The motivation behind expressing constraints models in UML is formalization. It is expected that formalization of the model would lead to the development of sound tools for analysis and synthesis. The correspondence between the extended model and a standard Object database model developed by ODMG has also been established. This also calls for extension of the standard described by ODMG.

We are in the process of developing a pre-processor [3] for incorporating code to check constraints specified in the schema of an object oriented database. Expressing constraints in UML help us in formalizing the inputs to the pre-processor.

Acknowledgements. This work is partially funded by U.G.C sponsored M.R.P entitled "Performance Analysis of Distributed Component Platforms & Introduction of a Unified Distributed Architecture" (Ref. No. F.14-16 / 2000 (SR-I) dated Oct 12, 2000).

References

1. Domenico Beneventano, Sonia Bergamaschi, "Consistency checking in Complex Object Database Schemata with integrity constraints", IEEE Transaction on Knowledge and data Engineering, Vol 10, No 4, 1998.
2. N. Bassiiliades and I. Vlahavas, "Modeling constraints with exceptions in object-oriented Database", Proceedings of 13th international Conference on the Entity-Relationship Approach, Manchester, United Kingdom, December 1994, Lecture Notes in Computer Science, P.Loucopoulos(Ed.), Vol. 881,pp 189–201, 1994.
3. S. Chattopadhyay, C. Roy, S. Bhattacharya, Modeling of Constraints as Methods in Object Oriented Data Model, Proceedings of the 17th Monterey Workshop on Engineering Automation for Software Intensive System Integration, June 18-22, 2001, 220–227.
4. C.J. Date, "An Introduction to Database Systems", Sixth Edition, Addision-Wesley Publishing Company Inc., 1995.
5. P.M.D. Gray, K.G. Kulkarni, N.W. Paton, "Object Oriented databases – A Semantic Data Model Approach", Prentice Hall International,1992.
6. Jan L. Harrington, "Object Oriented Database Design clearly explained", First Edition, Morgan Kaufmann Publishers, 2000.
7. H. Ishikawa, Y. Yamane, Y.Izumida & N. Kawato, "An Object Oriented Database System Jasmine: Implementation, Application and Extension", IEEE Transaction on Knowledge and data Engineering, Vol 8, No 2 April 1996.
8. H.V. Jagadish, X. Qian, "Integrity Maintenance in an Object Oriented Database" Proc. Of the 18th International conference on Very Large Databases, Vancouver, BC, Canada, August, 1992.
9. S. Khoshafian, "Object Oriented Databases" John Wiley & Sons ,Inc, 1993.
10. Q. LI, F. H. Lochovsky, "ADOME : An advanced object Modeling Environment", IEEE Transaction on Knowledge and Data Engineering, Vol 10, No 2, March/April 1998.
11. Pierre-Alain Muller, "Instant UML", First Edition, Wrox Press Ltd., 1997.
12. T.K. Nayak, A.K. Majumdar, A. Basu & S. Sarkar, "VLODS : A VLSI Object Oriented Database System", Information Systems Vol 16, No 1, pp 73–96, 1991.
13. Y.Ou, "On using UML Class Diagram for Object Oriented Database Design – Specification of Integrity Constraints", International Workshop, UML '98', Mulhouse, June 1998.
14. Y. Ou, "On mapping between UML and Entity Relationship Model", International Workshop, UML'98', Mulhouse, June 1998.
15. OMG. Object Constraint Language Specification, OMG, Inc. Sept. 1997, OMG document ad/97-08-08.
16. OMG. Unified Modeling Language – VI.3 alpha R5, OMG, Inc., March 1999.
17. Mark Richtors, Martin Gogolla, "On formalizing the UML Object Constraint Language OCL",Proc. 17th International Conference on Conceptual Modelling (ER'98) , Tok-Wang Ling(ed.), Springer LNCS, 1998.
18. Rational Software Corporation, Unified Modeling Language(UML) version 1.1, http://www.rational.com, 1997.

Grid Computing: The Future of Distributed Computing for High Performance Scientific and Business Applications

Soumen Mukherjee, Joy Mustafi, and Abhik Chaudhuri

Students of MCA Final Year, RCC Institute of Information Technology, Kolkata, INDIA

Abstract. Grid computing offers an efficient method of coordinating resource sharing and problem solving in or between physically dispersed virtual organizations. It offers an opportunity to access greater computing power at a fraction of current cost of technology. Grid computing provides a powerful aggregated computing facility useful for high performance scientific and business activities. Universities and research communities have already started using the grid for solving complex and difficult problems that was previously unsolvable. Grid computing will have a great impact on the education, research and business activities of the developing nations. It is high time for the academic and business communities to work together and realise this promise.

1 Introduction

Driven by increasingly complex problems in nature and propelled by increasingly powerful technology, today's science, research and business activities are as much more based on computation, data analysis, and collaboration as on the efforts of individual experimentalists, theorists and scientists. But even as processor power, data storage capability, and communication technology continue to improve, computational resources are failing to keep up with what we demand from them. Till now, we have relied mainly on human administration to manage this complexity. This unfortunately, will not be sufficient in the near future. These evolutionary pressures have led to the development of Grid technologies. Grid provides an extensible set of services that can be aggregated in various ways to meet the needs of virtual organizations, which themselves can be defined in part by the services they operate and share.

2 About the Grid

"Grid computing" refers to an ambitious global effort in developing an environment in which users can access computers, databases, resources and facilities simply, quickly and transparently, without having to consider where those facilities are located. It is distinguished from conventional distributed computing by its focus on large-scale resource sharing, data sharing, innovative applications and high quality performance. Grids are formed with clusters of servers, which are joined together

S.K. Das and S. Bhattacharya (Eds.): IWDC 2002, LNCS 2571, pp. 339–342, 2002.

over the web, using some protocols provided by the "Globus" open source community and other open technologies, such as Linux.

2.1   Grid Environment for Science and Business

"Grid computing" and the Internet are revolutionizing scientific and business processes. The scientific process has evolved from theorizing and experimenting alone or in small teams and then publishing results, to constructing and mining very large databases of observational or simulation data, developing computer simulations and analysis, accessing specialized devices remotely, and exchanging information instantaneously within distributed multidisciplinary teams.

To be useful, Grid computing and Web services may eventually converge until there is no distinction between the two. A Grid infrastructure needs to provide more functionality than the Internet on which it rests, but it must also remain simple. And of course, the need remains for supporting the resources that power the Grid, such as high-speed data movement, caching of large datasets, and on-demand access to computing. But the Grid goes beyond sharing and distributing data and computing resources. For the scientist, the Grid offers the computing power for collaborative problem formulation, data analysis and high performance research activities.

3   Application of Grid in Business and E-sourcing

Businesses will soon be able to tap into the power of a virtual supercomputer by harnessing the energy of idle PCs anywhere in the world due to the breakthroughs in grid computing. The systems would work much like electrical utilities, giving companies access to virtually unlimited surplus computing power, regardless of where it is stored, and make it easier to share stored data and specialized software with partners on the grid. All kinds of business will benefit from the technology. This emerging type of computing format lets companies tap into more computing power at a low cost by sharing resources among its departments and with other companies. The core of the e-Sourcing revolution is Grid computing. We believe that Grid computing and the emerging Grid protocols will grow beyond their current position in the academic world and become a foundation for the delivery of computing to business customers as a utility-like service over the Internet.

4   The Concept of E-learning through Grid

Using the electronic media for learning and teaching is widespread. e-Learning offers opportunities for staff to convey material in a variety of ways –anytime and anyplace. e-Learning materials can range from the simple act of putting lecture notes online to simulating real life. This means that distance learning (both off and on campus) is a realistic possibility, with students able to take part in class discussions and lectures via email and online discussion forums, and at the same time being able to remotely access materials and information. By providing scalable, secure and high-performance mechanisms for discovering and negotiating access to remote resources, the Grid promises to make it possible for scientific collaborations to share resources on an unprecedented scale, and for geographically distributed groups to work together in ways that were previously impossible.

5   The Security Issue in Grid Computing

Businesses has been slow to adopt grids, mostly for two reasons:

Reason 1: Security - The corporate world does not want to test the grid until security of the grid improves.

Reason 2: Friction - The friction that grid computing can stir up among departments that are forced to share computers.

If any fault is sensed in the grid system it needs to be recovered at the minimum possible time so as to obtain maximum possible normalcy within the system. It is the self governing operation of the entire system, and not just parts of it that delivers the ultimate benefit. IBM has named this vision for the future of computing as Autonomic Computing.

6   Software for Grid Applications

The "Globus" Toolkit which is free, downloadable software provides some security protocols and also a set of services and software libraries to support grids and grid applications. This tool kit is the brainchild of an open-source research project based in the University of Southern California (USC) and Argonne National Laboratory. An open source implementation of the Globus tool kit software makes it important to the industry. It represents an interoperable standard so that one company does not have an advantage over the next.

9   Importance of Grid Computing to the Developing Nations

The ability to share technology resources and its corresponding costs by setting up the grid will give a tremendous boost to the scientific and business activities of the developing nations. The universities and research organization of these countries, which lack proper technological infrastructure for high performance research, will benefit from the grid based computing environment. The small and medium scale business enterprises will be able to expand their business activities with the help of the grid. Thus the grid approach will prove to be a very attractive proposition for this part of the world.

References

1. Foster, I.: The Grid - A New Infrastructure for 21st Century Science (April12,2002)
2. Shread, P.: Grid Computing Will Drive Future Internet Growth, Economist Says (Feb19,2002)
3. Shread, P.: A Future When Grid Computing, Web Services Are One (February 22, 2002)
4. Shread, P.: Solving The World's Problems, One PC At A Time (April 9,2002)
5. Shread, P.: Grid Revolutionizing Scientific, Business Processes (May 21,2002)
6. Sloan, M.: E-Learning and Legislation (March 14, 2002)
7. Medicoff, Z.: Businesses gird for grid computing breakthroughs (September 4, 2002)
8. Waldrop, M.M.: Grid Computing, May 2002
9. J. Bonasia Investor's Business Daily: Grid Computing Aims to Harness 'Clusters', August, 2002
10. Foster, I., Kesselman, C.: The Grid: Blueprint for a New Computing Infrastructure, Morgan Kaufmann, San Francisco, Calif.

Contacting author:

Abhik Chaudhuri,
C-23/7, Kalindi Housing Estate,
Post Office- Lake Town,
Kolkata-700089,India.
Email: cabhik74@rediffmail.com

Email of other authors: soumou_601@rediffmail.com
Must143@rediffmail.com

A Token-Based Distributed Algorithm for Total Order Atomic Broadcast

Sandip Dey[1] and Arindam Pal[2]

[1] Department of Computer Science and Automation, Indian Institute of Science,
Bangalore 560 012, India
sandip@csa.iisc.ernet.in
[2] Microsoft Corporation, Hyderabad, India
arindamp@microsoft.com

Abstract. In this paper, we propose a new token-based distributed algorithm for total order atomic broadcast. We have shown that the proposed algorithm requires lesser number of messages compared to the algorithm where broadcast servers use unicasting to send messages to other broadcast servers. The traditional method of broadcasting requires $3(N-1)$ messages to broadcast an application message, where N is the number of broadcast servers present in the system. In this algorithm, the maximum number of token messages required to broadcast an application message is $2N$. For a heavily loaded system, the average number of token messages required to broadcast an application message reduces to 2, which is a substantial improvement over the traditional broadcasting approach.

1   Introduction

Various distributed applications require that a group of processes receive messages from different sources and take actions based on these messages. These actions can be updating a replicated database or executing a method on a replicated object etc. *Broadcasting* is a technique, in which an arbitrary one among N processes sends a message to the other $N-1$ processes. Although broadcasting can always be achieved by sending $N-1$ *unicast* messages and waiting for the $N-1$ acknowledgments, this algorithm is slow, inefficient and wasteful of network bandwidth.

By *atomicity* we mean that, if a message is delivered to one among a group of processes, then it will be delivered to all other processes in the group. By *total ordering* we mean that, if a process receives a message p before a message q, then all other processes in the group will also receive message p before message q. A message delivery rule is considered *safe*, if before a broadcast server delivers a message, it ensures that every other broadcast server has received that message. A message is considered *stable*, if every broadcast server in the system knows that every other broadcast server has received the message.

Various issues of broadcasting are addressed in [1,2,3]. In [4], a centralized broadcast protocol has been described. Here, application processes send messages to a central entity called *sequencer*. If the *sequencer* fails, a new *sequencer* has

S.K. Das and S. Bhattacharya (Eds.): IWDC 2002, LNCS 2571, pp. 343–347, 2002.

to be chosen before messages can be broadcasted. So, this algorithm has a single point of failure.

In this paper, we propose a total order, atomic broadcast protocol that allows broadcasting of messages using a unidirectional ring. A set of *broadcast servers* deliver messages on behalf of *application processes*. The broadcast servers are organized in a unidirectional logical ring and a *token* carrying broadcast messages circulates around the ring. The algorithm does not use any broadcast primitive. Instead it uses *unicasting* between broadcast servers to broadcast messages. The algorithm is fully distributed and there is no single point of failure.

The rest of the paper is organized as follows. In section 2, the system model is described. Section 3 presents the algorithm. In section 4, we have stated and proved the properties of the algorithm. Finally, section 5 concludes the paper.

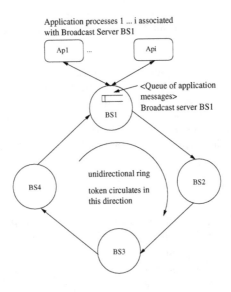

Fig. 1. System Model

2 System Model

The system consists of a set of broadcast servers and a set of application processes, where each application process is associated with a unique broadcast server. We consider an asynchronous distributed environment where processes communicate with each other by explicit message passing only. Send primitive is non-blocking and receive primitive is blocking in nature. The broadcast servers are failure-free and no messages are lost in transit. The communication channels between a broadcast server and its associated application processes are assumed to be first-in first-out (FIFO). The system model is depicted in Fig. 1.

3   The Algorithm

Our algorithm implements a broadcast protocol, which in essence uses unicasting to communicate between processes. Broadcast servers take the responsibility of broadcasting messages received from a group of application processes. Each broadcast server knows its identity, the identity of the neighboring broadcast server and the total number of broadcast servers present in the system. These informations are required to connect the broadcast servers in a unidirectional logical ring. Once the ring is established, each broadcast server starts a new thread called *ring handler* which takes care of broadcasting issues. The main *broadcast server* thread waits for a *connection* from some application process. When a *connection* is received, it invokes an *application client handler* thread which handles the communication with that particular application process. The main server thread continues waiting for other connections. So the broadcast servers are concurrent in nature, i.e., they can handle several client requests simultaneously.

An application client may dynamically join a new broadcast server. When a new application client starts execution, it first establishes a *connection* with a broadcast server. The main *application client* thread then invokes a new thread called *broadcast message receiver* which waits for application messages from the associated broadcast server. These application messages are generated by other application processes in the system and are now being broadcasted. The main *application client* thread runs simultaneously with the *broadcast message receiver* thread and generates application messages to be broadcasted. Each application client keeps an application message counter. A value of i for this counter indicates that this is the ith application message generated by this application client. Application messages are generated randomly i.e., after generating a message the application client sleeps for a random time and then generates another message. All these application messages are sent to the associated broadcast server.

A broadcast server stores messages from its application clients in a queue. There is no limit on the length of the queue. Whenever a broadcast server receives a message from an application client, it puts the message in the queue. A token circulates around the logical ring and it carries with it N number of application messages, where N is the number of broadcast servers present in the ring. The *ring handler* thread running at each broadcast server checks whether the message queue is empty or not. If the queue is empty, the broadcast server is currently not *interested* to broadcast. If the broadcast server is *interested*, has the token and the token has no previous message (still undelivered) from this broadcast server, it picks a message from the queue and puts the message in the token. This message gets a sequence number equal to the value of the sequence number in the token and the sequence number in the token is incremented. In other words, the token is carrying a unique sequence number generator with it. The *circulation count* for this message is initialized to 0, indicating that it has been just put into the token. The broadcast server then forwards the token to its neighbor. Whenever a broadcast server receives an application message for the first time, i.e., with a *circulation count* equal to 0, it copies the application message in a local buffer. This is important to satisfy the *safe* delivery rule. If the broadcast server is *interested* but the token has a previous message from this broadcast server which is not delivered to all the application processes yet, the broadcast sever just increments the *circulation count* of its message in the token and forwards the token to its neighbor. After forwarding the token it simply waits for the token to arrive again. When an application message circulates twice around the ring, it becomes stable. Once an application message becomes stable, it can be removed from the token. Each broadcast server delivers all the application messages with *circulation count* equal to 1, to associated application processes. The token has N slots for N application messages for each of the N broadcast servers. When a message needs to be delivered to the application clients, the *ring handler* thread starts a *broadcast message sender* thread which delivers the message to all the application clients associated with the broadcast server.

4   Properties of the Algorithm

Theorem 1. *The algorithm ensures atomicity and total ordering of messages.*

Proof. A broadcast server delivers an application message to all its associated application clients. Also, safe delivery rule ensures that every other broadcast server has received that application message. So, if an application process receives an application message, others will also receive it. This ensures atomicity.

Now, if a broadcast server delivers a message p before a message q, then every other broadcast server does the same because messages are delivered by a broadcast server only when the token completes one full circulation with respect to that broadcast server. Hence, every application process associated with a broadcast server will receive message p before q. This way the total ordering of messages is ensured.

Theorem 2. *The maximum number of token messages required to broadcast an application message is $2N$, where N is the number of broadcast servers in the system. For a heavily loaded system, the average number of token messages required to broadcast an application message reduces to 2.*

Proof. A message is stable when the token completes two full circulations. When a message is stable it has been delivered by all the broadcast servers. Hence the maximum number of token messages required to broadcast a message is $2N$.

For a heavily loaded system, each broadcast server will put one message in its slot. Hence, in two full circulations of the token N messages will be delivered. In other words, $2N$ token messages will be required to deliver N messages. Hence, the average number of token messages required to broadcast a message is 2.

Compare this with the number of messages required for a complete network of N broadcast servers. Here, a broadcast server which wants to broadcast a message will send it to $N - 1$ other broadcast servers. They will send acknowledgement messages back to the original broadcast server. The original broadcast server will send replies to all of them and every broadcast server will know that every other broadcast server in the system has received the message. Thus to satisfy the safe delivery rule $3(N - 1)$ messages are required. Hence, even for a lightly loaded system, our algorithm requires $3(N - 1) - 2N = (N - 1)$ messages less for broadcasting.

5   Conclusion

In this paper, we have designed a fully distributed algorithm for total order atomic broadcast and have shown that our algorithm requires lesser number of messages compared to the algorithm where broadcast servers use unicasting to send messages to all other broadcast servers.

Here, we have not considered any fault-tolerance issue. However, our algorithm can be modified to handle token loss. This can be achieved by using extra sequence numbers in the token and keeping a timer at each broadcast server. Two consecutive application messages having non-consecutive sequence numbers will indicate a message loss.

References

1. H. Garcia-Molina, N. Lynch, B. Blaustein, C. Kaufman, and O. Schmueli. Notes on a Reliable Broadcast Protocol. Technical report, Computer Corporation of America, July 1985.
2. J. M. Chang and N. F. Maxemchuk. Reliable Broadcast Protocols. *ACM Transactions on Computer Systems*, 2(1):39–59, February 1984.
3. P .M. Melliar-Smith, L. E. Moser, and V. Agrawala. Broadcast Protocols for Distributed Systems. *IEEE Transactions on Parallel and Disributed Systems*, 1(1):17–25, January 1990.
4. M. F. Kaashoek, A. S. Tanenbaum, S. F. Hummel, and H. E. Bal. An Efficient Reliable Broadcast Protocol. *Operating Systems Review*, 23(4):5–19, October 1989.

Task Allocation in Heterogeneous Computing Environment by Genetic Algorithm

Soumen Dey and Subhodip Majumder

Department of Computer Science and Engineering
University of Calcutta
92, A. P. C. Rd., Kolkata-700009, India
{sdcompsc, m12subho}@yahoo.co.in
Contact Ph. No. +91(033) 543-4970, +91(033) 565-0758

Abstract. This paper presents an efficient technique for mapping a set of tasks onto a set of heterogeneous processors. The tasks require data communication between them. The system is assumed to be completely heterogeneous, where the processing speeds, memory access speeds, communication latency between processors and the network topology are all considered being non-uniform. Typically, the numbers of tasks are much larger than the number of processor available. The problem of optimal mapping of the tasks to the processors such that the application run –time is minimized is NP-Complete. The searching capabilities of genetics algorithms are utilized to perform the optimal/near optimal mapping.

1 Introduction

Heterogeneous computing (HC) environment utilizes a distributed suite of existing machines along with their interconnection links to provide a cost effective approach to solve computationally intensive applications. In grid computing infrastructures geographically distributed heterogeneous resources are coupled to provide a meta-computing platform. A major challenge in meta-computing environment (grid computation) is to effectively use shared resources such as compute cycles, memory, communication network and data repositories to optimize desired global objective.

We present a genetic algorithm based approach for solving this problem on fully heterogeneous systems in terms of processors and memory speeds, communication latencies, and network topology.

2 Problem Definition

2.1 Application Model

In meta-computing system each application task consists of a set of communicating subtasks. The data dependencies among the subtasks are assumed to be known and

S.K. Das and S. Bhattacharya (Eds.): IWDC 2002, LNCS 2571, pp. 348–352, 2002.
© Springer-Verlag Berlin Heidelberg 2002

are represented by a weighted Directed Acyclic Graph (DAG), G=(V,E), which we refer to as the _workload graph or task graph_. The set of subtasks of the application to be executed is represented by V=($v_1, v_2, \ldots \ldots v_n$) where $v_k > 1$, and E represents the data dependencies and communication between the subtasks. Each vertex v has a computation weight, W^v, which reflects the size of computation at vertex v. An edge from vertex u to v has a computation weight, $C^{u,v}$, which reflects data dependency from u to v.

2.2 System Modeling

This heterogeneous system can be represented as a weighted undirected graph, S=(P,L), which we refer to as the _system graph_. The system graph consists of a set of vertices, P = $\{p_1, p_2, \ldots \ldots p_n\}$, denoting processors and a set of edges L={(p_i, p_j)| $p_i, p_j \in P$} denoting links between processors. Each processor (vertex) p has two weights, processing weight s_p and memory weight m_p. These reflect the cost associated with per unit of computation and per unit of memory access respectively. Each link (edge) has a link weight, $c_{p,q}$ that denotes the communication between processors for our experiments. Network heterogeneity implies some processor with no direct links between them. In this case, we weight a link between two processors with no explicit connectivity between them as the sum of the weights of links on the shortest path between them using _Dijkastra Algorithm_. Thus we find the "communication cost matrix". The communication cost matrix in our case is symmetric, as we assume full duplex links between nodes. In order to reflect total heterogeneity in the system model, vertex and edge weights in the system graph should take random values.

2.3 Processing and Computation Cost

When a vertex 'v' is assigned to a processor p it incurs a processing cost, W^v_p. It reflects time units required by p to process v and is given by, $W^v_p = W^v * s_p$. When 'u' and 'v' are assigned to the same processor p, data set for transfer to 'v' is present at the local memory of p. Thus internal communication cost involves simply a memory access and is given by $C^{u,v}_n = C^{u,v} * m_p$. When '$u$' and '$v$' are assigned to different processors, the communication latency between the processors comes into play. Suppose, 'u' is assigned to processor p and 'v' is assigned to processor q. Data set for transfer to 'v' is present at the local memory of p . Data is transferred from the local memory of p to local memory of q via an inter-process message. Vertex 'v' now involves simply a memory access from the local memory of q. In this case, the external communication cost is given by $C^{u,v}_{p,q} = C^{u,v} * (c_{p,q} + m_q)$. The execution time of processor, expressed as ET_p, with an assignment of vertices, and is given by the sum of three costs discussed above, namely processing cost, internal communication cost, and external communication cost & mathematically expressed as

$$ET_p = (\Sigma_{v \in \text{all processors } p} W^v * s_p) + (\Sigma_{u,v \in \text{all processors } p} C^{u,v} * m_p) +$$
$$(\Sigma_{v \in \text{all processors } p \ \& \ u \in \text{all processors } q} C^{u,v} * (c_{p,q} + m_p))$$

2.4 Problem Statement

GIVEN (1) A meta-computing environment with 'm' processors with their detail description & (2) A interconnection network between the processors with the communication weights in between them.

FIND an optimal or near optimal schedule such that minimum (ET $_{application}$) i.e. minimize { max $_{p \in P}$ (ET$_p$) } , where P is the processor set.

SUBJECT to the following constraints (1) Only one task can execute on any machine at any given time, i.e. the schedule is non preemptive & (2) A sub task can execute only after all its predecessors have been completed & all input data items have been received from its predecessors.

3 The Genetic Algorithm Approach to the Task Allocation Problem

3.1 Encoding Scheme

In our problem the chromosomes are string of integers. The length of a chromosome is determined by the number of tasks to be allocated. The processors in the network are each assigned with an integer number. The value in each slot is the processor number to which the corresponding task is to be allocated.

3.2 Selection and Reproduction

Selection for reproduction was performed with a bias towards choosing the better solutions in the current population. We chose to select proportional to objective function value, as is done with the traditional biased Roulette-Wheel approach.

Reproduction is done with the help of two genetic operators, crossover and mutation. Crossover is done in traditional way. At first two chromosomes are selected by the Roulett-Wheel selection process depending on the fitness values of the chromosomes. Crossover is then done at a randomly generated site. We selected chromosomes for mutation from the entire population with uniform probability. Mutation took the form of selecting one site at random and changing the value at the site randomly.

For each generation, the number of children to be produced was selected in advance, as was the probability of a given individual generating a mutant. As children and mutants were created, the strings with worst fitness were culled to keep a constant population size. To maintain enough diversity, mutants were inserted into the population after members of the current generation had been culled. In this way, mutants, no matter what their fitness, were assured to survive at least one generation and be available for reproduction selection.

4 Program Outline

The initial pool of chromosomes is taken at first and their fitness values are calculated. Here the pool of chromosomes is kept sorted with respect to their fitness values. New chromosome is inserted in the pool if its fitness value is greater than the last chromosome in the pool. In this way elitism is applied in the process of generating new generation.

GA takes its usual course in our program also. It generates new chromosomes by genetic operators like crossover and mutation. Crossover and mutation operators used here works conventionally. The whole process continues as many times as required by the user. In each iteration either crossover or mutation is applied depending the probability assigned to them by the user. Another feature of GA used in our program is that the chromosomes present in the pool at any instant are unique with respect to each other. At the end of all such iterations we end up with a pool of chromosomes showing different allocation schedule. This pool consists of best chromosomes found in the whole process. The chromosome with highest fitness value gives the best solution obtained till that number of iteration.

5 Result & Analysis of the Result

The conventional GA & our algorithm are applied on the same graphs (system & task graphs).

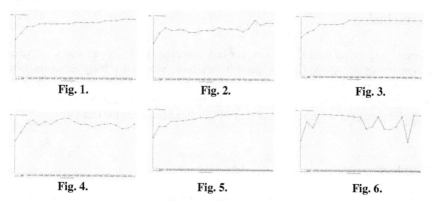

Fig. 1.   Fig. 2.   Fig. 3.

Fig. 4.   Fig. 5.   Fig. 6.

The following table gives the details of the above figures:

Fig No.	Method	Iteration No.	Crossover Prob.	Mutation Prob.	Best Fitness	Load Imbalance
1	Conventional	1000	0.8	0.08	11.904	1.680
2	Nonconventional	1000	0.8	0.08	13.333	1.471
3	Conventional	1000	0.4	0.08	11.904	1.680
4	Nonconventional	1000	0.4	0.08	13.333	2.684
5	Conventional	10,000	0.8	0.08	13.333	1.229
6	Nonconventional	10,000	0.8	0.08	13.333	1.304

The specifications used are Operating system :- Windows-98, Programming Language =Turbo C++, Processor Family= Pentium IV, RAM=32MB.

In all the output sets the curves for conventional GA have shown steady increase but the curves for non-conventional GA (our algorithm) have shown more ups and downs. It may be due to the fact that in our algorithm the crossover and mutation operators always generate unique chromosomes. If crossover fails to generate unique chromosomes for 100 times then it comes out of the process by applying mutation operator which may cause the abrupt change in the average fitness. Increasing this number to 1000 times or more can smooth the curve out. The conventional algorithm runs faster and not prone to abrupt change in the fitness value. The advantage of our algorithm may be that this algorithm is less prone to stick at local optima since it allows abrupt changes. But this claim can only be made strong if this algorithm is applied on larger graphs and with larger population strength.

6 Scope of Further Improvement

In our problem we have done static off-line allocation of tasks onto a Heterogeneous Computing Environment. But to obtain a more efficient allocation there are some other constraints, which may be taken into consideration such as *Deadlines, Preferred allocation, Synchronization etc.*

7 Conclusion

A Genetic Algorithm based technique for task mapping in Heterogeneous Computing Environments is developed in our project. We have modeled a truly Heterogeneous Environment and devised metric to determine the potential of a system. Since the general problem of optimally mapping tasks to non-uniform processors is known to be NP-complete, the searching capability of Gas has been used for this purpose.

References

[1]   Proceedings of SOFTCOMP'98–International Workshop on Soft Computing & Intelligent System, January 12-13,1998.
[2]   Handbook of Genetic Algorithms – Edited by Lawrence Davis.
[3]   Genetic Algorithm in search optimization &Machine Learning–David E. Goldberg.
[4]   C++ Programming Language – Bjarne Stroustrup.
[5]   Heterogeneous Computing : A New Computing Paradigm by Raju D. Venkataramana Department of Computer Science & Engineering, University of South Florida, Tampa
[6]   A Heuristic model for task allocation in heterogeneous distributed computing systems: by A. Abdelmageed Elsadek B. Earl Wells, Electrical and Computer Engineering The University of Alabama in Huntsville, Huntsville, AL 35899, U.S.A.

Author Index

Lecture Notes in Computer Science

For information about Vols. 1–2476

please contact your bookseller or Springer-Verlag